AFRICAN HISTORICAL DICTIONARIES
Edited by Jon Woronoff

Historical Dictionary
of
ZAIRE

by
F. SCOTT BOBB

African Historical Dictionaries, No. 43

The Scarecrow Press, Inc.
Metuchen, N.J., & London
1988

British Library Cataloguing-in-Publication data available

Library of Congress Cataloging-in-Publication Data

Bobb, F. Scott, 1950–
    Historical dictionary of Zaire.

    (African historical dictionaries ; no. 43)
    Bibliography: p.
    1. Zaire--History--Dictionaries. I. Title.
II. Series.
DT643.B63 1988   967.5'1'00321   88–11410
ISBN 0–8108–2109–5

DEDICATION

This book is dedicated to one of the founding fathers of Zaire who, for reasons of privacy, shall remain anonymous.

CONTENTS

v

ACKNOWLEDGMENTS

A work of this nature owes a great deal to the research and scholarship of others which, in some cases, was carried out decades ago. However, a number of works deserve special mention: The three country studies of Zaire, edited by W. MacGaffey, G. McDonald and I. Kaplan, respectively, and the more recent works of T. Callaghy, G. Nzongola-Ntalaja, C. Young and T. Turner, and J. Vanderlinden.

The assistance of a number of Zairians in government, at AZAP and at the Makanda Kabobi Institute is gratefully acknowledged. The comments of Mr. Nzongola and Mr. Young at certain points during the preparation of the book were especially appreciated. Nevertheless, any errors in this work are my responsibility and any opinions, however unintentioned, are entirely my own.

F. Scott Bobb

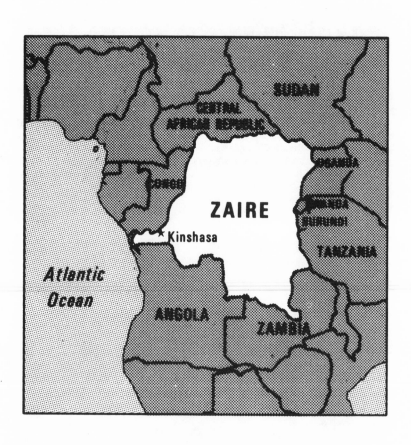

EDITOR'S FOREWORD

Although it is one of the last volumes in this series of African Historical Dictionaries, the Zaire book is certainly not one of the least.
That is obvious to anyone who studies Africa. The country is one of
the largest in size, population and wealth. It has played a very significant role in recent African history and enjoys considerable influence abroad. It remains one of the most crucial states, located in
the center of the continent and bordering nine other countries.

Although it has appeared frequently in the foreign media, perhaps too frequently given the sensational nature of most stories,
Zaire is not that well known. The country is vast and it is hard to
get around the rural areas. So what we know, as all too often in
Africa, reflects the capital city and the life of its elite. This book
breaks those binds and tells us much more about the broader situation of Zaire. It also reaches back into earlier history and delves
into its cultural traditions and ethnic mores.

Writing such a comprehensive book is not easy. It took the
unstinting efforts of someone who really cares like F. Scott Bobb.
Brought up by missionary parents in the then Belgian Congo, he
spent a decade in various regions before and after independence.
He has returned many times since and followed events while he was
away. As of 1977, Bobb worked as a reporter-broadcaster for the
African Division of the Voice of America and wrote articles on African
topics for Africa Report and other publications.

> Jon Woronoff
> Series Editor

NOTE TO THE READER

Given the varied orthography and nomenclature used by scholars of Zaire, a few clarifications on the usage of names and spellings in this work are in order. Although international cartographers generally prefer the name "Congo River" to describe Zaire's major river, I have used the official Zairian name, "Zaire River." Likewise I have used Lake Edouard to describe the eastern lake that for a time was called Lake Idi Amin but was changed by Ugandan authorities following the demise of the Amin government.

Many Zairian names were changed under authenticity between 1966 and 1971. The Guide to Former and Present Names provides a reference to the major changes of geographical names. Zairians themselves dropped their Christian names in the early 1970s (e.g., Joseph-Desiré Mobutu became Mobutu Sese Seko). In passages referring to specific times, particularly before authenticity, I have tended to use the name(s) in current use at that time (e.g., the "Katanga Secession" or the "Shaba Wars"), but in general or multiple time-frame references, I have opted for the name presently in use.

Concerning the names of ethnic groups, I have adopted the increasingly common anglophone practice of dropping prefixes thus using "Kongo" instead of "Bakongo" and "Zande" instead of "Azande." I have also eschewed for the most part the use of the term "tribe," since it currently is considered pejorative by many Africans. When the term is used, however, it is meant in the sense of ethnic group or nation with no negative connotations intended. I have used English spellings of French names that are well known in English, a practice that has meant dropping many orthographical accents, as in Zaire and Leopoldville, for example, as opposed to Zaïre and Léopoldville. However, I have used French spellings when referring to official names of organizations, such as "Office National du Café" and "Mouvement de la Révolution Populaire," unless they have commonly used English translations, for example, "Central Committee" and "Organization of African Unity."

CHRONOLOGY

1000 B.C. (circa)	Arrival in western and southwestern regions of the forerunners of Bantu-speaking people from West Africa.
1000 B.C. to 200 A.D.	Bantu-speaking peoples spread throughout Congo Basin.
500 to 1000 A.D.	Bantu-speaking people spread to the savannas and toward the Indian Ocean through what are now the Kasai, Kivu and Shaba Regions.
900 A.D.	Migration of other people from Lake Chad south into central Zaire.
1200 to 1500 A.D.	Emergence of the Kongo, Kuba, Luba and Lunda kingdoms and the Zande and Mangbetu dominions.
1483	Portuguese admiral Diogo Cao arrives at the mouth of the Congo River, which he names the Zaire. Cao returns in 1485 and 1487 to establish trading posts.
1500 A.D.	Zande people arrive in north and central Zaire. Nilotic people migrate into northeastern Zaire.
1640	Dutch replace the Portuguese as leading traders. The French and English establish a large presence, leading to the decline of Portuguese power toward the end of the 1600s.
1700	The slave trade with the Americas begins to flourish.
1789	Jose Lacerda e Almeida makes the first scientific exploration of the Congo Basin, penetrating as far as Katanga where he discovers copper mines.
1800	The Afro-Arab trade begins to flourish in eastern Zaire.

mid-1800s	Slavery is officially ended in most European countries.
1865	The defeat of the Confederacy in the United States closes the mass market for slaves in North America.
1870-88	Slavery is abolished in South and Central America.
1890-94	Military campaign drives Afro-Arab traders from Zaire and ends slave trade with the middle east.
1816	British expedition led by James Tuckey sails up the mouth of the Congo River.
1854	Scottish missionary/explorer David Livingstone reaches Lake Dilolo in Katanga and crosses the Kasai and Kwango River basins into Angola.
1858	British explorers Richard Burton and John Speke reach Lake Tanganyika, travelling from East Africa.
1860	Explorer Samuel Baker reaches Lake Albert (now Lake Mobutu).
1867-68	Livingstone reaches Lakes Mweru and Bangwelu, arriving at Lake Tanganyika in 1869. Seeking the headwaters of the Nile, he sails down the Lualaba River and reaches Nyangwe in southern Kivu in 1871.
1871	Journalist/explorer Henry Morton Stanley locates Livingstone at Ujiji on November 10 after an expedition of 236 days.
1870s	Christian missionaries return to Zaire.
1874	Stanley, commissioned by the New York Herald and Daily Telegraph newspapers to continue Livingstone's explorations, sets out to sail down the Congo River, in part to prove that the Lualaba is not the headwaters of the Nile. The trip takes 999 days. Stanley arrives at the Atlantic Ocean on March 12, 1877.
1878-87	Stanley, hired by Belgium's King Leopold II, sets out to establish trading posts and make treaties with local chiefs along the Congo River. He eventually returns with 450 treaties.

1884
At the Berlin Conference from November 15, 1884, to February 26, 1885, the European powers partition Africa. Leopold obtains personal sovereignty over the Congo, which soon becomes the Congo Free State.

1904-05
Reports by missionaries and diplomats in the Congo of forced labor and brutalities by the CFS authorities lead to a public outcry in Europe and the United States.

1908
Faced with international condemnation of human rights abuses in the CFS, Leopold II agrees to hand it over to the Belgian government and the Belgian parliament reluctantly agrees to annex the territory as a colony on September 9. On November 15, the CFS becomes the Belgian Congo.

1910-25
A large portion of the existing railway network is completed at great cost and with large material and human sacrifices.

1914-45
The economic fortunes of the colony largely follow the world economy, experiencing a boom in the 1920s and a depression in the 1930s. Congolese minerals aid the war efforts and Congolese soldiers fight with the Allies in the African Theater in World Wars I and II.

1945-55
The "évolués" class of educated and primarily urban, white collar workers begins to emerge. Although political activity is banned, "évolués" gather in "associations" based primarily on ethnic and alumni groups. Calls are made for greater equality and advancement opportunities for African workers. Trade unionism begins to emerge.

1957
The colonial authorities allow elections for local urban districts and colonial councils. However, authorities publicly say independence is at least 30 years away.

1958
Belgium holds the Brussels World Fair and brings hundreds of Congolese to Brussels. De Gaulle, speaking in Brazzaville, offers France's colonies autonomy within a French community. The All-African People's Conference is held in December in newly independent Ghana. Lumumba and other Congolese leaders attend and return home fired with the idea of independence.

1959 At a rally in Leopoldville on January 3, Lumumba calls for independence for the Belgian Congo. A confrontation with police erupts in violence that leads to two weeks of rioting in the capital and several other cities. The colonial authorities agree to hold local elections. Elections are held in December but are boycotted by many of the emerging parties. The Belgian government, in the face of continued unrest, agrees to hold a Round Table Conference in Brussels.

1960 The Round Table Conference begins on January 20 with 45 delegates from various Congolese parties in attendance. The Belgian delegates reluctantly agree to set June 30 as the date for independence. Elections are held on June 25, but they are inconclusive. Talk of secession is heard in various regions. A compromise is struck through which Kasavubu becomes president and Lumumba becomes prime-minister.

 The Congo becomes independent on June 30. On July 4, the Force Publique mutinies for higher pay and better promotion opportunities. The violence leads to the evacuation of foreigners and the arrival of Belgian paratroopers. The Congolese government, fearful of Belgian occupation, asks the United Nations for military and administrative assistance. On July 11, Katanga secedes, followed by South Kasai. Lumumba is dismissed on September 5 and is later captured while trying to join supporters in Stanleyville.

1961 Lumumba and two colleagues are killed on January 17 shortly after arriving in secessionist Elisabethville under ANC custody. The assassination leads to the secession of Orientale and Kivu Provinces. Adoula forms a government of reconciliation in February and the South Kasai secession is ended. U.N. relief efforts are necessary to aid victims of famine and internecine fighting in Kasai and Katanga.

1963 Following U.N. military intervention, the Katanga secession is ended and Tshombe goes into exile.

1964 Tshombe returns at the head of the CONACO party and is appointed prime minister on July 6 at the head of a southern dominated coalition. The country's first constitution is passed on August 1. The People's Republic of the Congo is proclaimed in Stanleyville on September 7 and is recognized by 13 foreign nations. Reports of atrocities by Stanleyville-based troops against Congolese and foreign hostages leads to the Belgian paratroop drop on Stanleyville on November 24. Over the next several weeks, the central government regains control over most of eastern Congo. Meanwhile, the Kwilu rebellion led by Mulele gathers force.

1965   Elections are held in March in which Tshombe's CONACO party makes significant gains. Tshombe is dismissed by Kasavubu on October 13, but parliament refuses to accept his designated successor. In the face of the political standoff and a resurgence of the eastern rebellion, the military decides to take command on November 24 and installs Mobutu as head of state with powers of decree. The Kwilu rebellion is put down.

1966   The MPR is formed on April 17. An army rebellion in Orientale Province is put down by the central authorities.

1967   UMHK is nationalized on January 2. The N'sele Manifesto is issued on May 20. An attempt to return Tshombe to power by fomenting a rebellion in eastern Congo is thwarted by the central authorities. The second constitution, promulgated on June 24, reduces regional autonomy and grants increased powers to the president. Tshombe is kidnapped on June 30 and imprisoned in Algeria. Kinshasa hosts the OAU summit and Mobutu becomes OAU Chairman. The last eastern rebellion is ended, although the PRP continues to control some territory in Kivu.

1969   Kasavubu dies. Algeria announces Tshombe's death in prison on June 30.

1970   Elections are held in November and Mobutu, the sole candidate, is elected president. The MPR is declared the sole political party and supreme institution of the country on December 23.

1971   On October 27, the Congo becomes the Republic of Zaire.

1973   On October 4, Zaire breaks relations with Israel. Mobutu announces the Zairianization of major foreign-owned companies on November 30.

1974   The third constitution is promulgated on August 15; it further centralizes power in the presidency and creates the party-state. Retrocession is decreed on December 30, returning portions of Zairianized farms and companies to private ownership.

1975   Following a drastic fall in copper prices, economic recession sets in and the government begins to fall in arrears on its foreign debt. The MPLA faction that is fighting a civil war for control of Angola takes control of Luanda. Zaire, which opposes the MPLA, continues to support the FNLA and UNITA factions.

1977   FNLC guerrillas enter Shaba Region from bases in Angola on March 8. They advance to the outskirts of Kolwezi but are forced back into Angola by Zairian and Moroccan troops 80 days later.

                          Foreign Minister Nguza and other Lunda leaders are imprisoned and convicted of complicity. Nguza is later pardoned and returned to government. Zaire holds national and local elections in October. Mobutu is elected to a second term on December 2.

1978   FNLC guerrillas attack Kolwezi on May 3 and occupy the town. Reports of looting and killing lead to a paratroop drop by Zairian, French and Belgian troops that regain control after two weeks. A Pan-African peacekeeping force is established in the region and the government, stung by international criticism of its economic and political policies, enacts some reforms.

1981   Nguza resigns unexpectedly in April and goes into exile. The Zairian government comes under severe criticism in the U.S. and West European legislatures.

1982   Zaire re-establishes diplomatic relations with Israel in May. Legislative elections are held on September 18 and 19 in which multiple candidates are allowed. Three-fourths of the incumbents are turned out. Thirteen parliamentarians attempt to form a second party, the UDPS, and are arrested and convicted of treason.

1983   Mobutu proclaims a general amnesty on May 21 whereby exiled dissidents may return if they cease opposition activities. On September 9, following nearly a decade of recession and debt arrears caused by low copper prices and mismanagement, the government announces a monetary reform, floating the currency on the free market, and removes overall subsidies on petroleum and agricultural products. Annual inflation reaches 100 percent. Labor protests are put down.

1984   Mobutu is elected to a third term on July 29. PRP guerrillas attack Moba in November demanding the end of the Mobutu government. The army re-occupies the town two days later.

1985   Zaire celebrates 25 years of independence on June 30. Many former exiled dissidents, including Nguza, are present. However, PRP guerrillas attack Moba on the eve of the celebrations. International creditors praise Zaire for remaining current on debt repayments and liberalizing its economy. Annual inflation has been reduced to 20 percent and the recession is considered ended, although the purchasing power of most Zairians is still low.

1986   Following a month-long meeting of the MPR Central Committee, the government, saying IMF economic stabilization programs are strangling the economy, announces it will limit payments on its foreign debt to 10 percent of export revenues and 20 percent of government revenues. Responding to persistent criticism of its human rights record, Mobutu announces the creation of a ministry of citizens' rights.

1987   Zaire announces on May 22 that despite the reduction of payments on its foreign debt, it has reached agreement with the Paris Club to defer payment on $846 million dollars of debt and also has received pledges of $1.48 billion dollars in aid from donor nations over the next two years. In June, clashes are reported along the border with Uganda.

GUIDE TO FORMER AND CURRENT NAMES
(most of which were changed between 1966 and 1971)

Former Name	Current Name
Albertville	Kalemie
Albert, Lake	Mobutu Sese Seko, Lake
Bakwanga	Mbuji-Mayi
Banningville	Bandundu
Bas-Congo Province	Bas-Zaire Region
Baudoinville	Virunga
Centime (currency)	Likuta (plural: makuta)
Congo Franc (currency)	Zaire (currency)
Congo, Republic of	Zaire, Republic of
Congo River	Zaire River
Coquilhatville	Mbandaka
Costermansville	Bukavu
Districts	Sub-Regions
Elisabethville	Lubumbashi
Jadotville	Likasi
Katanga Province	Shaba Region
Leopold II, Lake	Mai-Ndombe, Lake
Luluabourg	Kananga
Ministries	Departments
Ministers	State Commissioners
Orientale Province	Haut-Zaire Region
Paulis	Isiro
Port Francqui	Ilebo
Provinces	Regions
Stanley Pool	Malebo Pool
Stanleyville	Kisangani
Thysville	Mbanza-Ngungu

LIST OF ABBREVIATIONS AND ACRONYMS

ABAKO	Alliance des Bakongo
ANC	Armée Nationale Congolaise
APIC	Association de Personnel Indigène de la Colonie
APL	Armée Populaire de Libération (simbas)
AZAP	Agence Zaïroise de Presse
BALUBAKAT	Association des Baluba du Katanga
CAR	Central African Republic
CELZA	Cultures et Elevages du Zaïre
CEPGL	Communauté Economique des Pays des Grands Lacs
CFL	Chemin de Fer des Grands-Lacs
CFM	Chemin de Fer de Mayumbe
CFMK	Chemin de Fer Matadi-Kinshasa
CIMA	Cimenterie Nationale
CIZA	Société des Ciments du Zaïre
CND	Centre National de Documentation
CNL	Conseil National de Libération
CONACO	Confédération Nationale des Associations Congolaises
CONAKAT	Confédération des Associations Katangaises
CRISP	Centre de Renseignements et d'Information Socio-Politiques
CSK	Comité Special du Katanga
CSLC	Confédération des Syndicats Libres du Congo
CVR	Corps des Volontaires de la République
CVZ	Chemin de Fer Vicinaux du Zaïre
ECOCAS	Economic Community of Central African States
EEC	European Economic Community (Common Market)
ENA	Ecole Nationale d'Administration
FAZ	Forces Armées Zaïroises
FGTK	Fédération Générale du Travail du Kongo
FLEC	Frente de Libertaçao do Enclave de Cabinda
FLNA	Frente Nacional de Libertaçao de Angola
FLNC	Front pour la Libération Nationale du Congo
GECAMINES	Générale des Carrières et des Mines
GDP	Gross Domestic Product

IBRD	International Bank for Development and Reconstruction (World Bank)
IMF	International Monetary Fund
INEAC	Institut National pour l'Etude Agronomique du Congo
IRES	Institut de Recherches Economiques et Sociales
JMPR	Jeunesse du Mouvement Populaire de la Révolution
KDL	Chemin de Fer Kinshasa-Dilolo-Lubumbashi
MARC	Mouvement d'Action pour la Résurrection du Congo
MIBA	Société Minière du Bakwanga
MNC	Mouvement National Congolais
MNC/L	Mouvement National Congolais/Lumumba (wing)
MPLA	Movimento Popular de Libertaçao de Angola
MPR	Mouvement Populaire de la Révolution
OAU	Organization of African Unity
OKIMO	Office des Mines d'Or de Kilo-Moto
ONATRA	Office National des Transports du Zaïre
ONC	Office National du Café
ONP	Office National de Pêche
ONS	Office National du Sucre
OTRAG	Orbital Transport und Raketen Gesellschaft
PRP	Parti de la Révolution Populaire
PSA	Parti Solidaire Africain
PUZ	Presses Universitaires du Zaïre
REGIDESO	Régie de Distribution d'Eau et d'Electricité
SMK	Société Minière de Kisenge
SMTF	Société Minière de Tenke-Fungurume
SNCZ	Société Nationale des Chemins de Fer Zaïrois
SNEL	Société Nationale d'Electricité
SODIMIZA	Société de Développement Industriel et Minier
SOMINKI	Société Minière et Industrielle du Kivu
SONAS	Société Nationale des Assurances
SOZACOM	Société Zaïroise pour la Commercialisation des Minerais
SOZIR	Société Zaïro-Italienne de Raffinage
UDEAC	Union Douanière et Economique de l'Afrique Centrale
UDPS	Union pour la Démocracie et le Progrès Social
UEAC	Union des Etats de l'Afrique Centrale
UMHK	Union Minière du Haut-Katanga
UN	United Nations
UNAZA	Université Nationale du Zaïre
UNITA	Uniao Nacional para a Independência Total de Angola

UNTC	Union Nationale des Travailleurs Congolais
UNTZa	Union Nationale des Travailleurs Zaïrois
USAID	U.S. Agency for International Development
UTC	Union des Travailleurs Congolais

TABLES

TABLE 1:   AREA AND POPULATION OF ADMINISTRATIVE
REGIONS, 1970 AND 1982

Regions	Area (sq.km.)	Pop. 1970	Pop. 1982
Kinshasa	2,016	1,308,361	2,124,127
Bandundu	295,658	2,600,556	4,141,758
Bas-Zaire	61,869	1,519,039	1,726,608
Equateur	403,293	2,431,812	3,288,353
Kasai-Occidental	156,967	2,433,861	2,933,528
Kasai-Oriental	168,216	1,872,231	2,335,951
Kivu	256,662	3,361,883	4,361,736
Haut-Zaire	503,239	3,356,419	4,524,467
Shaba	496,975	2,753,714	3,762,806
TOTAL	2,344,895	21,637,876	29,198,334

Source: Government of Zaire, Bureau de la Statistique, and Makanda
Kabobi Institute.

TABLE 2:   POPULATION GROWTH OF
MAJOR CITIES, 1960-1982

Cities	1960	1970	1982
Kinshasa	403,310	1,308,361	2,124,127
Bandundu	11,500	74,467	103,513
Bukavu	60,850	134,861	158,465
Kananga	121,113	428,960	493,156
Kikwit	16,126	11,960	152,052
Kisangani	126,930	229,596	328,476
Likasi	80,212	146,394	191,606
Lubumbashi	184,126	318,000	592,111
Matadi	60,361	110,436	146,930
Mbandaka	51,397	107,910	153,440
Mbuji-Mayi	39,038	256,154	334,875

Source: Government of Zaire, Bureau de la Statistique, and Makanda
Kabobi Institute.

TABLE 3: KEY ECONOMIC INDICATORS
(in millions of U.S. dollars unless otherwise indicated)

Item	1974	1976	1981	1983
GDP (1970 prices)	2,366	2,218	2,024	1,982

BALANCE OF PAYMENTS AND TRADE

	1974	1976	1981	1983
Total Exports	1,283	1,000	1,499	1,500
Total Imports	911	800	1,290	1,150
Balance of Trade	+ 372	+ 200	+ 209	+ 350
Balance of Payments	- 237	- 155	- 721	- 462

EXTERNAL PUBLIC DEBT (including arrears)

	1974	1976	1981	1983
Total Debt	1,216	1,793	4,330	4,193
Total Payments Due	162	213	229	557
Service Paid	n.a.	n.a.	229	222

EXCHANGE RATE

	1974	1976	1981	1983
($1 = zaires)	0.5	0.9	5.5	30.1

MONEY AND CREDIT (millions of zaires)

	1974	1976	1981	1983
Money Supply	389	610	4,644	14,000
Net Credit to Govt.	328	676	3,784	10,400
Net Credit to Business	234	345	1,342	3,000

GOVERNMENT BUDGET (millions of zaires)

	1974	1976	1981	1983
Receipts	538	490	4,802	11,500
Expenditures	745	800	6,524	13,800
Deficit	207	310	1,722	2,300

Sources: Banque du Zaire, IBRD, IMF, as compiled by the U.S.
Department of Commerce.

TABLE 4:   PRODUCTION OF MAJOR MINERALS
(in metric tons unless otherwise specified)

Minerals	1960	1970	1980	1984
Copper	302,252	385,500	425,700	500,674
Cobalt	8,222	13,958	14,482	9,142
Diamonds				
(1,000 carats)				
Gem	415	1,649	345	4,873
Industrial	13,040	12,438	9,890	13,586
Gold (ounces)	314,145	177,128	40,864	80,335
Silver				
(1,000 ounces)	3,963	1,709	2,733	1,200
Petroleum				
(1,000 barrels)	0	0	6,566	11,704
Tin (before				
smelting)	8,775	6,356	3,159	4,120
Zinc (concentrate)	109,182	104,200	67,000	78,600
Manganese ore	381,630	346,950	6,321	15,518
Coal (bituminous)	163,000	102,000	287,000	104,349
Cement	200,055	419,000	443,000	400,000
Cadmium (metal)	505	317	168	317
Tungsten	274	189	134	47
Columbium-tantalum	254	146	92	46
Germanium (con-				
centrate)	25	21	0	0

Source: U.S. Bureau of Mines.

TABLE 5: PRODUCTION OF MAJOR CROPS
(in 1,000 metric tons)

Crops	1959	1968	1976	1982
Palm oil	244	206	128	88
Palm kernel	61	48	23	21
Coffee (Robusta)	52	46	88	64
Coffee (Arabica)	10	9	20	n.a.
Sugarcane	277	363	614	543
Timber (sawed)	212	119	81	n.a.
Cotton fiber	63	11	11	8
Rubber	40	41	28	17
Manioc	1,780	n.a.	819	883
Maize	115	n.a.	128	147
Cocoa	4	5	5	n.a.
Tea	4	4	6	6
Rice (unmilled)	110	n.a.	137	145
Tobacco	2	1	1	2

Source: Banque du Zaire annual reports.

TABLE 6:   INDICES OF WAGES AND PRICES
IN KINSHASA (1960 = 100)

Date	Wage Index	Price Index	Real Wage Index
June 1960	100	100	100
June 1963	235	342	69
June 1965	294	465	63
April 1968	549	842	65
June 1970	726	1,451	50
December 1973	956	2,065	46
December 1975	1,274	4,297	30
May 1977	1,529	9,484	16
December 1979	1,990	34,125	5

Source: Government of Zaire (for wage indexes) and UNAZA (for price indexes) as reported in Du Congo au Zaire, 1980, J. Vanderlinden, ed.

TABLE 7:   AMOUNT OF EXPORTS AND IMPORTS WITH
MAJOR TRADING PARTNERS IN 1976 AND 1985
(in millions of U.S. dollars)

Country	Exports 1976	Imports 1976	Exports 1985	Imports 1985
Belgium	174.5	126.1	499.4	259.7
United States	94.0	123.5	376.8	115.3
West Germany	33.1	74.3	190.5	97.4
France	53.5	85.1	83.9	134.7
Brazil	1.5	5.2	....	148.6
Italy	84.2	45.2	121.6	62.1
Japan	11.2	23.7	46.2	48.4
United Kingdom	174.9	38.1	42.4	50.1
Netherlands	12.8	34.1	28.8	50.9
China, People's Rep.	....	3.4	41.3	26.2
Sweden	....	8.6	29.4	12.3
Spain	9.5	25.5	20.7	13.6
Canada	2.6	6.7	12.1	17.5
Zimbabwe	....	34.2	0.4	22.1
Switzerland	52.9	16.0	2.4	17.0
Hong Kong	....	5.2	....	13.8
Malaysia	....	....	13.5	....
Portugal	0.2	3.5	5.5	6.9
Yugoslavia	....	0.5	10.6	0.5
Egypt	0.3	....	8.4	0.7
Central African Rep.	0.9	....	1.6	4.9
Argentina	0.1	2.4	....	6.3
Korea	....	....	2.4	4.0
Congo	2.7	....	6.2	0.1
Thailand	....	....	1.9	4.0
Greece	8.6	4.3	2.4	1.9
Malawi	....	....	....	5.3
Burundi	0.5	....	1.8	2.5
Romania	3.8	1.8	....	4.0
Rwanda	....	....	3.2	0.3
Zambia	0.4	11.0	1.2	1.9
Morocco	0.3	3.9	0.4	2.6
Israel	....	0.9	....	2.4*

* = Figure for 1984.

.... = Negligible or no trade reported.

Source: International Monetary Fund, Direction of Trade Statistics Yearbook.

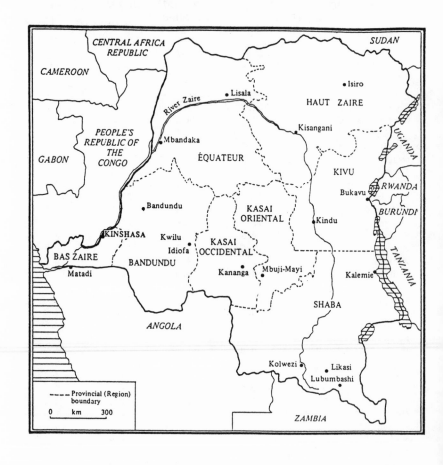

Political Map of Zaire

INTRODUCTION

Zaire entered its second quarter-century of nationhood on June 30, 1985, amid pomp and ceremony that celebrated a growing sense of nationhood, considerable political stability, and the reversal, at least at the macro-economic level, of more than a decade of economic decline. The previous 12 months had marked a significant decline in the rate of inflation. It also was a year in which the government had remained current on servicing its foreign debt for the first time in nearly a decade. And it was a year in which, despite continued hardship for the average Zairian worker, significant increases in agricultural production and gross domestic production had been achieved. Moreover, the independence ceremonies were attended by a number of political dissidents who had returned to Zaire, some of them after more than 20 years of exile, to participate in the festivities.

The political and economic improvements were applauded by the international community. However, it was apparent--and duly noted by many--that the achievements at the "macro" levels had yet to filter down to the average Zairian. For example, it was noted that although agricultural and mineral production had returned in many cases to pre-independence levels, per capita production, partly because of a 2.6 percent annual growth in population, still remained low, lower in fact than all but the landlocked countries of the Sahel.

Nevertheless, for a country born amid economic and political disruption, the historical development of which had been characterized primarily by the motive of plunder, the achievements were noteworthy. Even more impressive, moreover, was the fact that a nation had been forged from the disparate peoples speaking 250 different languages and 400 dialects who live in a land that, straddling the heart of Africa, stretches from the savannas of southern Africa and the highlands of eastern Africa to the woodlands bordering the Sahel and the sandy plains of the West African coast.

The shape of Zaire has often been compared to that of a heart. And although the physiological comparison may be debated, there is no doubt that it is the heart of Africa. Its 2,344,895 square kilometers of territory cover one-half of the Congo Basin, an area with one of the highest rates of rainfall in the world. The Basin is drained by the mightiest river in Africa, the Zaire, or Congo, River that is second in volume of flowing water only to South America's Amazon

1

River. Because of its location, Zaire has long been considered one of the most geo-politically strategic countries in Africa. It borders nine countries--Angola, Zambia, Tanzania, Burundi, Rwanda, Uganda, Sudan, Central African Republic, Congo--and the Angolan enclave of Cabinda. It also borders the lakes of the Great Rift Valley which form the headwaters of the White Nile River.

Zaire's mineral wealth is also considered of strategic importance. It produces two-thirds of the non-Communist world's cobalt, which is used to produce super-alloys for the aerospace industry; two-thirds of the non-Communist world's industrial diamonds; and 7 percent of its copper. The hydroelectric potential of the Zaire River and its tributaries is more than one billion kilowatts, or more than that of the rest of Africa combined. In addition, environmentalists say it is one of the largest remaining repositories of primary, tropical rain forest in the world. The country contains significant portions of the world's remaining elephants, gorillas, and wildfowl, as well as hundreds of thousands of species of animal and plant life still unknown to science.

Ranging from five degrees north of the Equator to 14 degrees south of the Equator, a great deal of Zairian territory is characterized by the hot, humid climate of the Congo Basin, where an average of more than 2,000 millimeters of rain falls per year. The low-lying terrain generally contains relatively poor soils but the region is rich in game, fish, and hydroelectrical potential. In the southeast, the terrain is characterized by more temperate savannas and woodlands that allow the cultivation of maize and millet as well as the raising of cattle. Cattle raising is not possible in the Basin because of the presence of the tsetse fly and other parasites. Woodlands and savannas also cover the northernmost parts of the territory, while fertile, densely populated forests cover the eastern highlands, where the temperate climate allows the growing of seasonal crops. The terrain lying to the west of Kinshasa is low, flat plainland, an ancient seabed that is relatively fertile and in the westernmost Bas-Zaire Region far enough away from the parasites of the rain forest to allow animal husbandry. Several mountain ranges cross Zairian territory: the Ruwenzori mountain range, which is the highest range in Africa; the Virunga mountains in western Kivu Region; and the Crystal mountains in Bas-Zaire. The mountains are largely responsible for the three series of cataracts that truncate the 3,000 navigable kilometers of the Zaire River: between Kongolo and Kindu in Kivu Region, between Ubundu and Kisangani in Haut-Zaire Region, and between Kinshasa and Matadi in Bas-Zaire Region. Despite the cataracts, which impede transportation between the Atlantic Ocean and most of the country, the 14,000 kilometers of navigable waterways in the country provide a natural transportation system that is navigable year-round. Railways were constructed between the 1890s and 1930s to circumvent the unnavigable portions of the river system and, during the first half of the twentieth century, 140,000 kilometers of roads were constructed to provide a feeder system for agricultural and mineral products.

Little is known about the early inhabitants of Zaire and archeological research has been impeded in many parts of the territory by the rain forest. However, anthropologists believe the first humans to arrive in the region were Bantu-speaking peoples from West Africa who moved into the western and southwestern parts of the Congo Basin area beginning in 1,000 B.C. Over the next 2,000 years they are believed to have spread throughout the Basin and toward the Indian Ocean and southern Africa. Migrations and counter-migrations helped produce the considerable mixture of west African, north-central African and east-central African strains of Bantu-speakers that are found today. Elements of Sudanic and Nilotic clusters of ethnic groups are believed to have begun migrating into northern Zaire beginning in 1500. They intermingled with Bantu-speaking groups in the areas, creating a mosaic of ethnic cultures. Meanwhile, the great kingdoms of the Kongo, Kuba, Luba and Lunda, with established hierarchies of paramount kings and lesser, tribute-paying kings and chiefs, began to rise in western and southern Zaire. It was these kingdoms that the European explorers encountered when they began arriving after the Portuguese explorer Diogo Cao sailed up the Congo River in 1483 and met the Kongo.

The Kongo, unlike some of the nations further inland, welcomed the European visitors. King Affonso I was converted to Christianity and the kingdom exchanged ambassadors with several courts in Europe. The Kongo also welcomed missionaries and traders. The former arrived seeking to save souls. The later came at first seeking gold and silver, but eventually settled for ivory and slaves in exchange for the cloth, manufactured goods and luxuries brought from Europe. The Europeans ventured a certain distance into the interior, but found the terrain and people there inhospitable and dangerous. As a result, they tended to prefer to trade with African middle men who brought the goods from the interior. Meanwhile, Africans and Arabs based in East Africa began developing overland trading routes into eastern Zaire. In the late 1600s, the greed of the traders, warfare between competing tribes, and fighting among the European powers led to a decline in the European presence. The abolishment of slavery in the western hemisphere in the mid-1800s also contributed to the decline, although the trade continued in the western part of the territory until the 1880s and in the eastern part of the territory until the late 1890s.

European interest revived in the mid-1800s and the writings of such explorers as Livingstone, Burton, Speke, Baker and Stanley whetted the appetites of European political leaders for markets and sources of revenue. One of the wiliest of the leaders at the time was Belgium's King Leopold II, whose dreams and ambitions far exceeded those of his relatively small kingdom. Under the mantle of associations (like the International African Association and the Survey Committee for the Upper Congo that espoused noble goals such as the exploration of central Africa and the abolition of slavery), Leopold II financed a number of expeditions into central Africa to explore the

Congo Basin and negotiate trading agreements with local chiefs. As a result, when thirteen European governments met in Berlin in November 1884, with the United States as an observer, in an effort to "negotiate an end to international rivalry over Africa and promote civilization and trade on the continent," Leopold was able to produce more than 400 treaties signed in his name with chiefs primarily along the Congo River. The treaties, the king's influence through the associations, and the greater interest by Britain, France and Germany in the coastal African territories, led the powers to agree to accept the Congo as the personal domain of Leopold II, codified in the Act of Berlin on February 26, 1885. Shortly thereafter the Congo Free State was formed and an administrative system was established to govern and develop the territory and "civilize" its indigenous inhabitants. However, Leopold II determined that the cost of developing the territory should be born by the territory itself. Consequently, the CFS granted European companies exclusive rights to trade and operate on large tracts of land in exchange for a percentage of the profits. More importantly, a labor law was passed that allowed the companies and CFS agents to forcibly employ indigenous labor or oblige them to provide a certain amount of marketable produce, particularly rubber, as payment of a "state tax." The labor law was abused to such an extent that entire villages were forced into the equivalent of slavery and the atrocities committed by agents of the state against groups that failed to meet their tax quotas raised a storm of protest in the international community. The outcry led a reluctant Belgian government to annex the territory in 1908 and the CFS became the Belgian Congo.

Under the Colonial Charter established by the Belgian parliament, the territory became a colony of the government. The king, nevertheless, remained sovereign, although his decrees had to be countersigned by the minister of colonies, who was answerable to parliament. Despite avowed intentions to improve human rights abuses in the Congo, the harsh labor laws persisted until the 1920s and numerous rebellions, sternly put down, were recorded. In addition, political activity was prohibited and a policy of paternalism evolved that regarded Congolese essentially as children, well-intentioned and potentially good citizens, but needing supervision and a firm hand. During the two world wars, Belgium was occupied by German forces, so Congolese material and human resources were contributed to the Allied war effort on Belgium's behalf.

Following World War II, colonial authorities and private companies began to regard Congolese labor as a resource to be developed and cultivated, and many of the harsher labor practices were abolished. Basic literacy was encouraged and in many cases the colonial government subsidized mission schools. However, training for Congolese was aimed primarily at filling semi-skilled blue-collar, or clerical white-collar jobs. As a result, secondary education was reserved for a small minority and the colony had no university until the 1950s. In addition, contact with Africans from other colonies was considered dangerous. As a result, few Congolese travelled outside the colony until the Brussels World Fair of 1958, when the Belgian government, eager to display its good works in the colony, sent hundreds of them to Belgium. Congolese were prohibited from forming political organizations, but in the early 1950s they began forming alumni associations and ethnically based "interest" groups. In addition, Congolese workers began organizing and calling for pay and advancement opportunities equal to those granted expatriate workers. Some Congolese began advancing their views in local periodicals. The articles were avidly read and were tolerated by the authorities who initially felt their audience to be too small to matter. These activities were encouraged by missionaries and "progressive" Belgian political leaders who argued that the Congolese should be preparing to assume control of their country one day. However, the activities were opposed by other Belgian leaders and many colonial administrators who felt they were premature. For example, a report in the late-1950s, considered daring, suggested independence be considered in 30 years' time.

Events began to move rapidly in 1958 following French President Charles de Gaulle's offer in neighboring Brazzaville of autonomy to France's colonies, and following the All-Africa People's Conference held in newly independent Ghana. Several Congolese leaders, including a fiery orator named Patrice Lumumba, attended the Accra conference and upon their return began calling openly for independence. During a rally in Leopoldville on January 3, 1959, a confrontation with security forces erupted into violence that led to two weeks of rioting. The Belgian government, in an effort to calm emotions, offered to move toward limited forms of self-government in the colony and elections were held for local councils in December of that year. The campaign for the elections led to the emergence of numerous parties, many of them based on the ethnic associations. However, some of the most influential parties boycotted the elections. In the face of continued unrest, the Belgian government called for a Round Table Conference in January 1960 to discuss some form of autonomy for the colony. Forty-five Congolese delegates from various parties attended. However, they surprised the Belgian delegation by making two demands before the conference: first, that a date for independence be set at the conference, and secondly, that all of the conference's resolutions be binding. The Belgian government was surprised but under pressure from both domestic and foreign sources, acquiesced. As a result, independence was set for June 30, five months away, and the Fundamental Law was hastily drawn up to serve as a constitution for the new nation.

In anticipation of independence, political activity blossomed and more than one hundred political parties were formed. Attempts to form nationally based parties foundered on ethnic tensions and personality conflicts and the larger coalitions splintered. Ethnic tensions degenerated into fighting in Kasai and Katanga Provinces and caused friction in the political parties and the ranks of the army.

Elections were held in May 1960 but no single party received a majority. A compromise was struck whereby Kasavubu of the ABAKO party was elected to the ceremonial office of president and Lumumba of the MNC was elected prime minister. The election of Kasavubu ended talk of secession in the ABAKO stronghold of Bas-Congo, but southern-based parties, particularly the CONAKAT led by Tshombe, left Leopoldville in anger over their relatively small representation in the Lumumba government.

The Belgian Congo became the Republic of the Congo on June 30, 1960, as many expatriate technicians and professionals were leaving the country for their annual summer vacations. Five days later, elements of the army, angry over low pay and the declared intention of their Belgian officers to remain in power, mutinied. The rioting, looting and atrocities that followed made headlines around the world, caused the evacuation of most of the remaining foreigners in the Congo, and led to the occupation by Belgian paratroopers of a number of Congolese cities. Fearful that the Belgian government intended to retake control of its former colony, the Congolese government asked the United Nations for security and administrative assistance. The United Nations subsequently began its first and, to-date, only "police action" in Africa. Following a series of resolutions, the U.N. Secretariat sent troops and police to re-establish security in the country, along with administrators, judges and technicians to re-activate government operations. In addition, relief supplies were sent to aid refugees who had fled famine and internecine fighting in Kasai and Katanga.

The mutiny by the army also brought a pay raise and promotions. The highest ranking Congolese soldiers at the time, master-sergeants, became colonels overnight. Meanwhile, Tshombe, whose CONAKAT party had swept the provincial elections in Katanga, led Katanga into a secession and, encouraged by foreign commercial interests, declared the Independent State of Katanga on July 11. Albert Kalonji, a southern leader who had split from the ANC, also declared South Kasai an independent state.

At the same time, the central government was finding it difficult to function as a unit. The Fundamental Law had established numerous checks and balances in government, but had failed to specify the extent of powers of the presidency and the parliament. On September 5, Kasavubu dismissed Lumumba after he threatened to seek military aid from Soviet-block countries to put down the secessions. However, Lumumba refused to accept his dismissal and his cabinet voted to "dismiss" Kasavubu. The "constitutional crisis" led Army Chief-of-Staff Joseph-Desiré Mobutu to "neutralize" all political activity and form a College of Commissioners, composed of young intellectuals and technocrats to run the government. Lumumba was placed under house-arrest. In November, he escaped and was heading to Orientale Province to join his supporters, led by former Vice-Prime Minister Gizenga, when he was captured and imprisoned in a military camp in Bas-Congo. In a move that has never been fully explained, the Congolese government ordered Lumumba and two senior officials in his government flown to Elisabethville. Subsequent investigations revealed the prisoners were severely beaten by their ANC guards during the flight and were killed shortly after their arrival in Elisabethville on January 17, 1961. Lumumba's assassination provoked an international outcry and led to the secession of Orientale and parts of Kivu Provinces. In February 1961, the College of Commissioners handed power back to a civilian government headed by Joseph Ileo. Kalonji ended the South Kasai secession and joined in the government. Gizenga and several MNC leaders were also named to the cabinet but did not immediately leave Stanleyville. U.N. troops took military action against foreigners believed to be aiding the Katanga government and the Katanga secession eventually was ended on January 14, 1963.

Tshombe went into exile but was called back to head a southern-dominated government in July 1964. The United Nations ended its action in the Congo that month. However, the Stanleyville group consolidated its hold on eastern Congo. It declared the People's Republic of the Congo in September and received diplomatic recognition from 13 countries. On November 24, 1964, amid reports of widespread atrocities committed against foreigners and the local population in Orientale, Belgian paratroopers in U.S. military transport planes dropped on Stanleyville. They recaptured the city but not before several hundred foreigners and several thousand Congolese "hostages" had been killed. The intervention prompted further indignation among supporters of the Stanleyville government and a rebellion began in Kwilu Province that included terrorist bombings and shootings in Leopoldville.

Under the Constitution of 1964, elections were held in 1965 and Tshombe's CONACO party made sizeable gains. Kasavubu dismissed the Tshombe government in October 1965. However, like Lumumba before him, Tshombe and his supporters in parliament refused to accept the dismissal and blocked the appointment of his designated successor, Evariste Kimba. Amid the latest constitutional crisis, the 14 senior military commanders gathered on the night of November 24, 1965, and decided to take over the government. The coup d'etat was carried out without bloodshed at dawn and Mobutu was named head-of-state with the power of decree. During the following months, civilian political institutions were stripped of their powers, the army was purged and military operations were launched to regain control of territory still under rebel control. In April 1966 the MPR party was launched and eventually proclaimed the sole legal party. Political power was gradually centralized by decree in the presidency and codified in the Constitution of 1967. Many of the early political leaders accepted the new regime. A number of them, however, did not and either went into exile or were imprisoned. By 1967, the Mobutu government had regained control over most of the territory. It began a program aimed at abolishing tribalism and regionalism and developing a sense of nationalism among the people. The program

became known as "authenticity." Under authenticity, former colonial
names were changed to "authentic" African ones. The Congo became
Zaire and citizens exchanged their Christian names for ethnic, Zairian
ones. In addition, European-style dress was discouraged and Zairian
fashions came into vogue. Efforts were made to rewrite Zairian history from a Zairian point of view and develop political institutions
that better reflected traditional patterns of leadership.

Economic policies followed the same course. Historically, the
Zairian economy, based at first on agriculture then on mining exports, had always tended to follow the business cycles of the world
economy, growing in the 1920s, experiencing a severe depression in
the 1930s, and rebounding following World War II. With the sudden
rise in mineral prices following the first Arab oil embargo of 1973,
the Zairian economy experienced a rapid expansion that led to excessive spending and heavy borrowing on international markets. In November 1973, at the height of the economic boom and amid popular
support for authenticity, the Zairian government nationalized all businesses with annual revenues of more than one million zaires and all
foreign-owned businesses in certain "strategic" sectors. (It should
be noted that the large mining consortiums had been nationalized as
early as 1967.) "Zairianization" led to a flight of foreign capital. In
addition, the nationalized establishments were redistributed primarily
on the basis of political connections, rather than business acumen.
As a result, productivity declined. In 1974, the price for copper,
Zaire's major export, plummeted to one-third its level of the previous
year. Government revenues tumbled and the government was obliged
to borrow increasingly large sums to cover a growing balance-of-
payments deficit. "Retrocession" was decreed in December 1974
which allowed up to 40 percent, and later up to 60 percent, foreign
ownership in Zairianized businesses. Despite this and other en-
couragements, foreign capital was slow to return. In the meantime,
accusations were growing of mismanagement and corruption in government. The Zairian government signed a number of economic stabilization agreements with the IMF, but for the most part was unable to
meet the requirements of the agreements. Annual inflation rose to
100 percent. Production continued to fall and foreign exchange became scarce enough on occasion to threaten productivity at the state-
owned mining companies, which provided more than one-half of government revenues.

Amid this background of economic conjuncture and political centralization, the first insurrection occurred against the Mobutu government since the end of the rebellions following independence. On March
8, 1977, FNLC guerrillas invaded southern Shaba Region from bases
in Angola, and over a period of several weeks marched to the outskirts of Kolwezi which, after Lubumbashi, is the most important mining center in the country. The Zairian army initially showed little
organization and only with the aid of Moroccan soldiers was it able
to drive the guerrillas back into Angola nearly three months later.
The incursion focused world attention on the Zairian government's

political and economic problems and led to a degree of liberalization of the political process and the launching of the Mobutu Plan for economic revival. The incursion also led to new purges of the army, the arrest of several prominent leaders from Shaba, including then-Foreign Minister Nguza Karl-I-Bond, and renewed efforts to induce exiled dissidents to return home.

In May 1978, the FNLC attacked again. This time, however, instead of marching through the sparsely populated countryside of southwestern Shaba, the guerrillas infiltrated Kolwezi, and in a surprise attack seized the town and stopped work at the mines and surrounding construction projects. The guerrillas then went on a looting spree. Amid reports of widespread killings and atrocities, a force of Zairian, French and Belgian paratroopers landed on Kolwezi and nearby towns and drove the guerrillas out. Two hundred foreigners and 1,000 Zairians were killed during the two-week occupation. However, work at the mines was quickly resumed, a pan-African peacekeeping force composed of troops from Morocco, Senegal and Togo was formed, and efforts were made to attend to some of the grievances of the local population which to a certain degree had supported the FNLC. In the same year, an insurrection also reportedly occurred in Idiofa, in Bandundu Region. It reportedly was harshly put down and fourteen village chiefs were publicly executed.

The Zairian government began a concerted effort to improve its image abroad. However, the effort was hampered by accusations of authoritarianism, corruption and human rights violations from exiled Zairian dissidents and certain members of the U.S. Congress and Belgian and French parliaments. Nevertheless, with the return of fighting in Chad, Ethiopia, Somalia, Western Sahara, Namibia and Angola, public attention was diverted elsewhere. Meanwhile, the Zairian government made an uneasy truce with the MPLA government in Angola, which it had opposed during the Angolan civil war and which it suspected of backing the FNLC. The truce led to the establishment of diplomatic relations between the two neighbors in 1978 and an agreement not to support each other's dissidents.

With the inauguration of the Reagan administration in 1981 and the departure of the human rights oriented Carter administration that had criticized Zaire and reduced U.S. military assistance to token levels, some of the political liberalizations began to be circumvented. Nevertheless, legislative elections were held in September 1982 in which multiple candidates were allowed within the MPR party and in which three-fourths of the incumbents were turned out. By that time, however, Zaire had become a party-state, as mandated by the Constitution of 1974. The Central Committee of the MPR had assumed most of the legislature's role as the government body for consultation and debate, and the legislature, known as the Legislative Council, had evolved into a body that met primarily to approve party initiatives. Under a system that had been evolving since the early 1970s, the Political Bureau, consisting of a handful of trusted political

lieutenants, assumed policy-making functions and undertook most of
the legal initiatives. The Executive Council of high commissioners,
or ministers, had become primarily an administrative body. And the
Judicial Council, composed of senior judicial officials and superior
court members, had become a politicized organization, the independence
of which at times was called into question by independent legal experts. Some political dissidence continued, most of it based outside
the country. However, two groups were active within Zaire. The
most notable was a group of 13 parliamentarians that in 1982 attempted to form a second party, an act which is against Zairian law.
They were convicted of treason and sentenced to lengthy prison terms.
They were amnestied but sent into internal exile when they refused
to cease their activities. Over the next few years, they were imprisoned and released several times. The other group consisted of
PRP guerrillas that had split from the Gizenga regime in Stanleyville
in 1964 and had retained control of a remote portion of mountainous
territory in northern Shaba and southern Kivu Regions near Lake
Tanganyika. The PRP staged attacks on the port town of Moba in
November 1984 and June 1985. Both attacks were quickly repelled
by the FAZ and appeared primarily intended to embarrass the Zairian
government.

        In the mid-1980s, faced with continued inflation, high indebted-
ness and low productivity, the Zairian government made significant
moves to liberalize its economy. In September 1983, the currency
was floated on the free market, ending 23 years of profiteering on the
parallel market, where the Zairian currency sometimes traded unofficially at rates as low as 15 percent of the official rate of exchange.
In addition, overall subsidies on petroleum and agricultural products
were ended and private participation was allowed in the mining and
air transportation industries. In addition, government budget deficits were slashed, imports were reduced and greater efforts were
made to honor debt servicing commitments. The measures greatly
impressed the international economic community. However, they also
caused a severe recession in the country. Real purchasing power
fell drastically, affecting all but the wealthiest of the elite. The
measures caused some labor unrest and many Zairians expressed concern over the declining ability of the government to provide health,
educational and social services.

        Mobutu was elected to a third, seven-year term in July 1984.
At his inauguration in December, he pledged to make his new term a
"social septennium" and outlined an ambitious plan to improve transportation and communications infrastructures, as well as education
and health services. In October 1986, following a month-long meeting
of the Central Committee, the Zairian government announced that it
could no longer abide by IMF stabilization programs which it said
were "strangling" the Zairian economy. The government said it no
longer could devote 50 percent of government revenues to servicing
its $4.5 billion foreign debt and would henceforth limit servicing to
10 percent of export revenues or 20 percent of government revenues.

The government also acknowledged that human rights abuses had occurred in Zaire and announced the creation of a ministerial-level post, called State Commissioner for Citizens Rights, to attend to complaints of abuses of personal freedoms.

Zaire's move to peg foreign debt repayments to export revenues was unprecedented in Africa. Peru had taken similar steps in 1985 that had virtually eliminated new infusions of foreign capital for that South American nation. However, many foreign donors expressed understanding for Zaire's situation and what were termed its "heroic" economic efforts. On May 22, 1987, following a two-day meeting in Paris, the Zairian government announced it had reached agreement with the Paris Club to defer payment on $846 million dollars owed to foreign governments. The government also announced it had received pledges from donor governments of $1.48 billion dollars over the next two years. The reported purpose of the aid was to help Zaire continue its economic reforms, which included privatization or liquidation of money-losing state companies and further investment in agricultural development.

Many Zairians remained skeptical over the reforms and doubtful that the political rhetoric would ever translate into actions that would be felt at the individual level. Nevertheless, the small measure of economic improvement, coupled with promises of greater prosperity and evidence of a growing maturation of the government and political systems, despite their flaws, led a number of exiled political dissidents to take advantage of the general amnesty and return home. Many of them were aging and in virtual retirement. They were being replaced in many cases by younger leaders, trained at the country's university campuses, professional schools and party institute. Political dissent remained a dangerous activity for anyone wishing to rise through the system. However, there was some appreciation, at least among those who remembered the restrictions of colonialism and the chaos following independence, of the sense of order and continuity in what from many disparate peoples and territories had become a single nation.

THE DICTIONARY

ACQUIRED IMMUNE DEFICIENCY SYNDROME see AIDS

ADMINISTRATION. The administration of the government and state
is nominally the responsibility of the various ministries. However, the Office of the Presidency retains most of the final authority for policy making. The Bureau du Président consumes
as much as one-third of the government's operating budget, and
the fact that the President has held the portfolios of Defense
and the Interior since the early 1970s has added to the office's
influence. In addition, the administration traditionally has been
highly centralized in Kinshasa, leading to complaints of neglect
from the remote regions, particularly in eastern Zaire. However,
since the beginning of the reforms of the 1980s, some attempts
have been made to decentralize the administration by increasing
the authority and staffing of the regional administrations.
    Politically, Zaire is divided into the capital of Kinshasa and
eight "regions": Bas-Zaire, Bandundu, Equateur, Haut-Zaire,
Kasai Occidental, Kasai Orientale, Kivu, and Shaba. The regions are divided into 14 urban sub-regions and 29 rural sub-
regions. The rural sub-regions are further divided into zones.
The government and party are organized along the same regional
and sub-regional lines, and rivalries sometimes arise among
representatives of the party, the executive (presidency), and
the legislature.

ADOULA, CYRILLE. The prime minister who headed the Congolese
government during most of the period of the U.N. presence in
the Congo, Adoula is best remembered for his belief in a united
Congo and his tireless efforts to negotiate between the central
government and the various secessionist factions. Adoula was
an "évolué" who in 1954 joined the Amicale Socialiste. He was a
co-founder of the MNC and a member of its first executive committee. Following the inconclusive elections of June 25, 1960,
Adoula was a major architect of the compromise that brought
Kasavubu and Lumumba to power. He served as Interior Minister
in the Ileo government formed in early 1961, following the dissolution of the College of Commissioners. Following Ileo's dismissal,
he was chosen Prime Minister on July 25, 1961. During the following three years, he attempted to negotiate an end to the
Katanga secession and the rebellions in northeastern Congo and

the Kwilu. In June 1964, a few days before the departure of
the U.N. forces, Kasavubu dismissed him and appointed Tshombe
to head a new government. He went into exile for two years,
but returned following the Mobutu coup and served as ambassador
to Brussels and Washington. In August 1969, he returned to the
government as Foreign Minister, but was removed from the post
in a cabinet reshuffle shortly thereafter. He died of illness a
few years later.

AFFONSO I. King of the Kongo from 1506 to 1541, King Affonso
welcomed the Portuguese explorers, traders, and missionaries
who sailed up the Zaire River during the first half of the sixteenth century. He converted to Christianity, along with a
large number of his people, and sent members of his court to
Europe. He established diplomatic relations with a number of
European powers and corresponded with European leaders. His
hospitality and desire for European goods are said to have led
to exploitation by the traders and in particular the spread of
the slave trade.

AFRICANIZATION. A term used in the late 1950s and early 1960s
to denote a policy of advancing Congolese quickly into positions
of responsibility in government, military, civil service, and private enterprise. However, resistance by entrenched colonial
bureaucrats and the lack of preparation for independence meant
that when the colonial era ended, few Congolese were serving in
positions above the clerical level. See ZAIRIANIZATION.

AFRO-ARABS. Traders and slavers originally from Zanzibar and the
east African coast who spread west, reaching Zaire in the second
half of the nineteenth century. Most of the Afro-Arabs were
driven out of Zaire by 1900.

AGENCE NATIONAL DE DOCUMENTATION (AND). Formerly called
the Centre National d'Enseignement et d'Information (CNEI) and
before that the Centre National de Documentation (CND) and the
Sûreté Nationale, the AND is Zaire's secret police, responsible
directly to the president. It is in charge of internal security
and counterespionage and is credited with having foiled at least
a half-dozen coup attempts. The organization was established
by the colonial administration originally to watch potential trouble-
makers. It was retained as part of the Interior Ministry following independence to control immigration, supervise resident
aliens, and protect key government figures. The organization
was transferred to the office of the President shortly after Mobutu
took power. Secretive and feared, the AND reportedly uses a
large network of informers and its own separate communications
system to monitor the activities of dissidents and potential chal-
lengers of the authority of the president. It is believed to have
played a significant role in allowing Mobutu to outmaneuver potential rivals.

AGRICULTURE. Agriculture and the achievement of self-sufficiency
in food supply has been the "priority of priorities" of the Mobutu government since the mid-1970s. However, because of the
disruption caused by instability during the post-independence
period, weak infrastructure and counterproductive government
policies, agricultural productivity declined during the first
quarter-century of independence. Zaire at independence was a
net exporter of food. Today, it is a net importer. Nevertheless, government efforts in the mid-1980s improved agricultural
productivity, although mineral production remained the dominant
sector of the economy. Twenty-five percent of Zaire's land is
considered arable. However, 2 percent is under cultivation. And
although 80 percent of the population is engaged primarily in
agriculture (70 percent at the subsistence level), the sector contributes only one-sixth of the total GDP. Three climatic regions
lie within Zaire: an equatorial region where palm oil, coffee,
cocoa, banana, and rice are grown; a tropical region of wooded
savannas where cotton, peanut, and manioc are grown; and the
high plains where potatoes, leek, and arabica coffee are grown
and cattle are raised. Most of the soil is moderately fertile.
However, the eastern highlands of Ituri and Kivu contain fertile
soils largely of volcanic origin, and the cooler climate there permits the extensive cultivation of vegetables like cabbage, onion,
tomatoes, and even strawberries. Zaire's major cash crops are
palm products, rubber, coffee, tea, and sugarcane. In the
large subsistence sector, crops like manioc, maize, rice, bananas
and to a lesser degree, beans, peanuts, and cotton are grown.

At independence, colonial authorities had achieved net self-
sufficiency in food, partly through the use of taxation schemes
and forced growing programs. Indeed, cash crops earned 40
percent of the Belgian Congo's foreign exchange. Following independence, political instability and the subsequent flight of experienced technicians caused a large drop in production and private investment in agriculture. Mismanagement and the continued failure by the government to invest new funds in agriculture and the transportation, extension, and communications networks needed to support it, contributed to the decline. As a
result, average annual growth rates during the 1960s and 1970s
were 0 to 2 percent while population increased at an annual rate
of 2.7 percent.

A nationalization program, "Zairianization," further aggravated
the situation. In December 1974, the government, concerned over
falling production, announced it was nationalizing agricultural
operations with annual revenues of more than one million zaires.
More than 100 farms and plantations were affected. In less than
two years, however, Zairianization was officially judged to have
been a failure. The failure was attributed to several factors.
The Zairians who received the Zairianized properties were generally politically well-connected individuals who knew little about
farming. In addition, the operations often were divided among
several beneficiaries and there was little coordination among them.

The departure of the experienced managers also led to the disruption of the marketing system. And finally, the beneficiaries
tended to view their new property merely as a source of revenue
and did not invest in its maintenance and long-term growth. Production continued to decline; in December 1974, the government
announced a policy of "retrocession," whereby 40 percent private
participation would be allowed in the large operations but smaller
plantations would be reserved for Zairians. The lack of response
to these measures led the government a few years later to allow
up to 60 percent private ownership in the sector. Continued
stagnation led the government in mid-1977 to announce the Agricultural Recovery Plan for 1978-1980. Capital expenditures for
agriculture, which had fallen from 15 percent of GDP in 1958 to
3.7 percent, were gradually increased and reached 13 percent of
GDP in 1977. In addition, a series of measures were announced
in 1983 to encourage Zairians to invest in farming. Price controls on food products were eased and foreign currency disbursements by the central bank for imported food were severely restricted. The government also instituted programs to increase
the production of rice, manioc, vegetables, and meat, and it
launched projects to improve roads and bridges, particularly in
western Zaire, in order to improve the farm-to-market network.
As a result, the government announced in 1985 that Zaire annually was producing 50,000 tons of wheat, (or roughly one-half of
total demand) and 1.5 million head of cattle (or three-fourths of
demand). Zairian officials said production had returned to pre-
independence levels and they expressed hope that per capita
production also would soon return to the levels of 25 years ago.
See ZAIRIANIZATION.

AIDS (ACQUIRED IMMUNE DEFICIENCY SYNDROME). A disease
first diagnosed in 1980 that destroys the body's ability to fight
disease, making it vulnerable to a variety of illnesses. Believed
to have originated in central Africa, the disease strikes African
males and females in roughly equal numbers and consequently is
believed to be transmitted in Africa primarily through hetero-
sexual activity and blood transfusions. Studies by Zairian, Belgian, and U.S. teams in the early 1980s revealed that 5 to 15 percent of the urban populations of Zaire and as much as 30 percent
of the prostitute population had been exposed to AIDS, albeit a
variety not always lethal. A non-lethal strain of AIDS also was
found in a species of monkey inhabiting northern Zaire, leading
scientists to speculate the lethal form of the virus may be a mu-
tation of a milder form of the disease that was acquired from a
monkey bite or from eating poorly cooked monkey meat. In Zaire,
however, where other health problems already were straining
government budgets, AIDS was viewed as a disease brought in
by foreigners; its transmission in the industrialized countries
primarily by homosexual contact also discouraged official recognition of the danger. As a result, in early 1987 the Zairian
government officially acknowledged 150 cases of AIDS in the

country, while doctors at Kinshasa's Mama Yemo Hospital alone said they had recorded 300 cases of the disease and that 23 percent of newborn babies at the hospital carried AIDS antibodies. The findings led some scientists to speculate there might be thousands of undiagnosed cases of AIDS in the country.

AIR FORCE. The Zairian air force is a relatively small branch of the armed forces. Its primary mission is to provide close support in skirmishes and transportation for the much larger ground forces. The force consists of one fighter squadron and two counterinsurgency squadrons of aging French Mirage F-1 and Italian Aermacchi jets. It also has one helicopter squadron of French Alouettes and Bell 47 helicopters, and a transport wing of U.S. made C-130's. The air force's 3,000 active members are looked up to and the force is admired because of the relatively advanced technological field in which it operates. However, maintenance problems, a lack of spare parts and, at times, a dearth of fuel tended to keep a significant portion of the air craft on the ground.

AIR TRANSPORTATION. Because of the size of the country and the poor condition of some roads, air transportation is an important link to parts of Zaire and at times has been used to transport minerals and food. The national Air Zaire airlines provides regular service to 40 airports, three of which--Kinshasa, Lubumbashi, and Kisangani--are international airports and can accommodate wide-body aircraft. One hundred fifty mostly unpaved airfields and landing strips, some of which are privately maintained, are also available primarily for small planes. The privately owned Air Brousse and missionary and relief agencies also operate small fleets of single and twin-engine planes. State-owned SNEL operates a fleet of planes and helicopters to maintain the Inga-Shaba power line. In 1982, 1,683 million passenger-kms and 31.5 million ton-kms were logged in Zaire.

In the late 1970s, domestic air service was opened to private carriers and several small companies began operating routes to regional centers like Lubumbashi, Mbuji-Mayi, Kisangani and Mbandaka. In January 1985, the Zairian government announced a partial privatization of the heavily indebted Air Zaire.

AIR ZAIRE. Zaire's national air carrier, called Air Congo until 1971. Air Zaire operates one DC-10, two DC-8's and a fleet of smaller jet and propeller planes. However, a lack of foreign exchange, shortage of parts, and chronic indebtedness caused operating problems during most of the 1970s and 1980s. The carrier was also at times subject to scheduling delays because its planes would be summoned for important government travel. Its planes were also used to transport coffee from the Kivu in early 1978 and cobalt from Shaba in 1979-80. In 1977, in an effort to render the carrier more efficient, Mobutu announced that Air Zaire would no longer enjoy a monopoly on domestic travel and in the mid-1980s a few private companies were operating regional routes. In 1985, Mobutu announced Air Zaire would be partially privatized and a group of Israeli investors, headed by Leon Tamman, said they would invest $400 million to rebuild the fleet and restructure the operations of Air Zaire.

ALBERT I, KING. Third king of Belgium who visited the Congo as crown prince, advocating a more humane colonization. Born in 1875, Albert ascended the throne upon the death of his uncle, Leopold II, in 1909. He ruled during World War I and the Great Depression until his death in a mountain-climbing accident on February 19, 1934.

ALLIANCE DES BAKONGO (ABAKO). One of the major political parties that wielded power in the five years between independence and the coup d'etat that brought Mobutu to power. The ABAKO was one of a number of groups that formed in Kinshasa and a few other urban areas following World War II in response to interethnic tensions. Its original purpose was to defend the rights and interests of the Kongo people. At times its leaders also advocated re-creating the ancient kingdom of the Kongo by combining portions of Zaire, Angola, and Congo (Brazzaville). On August 23, 1956, following the publication of the "Conscience Africaine" manifesto calling for a greater African voice in the affairs of the Belgian Congo, the ABAKO issued its Declaration of Civil Rights, calling for immediate political rights of speech, association, and press for Congolese. The ABAKO adopted relatively tough positions against the colonial administrators and even boycotted the local elections of 1959. Its leaders were considered to be radical by the colonial authorities and were frequently imprisoned.

The ABAKO drew most of its strength from Bas-Zaire in the west. However, the relatively large numbers of Kongo living in the capital of Leopoldville added to its influence. The ABAKO scored impressive victories in the legislative elections leading up to independence. However, the victories were not enough to give it a majority in the legislature. In a compromise, ABAKO's leader, Joseph Kasavubu, assumed the primarily ceremonial post of president, and another major winner in the elections, Patrice Lumumba of the MNC, became prime minister. ABAKO was dissolved with all other political parties following the coup d'etat in which Kasavubu was overthrown.

ALUMINUM. Zaire is known to have deposits of alumina ore in Haut-Uele and the Bas-Zaire regions of the country. However, interest has focused primarily on Bas-Zaire, where deposits estimated at 132 million metric tons have been found near transportation routes and adequate sources of manpower and electricity. The Zairian government has drawn up a project to build an aluminum complex in the proposed Inga Free Trade Zone and a consortium of foreign companies was formed to participate in a joint venture

in the area. However, richer deposits have been found in neighboring countries and the continued oversupply of aluminum on
the world market has led the consortium to postpone the project
indefinitely.

ALUMNI GROUPS. Groups of former students of Catholic mission
schools which, with trade unions and social/ethnic associations,
began pressing for changes in the colonial system, including better representation of Congolese interests in local government,
equal pay for equal work, and an end to other forms of racial
discrimination. Many members of the alumni groups became
leaders in the independence movement and political parties. Some
of the most notable alumni groups were the Jesuits, Christian
Brothers, Scheut Fathers, and Marists.

ALUR. An ethnic group of Nilotic origin living in a remote part of
northeastern Zaire, northwest of Lake Mobutu. Ethnologists say
it is the only major group in Zaire that speaks an Eastern Sudanic language, although Zairian ethnologists cite the Kakwa,
Logo, and Lugbara as equally important groups of Nilotic descent.
Less warlike than some neighbors such as the Zande and Mangbetu, the Alur gained influence in their region because of a
reputation for being able to mediate interlineage disputes. The
group is characterized by relatively small political groupings.
Chiefs are religious figures who, through intercessions with the
ancestors, intercede in disputes and are said to control natural
phenomena such as rain.

ALUZAIRE. A consortium of nine companies formed in 1981 to construct an aluminum smelter planned to have a capacity of 150,000
to 200,000 metric tons per year. The smelter, to be built at
Moanda, was one of several projects aimed at utilizing surplus
electrical capacity of the Inga hydroelectrical complex east of
Matadi. However, the consortium announced in April 1985 that
it was suspending the project for the "indefinite future" because
of low prices for aluminum on the international market and transportation problems within Zaire.

ALVARO I. King of the Kongo who is credited with returning the
kingdom to stability following the "Jagga" invasion of 1568-70.
However, under his successors, Alvaro II, Alvaro III, and Garcia II, the Kongo kingdom continued to lose influence and suffered rebellions from outlying sub-kings. As a result, Garcia II,
who died in 1661, is considered to have been the last effective
Kongo king.

AMNESTY INTERNATIONAL. International human rights organization that has frequently accused the Zairian government of detaining, torturing, and killing political opponents, as well as
some ordinary criminals. The Zairian government usually denies
the charges and often blames them on information that is outdated

or obtained from dissidents trying to discredit the regime. In 1986, however, Mobutu acknowledged that "some abuses" had occurred and formed a government ministry to deal with them.

AMNESTY OF 1983. On May 21, 1983, the Zairian government announced a general amnesty for political dissidents, whereby exiled dissidents would be allowed to return home and would be pardoned if they ceased their antigovernment activities. Although the response was cautious at first, a number of prominent exiles eventually took advantage of the amnesty and at least visited Zaire. These included former Prime Minister Nguza Karl-I-Bond, former Foreign Minister Thomas Kanza, former Ambassador to Brussels Mungul Diaka, Tshombe Ditenj (son of the late Moise Tshombe), former Ambassador to Paris Mbeka Makosso, and former leader of the Stanleyville secession Christophe Gbenye. In addition, a number of the 13 parliamentarians sentenced to prison or internal exile for subversion also were pardoned. See DISSIDENTS.

"ANCIENS." Term, roughly translated meaning "veteran," given in the revolutionary days of the 1970s to Zairians who had been involved since independence in Zairian politics, business, administration, the military, or other leadership positions. Some Zairians admired them for their ability to survive. Others did not.

ANGOLA, RELATIONS WITH. Relations between Zaire and Angola have been improving since the Shaba wars. However, both governments continue to harbor suspicions that the other may be aiding exiled dissidents. Angola, with a population of 7 million sparsely spread over its 800,000 square kilometers of territory, has a 1,400-kilometer border with Zaire. The Portuguese arrived at the Angolan coast at the same time as in western Zaire and trading and missionary activities were carried out jointly in the area for centuries. The colonial period in Angola is considered to have been at least as harsh as in Zaire, but when nationalist sentiment arose and calls for independence began to be heard in Angola in the late 1950s, they were suppressed. After Zaire obtained its independence, it supported Angolan independence movements and allowed many Angolan refugees to live in western Zaire. The Zairian government in particular supported the FNLA, one of three major Angolan factions that was based in the Kongo ethnic area of northern Angola and Bas-Zaire. Following the Portuguese revolution, Portugal granted independence to Angola and the three factions entered into a civil war. The Soviet-backed MPLA took control of Luanda in June 1975 and installed a Marxist-based regime that was admitted to the OAU on February 11, 1976, and to the United Nations on December 11, 1976. However, the FNLA and UNITA factions, backed primarily by the United States and South Africa, continued a guerrilla war against the Luanda government. Zaire continued to back the

FNLA, the leader of which, Holden Roberto, was President Mobutu's son-in-law. However, following the Shaba incursions, in which former members of the Katanga Gendarmes based in Angola occupied parts of Shaba Region, Mobutu and then-Angolan President Agostinho Neto met and agreed to end hostilities. Zaire and Angola established diplomatic relations in July 1978. Neto visited Kinshasa in August and Mobutu returned the courtesy in October. Relations improved gradually thereafter. However, mutual suspicions remained that were exacerbated by the Cuban and Soviet military presence in Angola and by the economic ties between Zaire and South Africa, which was staging raids into southern Angola.

Attempts were made to reopen the Benguela Railway, closed since 1974, which provides the most efficient route to the sea for Zaire's mineral exports. However, UNITA kept the railway out of operation with selected acts of sabotage. In April 1987, UNITA announced it would no longer sabotage the Benguela, a move seen as aimed at encouraging negotiations with the MPLA. In December 1985, relations were strained when an Angolan plane carrying 40 Cuban and 3 Angolan soldiers to Cabinda landed in Zairian territory 280 kilometers southeast of Kinshasa. Angolan officials said the Soviet-built Antonov aircraft became lost. However, Zairian officials said the pilot failed to explain why, after the plane landed, it was set on fire and its documents destroyed. A visit to Kinshasa by the Angolan foreign minister appeared to resolve the issue.

ARAB COUNTRIES, RELATIONS WITH. Zaire's relations with Arab countries have been largely affected by its relations with Israel, which were substantial during the first decade of independence. On October 4, 1973, during the Arab oil embargo that followed the Israeli-Egyptian conflict known as the Yom Kippur War, Mobutu announced before the U.N. General Assembly that Zaire was breaking relations with Israel. A number of African governments followed suit. Relations with Arab countries improved markedly in the following years. Zaire signed agreements with a number of Arab governments exchanging oil for minerals and timber. In 1976 however, Zaire voted against expelling Israel from the United Nations and refrained from condemning Israeli ties with South Africa. Nevertheless, relations with moderate Arab governments, particularly Saudi Arabia and Iran (until the Shah was overthrown), remained warm. On May 13, 1982, Zaire reestablished relations with Israel, saying the Israeli return of the Sinai Peninsula to Egypt, an OAU member, had ended Africa's quarrel with Israel. Zaire began to receive Israeli assistance in the areas of security, agriculture, and transportation, and support from the Jewish lobby in the U.S. Congress, which had been holding embarrassing hearings on Zairian economic mismanagement and human rights violations. Although Zaire had received $444 million in aid from Arab countries from 1973 to 1982, the government was disappointed by what officials privately said was the lack of serious Arab investment in the country's economy and the lukewarm Arab support for such African issues as the efforts to end apartheid and South Africa's presence in Namibia. However, a number of Arab governments, including Saudi Arabia, Qatar, Libya, and South Yemen, broke relations with Zaire. Others reduced their diplomatic missions and virtually all aid was cut off. The Zairian leadership felt the political advantages of restoring relations with Israel exceeded the disadvantages of cooler relations with Arab nations. Zaire's action was followed that same year by Liberia and later by Cote d'Ivoire, Togo and Cameroon.

ARMED FORCES. The Forces Armées Zairoises (FAZ) include a 400-man navy and a 3,000-man air force, but they are dominated by the army, which consists of 30,000 men and, since 1976, women. They also include a Gendarmerie of 20,000 persons that has exercised police functions in the country since it absorbed the national police in 1972. The purpose of the armed forces as written in the constitution is to defend the territory and maintain internal order. Although in the years following independence the officer corps was dominated by soldiers from southern Zaire, the army since the 1970s has attracted members from all over the country. A conscious attempt has been made to assign soldiers and officers to areas outside their home regions. This policy has prevented the development of regional power bases, but observers say it also has contributed to incidents of abuse of the local population.

The president is the commander-in-chief, and since 1969 Mobutu has held the portfolio of Minister of Defense. The army, assigned to eight military districts, contains fourteen infantry, seven paratrooper, one mechanized, and four guard battalions. They have received training at different times from Belgian, French, U.S., Chinese, North Korean, and Israeli military technicians.

The Zairian armed forces trace their history back more than one hundred years to October 1885, when King Leopold II created the "Force Publique." More commonly known as the "Bula Matari" ("stone-cruncher"), the Force Publique was a feared corps, officered by Europeans, that in the 1890s drove the Arab traders out of eastern Zaire and established control over Katanga. According to historians, conditions were harsh in the corps and there were three mutinies by 1900. During World War I, the Force Publique was reinforced with Belgian soldiers and sent to Cameroon and Tanganyika to join the allied war effort against Germany. They were highly commended. During World War II, after Belgium surrendered to Nazi Germany, the corps was sent to Ethiopia. In 1942, it joined the West African Frontier Force in Nigeria and also fought in Egypt. Four thousand Belgian troops remained in Congo following World War II, primarily as officers.

In the 1950s, the colonial authorities launched a system designed to prepare young Congolese for officers' commissions. At

independence, however, when the Force Publique became the
Armée Nationale Congolaise, there were no Congolese above the
rank of master sergeant. Following the independence festivities,
there was some grumbling in the corps over low pay and the lack
of promotion opportunities. The Belgian commander on July 5,
1960, five days after independence, summoned the men and wrote
on a blackboard the famous phrase: "AFTER INDEPENDENCE =
BEFORE INDEPENDENCE." The mutiny that followed spread
rapidly. The atrocities committed primarily against Belgians
caused panic among the European population and prompted the
Belgian government to send paratroopers to restore order in a
number of cities. The Lumumba government quickly raised
salaries, sent most of the Belgian officers home, and promoted
Master-Sgt. Victor Lundula to general and commander of the Army.
Master-Sgt. Joseph-Desiré Mobutu was promoted to colonel and
made Chief of Staff. The new commanders began visiting garrisons around the country in an attempt to quiet the troops. They
succeeded in large part, but the task of organizing the forces
in the face of coming challenges to security proved more difficult. Ethnic tensions were rising within the corps and increasingly talk was being heard of secession in Katanga and other
regions that felt left out of the central government's power
structure. Subsequent instability brought many foreign soldiers
to Zaire, including U.N. troops from African, Asian, European,
and American nations as well as mercenaries said to be the first
soldiers of fortune employed in Africa.

By late 1965, although the secessions in Katanga and South
Kasai had been ended and the U.N. troops had left Congolese
soil, the country still faced a rebellion in eastern Congo and
Kwilu, guerrilla bomb attacks and organized banditry in Leopoldville, and yet another political crisis caused by a standoff
between the president and prime minister. In the face of these
events, official Zairian history tells that the armed forces' senior
command met on the night of November 24 and asked Mobutu to
take command of the country. The bloodless coup carried out the
following day appeared to have the backing of most of the armed
forces.

Following the coup, greater efforts were made to improve the
effectiveness of the armed forces. Training programs were increased and a National Security Council was established in 1969.
There were purges within the armed forces and in 1975 seven
senior officers were executed after a failed coup attempt.

The armed forces were renamed the "Forces Armées Zairoises"
(FAZ) when the Congo became Zaire in 1971. In March 1977,
former members of the Kantanga Gendarmes lead an incursion
from bases in Angola into southern Shaba province. The Zairian
armed forces were slow to respond and 1,500 Moroccan troops
were flown in on Egyptian planes to help the FAZ repel the attack in what came to be known as the Eighty Day War. One year
later, the Katanga Gendarmes returned. Only this time they
seized the important mining town of Kolwezi and called for the

end of the Mobutu government. When reports of atrocities by the rebels began to surface, French and Belgian paratroopers in U.S. military planes were sent to the region. Zairian paratroopers also landed in Kolwezi and distinguished themselves in a bloody battle to regain control of the airport. A pan-African peacekeeping force of Moroccan, Senegalese, and Togolese troops remained for several months after "Shaba II" and France, Belgium, and North Korea began new training programs with the demoralized Zairian troops.

Most military observers agree that the quality and professionalism of the FAZ has been improved over the years. In addition, higher salaries and better benefits have reduced a tendency by members of the force to prey on the local population. Nevertheless, small garrisons in remote areas are still vulnerable to surprise attacks, as the assault on the garrison at Moba on Lake Tanganyika in 1984 exemplified. In that incident a group of about 50 guerrillas overran a garrison of 20 soldiers and left only shortly before the arrival of several hundred FAZ troops two days later.

ARMEE POPULAIRE DE LIBERATION (APL). The official name given to the loosely organized fighters of the Orientale (Stanleyville) Province who waged an armed struggle against the central government during the eastern rebellions of 1961-1967. More popularly known as "Simbas" (Swahili for "lions"), the fighting force was composed primarily of adolescents who were given amulets and taught chants to protect them from bullets. Tens of thousands of Congolese and hundreds of foreigners were killed during their reign of terror and the military campaign to end it.

ASSOCIATION DE PERSONNEL INDIGENE DE LA COLONIE (APIC). A civil servants trade union founded in Leopoldville in 1946 that was one of the first to begin lobbying for better pay and working conditions for Conglese workers.

ASSOCIATION DES BALUBA DU KATANGA (BALUBAKAT). An association founded by Jason Sendwe in the 1950s to represent the interests of the Luba in Katanga, the BALUBAKAT, was often at odds with the Lunda-dominated CONAKAT, led by Tshombe, and during the Katanga secession the BALUBAKAT were persecuted to the point that many took refuge in camps protected by U.N. forces. In 1964, however, BALUBAKAT representatives in parliament joined with CONAKAT to elect Tshombe prime minister. However, Kasavubu dismissed Tshombe on October 13, 1965, and appointed another BALUBAKAT leader, Evariste Kimba, to form a government. The CONACO coalition twice blocked approval of the Kimba government, a maneuver that led eventually to a government crisis and the Mobutu coup.

ASSOCIATION DES CLASSES MOYENNES AFRICAINES (ACMAF). Literally translated, the Association of African Middle Classes, the ACMAF was an association of small Congolese businessmen and farmers that was founded in 1954 with encouragement from the colonial government. Some of its representatives were appointed to colonial, consultative government councils. It was one of the labor and professional organizations that began pressing for an end to discrimination against Africans and greater Congolese participation in government.

ASSOCIATION DES LULUA-FRERES. Literally translated, the Association of Lulua Brothers, an association formed in Kasai in 1953 in reaction to the growing political and economic influence of the rival Luba Kasai to which the Lulua are related. The Lulua had driven the Luba from western Kasai in the late nineteenth century. As a result, many Luba had migrated to Shaba, where they took jobs in the mines and colonial government. However, the colonial authorities began to view the Luba as radicals and consequently encouraged the Lulua to convene a congress in 1959 during which they called for autonomy rather than independence.

AUTHENTICITY. A concept emphasizing the value of all things Zairian that at one point was declared the official ideology of Zaire. Mobutu first mentioned authenticity in February 1971 in a speech in Dakar, Senegal, during which he defined authenticity as "being conscious of one's own personality and values and being at home in one's culture." In interviews Mobutu has said he formally launched the concept on February 12, 1972. In any case, the concept began to emerge during the late 1960s and early 1970s, partly in reaction to colonialism and the continuing influence of European and other non-African customs and values, partly because of rising nationalism and partly because of the idealism, optimism and rising economic and political expectations that characterized the early years of the Mobutu regime and the end of the rebellions. Authenticity sought to create a truly Zairian identity by developing Zairian institutions and Zairian forms of expression in the nation's political, economic, and cultural life. Colonial names of cities, streets, bridges, and boats were changed to Zairian ones. Christian names were dropped. Citizens were encouraged to abandon European dress for more traditional clothes, a policy that launched a wave of new fashions such as the "abacost" (for "A bas le costume," meaning "down with the suit"), the bou-bou and other clothes made from Zairian designed cloth and prints. The Zairian constitution was modified. Educational curricula were changed. School and history books were rewritten. Foreign-owned businesses were taken over by Zairians and companies were urged to replace expatriate personnel with Zairian trainees. Hundreds of studies, monographs, and documentaries on Zaire by Zairians were commissioned and published.

By the late 1970s, authenticity had lost some of its luster, in part because of Zaire's waning economic fortunes and in part

because of a reaction to its excesses (at one point, visitors who
arrived at Kinshasa's airport had their ties cut off with scissors).
Friends once again began calling each other by their Christian
names and dropped what had been the requisite title of "citizen."
The need for expatriate expertise was officially acknowledged and
many nationalized firms were returned to their previous owners
in a move called "retrocession." Nevertheless, many of the
changes brought by authenticity remain. Authenticity helped
form the concept of a national character, served to unify the
country in many ways and was widely admired and imitated in
other African countries. See ZAIRIANIZATION and RETROCES-
SION.

- B -

BAKAJIKA LAW (LOI BAKAJIKA). Promulgated on June 7, 1966,
the Bakajika Law granted all wealth above and below the ground
to the Zairian state. The law was aimed primarily at ensuring
public mineral rights went to the government.

BAKER, SAMUEL. British explorer who reached Lake Albert in 1860,
travelling from East Africa's Tanganyika coast.

BAKWANGA. Capital of secessionist South Kasai and center of the
diamond mining trade. Its name was changed to Mbuji-Mayi in
1966. See MBUJI-MAYI.

"BALADOS." Term in vogue during the 1980s to describe the young
men and women who populated the streets of Kinshasa, surviving
by doing odd jobs or in some cases engaging in petty theft. Derived from the French term "ballader," meaning to roam or "hang
out." Other, older names include "nguembo" and "bill."

BALANCE OF PAYMENTS. Zaire registered balance-of-payments surpluses in the 1950s, a mixture of surpluses and deficits during
the 1960s, and increasingly larger deficits in the 1970s. The
small deficits of the early 1970s were offset by capital inflows from
abroad due to high mineral prices and foreign investments. In
the mid-1970s, growing budget deficits were offset by large bor-
rowings from foreign creditors, but the balance-of-payments situation deteriorated in the late 1970s. It improved somewhat in
the 1980s, but remained under pressure from low mineral prices
and the large amount of foreign exchange exported to service the
foreign debt.

BANANA. Primarily a subsistence crop grown in the wet lowlands,
banana has come to the attention of the Zairian government as
a potential export crop. However, poor transportation links with
the areas where the banana tree grows best continued to be an
impediment.

BANANA (CITY). A port town near the mouth of the Zaire River that is one of Zaire's three deep-water ports. In the early 1980s, the Zairian government, in an effort to ease congestion at Matadi and Boma, proposed to enlarge the port and improve the road connecting it to Matadi. However, the project experienced financing difficulties.

BANDA. A large cluster of ethnic groups considered a sub-group of the Zande, speaking a language of Adamawa-Eastern origin, living in northernmost Zaire near the Ubangi River.

BANDIA. One of two major groups of the Zande nation living in northernmost Zaire, speaking a Sudanic, Adamawa-Eastern-related language. The Bandia live in the western part of Zande land near the confluence of the Uele and Ubangi Rivers, between the towns of Ango and Bondo.

BANDUNDU. Bandundu is the name of the region formerly known as Kwilu Province as well as its capital (Kikwit once was the capital of Kwilu Province). The topography of Bandundu Region, lying in the west-central part of Zaire, consists primarily of sandy and relatively infertile soils of the Congo basin. However, some fertile areas exist, allowing the cultivation of oil palm and cassava, and cattle and hog raising. A large segment of the population of 4,141,758 (1982), however, lives primarily from river fishing and river trade. Bandundu city lies 400 kms up-river from Kinshasa, near the confluence of the Kwango and Kasai Rivers. Formerly called Banningville, the city was a small river port and fishing town until it became a regional capital, partly due to the rebellions and antigovernment activity in the southern part of the region. Its population was 103,513 inhabitants in 1982.

BANQUE NATIONALE DU ZAIRE (BNZ). Zaire's central bank, called the Banque Centrale du Congo during the 1960s and the Banque Centrale du Congo Belge et du Ruanda-Urundi during the colonial era. From 1961 to 1964, it was replaced by the Conseil Monétaire du Congo. In the late 1970s, as part of an economic stabilization argreement with the IMF, Zaire permitted an official chosen by the IMF to assume the position of Principal Director (second to the Director) in order to curb excessive and unofficial disbursements of scarce foreign exchange. The bank adopted austerity measures and restricted the ability of some well-connected businessmen to borrow or purchase foreign exchange for luxury items. The attempts, however, were considered largely ineffective until 1983 when, as part of a package of fiscal and monetary reforms, the government began to allow private banks to sell foreign exchange and the Zairian currency was floated on the free market.

BANTU. Eighty percent of the Zairian people are considered to

belong to the Bantu African grouping of people. Although debate still continues on the origins of the Bantu, due in part to
the dearth of archeological evidence, many anthropologists believe
they immigrated into the Congo Basin during the first millennium
A.D. from the Nigeria/Cameroon/Chad area and spread south and
east along the Congo Basin tributaries, eventually reaching both
coasts and developing a language system that could be called
"Bantu." Later, some began to emigrate toward southern Africa,
while others moved back through the forest in the direction from
which their ancestors had come. Hunters, gatherers, and cultivators, they initially formed small villages, usually organized
loosely around clan, descent, or lineage groups. By the 1500s,
some of the groups had evolved into large states such as the
Kongo kingdom and, later, the Luba and Lunda empires. Except for the coastal areas, the Bantu did not enter into contact
with Europeans until the mid-1800s. Arab slavers, however,
penetrated into what is eastern Zaire in the 1800s, trading cloth,
guns, and other goods for slaves, gold, and ivory. The Bantu
encountered the Pygmies, believed to be the first settlers of the
rain forest, and used them as workers or slaves. The Bantu developed stone and, eventually, iron tools. Sometime after 1500,
two groups of non-Bantu speakers entered the savannah north
of the forest. Some were assimilated by the Bantu and some
were repulsed, leading to the mosaic pattern of ethnic groups
in northern Zaire. According to oral tradition, Bantu groups
entered the Kasai/Katanga from the north about 1500 A.D. and
formed small states. Others entered the Sankuru/Lulua area
about the same time, perhaps fleeing the "Jagga" wars. They
hunted and fished and eventually developed buildings, tools,
and methods of food storage. By 1700, Bantu speakers were
established along the Congo River from the Stanley Pool to Bolobo, above the confluence with the Kasai River.

By the time the Europeans came into contact with the Bantu,
their societies had developed political systems that varied considerably in the hierarchy of their chiefs, their degree of authority, and their religious or ritual responsibilities. The chiefs,
however, usually made decisions upon the advice of counselors
and often after spiritual consultations with the ancestors. Another common characteristic was the tradition of paying tribute
to a higher king. Some groups had officials with judicial powers
in addition to a chief with ritual responsibilities. Others had a
war leader or officers with specific responsibilities.

BAS-UELE. A sub-region of northern Haut-Zaire Region, lying
    south of the Uele River, the Bas-Uele is a remote area with a
    sparse population of 567,040 (1982) of mostly Zande people, en-
    gaged primarily in subsistence farming and hunting and some
    river commerce.

BAS-ZAIRE. Zaire's westernmost region covering the territory rough-
    ly from Kinshasa to the Atlantic Ocean, Bas-Zaire boasts three

ports--Banana, Boma, and Matadi--that are the major gateways
for Zaire's imports and exports. Bas-Zaire is one of the most
developed regions of Zaire, with the third highest per capita
income, after Kinshasa and Shaba. The region is a major supplier of food for the Kinshasa area. It produces manioc, maize,
palm oil, sugarcane, coffee, some cocoa and timber, and is a
major cattle and hog raising area. In addition, petroleum wells
and a refinery off the Atlantic shore also provide jobs and cash
for local markets. The region produces one-third of Zaire's
manufactured goods and was home to industries in the metal,
woodworking, cement, textile, iron and steel and sugar refining
sectors. In addition, the construction of the Inga hydroelectric
complex 40 kilometers up-river from Matadi has contributed to
economic development in the area. The Zairian government,
wishing to utilize a surplus of electrical power and take advantage
of the transportation links and human resources in the region,
has proposed a free trade zone in the Inga area. The project
has attracted interest from foreign investors, but implementation
has been slow because of low prices for Zairian products on the
world market.

Bas-Zaire already was a densely populated area with a structured society (see KONGO) and an educated elite when the Portuguese arrived in 1483. The residents were farmers, herders,
and traders with other peoples further inland. The influx of
missionaries and considerable contact with Europe and the Americas over the subsequent centuries contributed to the region's
status at independence as one of the largest sources of professional and skilled labor. It also was one of the most politically
active regions and one of the earliest to form associations to
lobby against discrimination and other inequities of colonialism.

BAUDOIN, KING. The reigning monarch of Belgium since July 17,
1951, following the abdication of his father, King Leopold III.
Baudoin oversaw the end of the Belgian colonial experience in
1960 and the debate it caused in Belgian society with what many
considered to be tact and diplomacy. He paid an official visit
to the Belgian Congo in 1955, during which he foresaw independence in a speech, but said, "Before we realize this high ideal,
much remains to be done." In December 1959, however, he returned to consult with Congolese leaders on independence and
returned again in 1960 to witness the lowering of the Belgian
flag in the Congo. King Baudoin was born on September 7,
1930, in Brussels, the son of King Leopold III and Queen Astrid,
who died in a car accident when he was four years old. After
the Belgian surrender to Germany in World War II, he accompanied
his father and family to Austria. Following the war, the Belgian
government, angry over what was perceived to have been Leopold III's collaboration with Nazi Germany, refused to allow the
royal family to return to Belgium. As a result, the family lived
in Switzerland until 1950, when Leopold III asked parliament to
pass a law delegating his powers to his son in order to allow the

return of the royal family. Baudoin married Dona Fabiola de
Mora y Aragon of Spain on December 15, 1960.

BELGIUM. Zaire's colonial ruler from November 14, 1908, until independence on June 30, 1960. The Belgian parliament annexed
the territory from King Leopold II, who had ruled as sovereign
over the Congo Free State following the Berlin Treaty of 1885.
Belgium is a western European constitutional monarchy bordered
by the Atlantic Ocean to the northeast, the Netherlands to the
north, France to the south and West Germany and Luxembourg
to the east. A small country of only 30,507 square kilometers,
it is densely populated with 10 million inhabitants. Belgium is
deeply divided along ethnic and linguistic lines between the majority Flemish, who are related to the Dutch, and the Walloons,
who are a French-speaking minority. The Flemish in general
took a greater interest in the study of the Congo, although aspects of their personality often made them unpopular. Belgium,
small and militarily weak, was dominated over the years by the
Romans, the Dutch, the German monarchy, Spain, France, and in
the early 1800s, the Netherlands. A revolt, not the first, in
1830 brought independence, as Belgian teachers in the Belgian
Congo were fond of saying, after 2,000 years of colonial rule.
A constitutional monarchy was established in 1831 with executive
power invested in the king and legislative power invested col-
lectively in the house of representatives, the senate and the
monarchy. In 1914, despite a neutrality treaty signed in 1839,
Belgium was invaded by Germany. It only regained its sovereignty at the end of World War I in November 1918. Belgium was occupied again in 1940 by Nazi Germany, this time with little resistance; it was liberated by the Allies in 1944 and reconstructed
under the Marshall Plan. The primary motors of the Belgian
economy are agriculture from the plains of northern Flanders and
coal mining and heavy industry in southern Walloons. Belgium
is also an international banking center and Brussels, the capital,
is headquarters of NATO and the EEC. Belgium, like many
Western European countries, was preoccupied in the 1980s by declining industrial productivity, high taxes, a heavy social service
burden, and the advantages and disadvantages of immigrant labor
(in particular from Turkey, Portugal, and Zaire).

BELGIUM, RELATIONS WITH. Relations between Zaire and Belgium
vary between normal and stormy. As the former colonial power,
Belgium is still resented in Zaire and often made a whipping boy
for domestic problems for which it may be only partly responsible. Belgium often appears to react with the shock and hurt-
pride of a parent confronted by a rebellious child. The nature
of relations often reflects the state of commercial relations. Relations suffered under populist leaders like Lumumba and prospered under pro-business leaders like Tshombe. Following the
Mobutu coup, relations were generally good. In 1966, however,
in what was to be a precursor of the wave of nationalism soon to

strike the continent, Zaire broke relations with Belgium over the restructuring of UMHK. In December 1966, Zaire announced the nationalization of UMHK and formed GECOMIN to replace it. Under agreements signed later, Belgian companies continued to provide technical assistance and marketed some of the mineral products. A great deal of semirefined minerals continued to go to Belgium for further refining.

In the late 1960s, relations improved. Mobutu visited Belgium in June 1968 and was received as a house guest by King Baudoin. The Belgian monarch and his wife visited the Congo in June 1970. Later that year, however, relations deteriorated when Belgian companies were accused of dealing in the Congo's parallel currency market. The imprisonment of some Belgian executives during the scandal created an uproar in Belgium. The issue was resolved but relations suffered again in 1974 when Zairianization was launched and numerous Belgian properties were seized. Later, relations were further strained by the activities of Zairian dissidents based in Belgium. Relations improved again in 1985 when a number of vocal Zairian dissidents living in Belgium returned home under a general amnesty. However, they soured again in April 1986 when a Belgian judge ordered an Air Zaire DC-8 passenger plane grounded at Ostende airport. The judge, responding to a complaint by a Belgian former pilot of Air Zaire that he had been unfairly dismissed, ordered Air Zaire to pay $100,000 in damages and back pay. The Zairian government accused Belgium of continuously humiliating its former colony; banned all flights to Zaire by the Belgian national carrier, SABENA; said it was moving Air Zaire's European headquarters from Brussels to Paris; and threatened to sever all trade links. The dispute was resolved and the headquarters remained in Brussels.

BEMBA. A Bantu ethnic group living near northern Zambia west of Lake Tanganyika and Lake Mwero. Vansina identified the "Bemba cluster" as a group of three sets of similar communities that included the Hemba and Bemba-Haut Katanga.

BENGUELA RAILWAY. A railroad built by the Portuguese in the 1920s and opened in 1931, nearly 2,000 kilometers long, which links Shaba Region to the Angolan port of Benguela, near Lobito, on the Atlantic coast. At Dilolo, the railway meets a Zairian rail network that links southern Shaba and the Kasai regions to Zambia. The Benguela route to date is the most cost-effective way to transport minerals from Shaba to the coast. However, it has been closed since 1975 by UNITA guerrillas fighting to overthrow the Angolan government. When Zaire and Angola established relations in 1978, they officially reopened the route and a few trains travelling under heavy guard passed through. However, UNITA guerrillas have demonstrated the ability to sabotage the track at will and have even attacked train shipments. As a result, minerals from Shaba are exported via the National Way and through Tanzania and Zambia/Zimbabwe. UNITA announced in 1987, however, that it would allow the reopening of the railway. See ANGOLA, RELATIONS WITH; NATIONAL WAY; and RAILWAYS.

BENUE-CONGO. A term used by linguists to denote a group of African languages that include the Bantu tongues. Bantu and Adamawa-Eastern, which is spoken by a small portion of the Zairian population, together form the Niger-Congo linguistic division of Benue-Congo.

BERLIN CONFERENCE (1884-1885). The international conference that led to the European partition of Africa and the recognition of King Leopold II's Congo Free State. On November 15, 1884, 13 European nations gathered in Berlin, with the United States as an observer, to settle border disputes and "ensure the peaceful exploitation of Africa." During the meeting they divided the Congo Basin among France, Portugal, and the Belgian monarchy. The participants recognized Leopold II's International Association of the Congo and King Leopold as sovereign of the territory that would become the Congo Free State. The conference ended with the General Act of Berlin, signed February 26, 1885, under which the powers agreed the Congo should be governed by certain principles: freedom of trade and navigation, neutrality in the event of war, suppression of slave traffic, and improvement of the condition of the indigenous people. History shows that these principles were widely disregarded in the Congo as well as in many of the other colonies. The Act of Berlin formally ended the scramble for Africa and launched the colonial era. It also institutionalized a partition that left as its heritage 50 balkanized African states, the borders of which cut across traditional African political and ethnic boundaries, creating a mozaic of unrelated linguistic, judicial, political, and economic systems.

BINZA GROUP. Named after a suburban neighborhood of Kinshasa in which a number wealthy Zairian leaders lived, the Binza group was an association of young, educated intellectuals considered close to Mobutu that gathered in the years prior to the 1965 coup d'etat. The group included Adoula, Bomboko, Kamitatu, and Nendaka, some of whom had served in the College of Commissioners that replaced parliament for six months in 1960-61. The Binza group for the most part was critical of the Kasavubu presidency and the fractiousness of parliament. Following the Mobutu coup, many of its prominent members were sent abroad as ambassadors, ostensibly to explain the goals of the new regime, but in reality to weaken the influence of the Binza group. Some of the members were later arrested and accused of plotting against the Mobutu government.

BLACKMARKET see CURRENCY

BLUMENTHAL, ERWIN. A former director of West Germany's central bank who was the first foreigner appointed Principal Director
of Zaire's central bank as part of an IMF agreement in 1978-79
and later provided evidence of corruption in the Zairian government. Blumenthal's job was to help bank officials control irregularities in the disbursement of Zaire's scarce foreign exchange.
However, it turned into a quixotic attempt to prevent the barons
of the regime from raiding the state coffers. In December 1978,
he shocked Zairian business and political leaders by prohibiting
51 prominent Zairian businessmen from drawing foreign exchange
from the Central Bank because of their debts to the bank and
irregularities in their transactions with the bank. One businessman, Litho Moboti, was Mobutu's uncle and head of the family
financial empire. Seven others were members of the MPR's Political Bureau. Blumenthal left in 1979 and was replaced by another, less flamboyant IMF executive. In 1983, however, he
shook the Zairian government when he gave fuel to the opposition movement in a report in which he detailed incidents of corruption linked to senior Zairian officials and the presidency.
The report was meant to be confidential, but was leaked to the
public and became an important piece of evidence in hearings
by the U.S. Congress on corruption in the Zairian government.

BOA. An influential ethnic group living near Kisangani in Haut-
Zaire. In an extensive study, Vansina noted they were primarily
a patrilineal group that had no clans, but operated on a system
of lineages, each with its senior male member and usually including slaves. Newcomers to the region, if in a large enough group,
were allowed to form their own lineage.

BO-BOLIKO, LOKONGA MONSE MIHOMO. A union leader considered
by many to be the father of trade unionism in Zaire. Boboliko
was born August 15, 1934, at Lobamiti in Bandundu Region. He
attended Catholic secondary schools in Leopoldville and worked
at a printing shop there until he was sent on a scholarship to
Louvain, Belgium, to study social work. In 1959, he returned
to Congo and was elected Secretary-General (Administrateur National) of the Confédération de Syndicats Chrétiens du Congo, a
major union. In 1960, he was elected Secretary-General of the
Union des Travailleurs Congolais (UTC), one of three major
Congolese trade unions. He was a member of the College of
Commissioners that replaced parliament in 1960-61 and was elected
President of UTC in 1961. When the trade unions were united
under the banner of the UNTC in 1967, he was elected Secretary-
General. He was appointed to the Political Bureau of the MPR
in 1968 and has been a member of the Central Committee of the
party since 1980.

BOBOZO, SALELO, GENERAL (LOUIS). A war hero who headed the
FAZ from the 1970s until his death in July 1982, Bobozo began
his army career in the Force Publique in 1933 at the age of 18

years. He rose through the ranks and at independence was one of the highest ranking Congolese officers. He was an adjutant stationed at Camp Hardy in Thysville when the army mutinied following independence. He was promoted to Colonel and made Commander of Camp Hardy following the mutiny.

BOKELEALE, ITOFO, (ARCHBISHOP). Head of the Eglise du Christ au Zaire that groups most of the Protestant denominations in the country. Originally from the Equateur Region, Bokeleale was educated and ordained in the Disciples of Christ denomination.

BOLIKANGO, AKPOLOKAKA-ABUKULU-NZUBE (JEAN). A regional political leader who attended the Round Table conferences and served in a number of governments following independence. Bolikango was born in February 1909 in Leopoldville to parents originally from the Equateur Region. He studied and later taught with the Scheut Fathers. He joined the MNC and led its conservative wing for a short time, but split to form the Parti de l'Unité Nationale (PUNA) of which he was elected president. In 1960, he ran for president under the PUNA banner. He was arrested when Lumumba declared martial law in August 1960. He served as vice-prime minister and information minister in the Ileo government, and as vice-prime minister in the Adoula government. Following the Mobutu coup, he served as minister of public works in the Mulamba government and was appointed to the Political Bureau of the MPR in 1968 and to the Central Committee in 1980. He died of illness in February 1982.

BOMA (1). An early capital of the Congo Free State and one of Zaire's three ports accommodating oceangoing ships, Boma lies on the north side of the Zaire River, about halfway between Matadi and the Atlantic Ocean. As part of the administrative reorganization of 1978, Boma was made an urban sub-region. According to government figures (1982), Boma's population of 182,930 is actually larger than Matadi's, but Matadi's location at the head of the railway leading to Kinshasa has made it a more important commercial center. Nevertheless, Boma acts as a transport center for the agricultural and textile products arriving from the Bas-Fleuve sub-region and its links to Kinshasa have been improved by the paving of the road to Matadi and the construction of the bridge over the Zaire River.

BOMA (2). A Bantu ethnic group living in the Mai-Ndombe area along the Zaire River north of the Kwa/Kasai River. The Boma are considered a relatively heterogeneous group that traces its origins to the Tio Kingdom of the pre-colonial era.

BOMBOKO, LOKUMBA IS ELENGE (JUSTIN-MARIE). Longtime foreign minister who headed the College of Commissioners in 1960-61. Bomboko was born September 22, 1928 in Boleke, Equateur Region, and attended Catholic schools in the region before studying

at Lovanium's administrative school from 1945-51. He studied
political science at the Université Libre de Belgique and was
head of the student association there before returning to Congo
shortly before independence. He headed the College of Commissioners, a group of young intellectuals that governed during
the "neutralization" of parliament following the first Kasavubu/
Lumumba standoff, and served as foreign minister in the Ileo
government formed after Lumumba's death. Except for the period
in 1964-65 when Tshombe was prime minister, Bomboko remained
as foreign minister until 1969, when he was named ambassador
to Washington. He was recalled in 1970 and was arrested following the unrest of 1971. He remained out of politics for nearly
ten years thereafter, but was appointed vice-first state commissioner (equivalent to deputy prime minister) in 1981 for a brief
period.

BOSHONGO (or BUSHONG). A major sub-group of the Kuba nation
living in the Kasai region around Dekese, north of Ilebo. Kaplan says the Boshongo (the spelling used by official Zairian
ethnographers) initially were fishermen, but in the seventeenth
century they began to grow maize, manioc, and tobacco, and
eventually conquered some of the neighboring Lulua and Mongo
groups.

BRUSSELS, TREATY OF (1890). A treaty signed following a conference convened in Brussels to address the problem of slavery
in the Congo Free State. The conference was called partly in
reaction to the public outcry in Europe and the United States
over reports of mistreatment of Congolese by officers of the state
and private companies. Leopold II agreed to reforms but also
won the right to impose a 10 percent import tax to defray administrative costs.

BRUSSELS WORLD FAIR. The Brussels World Fair was held in the
fall of 1958. The Belgians, anxious to show their accomplish-
ments in one of Africa's largest colonies, brought large numbers
of Congolese to Brussels to be a part of the fair. These individuals ranged from traditional chiefs to the up and coming
évolués. During the fair, young Congolese like Lumumba and
Mobutu, as well as those studying in Brussels, began to realize
how isolated they had been kept from the rest of the world.
They came into contact with fellow Africans from other colonies:
with leaders from Ghana, which had been granted independence
the previous year, and with leaders in the French colonies that
had elected representatives to the French government and appeared to be on the verge of receiving some form of autonomy.
The contact with leaders of more mature independence movements
is said to have been one of the major factors in setting the stage
for the unexpected demands by the Congolese for total and rapid
independence.

BUKAVU. The capital of Kivu region located on the southern shore
of Lake Kivu near the border with Rwanda. With an area of
about 60 square kilometers and a population of 158,465 (1982),
Bukavu is one of the most densely populated areas in Zaire. Located in the mountains along a major trade route with east Africa,
Bukavu was a major trading center until the 1970s. However, by
the 1980s it had become somewhat isolated from most of Zaire.
Air carrier flights were infrequent and mail service was irregular. Many inhabitants were obliged to travel to Goma on the
northern tip of Lake Kivu for supplies. In addition, deteriorating
economic conditions in Uganda and Tanzania choked off trade
with eastern Africa. However, the Zairian government announced
in 1985 a plan to construct a road linking Bukavu to Shaba and
Eastern Kasai, as well as to improve telecommunications and other
links to western Zaire.

BUMBA. A river port on the Zaire River in northern Zaire, Bumba,
sometimes called the gateway to the northeast, is located between
the two regional capitals of Mbandaka and Kisangani. It is also
the port of embarkment for goods travelling along the railway
from Isiro, Buta, and Bombo in the northeastern corner of the
country.

BUMBA, NATHANIEL, BRIGADIER-GENERAL. Leader of the Front
National pour la Libération du Congo (FNLC) that launched the
two incursions into southern Shaba Region in 1977 and 1978.
Bumba was an officer with the Katanga Gendarmes that supported
the Katanga secession and later attempted to spark an army rebellion in Kivu and Haut-Zaire Regions. At that time, Bumba expressed support for Tshombe. However, during the Shaba uprisings, Bumba said he wished only to bring about the fall of
Mobutu and the advent of democracy in Zaire. Ten years after
the Shaba wars, he reportedly was living in exile in Europe and
did not take advantage of the general amnesty of 1983.

BURTON, RICHARD. An English explorer who, with John Speke,
reached Lake Tanganyika in 1858, the first Europeans to do so,
by crossing eastern Africa from the Indian Ocean.

BURUNDI, RELATIONS WITH. Burundi is a small densely populated
country, originally colonized by the Germans but administered
by Belgium following the end of World War I. It lies along Zaire's
eastern border and on the banks of Lake Tanganyika, where its
remote location caused it to be somewhat neglected by Belgium.
Relations between Zaire and Burundi have been close since the
two countries gained independence in 1960. Mobutu helped mediate a dispute between Burundi and Tanzania in 1972 after a group
of dissidents took refuge in Tanzania following a failed attempt
to overthrow the government of Michel Micombero. Relations
were further strengthened in 1976 when Burundi joined Zaire and
Rwanda in forming the CEPGL. Relations continued warm through

the 1980s with Presidents Mobutu and Jean-Baptiste Bagaza exchanging numerous visits. Mobutu also supported Burundi's
bid to host the Franco-African summit in December 1984, which
was attended by nearly two dozen heads-of-state.

BUSHMEN. A group of Khoisian-speaking people that migrated
through central Africa near Zaire's eastern border, although there
is no record of their having settled on Zairian territory. It is
to be noted that the term "bushman" is rarely heard in Zaire,
and usually only in Shaba Region, where anglophone terms from
southern Africa are occasionally used.

- C -

CABINDA. The Angolan enclave of Cabinda encompasses a mere 600
square kms of territory along the Atlantic coast north of the 30-
km strip of Zairian coastline surrounding the mouth of the Zaire
River. The port of Cabinda was a major central African Atlantic
port during the eighteenth and nineteenth centuries and competed
with Pointe Noire before being destroyed by the French in 1783.
Cabinda formally came under Portuguese rule in 1885 and was
administered separately until 1956 when it began to be administered as part of Angola. The area contains considerable offshore deposits of petroleum that provide the Angolan government
with most of its foreign exchange earnings. Two hundred wells
were operating in the mid-1980s, as a joint venture by the state-
owned SONANGOL (51 percent ownership) and the U.S. company
Chevron (49 percent ownership), which in 1984 bought the Gulf
Oil Corp. that had launched the venture. A nationalist liberation group calling itself the Frente para a Libertaçao do Enclavo
de Cabinda (FLEC) was formed in the 1970s aimed at liberating
the territory from Portuguese rule. Following Angola's independence, however, FLEC guerrillas continued their attacks, primarily against the oil installations. Zaire supported FLEC until
following the Shaba wars, Angola and Zaire agreed to stop supporting each other's opposition movements. Contingents of the
25,000-strong Cuban military presence in Angola guard the oil
installations against attacks attempted at various times in the past
by FLEC, UNITA, and South Africa. See ANGOLA, RELATIONS
WITH.

CABINET see CONSEIL EXECUTIF

"CADRES." A French term denoting the executive staff of an administration or the officer corps of a military unit. In Zaire,
however, the term has taken on a broader meaning with political
connotations: young intelligent elites who are being taught how
to actuate the levers of power and who, through political fidelity
and purity, expect and are expected to attain senior positions by
rising through the political ranks.

CAO, DIOGO. A Portuguese explorer who was the first European to land at the mouth of the Zaire River, in 1483, nearly ten years before Columbus reached America. In the 1480s, Cao visited the area several times, establishing contacts with the kingdom of Kongo, bringing Portuguese missionaries to the kingdom, and taking nobles from the Kongolese court to Portugal. See KONGO, KINGDOM OF.

CASABLANCA GROUP. The name given in the 1960s to what were considered the "radical" African nations: Ghana, Guinea, Mali, Morocco, and the United Arab Republic (Egypt). The Casablanca Group supported a strong central government in the Congo, as advocated by Lumumba. Following Lumumba's death, they met in Casablanca, Morocco, and announced they were withdrawing their troop contingents taking part in the U.N. operation in the Congo. All except Ghana did so.

CASEMENT, ROGER. British consul to the Congo Free State who was commissioned by the British government in the early 1900s to report on labor conditions in the Congo. His report, published in 1904, was one of those that, along with missionary reports and the works of E. D. Morel, aroused public opinion in Britain and the United States against the abuses in the CFS and Leopold's sovereignty over it.

CASSAVA. A food crop of the tubular family, more commonly called manioc in Zaire, that is a major staple of most Zairian diets. The plant grows well in poor soils, but it contains relatively low protein levels and some varieties contain poisons that produce goiter and tumors. Traditional methods to remove the poisons include soaking for several days and drying in the sun before pounding the root into a powder from which a paste is made. Scientists in Zaire and Congo are developing strains without the poisons. Efforts also are underway to produce strains with higher contents of protein. See MANIOC.

CATARACTES. A sub-region of Bas-Zaire Region named after the cataracts formed by the Crystal Mountains that render the Zaire River unnavigable for some 200 kms and contribute to the country's status as a "semi-enclaved" state. The sub-region is a relatively fertile area with a population of 590,793 (1982) that engages in farming, cattle raising, and some trading.

CATHOLIC CHURCH, ROMAN. The Roman Catholic Church has been the largest organized religious system in Zaire since the turn of the century. The Vatican's Annuario Pontificio states that 40 percent of the population of Zaire is Roman Catholic. In addition, the Catholic Church has played a significant role in political life, sometimes acting as the conscience of the nation.
     Roman Catholic missionaries first arrived in Zaire in the 1480s and heavily influenced life in the Kongo Kingdom for nearly 100

years. They converted a number of kings and chiefs to Christianity and established missions, churches, and schools. Kaplan writes that "Most Roman Catholic missionaries, themselves Belgians, shared the view of the colonial authorities that they had a civilizing mission, the task of inculcating in Zairians those virtues ... the capacity for hard work, decency, and reliability ... that would mark them as black Belgian burghers." The missionaries' influence declined in the 1600s, but organized missionary activity resumed in 1870, as European interest in Africa reawakened. The main task conferred upon the missions by the colonial authorities was in the field of education. Hundreds of parochial schools were set up during the first decades of this century and beginning in 1925, the colonial government further encouraged the efforts by subsidizing (primarily Catholic) mission schools to train Zairians. The Catholic Church also founded Zaire's first university, Lovanium, in the early 1950s. In addition to the educational work, the Church established clinics and hospitals, carried out large-scale baptism programs and built many churches. Many sects arose around the Catholic teachings, most notably the Jamaa and the Katete, that attempted to meld Catholic principles with African sensibilities and customs. However, these sects were frowned upon by the church hierarchy. In 1917, the first Congolese priest was ordained and the first bishop was installed in 1956. By the 1980s, there were more than 700 missions in the country working primarily in education, health care, and to a lesser degree in agriculture.

The Roman Catholic Church has long been a political power in Zaire and alumni groups of the mission schools were among the first to condemn discrimination against Congolese and other abuses of colonialism. However, the Church as an institution usually worked with the authorities, both before and after independence, and often played a stabilizing social role. The Church came into open conflict with the state in the 1970s. The state nationalized Lovanium University in 1971 following student unrest. The authenticity program also irritated the Church, particularly a decree ordering Zairians to abandon their Christian names for "authentic" African ones and the attempts to convert parochial schools into lay institutions. The decrees outlawing all youth movements but the JMPR, the youth wing of the MPR, and ordering the establishment of JMPR branches in all schools and seminaries also irked the Church. The Church responded by threatening to close its seminaries. In March 1972, the Political Bureau of the MPR announced religious services would no longer be a part of official state functions. On January 12, 1972, the journal Afrique Chrétienne questioned the policy of authenticity and was closed down. The leader of the church, Cardinal Malula, also objected at that time to the use of hymns with the lyrics changed to substitute the word "Mobutu" for "God." Malula was forced to leave the country and his residence was sacked. Later in the year, the government banned all religious television and radio broadcasts and prohibited religious church groups from meeting.

In February 1973, 31 religious publications were banned. The moves came at a time when Zairian political leaders, influenced by the People's Republic of China and North Korea, wished to establish the unquestioned supremacy of party and state in Zaire. However, the measures were resented by many Zairians who remained highly religious and many of the decrees were eventually relaxed. Relations soured again a few years later when the Catholic Church condemned corruption and the decline of morality in government and society. However, efforts were made to accommodate some government policies and Pope John Paul II's visit in 1980 sealed the rapprochement. The Pope paid a second visit to Zaire in 1985, this time beatifying a Zairian nun who was killed by Simba rebels during the eastern rebellions of the early 1960s. See POPE JOHN PAUL II.

Cardinal Malula is the head of the Roman Catholic Church in Zaire and the Interdiocesan Center in Kinshasa is the primary coordinating body. Major orders present in Zaire include Jesuit, Dominican, Paulist, Sacred Heart, Capuchin, Marist Brothers, Brothers of the Christian Schools, Sisters of Mary, Sisters of the Sacred Heart of Mary, and Sisters of Saint Joseph.

CEMENT. Five cement companies currently operate in Zaire with a total capacity of 1.1 million tons per year. However, output in the 1980s was less than 50 percent of capacity because of fuel shortages and the economic recession.

CENTRAL AFRICAN REPUBLIC, RELATIONS WITH. This small landlocked country of 2.5 million people and 241,313 square kilometers of territory lies along Zaire's northern border. The CAR historically has had warm ties with the Mobutu government. Mobutu is from a small town on the southern side of the Ubangi River that forms a great part of the border between the two countries and some of his family is said to have originated in CAR. In addition, the CAR depends on the Ubangi and Zaire rivers (the former navigable only six to eight months out of the year) for most of its overland transportation and commerce; as a result, the CAR tries to maintain good relations with Zaire and Congo.

CENTRAL COMMITTEE. The Central Committee is a 120-member body of the MPR that was established on September 2, 1980. It gradually assumed the legislative functions within the party/state. It became the basic consultative body for the president and the Political Bureau, responsible for debating laws proposed by the Political Bureau. Members were appointed by the Political Bureau. The Legislative Council, the members of which were chosen in popular elections, remained but primarily as an organ that ratified the laws emanating from the executive branch and the party.

CENTRAL INTELLIGENCE AGENCY (CIA). U.S. government intelligence agency that has been linked by researchers and the news media to many events in the Congo, particularly in the early 1960s when, according to declassified cables, it had license to engage in covert activities to counter communist activities in the country. Declassified secret documents have revealed that the CIA had a code name for Lumumba and ordered then-Bureau Chief Lawrence Devlin to study ways to eliminate him. Devlin has said he never carried out the plans. Some Zairian dissidents say Mobutu has collaborated with the agency, but various Zairian leaders, including Mobutu, have on occasion accused the CIA of seeking to destabilize the government. In 1975, Mobutu accused the agency of involvement in the "Ndele" plot, following which three generals and two Zairian army majors were executed for seeking to overthrow the government. However, the charges were never substantiated. At other times, the agency has been credited with warning Mobutu of impending plots against him.

CHAD, RELATIONS WITH. Zaire and Chad historically have had close relations virtually since independence. Zaire sent troops to Chad in the late 1960s to bolster the Tombalbaye government in the face of a northern rebellion. In 1981, Zaire supplied troops as part of the OAU Peacekeeping Force sent to Chad to protect the government of Goukouni Oueddai. In 1983, Zairian troops were dispatched once again after the Goukouni forces, which had been driven from Ndjamena the year before by the forces of Hissen Habre, threatened the Habre government in an offensive backed by Libya. The Zairians remained for two years. Chadian soldiers have frequently been sent to Zaire for training and Presidents Mobutu and Habre have visited each other's countries a number of times. On the economic front, Zaire, Chad, and CAR joined in 1968 to form the Union des Etats de l'Afrique Central (UEAC), a move that was greeted with hostility by Cameroon, Congo, and Gabon which already had joined Chad and CAR in the French-backed UDEAC customs union. CAR, under pressure, withdrew from UEAC, but Chad remained until the organization's demise in the 1970s. Chad and Zaire eventually joined UDEAC in the 1980s and also were founding members in September 1983 of the 11-nation Economic Community of Central African States.

CHANIMETAL. The largest metal works in Zaire, which builds and repairs large river boats at its yards in Kinshasa and makes a variety of consumer items ranging from pots and pans to farming tools. See STEEL.

CHIEFS. The "titular" head of a political entity ranging in size from the small village to a feudal state. Kaplan notes that with few exceptions, every community had a chief of some kind. Often the chief's most important function was to perform religious rituals or settle disputes. Among the Alur of northeastern Zaire, for example, chiefs controlled the weather and interceded with the ancestors to settle disputes. Some societies developed elaborate chieftaincy structures. For example, in the Luba and Teke empires, groups of villages formed chiefdoms, several chiefdoms formed a province, and all of the provinces formed a kingdom. Chiefs rarely made decisions alone and usually with a council of elders, with the notable exception of the Zande, who developed a system of supreme chiefs who delegated their power and privileges to subordinates. Some chiefdoms, such as those of the Lopwe and Teke, were hereditary. Some were appointed, as in some Luba societies. Some were elected and some were a combination of the two. A major duty of the chief was to collect tribute for a king or higher chief.

Under colonial rule, chiefs were expected to provide links between the administration and the traditional societies. Before World War I, the Congo was divided into chiefdoms ("chefferies"); the chiefs were appointed and paid by the administration and were given administrative and police powers. The chiefs' major responsibility was to administer customary law which was a separate legal system from colonial law. A European could not be tried under customary law, but an African could be tried under either of the two, depending on the nature of the charges. In the 1920s, the chiefdoms were consolidated into sectors that did not coincide with traditional political boundaries and as a result, created confusion. Following independence, chiefs continued to exercise their functions although the extent of their influence depended on their own prestige and amount of influence over local administrative authorities.

During the administrative reforms of 1972-73, the Zairian government tried to transfer traditional chiefs to other areas, as it had been doing with regional governors and military commanders, but it was obliged to abandon the policy because of public protest. Since then, the Zairian government for the most part has avoided broad, centralized attempts to develop policies toward or regulate the activities of the chiefs. Instead it has tended to approach chiefs individually, or within a certain area, to help solve specific problems and achieve specific goals, such as acquiring land for public use or obtaining local manpower for public works.

CHINA, PEOPLE'S REPUBLIC OF, RELATIONS WITH. Following independence, relations between Zaire and China were cool because of Chinese support for the Mulele uprising and other rebellions. In 1972, however, several years after the rebellions were ended and as China was being admitted to the United Nations, Zaire recognized and established diplomatic relations with China and East Germany. The friendship between Zaire and China deepened when both discovered they opposed the Soviet-backed MPLA faction in the Angolan civil war. Mobutu visited Beijing and North Korea in 1973 and, upon his return, announced he would radicalize the Zairian revolution. He said that henceforth he would be addressed as "citizen" and that he would establish cooperative systems of production. The nationalization of foreign-owned businesses with annual gross incomes over one

million zaires and an increased emphasis on cultural authenticity
followed shortly thereafter. The Chinese government backed
Zaire during the Shaba invasions which it said were the work of
the Soviet-backed government in Angola. The Chinese built a
convention hall called the "People's Palace" in Kinshasa and provided assistance and training in agricultural, particularly rice,
projects in Zaire.

CHOKWE. A Bantu ethnic group related in many ways to the Lunda,
with whom they are often at odds. The Chokwe were originally
a seminomadic, matrilineal society of hunters and some traders
from northeastern Angola who were largely unknown to Europeans
until the mid-1800s when they began expanding rapidly into Katanga, Kasai, and the upper Kwango and Kasai rivers area. A
people of the savannas, they were organized into groups of small
chiefdoms that, some speculate, enabled them to raid Lunda set-
tlements, and at one point take over the Lunda capital near what
is now the Zaire/Zambia-border area. The Lunda halted the
Chokwe expansion in the 1890s but did not move them back. Following independence, the Chokwe were an important political
force in southern Zairian politics. For a time, they allied themselves with BALUBAKAT because of their conflicts with the Lunda,
who dominated CONAKAT. In later years, however, their politics
were characterized primarily by a lingering resentment against
the national government in Kinshasa which they felt appropriated
the wealth of Shaba for its own uses and returned little of it to
the region.

CHRISTIANITY. An estimated 50 to 65 percent of the Zairian population is considered Christian, though Christianity is often mixed
with local religious practices and liturgy. Roman Catholicism
predominates, claiming 60 to 70 percent of Zaire's Christians.
Twenty to 30 percent are estimated to belong to Protestant denominations, and the remainder adhere to African offshoots of
Christianity, such as Kimbanguism. Christianity arrived in Zaire
during the 1480s when missionaries brought by explorer Diogo
Cao converted the brother of the reigning king, who later became King Affonso I. Affonso I proved receptive to Catholicism
as well as to aspects of European culture. Christianity began
spreading slowly eastward with the European traders and missionaries. The influence of Christianity, however, declined in
the 1600s with the rise of the slave and ivory trade boom. However, it returned beginning in 1880 with the arrival of the France-
based Fathers of the Holy Spirit in Boma and the Order of Missionaries in Africa ("White Fathers") on the shores of Lake Tanganyika. Belgium's Scheut Fathers arrived in 1888 and the number of Catholic missions grew to 17 by 1900. The first Protestant
mission was founded in 1878 and expanded quickly following the
Berlin Treaty, with British, Americans, Swedish, French, and
Belgian churches sending missionaries to build schools, churches,
and hospitals. There were 46 Protestant missionary groups in

Congo at independence. That figure has nearly doubled since then. Kimbanguism, the church of followers of Simon Kimbangu, mixed African traditions with Christianity. The church was harshly repressed in the early years but eventually was accepted and admitted to the World Council of Churches in 1969. Its membership has grown steadily and may now constitute 10 percent of all Zairian Christians.

The Christian Church was influential in politics during the early years of the Mobutu regime. However, with the advent of authenticity and the nationalistic policies of the 1960s and early 1970s, the church entered a period of confrontation with the government. In 1972, Mobutu decreed that all Zairians born after February 16, 1972, would bear, instead of Christian names, the names of their ancestors. In March, the government announced that religious services would no longer be a part of official state functions. Other measures were taken to lessen the influence of the church in politics, including the suspension of the journal Afrique Chrétienne, the banning of all Christian broadcasts, and the temporary exile of the head of the Roman Catholic Church, Cardinal Joseph Malula, in 1972. At its peak, some hymns were adapted by the government with the word "Mobutu" substituted for "God," just as early missionaries had substituted "God" and "Jesus" for the names of traditional African gods in indigenous religious songs when they began their evangelical work. In the mid-1970s, the government loosened some of its anti-church policies and in October 1976 rescinded an earlier decision to take over all church schools. In the 1970s, in the face of a decline in government services, church agencies assumed a large role in distributing foreign food shipments and the development of educational facilities and texts. Church and State had reached a relative peace by the time Pope John Paul II visited Zaire in 1980 and again in 1985. In the 1980s, the church devoted itself less to trying to influence the government and concentrated more on tending the needs of those suffering because of economic decline, migration to the cities and the loss of family support-systems. See CATHOLIC CHURCH, ROMAN and PROTESTANTISM.

CIMENTERIE NATIONALE (CIMA). A cement plant in Bas-Zaire begun in 1978 with 51 percent government ownership and the remainder owned by a private West German firm.

CITE. Term coined by the Belgians to denote the "inner city" or indigenous sections of Zaire's cities. In Kinshasa in particular, the cité is a teeming neighborhood of crowded homes, some of which are government-built housing projects, others individually built shacks. The cité is a vigorous economic and political sector of the city and no politician ignored the mood and the rumors of the masses that dwell there.

CIVIL RIGHTS, DECLARATION OF (DECLARATION DES DROITS

CIVILS). A document published by ABAKO on August 23, 1956, partly in reaction to a more cautious "manifesto" published in Conscience Africaine on June 30, 1956. The declaration called for immediate political rights of association, speech, and press for Congolese. It is often considered the first public manifestation of the growing pressure among Zairian intellectuals for political freedom and, eventually, independence.

CIVIL SERVICE (FONCTION PUBLIQUE). A system of public employment by the government that was essentially inherited from the Belgian colonial structure but that has been modified somewhat since independence. The government-wide civil service was abolished in 1972 in order to give the state commissioners (ministers) greater leeway in hiring and firing employees within their departments. However, significant constraints were maintained and the Department of Finance and the Permanent Commission for Public Administration continued to oversee employment practices in order to control abuses. The concept of civil service resembles that of many other countries. Government jobs are viewed by many as a reward for political service and political appointments run deep. A job with the government is considered relatively secure although the paycheck is not always on time. Most civil servants must profess "militantism" within the party. They, like all Zairians, are automatically members of the MPR. At the lower levels of the service, career stagnation, boredom and inefficiency are evident in many departments.

CLANS. Clans are relatively close-knit groups, usually within the extended family, often organized around one or two veteran family members, their children, grandchildren, spouses, and sometimes members of the spouses' families. Clans, by most definitions, are usually within the same ethnic group, but often spread further out than descent groups, particularly for political purposes and in situations where greater numbers were needed for survival. See DESCENT GROUPS.

CLIMATE. Zaire's climate is tropical. It is characterized by a long (four months) and short (two weeks) hot, wet season called the rainy season that alternates with a long and short temperate, dry period called the dry season. The country straddles the equator, with one-third of the territory in the northern hemisphere and two-thirds in the southern hemisphere. As a result, farming is carried out year-round and most rivers enjoy relatively stable water levels. Average annual rainfall is 1,000 to 2,220 millimeters, depending on the season. Rainfall north of the equator is usually heaviest between May and September, and heaviest in the southern hemisphere from November to March. With some variations, dry season in the north is from November to March and in the south from May to September. In some areas, like parts of the Congo Basin and central Kivu, it rains almost every day of the year. Temperatures generally range from 20 to 35

degrees Celsius, or 68 to 95 degrees Fahrenheit, although temperatures in parts of Shaba sometimes fall below 10 degrees Celsius
(50 degrees Fahrenheit). Temperatures average 26 degrees
Celsius (78 degrees Fahrenheit) in coastal areas and 18 degrees
Celsius (64 degrees Fahrenheit) in mountainous areas. Depending on the season and the region, humidity ranges from 35 to
95 percent.

CLOTH. In Zaire and other Francophone African countries, the word
"pagne" is used to denote the colorful print fabrics used to make
everything from bedsheets and curtains to clothes and head-
dresses. Although the cloth originated primarily in Dutch controlled parts of Malaysia, where the use of wax and dyes to
create colorful prints created some of the most valued pieces of
cloth in the world, the manufacture of the prints spread through
Africa quickly and became identified as one of Africa's major
contributions to fashion. Today most African countries, including
Zaire, have textile factories producing the fabrics which are a
mainstay of the small traders. The cloth, made in bolts two
yards wide, is usually cut for resale into strips two to six yards
in length. The cloth may be hemmed and worn as a robe or
body wrap, or cut to make shirts, blouses, and the pajamas-
style outfits. A staple of African culture and dress, many prints
are given a name. Some are designed and marketed for special
puposes, whether it be to praise a leader or to mark a special
event such as a summit meeting, a soccer tournament, a cultural
festival, or a visit by a foreign head-of-state.

COAL. Zaire contains deposits of coal estimated at 60 million metric
tons. However, a great deal of the deposits are of relatively poor
quality and are located in isolated areas where transportation
costs are prohibitive. The country produces 110,000 metric tons
of low grade coal primarily in Shaba that is used by a cement
factory at Kalemie. High quality coke and coal that are used for
mineral processing are imported from Zimbabwe. Imports average
130,000 tons per year. Because electrical usage is well below
capacity since the completion of the Inga hydroelectrical complex
and Inga-Shaba power line, electrical power is the preferred
form of power.

COBALT. Cobalt, a by-product of some copper ores, is used to make
super-alloys, particularly for the aerospace industry. Zaire produces two-thirds of the non-Communist world's cobalt from two
GECAMINES-operated refineries at Likasi and Kolwezi. From
1980 to 1984 Zaire supplied 46 percent of U.S. cobalt imports.
Production rose steadily during the 1970s and peaked at 14,500
tons in 1980 when the price reached $40 per pound on the spot
market. Production fell over the next three years, to 5,400
tons, in part because of a lack of spare parts for mining equipment and the exhaustion of easily accessible ores. Production
began rising again in the 1980s and reached 1,000 tons in 1985.

Since the reorganization of GECAMINES in 1984, Zaire has been
pursuing a policy of "swing" production of cobalt. Because
it produces such a great proportion of the world's cobalt, Zaire
has decided to seek with Zambia, another major cobalt producer,
a buffer stock system in an effort to maintain a world price of
at least $11.70 per pound. Demand, however, remained low. In
November 1986, Zaire and Zambia announced an agreement to
seek to stabilize the price at $7 per pound and said they would
withhold exports from the market when the price fell below that
level.

COFFEE. In the 1980s, coffee was Zaire's largest agricultural export. The government agency, Office National du Café, said
production reached 100,000 tons in 1985, of which 80,000 tons
were "exportable." Production reached that level before independence but fell when the large coffee estates were abandoned
during the political instability of the early 1960s. Production
rose from fewer than 50 thousand tons in 1967 to 110 thousand
tons in 1976, but declined for several years before the government launched new incentives for growers in 1983. Two major
varieties are grown in Zaire: the hearty robusta that is grown
in the Ubangi, Uele, Kivu, Kasai, and Bas-Zaire areas; and the
lighter Arabica, which constitutes one-fifth of the total crop,
that grows in the higher altitudes of eastern Kivu and Ituri.

COLLEGE OF COMMISSIONERS. A group of young technocrats and
intellectuals formed to direct state affairs after Mobutu "neutralized" the Congolese government in September 1960, following
the constitutional crisis created by the political standoff between
Kasavubu and Lumumba. The commission, headed by Justin-
Marie Bomboko, was formally installed September 29, 1960. It
too, however, was wracked by factionalism and was dissolved
February 9, 1961, following the formation of the Ileo government.

"COLON." A French term that means, when literally translated,
"colonialist." The colon was usually an agent or other secular
representative of the colonial administration or the Belgian government. The term, however, came to be used to describe other
European residents of the Congo who, through manner and attitude, seemed to personalize the European attitude of superiority
over Africans. See COLONIALISM.

COLONIAL CHARTER. A law passed October 18, 1908, by the Belgian parliament that formally ended the Congo Free State and
King Leopold II's personal sovereignty over the territory. The
charter, passed partly in reaction to the international outcry over
human rights abuses in the CFS, set out goals for the colonializa-
tion of what would become the Belgian Congo. The goals included a "civilizing" mission of educating and Christianizing the
indigenous people, and the charter guaranteed that the abuses of
the CFS would not reoccur. In response, however, to a reluctance

among some Belgian political leaders to assume so heavy a financial burden, it was also determined that the colony would earn a "profit" for the metropole. Under the charter, Leopold II lost his sovereignty over the territory, but still retained a great deal of authority. He governed with the Belgian parliament and executive branch and ruled by decree, although the decrees required the approval of the minister of colonies. See CONSTITUTION.

COLONIALISM. Although Europeans had been carrying out colonizing activities, such as exploration, trade, and evangelization for centuries, the African colonial period only formally began with the signing of the Berlin Act on February 26, 1885. The act, often called the European partition of Africa, divided the Congo Basin among France, Portugal, and the Belgian monarchy, and recognized what was to become the Congo Free State and King Leopold II's personal sovereignty over it. The Congo Free State became the Belgian Congo 23 years later when, on November 15, 1908, the Belgian parliament annexed the territory following an international outcry over abusive labor practices against Africans by traders and corporate monopolies. Colonialism officially ended with independence on June 30, 1960.

The topic of colonialism probably always will remain controversial. Most Africans view colonialism as a period of occupation of their soil by a foreign power, a period of humiliation and of repressed rights and freedoms. Many "colons," however, saw colonialism as a flawed but well-intentioned attempt to administer a vast, ungovernable land by dedicated, self-sacrificing individuals whose pioneering work led to the rise of Africa's independent states, albeit too suddenly and 20 to 50 years too early. In Zaire, colonial rule was imposed primarily because of excessively harsh labor practices. It was also said to have resulted from the growing realization in Belgium that the territory possessed vast riches and could be made "economically viable," that is, that the cost of developing an infrastructure in the territory could be amortized with the profits from its exploitation. Belgian colonial rule ended some of the forced labor and some of the mining and farming monopolies. However, exploitation continued nevertheless in order to provide revenues to the metropole. Under the Colonial Charter, the colony was administered by a governor-general, appointed by the king, who acted in consultation with a council but ruled by ordinance. Political activity was outlawed. According to many historians, the "colons" considered the African to be a child, superstitious, slow to learn, and generally in need of supervision. The role of the colonizer, they felt, was paternal. The colonizer, like a parent, should seek to educate and prepare the children for their eventual independence by teaching them the harsh merits of hard work, productivity, and responsibility.

Colonialism ended much earlier than most Belgians expected, the aftermath of a revolt by the colonized who preferred to

develop as free individuals their own version of the modern
state. And because the repression of political and personal
freedoms had prevented the development of any political experience or administrative tradition among the indigenous societies,
the colonizer was left with a sense of responsibility for having
failed to complete a promised duty. Only a few realized that as
a result, any progress toward fulfilling that promise would have
to be made in partnership with the Congolese leaders who previously had been repressed for opposing colonialism and who could
not forget the self-styled father-figure who had been the op-
pressor.

COMITE SPECIAL DU KATANGA. A large private mining consortium
established by King Leopold II on June 19, 1900, to explore
Katanga for minerals. It was one of a number of large companies
allowed by the CFS to administer monopolies over vast areas of
territory. The CSK, which held large amounts of stock in the
Union Minière du Haut-Katanga mining company, was technically
dissolved on the eve of independence by Belgian decree. However, its affairs were not settled until 1965 following negotiations
with the Tshombe government. See UNION MINIERE DU HAUT-
KATANGA.

COMITE ZAIRE. A group of primarily Belgian opponents of the Mobutu government with enough financial support to provide a semi-
regular newsletter detailing corruption, human rights violations,
and abuses of power in Zaire. Some Zairian political exiles associated with the Comité Zaire and utilized their facilities, but most
dissidents preferred to form their own organizations.

COMMERCE see TRADE and ZAIRIANIZATION

COMMITTEE FOR THE STUDY OF THE UPPER CONGO (COMITE
D'ETUDES POUR LE HAUT CONGO). An association of entrepreneurs formed by King Leopold II in 1878 to finance expeditions by Stanley and other explorers into the Congo aimed at
establishing profit-making enterprises in the territory. At the
time of its formation, the Committee was viewed as a noble and
even daring venture. However, modern historians have called
it a maneuver by a wily monarch to grab as much of central
Africa as possible while camouflaging his designs under the noble
guise of scientific, geographical, and anthropological research.
The Committee declined in influence after the Berlin Conference
in 1885 when Leopold II was recognized as sovereign of what was
to become the Congo Free State.

COMMUNAUTE ECONOMIQUE DES PAYS DES GRANDS LACS (CEPGL)
(ECONOMIC COMMUNITY OF COUNTRIES OF THE GREAT LAKES).
An economic community established in September 1976, grouping
Zaire, Burundi, and Rwanda. With its headquarters at Gisenye,
Rwanda, the Community aimed to increase economic integration

by harmonizing tariffs, trade, and economic policies. It was dominated by Zaire, however, and in its early years served mainly to legalize some of the smuggling of contraband goods across Lakes Tanganyika and Kivu.

COMMUNICATIONS. In the early days, communications in Zaire consisted mainly of messengers travelling from town to town on foot and by canoe. "Talking drums" were a major form of communication among the indigenous societies of the forest that came to be used by some early missionaries. The drum, usually a hardened tree trunk or other form of hollowed wood, in many ways imitated the tones and vowels of some of the Bantu languages. As a result, the "talking" drums could be understood by ethnic groups speaking different languages. In the mid-1900s, the two-way radio came into use and fairly complex communications networks were set up by colonial officials, missionaries, and private companies. Telephone lines linked some parts of the country, notably Bas-Zaire and Shaba Regions beginning in 1950, but their effectiveness was hindered by heavy rains and dense forest. Beginning in the 1970s, the Zairian government began a program to link major urban centers through a combination of long lines, microwave, and satellite communications. In 1984 the government announced an ambitious program to install thousands of telephones throughout the country by the end of the century. Except for a few large commercial entities, however, Zaire's major urban areas remained the only centers with established telecommunications links. According to government figures, in 1982 there were 8,000 television sets in Zaire, 150,000 radios, and daily newspaper circulation was one per 1,000 inhabitants. There were 30,300 installed telephones in 1980.

COMMUNISM. Communism has never played a large role in Zairian life or politics although its influence was felt in the 1960s. Patrice Lumumba espoused some socialistic ideological tenets and sought to play the Marxist nations against the western nations. The policies led to his dismissal by Kasavubu and eventually to his arrest and death. Following the polarization of politics due in part to the assassination of Lumumba, Gizenga, backed by the Soviet Union, declared a People's Republic at Stanleyville in 1964. Some aspects of scientific socialism, such as the concept of communal property and the elimination of the gap between rich and poor, appealed to some Zairians. However, most felt uncomfortable with an ideology that placed state bureaucracy over family and religion. Nevertheless, Marxist nations cultivated Zaire and their concepts of revolution and their history of opposition to colonialism appealed to some Zairians. China backed Mulele. The Soviet Union supported Lumumba, Gizenga, and Gbenye. When Mobutu took power relations with the communist powers were poor for years. During the authenticity campaign of the early 1970s, however, Mobutu sought to avoid alignment with either communism or capitalism. He frequently used the phrase, "Neither to the left nor to the right, but straight ahead."

Although China and North Korea eventually developed trade and economic assistance ties with Zaire, the Soviet Union made few inroads during the 1960s. Its ambassador repeatedly was expelled from Zaire and accused of interfering in the country's internal affairs. Zaire condemned the Soviet invasion of Czechoslovakia in 1968. Following the Shaba wars, it accused Moscow of financing the FNLC and broke relations with Cuba and East Germany. At the same time, relations warmed with the Marxist regimes of Asia. Mobutu visited Beijing in 1973 after recognizing the governments of China and North Korea. In the 1970s, the Soviet Union was allowed to develop and maintain a discreet though sizeable diplomatic presence in Zaire. Chinese Premier Zhao Ziyang visited Zaire during a trip to Africa in December 1982-January 1983.

COMPAGNIE DU CONGO POUR LE COMMERCE ET L'INDUSTRIE (CCCI). Large Belgian holding company noted for its heavy investments in Congo following World War I.

CONACO (CONFEDERATION NATIONAL DES ASSOCIATIONS CON-GOLAISES). A coalition of primarily southern political groups that merged into a party headed by Tshombe upon his return to political life after a brief exile following the end of the Katanga secession. CONACO was the result of attempts by the leaders of the CONAKAT, BALUBAKAT, and MNC-Kalonji, as well as some dissatisfied Adoula backers, to form a nationally based party. Although they failed to attract significant support from northeastern and western parts of the country, CONACO supporters were able to elect Tshombe prime-minister on July 9, 1964, with Munongo as interior minister and Albert Kalonji as agriculture minister. Following elections in March 1965 in which CONACO scored significant victories, winning 122 of 167 seats in parliament, Kasavubu dismissed Tshombe and asked another southern leader, Kimba of the BALUBAKAT, to form a government. Kimba tried twice but was blocked both times by CONACO supporters. The deadlock, combined with renewed uprisings in eastern Congo, helped set the scene for the military coup that ushered in the Mobutu era. CONACO's activities were suspended along with those of all political parties following the coup.

CONAKAT (CONFEDERATION DES ASSOCIATIONS KATANGAISES). CONAKAT, more commonly known by its acronym, was a political association dominated by Lunda "évolués," formed in Katanga in the late 1950s by Moise Tshombe and supported by Belgian mining and financial interests. Reflecting the disaffection with Leopoldville that was common in Katanga among Congolese and Europeans alike, CONAKAT in 1959 began advocating autonomy for Katanga within a Congolese federation. It became a political party, and in the elections of 1960, succeeded in gaining the support of the

Luba-dominated BALUBAKAT, thus establishing a one-party
provincial government in Katanga. However, CONAKAT was unhappy with its representation in the Lumumba cabinet. Encouraged by Belgian commercial interests and spurred by moves for
autonomy and/or secession in the Stanleyville and Bakwanga
areas, the Katanga seceeded from the Congo in July 1960. Following reunification in 1963, CONAKAT was liquidated to form
the backbone of the southern-based CONACO that elected
Tshombe prime minister in 1964.

CONGO, BELGIAN. The formal name given to the Congo Free State
when it was annexed by the Belgian parliament on November 14,
1908, following an international outcry over abuses in the CFS,
and retained until the proclamation of independence on June 30,
1960, when it was renamed the Republic of the Congo. The
Belgian government only agreed to assume control over the territory after heated debate in which many leaders opposed the annexation saying it would be too costly to the government. However, the parliament finally agreed to assume responsibility for
the territory out of what it said was a religious belief in "civilizing Africa" and on the condition that it operate at a profit.
A Colonial Charter was passed on October 18, 1908, setting up
the guidelines for administering the territory. Under colonial
administration, many monopolies were reduced. However, a number of large companies, such as the Société Générale de Belgique,
the Comité du Kivu, and the Comité Spéciale du Katanga, retained special privileges.
    The king, as head-of-state, ruled by decree, but the de-
crees had to be countersigned by the minister of colonies. An
advisory council of government of older, conservative leaders
was established in 1911, but political activity was forbidden.
There was some resistance to the colonial administration, particularly by the Yaka, Zande, Luba-Katanga, and Lele. Congolese
were appointed to the council beginning in 1947. The king was
represented by a governor-general who, as chief administrator,
issued ordinances with the power of law. The territory was divided into chiefdoms, called "chefferies," that were grouped into
sectors. Chiefs, appointed by the governor, administered customary law, which was kept separate from colonial law. Historians say labor policies improved somewhat from the harsh practices that brought the end of the CFS, but nevertheless remained
oppressive for decades. See COLONIALISM and PATERNALISM.

CONGO, DEMOCRATIC REPUBLIC OF. Zaire was officially the Democratic Republic of the Congo from August 1, 1964, until October
27, 1971, when it became the Republic of Zaire. It was often
called "Congo/Kinshasa" to differentiate it from "Congo/Brazza-
ville," the former French Congo. The name was changed from
Republic of the Congo with the promulgation of the Constitution
of 1964, which replaced the Fundamental Law of the early years
of independence. The constitution that created the Democratic

Republic of the Congo was drafted following the secessions and considerably altered the principle of federalism established by the Fundamental Law. From the six provinces inherited from colonial rule, it created 21 semiautonomous provinces that were given their own governments. In an attempt to avert the constitutional crises that plagued earlier governments, the constitution granted the president power to appoint and dismiss the prime minister and other ministers, subject to parliamentary approval. It also combined the bicameral parliament inherited from the Belgian system into a single assembly. The Democratic Republic represented an attempt to set aside the disorder following independence. Although it brought some improvements, political fragmentation and administrative disintegration continued, leading to Mobutu's military coup 15 months after its promulgation. The name was retained, however, until the Republic of Zaire was proclaimed in 1971. See CONSTITUTION.

CONGO, PEOPLE'S REPUBLIC OF, RELATIONS WITH. Relations between the two riverine neighbors, which for eleven years following independence shared the same name, have fluctuated considerably. Periods of friendship have been broken by disputes, only to be mended months later. The former French colony of the Congo, Zaire's neighbor to the west, is a much smaller country, with 343,000 square kilometers of territory and a population of 1.8 million persons concentrated almost exclusively around the two urban centers of Brazzaville and Pointe Noire. Brazzaville was the capital of French Equatorial Africa during the colonial era and also was the headquarters of the free-French forces during World War II. Congo became independent on August 15, 1960. A military coup in September 1968 led to Marien Ngouabi's assumption of the presidency on January 1, 1969. Congo formalized its affiliation with Marxism/Leninism by becoming a people's republic on June 24, 1973. Ngouabi was assassinated on March 18, 1977, by a group of commandos. Former President Alphonse Massamba-Debat was executed after being convicted of responsibility for the crime. Joachim Yhombi-Opango was named president on April 4, 1977, and in June the new government resumed relations with the United States after a 12-year break. However, Yhombi-Opango resigned on February 4, 1979, in a power struggle and was replaced by Denis Sassou-Nguesso. Large-scale nationalizations seriously hurt the economy in the 1970s, but in the 1980s the country entered an economic boom due to the discovery of significant deposits of offshore petroleum.

Relations between Zaire and Congo were frequently broken and the ferry linking Brazzaville to Kinshasa often was shut down because of disputes over contraband, gun-running, and currency smuggling. Ideological and historical differences, however, also played a role in the sometimes stormy relations. Congo/Brazzaville supported the Stanleyville secession and has been the exile home of one of its major leaders, Gizenga. Brazzaville also supported the Mulele uprising in Kwilu and is said to have been the source of arms and explosives that for a time created security problems in Leopoldville. After the Kwilu rebellion was put down, Mulele fled to Brazzaville. He later accepted an offer of amnesty from Mobutu, and upon his return to Kinshasa was promptly executed. Furious, the Congolese government broke diplomatic relations. Zaire and Congo supported different factions in the Angolan civil war and often voted with opposing blocs at the U.N. General Assembly. However, as the very different "revolutions" of each nation matured, some of the mistrust began to dissipate. In 1976, the Congolese government began attempts to mediate the differences between Zaire and Angola by hosting a reconciliation meeting between Mobutu and then-Angolan President Agostinho Neto. In 1978, following the second Shaba war, the Congolese authorities mediated a series of talks that brought an agreement by Zaire and Angola to refrain from supporting each other's dissident guerrilla groups and to establish diplomatic relations. In April 1985, Zaire and Congo signed a protocol that signaled growing mutual trust, in which they agreed in principle to the construction of a 17 kilometer-long bridge across the Congo/Zaire River to link the capitals of the two countries.

CONGO, REPUBLIC OF. Zaire was called the Republic of the Congo from Independence on June 30, 1960, until the promulgation of the first Constitution on August 1, 1964. During that time, the country was governed by the Fundamental Law, a charter modeled on the Belgian system of government that provided for a bicameral parliamentary system, a president as chief-of-state elected by parliament but not responsible to it, and a prime minister and cabinet elected by and responsible to the parliament. The powers of the president and prime minister were not clearly defined for political reasons and the concept of checks and balances was liberally applied in the belief that it would prevent abuses of power. In addition, considerable authority was accorded to the six provinces inherited from the colonial era. The provinces no longer were administrative units, but regional governments with elected assemblies and presidents. The federalist structure, local autonomy, fragmentation and regionalism, as well as the weak condition of the army, led to numerous secessions and rebellions from 1960 to 1965. As a result the constitution of 1964 sought to remove the sources of weakness in the central government and established a considerably different system.

CONGO BASIN. Known in French as the "Cuvette Centrale," the Congo Basin is a topographical depression, lying at an altitude of about 400 meters above sea level that covers a total of three million square kms, including nearly two-thirds of Zairian territory and parts of Congo, Central African Republic, and southeastern Cameroon. The Zaire River and its tributaries drain most of the basin. An area of heavy rainfall, averaging 2,000 millimeters per year, the Basin is covered with swamps, marshes, and a lush tropical rainforest where the primary means of transportation is by riverboat and dugout canoe. The Congo Basin is the most sparsely populated area in Zaire, with five persons or fewer per square kilometer, and is inhabited primarily by Bantu language speakers--most of whom of the Mongo group-- pygmies, and some speakers of Adamawa-Eastern languages. At higher levels the ground is covered by clay-like topsoils that allow some forms of agriculture. However, the sandy soil with generally poor mineral content that covers most of the region makes farming difficult. The basin contains an estimated 100 million hectares of forest, but only 60 percent of it is considered accessible for timbering. Some oil exploration was carried out in the Mbandaka area, but it was halted in 1982.

CONGO FREE STATE. The Congo Free State came into existence on November 26, 1885, shortly after the Berlin Conference, where 13 European nations recognized King Leopold II's sovereignty over the territory. The Berlin Act stipulated that the territory be governed by the principles of free trade and navigation, neutrality in war and efforts to improve the lives of the indigenous people. Leopold was recognized as sovereign of the territory who acted with advice from the Belgian ministries of Foreign Affairs, Finance and Interior. The territory was divided into 15 districts, each headed by a commissioner. The authority of the local chiefs was reduced.

In order to pay for the administration of the territory and render a profit to the king, the CFS was protected from business competition by decrees allowing many commodities produced in the CFS to be sold only to the state. The state also decreed that all land not owned by Europeans belonged to the CFS and granted exclusive rights for exploitation and trade to various companies. A security force called the "Force Publique" was formed in order to curb the influence of the local chiefs, drive Arab traders from the eastern part of the territory, and prevent disruptions to trade. By 1900, concern was building in the international community over reports by missionaries of maltreatment of the Africans in the territory. A number of writers, most notably E. D. Morel, drew on these reports to describe atrocities in the CFS. A 10 percent labor tax, passed in 1890, had become an excuse for demanding large quantities of rubber from the indigenous populations. Failure to pay the tax was punished by flogging, execution, and occasionally the destruction of entire villages. Soldiers were required to produce the right hand of villagers who had been executed for not paying their taxes and the procurement of hands became an end in itself, reportedly leaving thousands of maimed victims. The reports led to the formation of an international commission of inquiry and U.S. Congressional hearings which substantiated the abuses. The public outcry led the Belgian parliament reluctantly to annex the territory as a colony. On November 14, 1908, the territory became the Belgian Congo. Labor conditions improved somewhat

but they remained harsh for decades and the end of the CFS
did not mean the end of the exploitation of Zaire and its people.
See CONGO, BELGIAN and COLONIALISM.

CONGO JAZZ. The name given to the rhythmic music popularized
by urban orchestras beginning in the late 1950s which has become popular throughout Africa. Also called "Soukouma." See
MUSIC.

CONGO REFORM ASSOCIATION. A group formed by Edmund D.
Morel at the turn of the century to lobby against the atrocities
being committed against Africans in the Congo Free State. The
outcry that followed the Association's reports led to the reluctant
annexation of the territory by the Belgian parliament and the beginning of the Belgian Congo.

CONGO RIVER. Zaire's major river (4,300 kms long) and Africa's
largest flowing body of water. It has been called the Zaire
River by Zaire since 1971 when Congo/Kinshasa changed its name
to the Republic of Zaire. The river is still called the Congo by
the People's Republic of the Congo and many cartographers.
(This dictionary has opted for the Zairian term.) The name
"Congo" was originally given to the river by explorers who named
it after the Kongo people they met when they landed at the mouth
of the river in the fifteenth century. However, the Zairian government says the term "Zaire" is derived from the name actually
given by the people to the river. The name change came amid
a move in Zaire to distance itself from the negative foreign impression associated with the Congo crisis and establish a new,
unified nation. It also came during a campaign against tribalism
and was considered to have been an attempt to find a name that
could be associated with more than one of Zaire's 250 ethnic
groups. See ZAIRE RIVER.

CONSCRIPTION. Draft conscription is allowed by Zairian law but has
not been necessary since the armed forces represent a relatively
good source of employment and soldiering is one way for poorer,
less-educated citizens to find their way into the power structure.
Student unrest on several occasions has provided conscripts for
the army. Dozens were inducted following demonstrations in 1969,
1971, and more recently in 1982. Other methods of recruitment
reportedly have included round-ups of young, unemployed males
in urban centers, and offers to prison inmates serving sentences
for lesser crimes of freedom in exchange for service in the armed
forces.

CONSEIL DE SECURITE NATIONAL (CSN) (NATIONAL SECURITY
COUNCIL). A little known organ established in 1969 to advise
the president on internal and external security matters. According to diplomatic observers, the organization remained primarily an informative body since most security decisions continued

to be made by the military high command and the presidential
secret service.

CONSEIL DU GOUVERNMENT (GOVERNMENT COUNCIL). A consultative group set up by the colonial authorities following World War
II to provide a source of ideas and information from persons outside the colonial power structure. The body was composed
primarily of civil servants, but included missionaries and social
workers who were considered the primary representatives of the
Congolese.

CONSEIL EXECUTIF (EXECUTIVE COUNCIL). The rough equivalent
of a ministerial cabinet, the organ was formed in 1972 by merging
the Council of Ministers and the National Executive Council of
the MPR and was given the name "Conseil Executif" on January
5, 1975. The formation of the Council was one of the first
moves to merge party and state. However, as the party became
the supreme organ of state, the Political Bureau and Central Committee assumed increasing importance and the Council became
primarily a committee of the chief administrators of the executive
branch. The Council is composed of the government's state commissioners (ministers) who are all appointed by the president.
With the rise in political and bureaucratic power of the Presidency, the Conseil Executif gradually has been overshadowed by
the Office of the President which is staffed with the brightest
and most loyal cadres.

CONSEIL JUDICIAIRE (JUDICIARY COUNCIL). A group of senior
judges of Zairian courts and the Supreme Court, presided over
by the president, that according to the constitution is one of
the main organs of government. See JUDICIARY.

CONSEIL NATIONAL DE LIBERATION (CNL) (NATIONAL LIBERATION
COUNCIL). An organization formed in Brazzaville in late 1963
which claimed to group all Zairian revolutionary organizations.
The council was created at a time of heightened interest by
China in central Africa and claimed Gizenga and Mulele as members. It gradually faded from view, however, as relations improved between Kinshasa and Brazzaville and as China lost interest in promoting peasant revolution in central Africa and
turned its attention to its own Cultural Revolution.

CONSTITUTION. Zaire has been governed in the past century by
three constitutions and two charters. The first document, the
"Charte Coloniale" (Colonial Charter), was adopted on October 18,
1908, by the Belgian parliament to guide the administration of
the Belgian Congo, which it had recently annexed following international criticism of human rights abuses in the Congo Free State.
Under the charter, the king continued to rule the territory by
decree, but the decrees had to be countersigned by the minister
of colonies and the parliament also shared responsibility for the

colony with the executive. A governor-general, appointed by the king, administered the colony with the help of a colonial council. The governor could issue ordinances that had the force of law. All political activity was banned. Following World War II, Africans were admitted to the Colonial Council and a Council of Government was established to provide input from groups working in the colony, such as civil servants and missionaries.

The "Loi Fondamentale" (Fundamental Law), was passed May 19, 1960, as the Belgian Congo approached independence. It was designed as a document to guide the Republic of the Congo during its early years. The Fundamental Law was modeled on the Belgian system of government. It provided for a bicameral parliament with a prime minister and cabinet responsible to it. Instead of a monarch, as in Belgium, the Fundamental Law provided for a president as chief-of-state who was elected by parliament but who was not responsible to it. The law also provided considerable autonomy for the six provinces, which ceased being administrative units and gained their own assemblies and executives. The Fundamental Law contained numerous checks and balances in order to prevent abuses of power. Some historians say, however, it failed to provide a clear-cut leader and consequently helped foment a bickering, ineffective leadership that was unable to address the country's economic and security problems.

Zaire's first constitution, which created the Democratic Republic of the Congo, was drafted partly in reaction to these weaknesses. Promulgated on August 1, 1964, the constitution creating the "First Republic" gave the president greater power and made it clear that he was above the prime minister and had the power to appoint and dismiss the cabinet. The Constitution of 1964 merged the two houses of parliament into one assembly. It also eliminated the state assemblies and, in an effort to diffuse separatist sentiment, divided them into twenty-one provinces. The 1964 Constitution, however, failed to resolve the inevitable power struggle between president and prime minister. The subsequent standoff created yet another power vacuum that was a major reason for the decision by the military to assume command and suspend political activity.

Zaire's second constitution was promulgated on June 24, 1967, less than two years after the coup that brought Mobutu to power. It responded strongly to what many saw as the failures of the previous document. The new constitution, which was approved by 98 percent of the voters, provided for a unicameral legislature and a strong, executive president and removed virtually all political power previously granted to the provinces. The president was granted the power to suspend parliament and political activity and rule by decree. With the power of decree, Mobutu moved to consolidate his power and launched the cult of personality which he felt was needed to provide the nation with strong leadership and a sense of nationhood. The Mouvement Populaire de la Révolution was launched in 1966 and on December 23, 1970, became the sole political party. Mobutu was elected unopposed to his first term that year. The number of provinces were gradually reduced and names of government institutions, cities and even the nation itself were changed in an attempt to bury the trauma of the years following independence. The ministries became departments. Ministers became Secretaries. Leopoldville became Kinshasa. The Congo became the Republic of Zaire.

The third constitution promulgated August 15, 1974, essentially codified the changes of the previous seven years. But it further concentrated power in the office of the president. There was no separation of powers, since members of the judicial and executive branches and candidates for the legislature were appointed by the president. Members of the Political Bureau, chosen by the president, selected the members of the congress of the party. The third constitution removed any distinction between party and government and established "Mobutism" as the official ideology and doctrine. Under the constitution, most terms of office were for five years except for the president's which was raised to seven. The political process was liberalized somewhat in 1977-78 under pressure from U.S. President Carter's administration. Local party cells were allowed a voice in the selection of legislative candidates, and for a brief time the legislature was allowed to summon ministers for questioning. In the legislative elections of 1982, multiple candidates were allowed. In addition, for a brief period, a minority of the members of the Political Bureau were elected. However, following the inauguration of the Reagan administration in the United States, many of the reforms were circumvented or phased out. The constitution was rewritten in 1983 to incorporate the changes and Zaire became the "party/state." All citizens were party members from birth until death. The 120-member Central Committee, created in 1980, became the de facto legislative/consultative body, while the Political Bureau remained the main policy-making body and continued to provide the inner core of direction. The legislature's role became one primarily of approving the Central Committee's decisions, while the Executive Council became in essence a committee of senior administrators. To outsiders accustomed to more open political systems, the Zairian constitution appeared to be a document that discouraged dissent and invited excesses. Nevertheless, it was apparent that some channels existed, primarily through the party structure, for new ideas and proposals and Zairian officials argued it was a framework that provided political stability and more closely resembled traditional Zairian political structures. These arguments were disputed, however, by a number of Zairian dissidents who, unable to endure the restrictions of the system, chose to live in exile.

COPPER. Copper, Zaire's major export, supplies about one-half of the government revenues and two-thirds of its foreign exchange. Zaire is the seventh largest producer of copper in the world and supplies 7 percent of total world output. The copper comes from a rich lode 100 kilometers wide, called the Zambia Copper Belt,

which runs for about 400 kms through the southern part of
Zaire's Shaba Region from Kolwezi to Sakamia. Important mines
are located at Kolwezi, Lubumbashi, Likasi, Tenge, Kipushi,
and Musoshi. In the nineteenth century, tales of rich copper
lodes brought explorers from the east and west coasts of central
Africa, but the discoveries were not deemed commercially viable.
However, discoveries by a British exploring team in 1901 led
King Leopold II to send engineers and start building a railway.
Production, of 1,000 tons, began in 1911, reached 100,000 tons
in 1928, and 300,000 tons in 1960. An expansion program in
the 1970s brought production to a peak of 460,000 tons in 1974.
A second expansion program was planned but was scuttled when
prices fell in 1975. Prices for copper rose sharply in 1973-74,
following the Arab oil embargo, reaching $1.75 per pound. In
less than one year, however, they dropped to $.50 per pound.
By the end of 1986, prices were in the $.60-.70 range, but pro-
duction had stagnated because of an oversupply on the world
market. Zairian production dropped to 370,000 tons in 1979 but
had returned to 464,000 tons by 1984.

During the first half of the twentieth century, copper pro-
duction was virtually monopolized by the Union Minière du Haut-
Katanga (UMHK), which operated a dozen mines. However,
UMHK was nationalized in 1967 and eventually replaced by
GECAMINES. A second venture, SODIMIZA, also owned by the
government but operated by a Canadian company, produced
80,000 tons per year. In 1970, a consortium of British, French,
Japanese, and U.S. companies organized a third venture with
20 percent state participation. Called the Société Minière de
Tenke-Fungurume (SMTF), the venture received a 1,500 square
kilometer concession, but low copper prices and the continued
closure of the Benguela Railway caused the company to be liquidated in 1984.

The first and only smelting plant, owned by GECAMINES and
located at Lubumbashi, was started in 1911 and produced 100,000
tons of refined copper by 1928. In the mid-1980s, it produced
150,000 tons of refined copper a year, 70 percent of which was
for export to Europe and 30 percent of which was for anode production in Zaire. The plant produced 98.5 percent pure ingots
of 225-250 kg. A wire plant and rolling mill, also in Lubumbashi,
produced approximately 1,500 tons of wire and rolled products
a year.

COQUILHATVILLE CONFERENCE. Conference organized by the
Congolese central government in Coquilhatville (now Mbandaka)
in April/May of 1961 as part of negotiations aimed at ending the
secessionist movements in the provinces. The Coquilhatville Conference followed a meeting in Tananarive, Madagascar, which called
for a confederal system of government in the Congo that would
have granted a large degree of autonomy to the provinces. However, the Coquilhatville Conference rejected confederalism in
favor of a federalist system. Neither system was adopted but

some elements of the two were used in drafting Zaire's first constitution in 1964.

CORPS DES VOLONTAIRES DE LA REPUBLIQUE (CVR) (VOLUNTEER
   CORPS OF THE REPUBLIC). A group created on January 9,
   1966, by Mobutu to galvanize the people into helping rebuild the
   Congo after years of chaos and deterioration. Conceived as a
   means to mobilize the people behind the Mobutu government,
   the CVR eventually gave way (some say, prepared the way) for
   the formation of the MPR and its youth wing, the JMPR.

CORRUPTION. Zaire has had a tradition of plunder since the sixteenth century when trading and slaving by the Arabs and Europeans began. It reached notorious levels during the Congo Free
   State and continued under the large monopolies during colonial
   rule. It was no accident, then, that many Zairians came to per-
   ceive the public coffers as a source of personal enrichment.
       Corruption has been seen in many forms, ranging from the
   acceptance of gifts for official favors and personal services to
   officially sanctioned smuggling and outright diversions of public
   funds. During the 1970s, Zaire gained considerable renown
   for its institutionalized system of "matabish" (Lingala for "tip").
   A former World Bank official who served in the Zairian central
   bank in the late 1970s estimated after leaving Zaire that less
   than one-third of the revenues from diamond sales were processed
   through the bank. The rest, he said, were smuggled. He also
   estimated that as much as one-half of Zaire's revenues were not
   recorded officially. Other officials with international institutions
   monitoring the Zairian economy said the budget of the presidency
   was virtually indistinguishable from the president's private accounts. Dissidents obtained published documents that they
   claimed came from the central bank, detailing illegal transactions
   such as funds withdrawn from the bank and deposited in private
   Swiss accounts. They also published receipts from exports like
   diamonds, copper, and cobalt showing payment had been made to
   private accounts in Europe. The situation led the Roman Catholic
   Church to issue a letter expressing concern over the decline of
   morals in private and public life. Whether viewed as a blight on
   the state or as a modern version of the traditional practice of
   spreading the wealth, the practice of diverting funds for personal
   use seriously affected the ability of the government to administer
   the country, especially after government revenues were cut by
   the fall in mineral prices. The Zairian government made several
   major drives to halt mismanagement. In 1978 and 1982, dozens
   of lower and mid-level officials were tried and dismissed for corruption. In 1983, 150 relatively senior officals were tried and
   punished. However, the greatest and most successful effort to
   curb mismanagement came following the fiscal and economic reforms of September 1983, when state commissioners became per-
   sonally accountable for overspending in their departments and
   the government began to carry out audits of bureaus. By the

mid-1980s the combination of greater controls and political pressure appeared to be having an effect although critics said many officials still viewed the public treasury as an inexhaustible source of money.

COTTON. Cotton has been a principal commercial crop in Zaire since the colonial period, when it was promoted by the colonizers as a crop to be grown by individual Congolese. The crop has traditionally been reserved for Zairians and is grown extensively on small plots of one-half to one hectare. Production reached 60,000 tons at independence, but had fallen to 5,000 tons by 1965. The Zairian government has begun a program to revive cotton production and return it to pre-independence levels. With domestic demand at about 25,000 tons, the government hopes to be able to export cotton once again.

COUP D'ETAT. Zaire has had only one successful coup d'etat, the one by the armed forces on November 24, 1965, which brought Mobutu to power. As with many military coups, the military decided to seize power following a constitutional crisis exacerbated by bickering among political leaders and the inability of the civilian government to deal with threats to the security of the territory. Mobutu also had assumed power on September 14, 1960, during the political standoff between Kasavubu and Lumumba. However, he made a point of stating he was not staging a coup, but only "neutralizing" the politicians until passions cooled and political order could be restored. When Mobutu did assume power in 1965, during a similar standoff between Kasavubu and Tshombe, it was during a period when Leopoldville was being rocked by urban terrorism and banditry and yet another rebellion was beginning in the east. Mobutu vowed to set up a new political order, which soon became a "revolution" that brought a one-party state to Zaire with Mobutu as its undisputed head. There have been a number of plots to overthrow the Mobutu government, usually with some collaboration from the Zairian military. All have failed, however, due in part to the president's rigorous internal security network and the practice of offering handsome rewards to informers. See NOVEMBER 24, 1965.

COURTS see JUDICIAL SYSTEM

CRIME. The Zairian government publishes no statistics on crime, court cases, or prison populations, so it is impossible to know exactly the extent of criminality or its incidence relative to other countries. Crime of all sorts is present in Zaire, and as in most of the world, appears to be worse in the cities were poverty has made burglaries, pickpocketing and petty theft common occurrences. Most middle- and upperclass households are protected by high walls and guards called "sentries." Tight controls on firearms have made their use relatively rare and as a result, violent and armed criminality is considered to be less

frequent than in many countries of the developing and industrialized world.

CROPS. Zaire's major crops include banana, coffee, cotton, maize,
manioc (or cassava), palm oil, rice, rubber, and sugarcane.
(See separate listings for details on these crops.) Other crops
include cocoa, millet, peanuts, potatoes, sorghum, tea, tobacco,
and vegetables. For the subsistence farmer, the major crops are
manioc, banana, and, in the high plains, maize. These are sup-
plemented in some cases by vegetable gardens. The ground is
usually cleared toward the end of the dry season and the crops
planted either just before or just after the first rains. The
hardy manioc, however, is often grown throughout the year.
Crops are harvested toward the end of the rainy season, or
when mature. Some years, when the rainy season is long, two
crops may be planted and harvested. When the rainy season
runs short, the crops are harvested early. There is little crop
rotation, but fields are sometimes left to lie fallow for several
seasons. During the colonial period, commercial farming was,
along with mining, the major source of income. Coffee, cotton,
palm oil and, in the earliest days, rubber, tea, and cocoa were
major cash crops. However, many plantations deteriorated following independence and the maintenance of hardy crop strains
suited to the Zairian environment often suffered. However, as
part of its focus on increasing agricultural productivity, the
Zairian government is seeking to develop new strains of crops
as well as to improve farming techniques and marketing infrastructures. See AGRICULTURE.

CUBA, RELATIONS WITH. Zaire's relations with Cuba have been
cool and at times hostile since the beginning of the Angolan
civil war, when Cuba sent an estimated 15,000 troops and advisers to Angola to back the MPLA faction that was opposed by
the Zairian government.
    Despite the MPLA's recognition as the legitimate government
of Angola by the United Nations and the Organization of African
Unity in 1976, Zaire continued to back the FNLA faction that was
fighting a guerrilla war against the MPLA. Zaire broke relations with Cuba following the first Shaba incursion in March 1977
by FNLA guerrillas based in Angola. Relations with Cuba improved gradually after Zaire and Angola established relations in
late 1978 and the activities of the FNLA diminished. However,
tensions remained as the civil war with UNITA continued and
the Cuban presence in Angola increased to more than 25,000
soldiers and advisers. A sizeable contingent of Cuban troops
were guarding Angolan offshore installations in Cabinda, only a
few kilometers from the Zairian border. Zaire expelled a Cuban
diplomat in October 1986 after accusing him of espionage.

CULTURE. The Zairian government has adopted a policy of trying
to preserve the traditional culture of the hundreds of ethnic

groups in the country. As a result, numerous studies, exhibitions, films, seminars and performances are sponsored with that purpose in mind. In addition, some members of Zairian artistic circles make concerted efforts to translate and propagate aspects of traditional Zairian culture in their work, whether it be literature, music, painting, or theater. Nevertheless, many Zairians feel the lack of funds and the disruption of the transmission of traditional culture to younger generations caused by urban life are creating an erosion of the sense of Zairian culture among the youth of the country. Modern, urban Zairian culture, however, is vibrant. Taking its roots from aspects of the traditional past and melding them with influences from abroad, it continues to influence fashion, music, and the arts throughout Africa as well as in parts of Europe and the Americas. The influence of central African sculpture on modern art is well documented. Today, Zairian influences are regularly felt on the international scenes of fashion and music as well. See CLOTH; DRESS; MUSIC; and CONGO JAZZ.

CURRENCY. The Zairian currency is called the "zaire." A smaller unit, worth 1/100th of one zaire is called the "likuta" (plural: "makuta"). Originally an even smaller unit was in circulation, the "sengi" equalling 1/100th of a likuta, but that unit has disappeared. Because of inflation, one zaire in the mid-1980s was worth 1/1,000th of its value at independence. The currency of the Kongo Kingdom, when the Europeans arrived, was denominated in a certain kind of shell that could only be found in the king's fisheries. During the colonial period and for a number of years after independence, the currency was the Congolese franc, pegged at a 1:1 ratio to the Belgian franc. However, at independence, the Congo franc began to lose its longstanding value of 50 francs = 1.00 U.S. dollar and was devalued a number of times. In September 1967, a currency reform was decreed and the currency was changed to the "zaire." One zaire became the equivalent of and could be exchanged for 1,000 francs. One zaire equalled two U.S. dollars. In January 1987, one dollar equalled 70 zaires. The currency never has been strong, in part because of a lack of demand and in part because of the tendency of the government to borrow from the treasury to meet budget deficits. Shortages of foreign exchange also gave rise to a healthy parallel market where, for example, the U.S. dollar usually traded at three to seven times the official rate of exchange. However, in September 1983, the Zairian government announced monetary reforms, allowing private banks to trade in the currency for the first time, and essentially floating the zaire on the free market. Under the new system, banks met weekly to set the exchange rate, based on supply and demand. After an initial plunge to one-fourth its previous level, the zaire has remained relatively stable and, bankers say, the parallel market has been virtually eliminated.

CUVETTE CENTRAL see CONGO BASIN

- D -

DEATH PENALTY. According to the Zairian constitution, the death
penalty may be accorded for the crime of murder and other ex-
tremely serious offenses, usually involving the death of the vic-
tim or victims. See PENAL SYSTEM.

DEBT, FOREIGN. Zaire was one of the first casualties of the developing world's debt crisis caused by falling commodity prices
and rising interest rates. During the early 1970s, as mineral
prices soared following the OPEC oil embargo and price increases,
prices for copper and cobalt rose to historic heights. Foreign
banks, basing their collateral estimates on the value of mineral
reserves estimated at the inflated price levels, lent large sums
to Zaire for large-scale development projects. In 1974, when
copper prices fell to one-third their previous level in less than
one year, the Zairian government began to fall behind in repayments on its foreign debt of 5 billion U.S. dollars, the rough
equivalent of its annual GDP. Zaire's debt problems and its attempts to reschedule debt payments received a great deal of
coverage in the news media during the 1970s. The government
signed a series of stabilization agreements with the IMF. However, most of the IMF standbys were aborted by the failure of
the Zairian government to reduce its budget deficit and to control inflation.
    In 1983, Zaire undertook a series of drastic fiscal and mone-
tary reforms that included floating its currency on the free
market and drastically reducing its budget deficits. The measures
caused a severe recession in Zaire, but they also brought renewed confidence and expressions of support from the IMF and
foreign creditors. By 1987, Zaire, which had seen some of its
debts written off by private creditors because of arrears, had
actually repaid some of the principle on its foreign debt, reducing it to $4.5 billion. However, staying current on its debt
repayments was costly. More than 50 percent of the government's
budget was allocated to debt repayment in 1984-85. The Central Committee of the MPR, following a month-long meeting in
October 1986, determined that debt servicing was creating social
hardships that could set the stage for political upheaval in the
country. Following the meeting, the government announced that
Zaire would limit debt repayments to 10 percent of export revenues and no more than 20 percent of the total budget. The
move, which resembled the actions taken by Latin American
debtors Peru and Mexico, startled foreign creditors but did not
create serious repercussions. In addition, it was widely acknowledged that easier debt repayment policies were needed in
the face of continued low prices for Zaire's major exports. See
ECONOMY.

DEMOCRACY. Like many African nations, Zaire was a multiparty democracy at independence, modeled on Western European principles of government. However, because of a variety of ethnic, economic, and cultural reasons, the nation was obliged to redefine its political ideology and restructure its political institutions. The Fundamental Law that established the political institutions at independence was largely influenced by the Belgian political system. It provided for a bicameral legislature with a president and prime-minister. Both president and prime minister were elected by parliament, but the Fundamental Law did not specifically establish the power-sharing relationship between the two leaders and the institution that chose them. The explosive growth of regionally and ethnically based political parties, estimated to have reached 125 in number prior to the elections of 1960, and the fact that no party or group obtained an absolute majority, both made government difficult and aggravated regional tensions. The constitution of 1964, which followed the quelling of most of the secessions and rebellions, addressed some of these problems. In addition, as parliamentary politics began to mature, some political coalitions began to emerge, leading to significant victories by the CONACO coalition in elections in 1965. However, power struggles between the president and prime minister and continued regionalistic tensions kept the political climate unsettled.

Amid new rebellions and yet another constitutional crisis caused by a political standoff between the president and the ruling parliamentary coalition, democracy was ended by a coup d'etat that brought Mobutu to power on November 24, 1965. The new president ruled by decree, suspended all political activity and promised to hold elections in five years. Following purges in the military and the exile of many opposition leaders, Mobutu established a single party (see MOUVEMENT POPULAIRE REVO-LUTIONAIRE), modeled primarily on the Chinese system, beginning in 1966. In what was to become a trend in many African countries, the sole legal party increasingly became the institution of the state, and the presidency assumed increasing political and administrative powers. Mobutu was elected to seven-year terms in 1970, 1977, and 1984. Each time, he ran unopposed and received nearly 100 percent of the vote. During the elections, observers noted many irregularities, such as a dearth of "No" ballots and the active presence at the polls of "pressure" groups of party militants or members of the military.

By the late 1970s, Zaire had become a "party-state." Candidates for public office had to be party members in good standing and were chosen by the Political Bureau or by the president himself. The president also appointed members of the Bureau as well as the occupants of most senior-level positions in party or government. Under pressure from U.S. President Carter's administration, however, some liberalizations were carried out. These included allowing some members of the Political Bureau to be elected, allowing multiple candidates for legislative elections, and allowing local party cells a voice in selecting the legislative

candidates from their region. Parliament was officially unmuzzled
and allowed to summon state commissioners (ministers) for questioning on the budgets of their departments. Parliamentary
freedom led to raucous political debate. In 1980, Mobutu created the party "Central Committee" that gradually assumed the
major debate and law-making functions of government. The
Legislative Council's role became one of approving decisions by
the Central Committee, Political Bureau, and the Presidency.
Many other liberalizations were either rolled back or sidestepped
in similar fashion and control of the political process once again
was returned to the president and a small group of his close
associates who, nevertheless, continued to consult frequently on
an informal base with other influential individuals in Zairian society. Many Zairian intellectuals who had lived abroad felt a harsh
dictatorship was being hidden behind the trappings of democracy.
However, others noted that the institutions had brought political
stability to a country that had spent its early years in virtually
constant crisis.

DEPARTMENTS. On January 5, 1973, the ministries of the executive branch were renamed departments, the ministers were renamed state commissioners, and the Council of Ministers became
the Executive Council. The names and functions of the departments changed over the years and their number varied between
20 and 30, but their basic responsibilities (Interior, Defense,
Foreign Affairs, Education, Agriculture, etc.) and their bureau-
cracies remained. As the power of the presidency became institutionalized, another trend developed. The departments became
increasingly subordinate to the party and the Office of the President, both of which maintained organizational substructures
similar to the executive branch. The Office of the President, in
particular, attracted the brightest "cadres" and appeared to experience the fewest restraints on spending.

DESCENT GROUPS. Although the nature and role of descent groups
vary considerably according to ethnic group, it is generally
agreed that to the central African, ancestry is one of the most
important aspects of heritage and, to some, individuality. Descent groups were important in the personal development and
identity of the individual, usually centering on descent, ranging
from two to sometimes dozens of previous generations. In traditional society, lineage groups sometimes assumed political functions,
particularly in areas where a chieftaincy structure was not present. The descent/lineage group often spread over a large area
because of the practice of marrying from another group and taking the spouse to the father's or the mother's village. In the
patrilineal societies, descent was traced primarily through the
male members of the society. The man would marry and often
take his wife to his father's village. In the matrilineal societies,
when a man married, he often moved to the village of his mother-
in-law's brother, who usually had more authority over him than

his own father. In these societies, a matrilineal uncle often took care of the education and coming-of-age rites of young males. Children often took the name of their mother or maternal uncle.

DEVELOPMENT PROJECTS. As one of the largest nations in Africa with a history of close ties to western Europe and the Americas, Zaire has been the recipient of numerous development projects. Many of these have focused on improving infrastructure, such as roads, railways, and electrical and water supplies. Others have focused on improving agricultural productivity. A few have focused on industry and the service sector. Large projects since independence have included the Inga I and II hydroelectrical complexes at Inga, 40 kilometers upriver from Matadi; the Inga-Shaba power transmission line that can carry up to 520 megawatts of current from Inga to the Shaba mining region; the deepwater port at Banana on the Atlantic Ocean; the Matadi-Banana railway project aimed at providing a rail link from eastern Zaire to the Atlantic Ocean; the suspension bridge over the Zaire River at Matadi to provide easier surface transportation links between the Atlantic Ocean and the rest of Zaire; the electrification of the Matadi-Kinshasa railway to make use of unused electrical potential at Inga and reduce petroleum consumption; the Kinshasa/Ilebo railway link aimed at supplementing the traditional river link; the Voix du Zaire telecommunications and broadcasting center which produces and beams radio and television programs via satellite to eight regional broadcasting centers; the World Trade Center aimed at providing a major central African trading forum; the Maluku metallurgy complex; cement factories in Bas-Zaire; the Kaniama-Kasese Maize Project and Géméne Agro-Industrial Complex aimed at installing agribusiness in distant and sometimes neglected regions; and various projects to refurbish and improve airports, roads, bridges, telephone networks, and water and electrical distribution systems.

Development observers noted that in Zaire, as in many developing nations, projects that set relatively simple goals tended to have a higher success rate than ambitious, complex projects aimed at installing an industry or agricultural complex in a remote, underdeveloped area. The larger projects tended to encounter maintenance problems following completion due to deterioration of imported equipment and decline in management quality due to the departure of the more experienced personnel.

DHANIS, BARON FRANCIS. One of the leaders of the military campaigns in the 1890s against the Arab slave and ivory traders in eastern Zaire, and particularly against slavers loyal to the Mahdi, prophet of Sudan, from 1894-96.

DIAMONDS. Zaire produces an estimated two-thirds of the non-Communist world's industrial diamonds, although official production levels have fluctuated considerably in recent years. The diamonds, a small percentage of which are of gem quality, come

primarily from the Mbuji-Mayi and Tshikapa areas in Kasai Orientale where they originate in Kimberlite deposits along several
rivers, but especially along the Lubilash River. Wildcat digging,
like that by students on vacation, is a tradition in the area and
on occasion has led to clashes with the authorities. Total official production fell from an average of 12 million carats in the
1970s to six million carats in 1981, due to theft, smuggling, and
shortages of spare parts for mining equipment. In 1982, the
Zairian government which, since independence had been the sole
legal diamond trader, announced that anyone could trade freely
in diamonds by depositing $50,000 with the state. The move
was aimed at countering diamond smuggling and a dozen wealthy
Zairians registered with the state as official traders. The
government said production rose to 6.9 million carats in 1985.

The government-owned Société Minière de Bakwanga (MIBA)
dominates the diamond industry in Zaire and is the country's
second largest corporation after GECAMINES. MIBA, which was
first established in the 1920s, is the world's largest single producer of diamonds, according to the Zairian government. MIBA
has traditionally worked alluvial deposits and eluvial deposits
where the river is diverted in order to allow digging. However,
with the discovery of nickel and chromium in MIBA concessions,
MIBA has begun examining underground mining. Production began to increase with the installation in 1983 of the "Mobutu Sese
Seko" dredge and floating processor. The Brit Mond subsidiary
of the DeBeers Central Selling Organization marketed Zaire's production from 1967 until 1981, when Zaire transferred the marketing responsibilities to SOZACOM, the state marketing board. That
arrangement, however, was short-lived. DeBeers resumed marketing through Brit Mond in 1984 and SOZACOM was dissolved on
July 2, 1985. MIBA assumed its own marketing in 1985 during a
period when Brit Mond was renegotiating its agreement with the
government. In 1986, MIBA was developing a new site at Tshi-
bua, 35 kms southwest of its current operations.

DIANGIENDA, KUNTIMA (JOSEPH). Son of the Prophet Simon Kimbangu and founder of an off-shoot of the Zairian Protestant
Church called the Church of Jesus Christ on Earth by the Prophet
Simon Kimbangu (L'Eglise de Jésus-Christ sur la Terre par le
Prophète Simon Kimbangu). The church grew following Kimbangu's
death in 1951 and was admitted to the World Council of Churches
in 1969, the first independent African church to be officially
recognized by the world body. See KIMBANGUISM.

DILOLO. A town of about 40,000 inhabitants lying in western Shaba
Region along the border with Angola where the southern Shaba
railway system connects with the Benguela Railway. During the
first Shaba incursion, Dilolo was the first town to be taken by
the FNLC and the last to be retaken by Zairian and Moroccan
troops nearly three months later. The Lunda ethnic group predominates on both sides of the border in the area and some local

residents were said to have aided the guerrillas. As a result there were reports of reprisals by Zairian troops who felt the residents had aided the rebels.

DIOMI, GASTON. One of the founders of the MNC party through which Lumumba rose to prominence. Diomi attended the Pan-African conference in Accra, Ghana, in December 1958 with Lumumba and Ngalula. He was one of the speakers who reported on the conference at a rally in Leopoldville on January 3, 1959, which led to two weeks of rioting in Leopoldville and accelerated the movement toward independence. Diomi, along with Kasavubu, was imprisoned following the riots.

DISEASE. Major diseases prevalent in Zaire include malaria, pneumonia, measles, tuberculosis, sleeping sickness, gastroenteritis, gonorrhea, syphilis, leprosy, schistosomiasis, and other parasitic diseases. Malnutrition is also common, especially protein deficiency. In its 1987 world report, UNICEF estimated total infant mortality in Zaire at 103 deaths per 1,000 births, down from 148 per 1,000 births in 1960. UNICEF also reported 170 of every 1,000 children died before reaching the age of five years, down from 251 per 1,000 births in 1960. Zaire was listed as having the 31st highest infant mortality rate of 130 nations surveyed. Life expectancy was estimated at 51 years, up from 42 years in 1960. The same study reported 8 percent of all Zairian children were born underweight, 11 percent of those aged 1-2 years suffered from severe malnutrition, and that less than one fourth of the children below the age of one year were immunized against the most common diseases. Forty-three percent of urban dwellers and 5 percent of the rural dwellers (20 percent of total population) were reported to have access to potable water, and 60 percent of urban dwellers and 17 percent of rural dwellers (20 percent total) were reported to have access to health services. Meanwhile, UNICEF reported 3.2 percent of the government budget was allocated to health services and ranked Zaire among the ten developing nations with the lowest proportion of their budget allocated to health services.

DISSIDENTS. Dissidents, organized and unorganized, have been perceived to be a threat to political stability virtually since independence. In fact, popular reaction against the factionalism and secessions of the early 1960s is one reason for the military coup d'etat and the considerable support it initially received. However, authoritarianism and the establishment of a one-party system in the 1970s led to increased opposition by dissidents. Some of the better known exiled dissident groups included the Front National pour la Libération du Congo (FNLC), which was involved in the Shaba incursions; the Forces Démocratiques pour la Libération du Congo (FODELICO), led by Antoine Gizenga involved in the rebellions in northeastern Zaire; the Movement d'Action pour la Résurrection du Congo (MARC), formed primarily by students, led by Munguya Mbenge, and involved in the university demonstrations of the 1970s; and the Mouvement National Congolais (MNC), led by Lumumba's son François Emery. Two groups could be described as internally based: the Parti de la Révolution Populaire (PRP), which controlled a portion of remote mountainous territory near Lake Tanganyika and attacked an army garrison at Moba in 1984; and the Union pour la Démocracie et le Progrés Social (UDPS), formed by 13 parliamentarians in the 1980s as a second party. In addition, the Comité Zaire, a group composed primarily of Belgian academics, published a newsletter in Brussels that often related the excesses of the regime.

Dissidents have plotted many times to overthrow the Mobutu government. However, his intelligence network is strong and the opposition is faction-ridden. Although many dissidents have been arrested and convicted of plotting against the government, executions have been relatively rare. Death sentences for subversion or treason often are commuted to life imprisonment, which in turn may be reduced or eliminated with presidential pardon. Among the most noted executions were those of Prime Minister-designate Evariste Kimba and three former ministerial-level collaborators who were hanged for reportedly plotting a coup in 1966. In addition, 14 plotters (nine military and five civilian) were reportedly executed in 1978 after a failed attempt on the president's life.

The exiled dissident movement has been characterized by disorganization and factionalism. The exiled movement of recent years appeared to have peaked in 1981-82 with the resignation and self-imposed exile of then-Prime Minister Nguza Karl-I-Bond. Nguza and his backers organized a series of highly publicized meetings in Europe and the United States that included an appearance before a hearing of the Africa Sub-Committee of the House of Representatives. During the hearing, Nguza detailed incidents of corruption in government and recounted his own torture while imprisoned following the first Shaba War. Mobutu issued a general amnesty on May 21, 1983, in which he offered to allow exiles return to Zaire unmolested if they gave up their anti-government activities. Over the next two years, many former leaders took advantage of the amnesty, including Nguza who returned in 1985 and one year later was appointed ambassador to the United States. Other former officials who benefited from the amnesty included former minister Thomas Kanza, former ambassador Mungul Diaka, former rebel leader Cléophas Kamitatu, and Tshombe Ditend (son of Moise Tshombe).

The group of 13 parliamentarians fared less well. Some of them published a 50-page letter on December 31, 1980, accusing the government of authoritarianism and corruption, and outlining proposals for a new form of government in Zaire. In 1982, they were convicted of treason for trying to form a second political party, an illegal act under the Zairian constitution. They were later amnestied, but were imprisoned again when they failed to cease their activities. They were released again on June 30, 1985,

as part of the festivities marking Zaire's 25 years of independence.
However, most soon were banished to their home villages. In
1986, Amnesty International accused the Zairian government of
increased human rights abuses, saying authorities had arrested
more than 100 government critics between October 1985 and January 1986. The organization said many had been tortured and
some had died. Later that year, Mobutu acknowledged that some
abuses had occurred and created a ministerial-level office in
charge of human rights. A great deal of the dissidence movement
had been weakened in 1986 by what appeared to be the beginnings
of an upturn in the Zairian economy, Mobutu's re-election to a
third, seven-year term, and the return to Zaire of many of the
most prominent dissidents. See HUMAN RIGHTS.

DRESS. In Zaire, dress and fashion tend to follow central African
and European patterns. The Arab-style robe as seen in north
and west Africa is rare. African garb includes the bou-bou (or
dashiki) and slacks for men, with sandals and rarely with hat.
Women's dress consists of a traditional wrap of two to four yards
of African print cloth, called "pagne," with a blouse and match-
ing headdress worn with sandals or high heels. During the hey-
day of authenticity, Zaire pioneered the modernistic, urban version of the traditional woman's garb, whereby the ample, loose
folds of the pagne were turned into a long, tight skirt and blouse
that emphasized the hips. For men, Zaire pioneered the "abacost" (acronym for "à bas le costume," meaning "down with the
suit"). The abacost was a tight-laced two-piece suit often of
dark, formal material with a Mao-type collar that was buttoned
at the throat. Ties were not worn, but among the stylish, a
silk, ascot scarf was permissible. For the politically conscious,
the MPR party lapel-pin was a required accoutrement. Among
the less political, European business suits later returned as
permissible wear. Among the well-to-do young, the sleek French
and Italian styles of casual dress remained popular, as did
American blue jeans.

DUTCH INFLUENCES. The Dutch arrived in the early 1600s and,
along with the Portuguese, are considered to have helped destabilize the Kongo Kingdom when Kongo leaders began to object to the uncontrolled activities of the traders. Motivated by
a desire for slaves that could not be satisfied through commercial
dealings with local African traders, the Dutch took Luanda in
1641 and for a time replaced Portugal as the leading slave traders
along the central African coast. The Portuguese retook Luanda
in 1648 and Dutch influence declined.
   The major Dutch contribution to central African society was
the printed "wax" cloth introduced by traders returning from
Asia. The print, originally made using the lost-wax method, was
first imported from Indonesia and Java. Today, virtually every
African nation possesses a textile industry that manufactures
the "wax" and it is the standard cloth for dresses, shirts, suits,

tablecloths, mats, and bedding among most Zairian and many
other African families. It has been a leading attraction of
Zairian fashion that also has gained popularity in the Caribbean
and parts of Europe.

- E -

EASTERN HIGHLANDS. The highest and most rugged region of
Zaire. The Eastern Highlands range for 1,500 kms along the
lakes of the Great Rift Valley and include the headwaters of
the White Nile. The backbone of the region is formed by a
series of mountain ranges 80-560 kms wide extending from the
Ruwenzori chain in northeastern Zaire to the Virunga volcanic
range in northern Shaba. The hills and mountains vary in
altitude from 1,000 meters to more than 5,000 meters, giving the
region a cool climate that has led some to call it the "Switzerland"
of Africa. The region produces gold, tin, iron ore, sugar,
textiles, methane gas, palm oil, tobacco, and coffee. Some light
industry has been developed around the two main urban centers
of Bukavu and Goma. The region is also known for its independent attitude toward the Kinshasa government, from which its
residents feel somewhat distant and by which they often feel
neglected. The government, however, has been trying to reduce the area's isolation by constructing a network of roads linking it to Shaba and Kasai Orientale.

EASTERN WAY. The term given to the transportation route taken by
mineral exports from Shaba to the Tanzanian port of Dar es
Salaam. The Zairian government views this route less favorably
than the Benguela Railway, the National Way entirely through
Zairian territory, or the Southern Way through Zambia and Zimbabwe. The Zairian government says 11 percent of the country's
copper is exported via the Eastern Way, by rail 1,300 kms from
Lubumbashi to Kalemie on Lake Tanganyika, by boat across the
Lake, and by rail once again to the port at Dar es Salaam. The
Eastern Way, 2,715 kms long, is no shorter than the National Way
and requires several transshipments. Furthermore, goods are
often delayed by maintenance problems with the rolling stock and
by congestion at the port.

ECOLE NATIONALE D'ADMINISTRATION (ENA) (NATIONAL SCHOOL
OF ADMINISTRATION). A professional school in Kinshasa,
founded in the early 1960s by the Zairian government and private
foundations in order to train Zairians for careers primarily in
the civil service.

ECONOMIC COMMUNITY OF CENTRAL AFRICAN STATES (ECOCAS)
(COMMUNAUTE ECONOMIQUE DES ETATS DE L'AFRIQUE CEN-
TRALE). Modeled on the larger, older, and more established
Economic Community of West African States (ECOWAS), ECOCAS

was first proposed in the early 1980s by Gabonese President Omar Bongo and President Mobutu in an attempt to form a central African common market. The organization seeks to integrate the disparate economies of nations ranging from the relatively large and more developed Zaire and Cameroon to the small, landlocked Rwanda and Burundi and the island nations of Equatorial Guinea and Sao Tome and Principe. In September 1983, ten nations formally signed the agreement to form the community: Burundi, Cameroon, Central African Republic, Chad, Congo, Equatorial Guinea, Gabon, Rwanda, Sao Tome and Principe, and Zaire. An eleventh, Angola, indicated its intention to join eventually, but postponed its formal entry because of its civil war and economic problems. Economists predicted, however, many obstacles to establishing a common market in the region, such as lack of infrastructure and widely diverging economic and political policies. Nevertheless, progress with the smaller, Francophone-dominated UDEAC had given central African leaders some hope of implementing at least such initial steps as an alignment of customs tariffs and the free movement within the region by citizens of member-nations.

ECONOMY. Zaire's economy, with an estimated gross domestic product of $5 billion, continues to depend heavily on the extraction of raw materials, such as copper, cobalt, industrial diamonds, and to a lesser degree rubber, timber, coffee, palm products, cocoa, and tea. Copper alone accounts for one-half of government revenues and nearly two-thirds of its foreign exchange earnings. Cobalt derived from some copper ores is an important by-product. Self-sufficient in food at independence, Zaire by the 1980s was importing large quantities of food products, consumer goods, transportation and construction equipment, and technological supplies. Less than one-third of the population participates in the formal economy and per capita income is $140 U.S. The Zairian economy has tended to follow the economic fluctuations of the world economy: severe depression in the 1930s, recovery after World War II, a boom during the early 1970s and recession with a fall of mineral prices in 1974-75. The one notable exception was the recession of the early 1960s, caused by secessions and rebellions, the departure of many technicians, the weakness of the central government, and the decline of a great deal of the infrastructure.

In the early 1980s, Zaire's economy was characterized by a severe foreign debt burden of nearly $5 billion, by an inability to meet debt repayment schedules, and by failure to abide by stand-by agreements with the IMF. These problems were aggravated by a lack of foreign exchange, low industrial production (10-30 percent of capacity), high inflation of 50-100 percent annually, declining standards of living, and continued government mismanagement of budget and fiscal affairs. In 1983, the Zairian government announced legal action against 150 functionaries for various forms of embezzlement and fraud, but the most powerful

were not affected. Mismanagement continued to drain government coffers. Economists estimated that smuggling roughly
equalled official trade figures. Most of the wealth remained in
the hands of a few important Zairians and foreigners.

On September 9, 1983, the Zairian government announced
drastic fiscal and monetary reforms, including floating the currency on the open market, allowing private banks to trade in
foreign currency and set the rate of exchange, and instituting
austerity measures among the ministries and local governments.
The result was a sudden and severe deflation of the economy.
Overnight the official exchange rate fell from a rate of six zaires
to one U.S. dollar, to 30 zaires to one dollar. Earning power
fell to less than one-fourth its previous level. Other reforms,
including the end to overall subsidies of petroleum and agricultural products, caused prices to rise even further and aggravated the squeeze on salaried workers. Measures to allow private participation in diamond and gold trading and domestic air
transportation were introduced in the following two years. The
measures were harsh but provided results. Inflation was reduced from 100 percent in 1983 to 20 percent in 1985. By 1985
Zaire was current on interest payments on its foreign debt. It
had reduced foreign debt principle and had received new loans.
Economic growth, according to the government, increased from
1.2 percent in 1983 to 2.6 percent in 1985; by 1986 a slow revival was being experienced as wage increases began to permit
wage and salary earners to recover some of their buying power.
However, the social cost of servicing the debt was high and on
October 29, 1986, following a month-long meeting of the Central
Committee, the government announced debt repayment would be
limited to 10 percent of exports earnings and 20 percent of
government revenues. The government said IMF austerity programs were strangling the economy and that political stability
would be threatened if greater attention was not paid to social
programs.

EDUCATION. Education in Zaire has made considerable progress
since independence, but has been hampered by a lack of funds,
qualified instructors, and curricula designed to train individuals
to address the country's most pressing needs. During the
colonial period, considerable emphasis was placed on primary
school programs and the Belgian Congo boasted one of the
highest literacy rates in Africa. The primary purpose was to
prepare Congolese for clerical and secretarial jobs. Few Zairians
were able to attend secondary schools or universities. As a result, at independence there were fewer than ten university graduates and fewer than 200 high school graduates. An emphasis on
education since independence raised literacy in 1985 to 79 percent
of males and 45 percent of females, according to UNICEF figures,
whereas in 1970, literacy was 61 percent for males and 22 percent
for females. In this case literacy was defined as those individuals
over the age of 15 years who could write. According to UNICEF

figures published in 1987, the proportion of Zairian children enrolled in primary school who completed first grade was 65 percent, while 33 percent of eligible males and 13 percent of the
females were enrolled in secondary school. By 1985, there were
20,000 university graduates, some of whom had been educated
abroad but many of whom had received their degrees from one
of three campuses of the Université Nationale du Zaire (UNAZA):
Kinshasa, Kisangani, and Lubumbashi.

Primary education, during the colonial period, was handled
mostly by religious organizations, although lay, "official," schools
were later established in urban centers. The dual system was
maintained after independence, although the government set certain standard curricula. The schooling consisted of six years
designed to impart literacy, computational skills, and basic knowledge of health, sanitation and nutrition. Textbooks were developed that used Zairians as role models and village, or "cité,"
settings as locations. However, many schools were hampered by
the poor quality of teachers, who were seriously underpaid, and
a lack of basic teaching materials. There was some instruction
at the primary level in the four "national" languages (Kikongo,
Lingala, Swahili, and Tshiluba), depending on the region.

Secondary education, available to a much smaller proportion
of the population, was conducted entirely in French, the "official" language. A great many of the secondary school teachers
were expatriates, until the recession of the mid-1970s obliged many
to leave. Secondary sequences consisted of either a four-year
university preparatory course or a two-year vocational course.
Secondary schools were afflicted with many of the material and
human resource problems of primary schools.

University education was conducted at the three campuses
mentioned above. The three campuses originally were separate
church universities: Lovanium founded outside Kinshasa by the
Catholic church, and Kisangani and Lubumbashi founded by
Protestant churches. The average length of course-of-study at
the universities was three to seven years. Students benefited
from government subsidies. In 1985, the government announced
plans to open a fourth campus at Kananga.

Vocational/Professional education was carried out by a number
of schools that focused primarily on agriculture and administration. They generally offered programs lasting two to four years.
In August 1971, following a period of antigovernment student unrest, the universities were nationalized. Subsequently, the universities were closed many times because of student unrest, often
organized to protest meager subsidies and poor food and living
conditions.

In the early 1970s most primary and one-half of secondary
schools were staffed and managed by religious groups, although
their administration was centered in the government's Department
of Education and they received government subsidies. In 1974,
however, during the height of authenticity, theological faculties
were abolished and religious instruction was phased out of primary

and secondary schools. By 1976 the government had assumed full administrative control. In the late 1970s, following the collapse of mineral export prices, a lack of government revenue left many public schools underequipped, sometimes even without desks and blackboard chalk. Teachers were often paid several months late. As a result they often left classes during the day to engage in commerce or charged fees before they issued grades. In the face of the deteriorating conditions and as relations with the church improved in the late 1970s, the Zairian government relaxed some of its controls over religious schools which continued to provide the bulk of the primary school graduates.

EGLISE DU CHRIST AU ZAIRE. An organization grouping most of the Protestant churches in Zaire, with 83 member churches in 1982. The Anglican and Plymouth Brethren churches were the only two major churches that did not join. The ECZ evolved out of a series of organizations formed near the turn of the century to avoid duplication and competition among Protestant churches working in the Congo. The Comité de Continuation Congolais (CCC--Congo Continuation Committee) was formed in 1911 by Protestant missions in the Congo to encourage contact and cooperation among the various denominations. The Congo Protestant Council (CPC) was created in 1924 from the CCC. In 1934, members of the CPC voted to rename themselves the Eglise du Christ au Congo, which became the ECZ when the Congo's name was changed to Zaire in 1971. The 1960s witnessed an Africanization of the leadership of the organization. Rev. Pierre Shaumba was elected the first Congolese secretary-general following independence. He was succeeded by Rev. Jean Bokeleale in 1968, who became Archbishop in 1970. See PROTESTANT CHURCH.

EIGHTY-DAY WAR. The name often used by the Zairian government to denote the first Shaba incursion, from March 8 until the end of May in 1977. During this period Angola-based guerrillas of the FNLC took the border town of Dilolo, in western Shaba Region, and marched east nearly reaching the mining center of Kolwezi. The attack took the authorities by surprise and because of the remoteness of the region, it was several weeks before a counteroffensive could be organized. See SHABA.

ELECTIONS. The first elections held in Zaire were the municipal elections of 1957 that followed colonial reforms designed to give Congolese a voice in the running of local affairs. Congolese candidates were allowed to run for posts in the "communes," subdivisions of the cities. In December 1959, elections were held to elect representatives to territorial and communal councils. The elections were inconclusive because they were boycotted by the MNC, ABAKO, and several other parties, but several personalities emerged during the campaigning who would play major roles following independence: Kasavubu, Lumumba, Tshombe, and Kalonji. In May 1960, as part of the preparations for

independence, more than 100 parties competed for seats in parliament and the provincial assemblies. The MNC received the
largest number of seats, but no clear majority. Lumumba and
Kasavubu tried to form a coalition, but failed. Lumumba succeeded on the second attempt with some other leaders and formed
a cabinet of 23 ministers. Under a compromise agreement, Kasavubu was elected president on June 25, 1960, ending talk of
secession in Bas-Congo. Tshombe, angered by the lack of representation of the CONAKAT leadership, withdrew to Katanga.

Elections were held for the first time as an independent nation in March 1965, under the newly promulgated constitution.
In that polling, the CONACO alliance of primarily southern-based
parties with some support from disgruntled Adoula supporters
won a clear majority of seats in the parliament, while ABAKO
and some recently formed coalitions gained little ground. The
CONACO ascendancy led to tensions between ABAKO and CONACO
and a constitutional crisis that contributed to the military's decision to seize power. When elections were held next, on November 11, 1970, the MPR had been declared the sole legal party.
Mobutu ran unopposed and won by an official vote of 10,131,699
to 157. Legislative elections were scheduled for November 1975,
but were cancelled by presidential decree. Instead the names of
the MPR candidates were read in public and approved by popular
applause. In October 1977, following a series of liberalization
measures, elections were held for the Legislative Council and urban councils and some members of the Political Bureau. Any
citizen was allowed to run, but party officials eliminated many
candidates on technicalities. On December 2, 1977, Mobutu was
re-elected president for a second seven-year term. Elections for
legislative and local councils were held again on September 18-19,
1982. Under the liberalization process, multiple candidates were
allowed within the party structure. Candidates were nominated
by MPR cells, then approved first by regional party leaders and
ultimately by the Political Bureau. Considerable changes were
made to some of the lists. However, the campaign was lively.
About one-half of the incumbents failed to make the nominations
lists and of those who did, one-half were not re-elected. The
results led to the youngest legislature in history, with an average
age of 35 years. However, they reflected to a degree the public's
dissatisfaction with the party barons. Many of the defeated incumbents, however, received in consolation posts in the party
hierarchy. Mobutu ran unopposed and was re-elected, again by
more than 99 percent of the vote, to a third term on July 29,
1984, in elections that were moved up by six months because,
according to the announcement, "The will of the people made it
evident that further campaigning was not necessary." As in
most elections since 1965, reports of irregularities surfaced, including a shortage of "No" votes, surveillance and harassment
of voters by soldiers and party militants at the polls, and the
lack of observers during much of the ballot counting. Nevertheless, the Zairian government demonstrated it could hold peaceful
elections and the world community recognized the results.

ELECTRICAL POWER. Zaire is estimated to hold 13 percent of the world's hydroelectrical potential, one billion kilowatts, the largest amount of any country in the world. Total installed capacity in 1984 was 2.4 million kilowatts, 90 percent of it from hydroelectrical complexes. Total annual generation in 1984 was 4.8 million megawatt-hours and home consumption was available to 500,000 customers. The largest site is the Inga hydroelectrical complex lying 40 kilometers upriver from Matadi where the Zaire River falls 100 meters in a series of cataracts two kilometers long. Two phases have been completed of a potential three-phase complex with a capacity of 40 million kilowatts. Shaba Region is the second largest producer of electricity with three complexes on the Lualaba River north of Kolwezi and two on the Lufira River northeast of Likasi. Shaba purchased power from Zambia from 1973 until the completion of the Inga-Shaba power line, a 500 kilovolt direct-current, high-tension line linking the Shaba grid to Inga. Smaller hydroelectrical complexes provided electricity to other, primarily urban, areas. These included complexes on the Inkisi River near Kinshasa, on the Tshopo River near Kisangani, on the Aruwimi River near Bunia, on the Ruzizi River supplying Bukavu and Burundi, and small stations near Punia, Piana, Mbuji-Mayi, Tshikapa, Kalima, Sanga, and Zongo.

The Société Nationale d'Electricité (SNEL) was created on May 16, 1970, to exploit and market power from Inga. In February 1974, the government ordered six private or mixed-ownership electrical complexes still operating in Zaire to be absorbed by SNEL. In 1979, REGIDESO, the national water management corporation, turned over to SNEL a number of small thermal units that supplied about 30 Zairian cities in the interior. SNEL, which employed 5,000 persons in 1984, has divided the distribution of electricity into six areas: the Kinshasa urban area, which sells some electricity to Brazzaville, Congo; Western Zaire, which supplies Bas-Zaire; the Central region, supplying Bandundu and the Kasais; Northern region, supplying Equateur primarily from thermal units; an Eastern region, which supplies Haut-Zaire and Kivu (and sells electricity to Rwanda and Burundi); and the Southern Region, which supplies most of Shaba. Some electricity is traded with Zambia across a 220-volt line. SNEL also manages the Inga-Shaba line. Among its expansion programs, SNEL has announced plans to add 90,000 electrical hookups by the end of 1988. Also planned is a hydroelectrical unit at Mobayi to supply Gbadolite by 1988. A line linking Bukavu to Goma via Katana reportedly was completed in 1985.

ELEPHANTS. Before the eighteenth century, Zaire had one of the largest elephant populations in the world, numbering in the millions. Since then the ivory trade--first legal, now illegal--has seriously reduced the population, currently estimated in the tens of thousands. Only herds in the remotest areas have been protected by the lack of roads. Poaching reportedly is carried on virtually unmolested in more accessible areas because of corruption and a lack of funds for patrols.

ELISABETHVILLE. The former name of the capital of the former
Katanga Province, now called Shaba Region. Elisabethville, now
called Lubumbashi, was the capital of secessionist Katanga in
1961-63. See LUBUMBASHI.

"ELITE." A French term, now widely used in English, to denote the
educated, often wealthy middle- and upper-class Africans usually
engaged in business, politics, or the professions. In Zaire, the
"élites" sprang in part from the colonial "évolués," but were
joined following independence by Congolese who rose to professional and political positions in the new state. In Zaire, the
term has assumed some negative connotations because of the wide
disparity of wealth between the elite and the rest of society, the
conspicuous consumption by some members of the elite, and the
supposed involvement of many of them in corrupt activites.

EMERY, FRANCOIS. The son of Patrice Lumumba who has led the
MNC-Lumumba party from exile since the mid-1960s. Emery is
perhaps best remembered for an article he wrote in Afrique-Asie,
commemorating the 17th anniversary of his father's death, in
which he called for the overthrow of Mobutu. He has been more
subdued since the Belgian and French governments, under pressure from the Zairian government, told Zairian dissidents they
could remain within their borders if they did not engage in public,
anti-Mobutu activities.

EMPLOYMENT. An estimated two-thirds of the Zairian population
lives outside the formal economy and consequently does not
figure in official employment statistics. According to the UNICEF
annual report of 1987, 80 percent of the rural population lives
in poverty and mainly from subsistence farming and hunting.
Membership in UNTZa, the sole trade union, is one million and
several million additional persons hold some form of regular job,
like maids, drivers, and guards. The largest employing sectors
are the public sector (39 percent), farming (25 percent), and
industry (12 percent). Unemployment in the cities is estimated
to vary between 10 and 20 percent, although that figure does
not include unemployed persons engaged in the marginal economy,
like street vendors, car washers, small traders, and artisans.

ENERGY. Zaire possesses relatively abundant energy. However, 98
percent of it is hydroelectrical and the lack of infrastructure im-
pedes delivery to remote areas. Hydroelectrical potential is
estimated at one billion kilowatts. Installed capacity is 2.4 million kilowatts. Known petroleum reserves are relatively poor,
estimated at 60 million barrels. There was no oil production until 1975 when several wells off the Atlantic coast came on line
and production was begun on an island in the mouth of the Zaire
River. Total production is eight million barrels of crude oil per
year, but most refined oil products have to be imported. Explorations in the Mbandaka area in the early 1980s were not

fruitful. There are significant deposits of low-grade coal located in northern Zaire. However, exploitation is uneconomic because of transportation costs. Small deposits in Shaba Region, between Likasi and Kamina, and near Kalemie produce 100,000 tons per year, all of which is used by local industry. Higher-grade coke and coal needed to power the copper refineries must be imported from Zimbabwe. See COAL; ELECTRICAL POWER; and PETROLEUM.

EQUATEUR. One of Zaire's eight regions, Equateur lies in the north-western corner of Zaire, in the heart of the Congo Basin. Its topography is dominated by vast rain forests and numerous swamps, rivers, and streams. However, in the northernmost parts, along the border with the Central African Republic, the terrain is higher and drier, providing for some wooded savanna. With an area of 403,293 square kilometers and a population of 3,288,353 (1982), Equateur is one of the most sparsely populated regions in Zaire. The region is largely inhabited by people of the Mongo ethnic family with some groups of Sudanese origin present in the northern parts. Most depend on hunting and fishing, although some groups have a tradition of gathering and cultivation. The regional capital is Mbandaka with a population of 153,440. The administrative sub-regions of Equateur Sub-Region, Tshuapa, and Mongala are the most populated with roughly one-half million persons living in each. Major products include palm oil, timber, herding, and some cocoa and rice from irrigated projects. The region is believed to have large deposits of iron ore, but these have yet to be exploited. Originally one of the more remote and neglected areas of Zaire, Equateur has received some attention in recent years, in part because it is the home region of Mobutu and many of his close collaborators and in part because of a government policy of attempting to develop the economies of more remote regions of the country.

ETHNIC GROUPS. Although estimates vary, ethnologists say at least 200 distinguishable ethnic groups live in Zaire, speaking as many distinct languages and another 250 dialects. Although no single group is believed to exceed 10 percent of the total population, a number of major groupings or "clusters" have been identified. They include the Kongo, Luba, Lulua, Lunda, Mai-Ndombe, Mongo, and Zande. However, there are ethnic groups distinguishable by language, customs, and traditions with only a few thousand members. In recent years, official Zairian ethnographers have cast the northwestern-based Mongo group as one of, if not the largest ethnic cluster in Zaire, classifying societies living as far away as the Kasais and Shaba as Mongo. Although some of the groups can trace their origins from the Mongo area, other ethnologists tend to view the Mongo group as covering a much smaller range of territory. They tend to view the more homogeneous societies of the Kongo, Luba, and Lulua as being the more populous of Zaire. Other ethnic groups, such as Lunda

and Chokwe, also are large societies, but ones with a considerable proportion of their populations living in neighboring countries. (See individual ethnic listings.)

ETHNICITY. Ethnicity, or the concept of identity based on ethnic
grouping, is as much a product of the European tendency to
classify groups of people for the purpose of study on the basis
of their most discernible traits (physical appearance, language,
religious practices, etc.), as it is a product of a natural human
tendency toward parochialism, regionalism, and the placing of
value on family and ancestry. Nevertheless, ethnicity, often
called by the currently unpopular name of "tribalism," was used
by the colonialists to divide a people and prevent the rise of
nationalism. It also was used by some Zairian leaders in an effort to build a base of power for their political ambitions. After
the political disruption following independence, caused in no
small part by regionally and ethnically based political parties and
their leaders, most African leaders began to criticize ethnicity
as a source of friction and factionalism. As a result, many have
sought to remove it from national politics through the promotion,
for example, of one-party states, while at the same time seeking
to preserve its cultural aspects through such concepts as authenticity and folklore. The effort to remove ethnicity from national
politics is one of the strongest signs of the fact that ethnic affiliation continues to play an important role in the political life
of modern Zaire. It continues to be a major factor in political
appointments, business contracts, and, to a degree, in housing
patterns. However, the rise of the one-party state and the concept of nationalism, as well as the official disgrace of "tribalism"
and "favoritism," may be contributing to a slow decline of some
of the more divisive aspects of ethnicity. For example, a decree
February 22, 1972, said the assistants of State Commissioners
could not be from the same region or ethnic group as the Commissioners. However, it has been noted that often the individuals most trusted by a political official are those from that
official's family, ethnic group, and region.

EUROPEAN ECONOMIC COMMUNITY (EEC). The EEC is Zaire's major trading partner, supplying one-half to three-fourths of
Zaire's imports and purchasing three-fourths to four-fifths of
Zairian exports. Belgium has remained the largest individual
trading partner, although trade with Belgium has been steadily
declining in recent years in favor of France and Japan. Zaire
signed the trade agreement between the EEC and the countries
of Africa, the Caribbean and the Pacific (ACP), often called
the "Lomé Convention" in 1975. The agreement provided prefer-
ential access to EEC markets for Zairian products while, in exchange, provided access for EEC products and technology to
Zaire and other markets in the developing world. Zaire also
signed the second, more broad-based Lomé II agreement and, with
members of the growing ACP group, negotiated a "Lomé III"

agreement in 1986 aimed at further increasing trade with the
Common Market.

"EVOLUES." A term used primarily in the 1950s and 1960s to describe Congolese who were the most assimilated into European-
style society and lifestyles, usually because of education at missionary schools or training and experience at European firms.
More European than the "immatriculés," most "évolués" were educated urban dwellers. Some of them were intellectuals who appeared to be largely disassociated from their traditional societies.
Most of them quickly moved into positions of leadership following
independence.

EXPLORERS. Recorded history knows little about the African, Arab,
and Asian explorers who travelled and traded across central
Africa well before the arrival of the Europeans. Tippo Tib is
perhaps the best known of these. The Europeans who arrived--
beginning with Diogo Cao at the mouth of the Zaire River in
1483--are better known: José Lacerda e Almeida and the British
explorers James Tuckey, Henry Morton Stanley, David Livingstone, Richard Burton, John Speke, and Samuel Baker. They
were forgotten while they were gone and adulated when they returned. Nevertheless, their travels and mappings helped spark
European interest in the continent. Greater knowledge of the
region came later with the traders, missionaries, and colonialists.

EXPORTS. Zaire's economy is considered export driven and dependent primarily on minerals: copper, cobalt, industrial diamonds,
gold, zinc, and tin. In fact, more than 80 percent of export
revenues come from minerals, 65 percent from copper alone. Agricultural products, primarily coffee and palm oil, form the second
largest export sector. Other agricultural exports include timber,
rubber, cocoa, tea, and cotton. Following independence, however, agricultural exports declined for many years because of
mismanagement and a brief period of nationalization (see ZAIRIAN-
IZATION). Nevertheless, privatization and more liberal policies
beginning in the early 1980s spurred agricultural exports. Smuggling continued to be a problem. However, the government attempted to address the problem by removing price restrictions on
domestically marketed commodities and by allowing the overvalued
Zairian currency to float freely on the open market. According
to IMF figures based on Zairian government statistics, Zaire
exported $1,568 million worth of goods in 1985, $104 million of
that to developing countries. The figures represented a significant increase from 1981, when $685 worth of goods were exported.
Major markets for exports were Belgium ($499 million), USA ($376
million), West Germany ($190 million), Italy ($121 million), France
($83 million), Japan ($46 million), United Kingdom ($42 million),
and China ($41 million). During the 1980s, exports more than
doubled to the United States, Japan, France, West Germany, and
Italy, and declined markedly to Switzerland and the United Kingdom.

Among the developing nations, the major customers were China, Malaysia ($13.5 million), Yugoslavia ($10.8 million), Egypt ($8.4 million), Congo ($6.2 million), and Rwanda ($3.2 million). See IMPORTS and Table No. 7.

- F -

FISHING. Zaire's vast network of lakes and rivers has endowed it with an abundant supply of fish, an important source of protein in the Zairian diet. A great deal of fishing is at the subsistence level or on a small commercial scale. There were some commercial fishing operations by European-owned companies on the great lakes, but these virtually disappeared after Zairianization. Fuel shortages in the years following retrocession hampered the renewal of activity. The Société des Pêcheries Maritimes du Zaire (PEMARZA) operated a small fleet of fishing boats at the mouth of the Zaire River, supplying Bas-Zaire and the Kinshasa area. The Agriculture Department estimated total production at 180,000 tons per year in the 1980s, of which approximately two-thirds was from the rivers, 20 percent from the lakes, and 10 percent from ocean waters. The Zairian government began a number of fisheries projects in the 1980s in conjunction with USAID and the Peace Corps.

FOOD SUPPLY. Zaire was self-sufficient in food at independence, but the civil unrest during the 1960s disrupted extension services and harvests, and a deteriorating transport sector accelerated the decline in productivity. In addition, new investment in agriculture during that period fell to negligible levels, choking off inputs and the establishment of new farms. By the early 1970s, overall agricultural production had returned to pre-independence levels, but an increased population meant per capita food production had declined. Agriculture was deemed the "priority of priorities" by Mobutu in 1973, but government policies failed to encourage an increase in production commensurate with the rapidly expanding population. In the late 1970s, for example, an international team of physicians studying nutrition levels in the relatively productive areas of Kinshasa and the Bas-Zaire determined that one-third of the children in the region were suffering from severe malnutrition. Because of the neglect of agriculture, Zaire was forced to import many food items, ranging from rice and maize to fish, meat, and dairy products. Zaire also received food aid from many donors, including U.S., EEC, and U.N. agencies. In 1982-83, Mobutu announced a liberalization of agricultural policies and the removal of restrictions on currency exchanges. As a result, by 1984, parts of Zaire were experiencing a small boom in agriculture, despite continuing transportation and marketing problems.

FORCE PUBLIQUE. The name of the armed forces of the colonial

Congo. The Force Publique, created in 1885 by Leopold II, was a feared corps of Congolese soldiers led by European officers and charged with maintaining order in the territory and ensuring compliance by local villages with tax and labor laws. Reports of excesses by the Force led to an international outcry that in large part was responsible for the annexation of the territory by the Belgian parliament in 1908. The name was changed to the Armée Nationale Congolaise following independence. See ARMED FORCES.

FORCES ARMEES ZAIROISES. Official name of the Zairian armed forces since the Congo became Zaire in 1971. See ARMED FORCES.

FORCES DEMOCRATIQUES POUR LA LIBERATION DU CONGO (FO-DELICO) (DEMOCRATIC FORCES FOR THE LIBERATION OF THE CONGO). An opposition movement-in-exile founded by Antoine Gizenga, the leader of the eastern rebellion and self-proclaimed spiritual successor of Patrice Lumumba. Gizenga announced the creation of FODELICO after he went into exile following the end of the rebellion. Gizenga's primary support is said to have come from Marxist and radical nationalist African regimes, but he claimed to be a nonaligned, leftist African patriot. The movement, which for a time was based in Brazzaville, has been inactive in recent years, in part due to an agreement between Congo and Zaire to avoid encouraging antigovernment activities by opposition groups based in each other's territories.

FOREIGN EXCHANGE. For 23 years following independence, Zaire's currency exchange rate was set at unrealistically high levels; consequently, foreign exchange, whether Belgian francs, U.S. dollars, or French-backed CFA francs, were always in high demand and short supply. Because of a shortage at the central bank, a parallel market in foreign exchange flourished, providing hard currency at three to seven times the official rate of exchange. The parallel market supported and enriched the political elite for nearly a quarter of a century. Those with political connections often were able to acquire foreign exchange through the central bank, at the official rate, ostensibly to import essential goods. However, many entrepreneurs used the foreign exchange to purchase luxury imports which were subsequently sold at parallel market rates. In some cases, the hard currency was merely dumped on the parallel market for an instant profit. However, in September 1983, following severe foreign exchange shortages, the Zairian government adopted a series of monetary reforms that allowed foreign and private banks to deal in foreign exchange for the first time since independence. In addition, the banks were allowed to set the rate of exchange according to supply and demand. Overnight, the value of the currency plunged from 6 zaires per one U.S. dollar to 30 zaires per dollar. The value of the zaire subsequently continued to drift downward, but at a rate much slower than expected. In January 1987, it stood at a value of 70 zaires to $1.00 at the official rate of exchange, and 80 zaires to $1.00 at the parallel rate, underscoring the virtual disappearance of the parallel market in Zaire. See CURRENCY.

FOREIGN INVESTMENT. Foreign investment in Zaire has varied since colonial times with world economic and business cycles, and with the incentives provided by the current government. Foreign investment reached its peak in the late 1960s and early 1970s, when foreign bankers granted large loans for ambitious infrastructure and industrial projects, based on projections of revenues from Zairian minerals, then at historically high prices. Following the collapse of commodity prices and subsequent recession in 1975, new investment virtually disappeared, despite increasingly attractive terms offered by the Zairian government and a trend toward privatization of the economy. However, following the economic and monetary reforms of 1983 and subsequent stabilization of the currency, some foreign investors began to return. Agreements were signed with Japanese and European firms for mineral exploration, and international consortia were formed to examine investment in light industry. Many investors, however, remained cautious because of uncertainty over the stability of the economy and the political future because of the absence of a designated successor to Mobutu.

FOREIGN RELATIONS. Officially, Zaire pursues a foreign policy of nonalignment and its government maintains diplomatic relations with such ideologically diverse governments as Belgium, the United States, France, North Korea, China, and a variety of East European nations. Relations with the Soviet Union, however, rarely have been good. By its votes at the United Nations and other world bodies and by its policies toward such regional disputes as the wars in Angola, Chad, and the Western Sahara, Zaire is seen as belonging to the moderate, more conservative group of African nations. Radical regimes have called it a U.S. puppet, although it often has been criticized by the U.S. Congress, which repeatedly has expressed concern over authoritarianism, mismanagement, and human rights abuses by the government. In the 1980s, the Zairian government strengthened relations with the Reagan and Mitterand governments and became a major spokesman among the Francophone African nations allied with France.

The Zairian government sees itself as a regional or sub-regional leader. It was the first sub-Saharan African nation to break relations with Israel following the 1973 war, and it was the first to re-establish relations after Israel completed its withdrawal from Egypt's Sinai desert. Zaire also was an early backer of such regional organizations as the Institute for Bantu Studies and the Economic Community of Central African States. It also has proposed the creation of an international organization of black-African states to supplement the activities of the Organization of

African Unity, which is seen as tending to focus too much on Arab problems. Zaire increasingly has exerted an influential role among central Africa's Francophone states, particularly after it hosted the Franco-African Summit in 1982.

FORESTRY. More than one-half of Zairian territory is covered by forest, or a total of 1.2 million square kilometers containing the world's largest reserves of African hardwoods. The forests dominate the Congo Basin area in the heart of Zaire, but also can be found in western Bas-Zaire and the mountainous areas of eastern Zaire. Exploitation of the forests has centered primarily on Bas-Zaire and the most accessible parts of the Congo Basin. In the early 1980s, one-half million cubic meters of wood were being cut for timber per year. The amount was considered relatively small, contributing less than 0.3 percent of the GDP, and the industry was considered "underdeveloped." The forestry industry was nationalized under Zairianization in 1973 and although up to 60 percent ownership was returned to the private sector with retrocession in 1975, 40 percent of each enterprise was reserved for the state.

FRANC, CONGO. The Congo franc was established in 1919 and, linked to the Belgian franc, was the Zairian currency for nearly 50 years. As part of a monetary adjustment in 1967, the name was changed to the "zaire" and one zaire was exchanged for 1,000 Congolese francs. See CURRENCY.

FRANCE, RELATIONS WITH. It could be said that France's interest in Zaire dates from the late 1880s, when Count De Brazza was sent to beat Stanley to what would become Stanley Pool and the city of Leopoldville. Although Zaire's colonial experience was under Belgium and considerably different from that of the French colonies, de Gaulle's offer of autonomy to France's African colonies in a speech in Brazzaville in August 1958 was one of several events that led Congolese in the Belgian Congo to call for independence. Zairian relations with France were friendly for the most part following independence and have become steadily warmer since the second Shaba War when 700 French paratroopers jumped on Kolwezi to help Zairian soldiers drive FNLC guerrillas from Shaba Region. Zaire's tempestuous relations with Belgium and the much greater capability of France to provide development aid, as well as France's status as the cradle of Francophone civilization and a growing sense of kinship with the former French colonies, contributed to Zaire's gravitation toward Paris. The rapprochement culminated in October 1982, when Zaire hosted the ninth Franco-African summit.

Relations following the inauguration of the Mitterrand government were initially cool and suspicious, primarily because of the socialist candidate's criticism during the campaign of incumbent Giscard d'Estaing's close ties with authoritarian regimes in Africa. However, within two years of Mitterrand's investiture, a policy of pragmatism had evolved and Mitterrand had mended fences with Mobutu and such traditional friends of France as Togo's Gnassingbe Eyadema and Gabon's Omar Bongo. The socialists appeared to have begun to appreciate the "moderates'" support of French policies in Africa and their continued status as receptive markets for French exports. Later, it would be the moderate African leaders who would persuade a reluctant French government to send military forces to Chad, exert moderation in the face of the revolution in Burkina Faso, and press for greater leniency on the part of international creditors toward Africa's debt problems. France has been Zaire's major foreign partner in telecommunications development and built the Voix du Zaire complex at an estimated cost of $1 billion. The complex, when it was completed in 1976, housed some of the latest television and radio broadcasting equipment in the world. France also has helped with military equipment and training, and has become one of Zaire's top three trading partners, after Belgium and the United States. The French government said 4,000 French citizens were living in Zaire, mostly in Kinshasa and Lubumbashi, in 1985.

FRANCK, LOUIS. Belgian minister of colonies in the 1920s who is credited with changes in the colonial administration following World War I that consolidated the chiefdoms into sectors. The measures are considered to have Europeanized, or de-Africanized, the colonial administration by separating it from the traditional African political and judicial structure.

FRENTE NACIONAL DE LIBERTAÇAO DE ANGOLA (FNLA) (NATIONAL FRONT FOR THE LIBERATION OF ANGOLA). One of three major guerrilla groups that fought for Angolan independence and, after it was granted, fought each other for control of the national government. The FNLA was a group based primarily in northern Angola, with strong ties to the Kongo people of Bas-Zaire. Its leader was Holden Roberto, the son-in-law of Mobutu. The smallest of the three factions, the FNLA was backed by Zaire during the civil war and for a number of years after the MPLA took control of Luanda. Following the Shaba invasions, which reportedly received the support of the MPLA government in Angola, Kinshasa and Luanda established diplomatic relations and Zairian support for the FNLA diminished. The FNLA virtually disappeared while a second group, UNITA, continued its guerrilla war against the MPLA. However, during U.S. President Reagan's administration, spokesmen for the FNLA sometimes resurfaced seeking financial support and demanding to be included in any peace talks between the MPLA and UNITA.

FRENTE PARA A LIBERTAÇAO DO ENCLAVE DE CABINDA (FLEC) (FRONT FOR THE LIBERATION OF THE ENCLAVE OF CABINDA). A group that surfaced in the 1970s demanding independence for Cabinda at first from Portugal and subsequently from independent

Angola. Cabinda, 600 square kilometers in size, is an enclave
that was a special Portuguese possession until it was attached
administratively to Angola in 1956. It lies along the Atlantic
coast separated from Angola by the mouth of the Zairian River
and the Zairian territory that surrounds it. Mobutu began supporting FLEC in 1974 and, at the time, Zaire was rumored to be
interested in annexing Cabinda, which has considerable off-shore
petroleum reserves. Zairian support for FLEC was officially
halted following an agreement between Zaire and Angola, reached
during a meeting in Brazzaville on February 26, 1976, to cease
hostilities. FLEC activities appear to have ended, although a
heavy guard of Cuban soldiers around Cabinda's oil installations
has been maintained, in part out of fear of attacks from UNITA
and South Africa.

FRONT NATIONAL DE LIBERATION (FNL) (NATIONAL LIBERATION
FRONT). An antigovernment group created in Brazzaville in the
late 1960s. It was said to be linked to the Conseil de Libération
du Congo, which had been formed earlier, and rumored to be
headed by Gizenga. The FNL was accused of responsibility for
alleged plots against the Zairian government in 1970 and 1971. It
faded from view with the consolidation of Mobutu's power and a
strengthening of relations between Zaire and the Congo in the
1970s.

FRONT NATIONAL DE LIBERATION DU CONGO (FNLC) (NATIONAL
FRONT FOR THE LIBERATION OF THE CONGO). An opposition
group created in 1968 by Nathaniel Bumba, a former member of
the Katanga Gendarmerie that supported the Katanga secession
and participated in an invasion of eastern Zaire in 1967 aimed at
returning Tshombe to power. The FNLC is best known for
launching the Shaba invasions of 1977 and 1978 that obliged an
embarrassed Mobutu government to seek foreign military troops
and equipment to repel them. The FNLC contained elements of
the former Katanga Gendarmerie, but also included younger individuals, primarily of the Lunda ethnic group, who resented
the imposition of authority from distant Kinshasa. The FNLC
also reportedly fought with the Portuguese against guerrillas
fighting for independence for Angola and after independence
were hired by the Angolan government to fight against UNITA
and the FNLA. The FNLC guerrillas expressed little ideology or
political orientation other than a desire to overthrow Mobutu.
The attention they initially received faded considerably after the
Shaba incursions, although the FNLC still was considered a major opposition group in the mid-1980s.

FRONT SOCIALIST AFRICAN (AFRICAN SOCIALIST FRONT). An
exiled opposition group, affiliated with the PSA, formed by
Cléophas Kamitatu in the late 1960s after the end of the eastern
rebellions. The group disappeared after Kamitatu accepted Mobutu's offer of amnesty and returned to Zaire.

FULERU. A small Bantu ethnic group living near Bukavu in the
eastern highlands. Kaplan reports it was the only ethnic group
in the region to be organized into a single state.

FUNGURUME. A small town in Shaba west of Likasi located in an
area reportedly containing large deposits of high-grade copper
and cobalt. A consortium of British, U.S., French, and Japanese
mining companies formed the Société Minière de Tenke-Fungurume
(SMTF) in 1970 with 20 percent government participation in order
to exploit the deposits. However, continued low prices for copper
and the closure of the Benguela Railway led to the liquidation of
the company in 1984.

- G -

GARCIA II. King of the Kongo from 1641 until his death in 1661,
Garcia II ruled over what many African historians believe were
the twilight years of the Kongo empire. He faced problems re-
conciling the recently introduced Christian religion with traditional Kongo religious practices. After his death, war broke
out in 1665 between the Kongo and Portuguese-ruled Angola,
resulting in the defeat of the Kongo and disruption of the al-
legiance by sub-chiefs of distant parts of the kingdom.

GARDE CIVILE see GUARD, CIVIL

GAULLE, CHARLES DE (GENERAL). President of France during the
African independence period. De Gaulle's speech in Brazzaville
on August 24, 1958, in which he offered autonomy to France's
African colonies, dramatized the difference, in the minds of
Congolese, between the Congolese prospects for independence
and those of their French-ruled neighbors. De Gaulle's speech,
along with the Pan-African Conference in Accra and the Brussels
World Fair, led to the calls for independence that sparked the
riots beginning January 4, 1959, and the setting in motion of
the march toward independence.

GBADOLITE. A town on the Ubangi River in Equateur Region, 400
kms upriver from Bangui, the capital of Central African Republic.
The Mobutu family originally is from Gbadolite, although he was
born and raised in Lisala. Gbadolite has become a model town
with electricity, paved roads, and relatively developed health
and social care facilities. It also is home of the shrine to Mobutu's mother, Mama Yemo.

GBENYE, CHRISTOPHE. Interior Minister in the Lumumba government, Gbenye was the acolyte of Gizenga, who assumed the control of the Stanleyville regime in its brutal, final days and in
1964 became President of the short-lived People's Republic of the
Congo. Fearing an offensive by government troops and mercenaries in late 1964, Gbenye declared the 200 European and
Americans living in the region hostages. Reports of atrocities

led to the Belgian paratroop jump from U.S. military planes on
Stanleyville on November 24, 1964. An estimated 10,000 Zairians
and 200 foreigners were killed during the final days of the rebellion. Gbenye fled to Uganda and Europe, but returned to
Zaire in 1984 following the general amnesty of 1983.

GECAMINES. The Générale des Carrières et des Mines, more commonly
known by its acronym, is Zaire's largest corporation, government-
owned since 1967. GECAMINES traces its history back to October 30, 1906, when it was formed as the Union Minière du Haut
Katanga by the Société Générale de Belgique and the British
Tanganyika Concessions Ltd. to exploit deposits of copper and
other minerals found in southern Katanga. The name was changed
to Générale Congolaise des Minérais (GECOMIN) when UMHK was
nationalized on January 2, 1967, following the refusal by UMHK
officials to move the company headquarters from Brussels to Kinshasa. Negotiations on compensation continued for several years,
but were resolved for the most part by the early 1970s in an
agreement through which the Belgian company Société Générale
des Minérais assumed technical operations in exchange for a portion (about 6 percent) of revenues. In 1972, as part of the
authenticity program, GECOMIN became GECAMINES. The company has one dozen subsidiaries operating several dozen mines
and several refineries. Historically, it has provided the Zairian
government with one-half of its total revenues and two-thirds of
its foreign exchange. The size of the company and the relative
power it can exert has made it a sort of state-within-a-state that
dominates the economic affairs of such cities as Lubumbashi and
Kolwezi. From 1975 until the early 1980s, GECAMINES was crip-
pled by low prices for copper and the shortage of foreign exchange that caused shortages of spare parts. In 1976, the
Zairian government granted the company the right to use one-
half of its foreign exchange earnings to refurbish and modernize
its plants. In 1983, faced with mounting shortages of spare
parts and supplies necessary for refining, the government granted
the company de facto permission to purchase foreign exchange on
the parallel market.

The company was restructured in 1984 and a great deal of
the top heavy, central management was redistributed among three
entities: GECAMINES-Exploitation, responsible for the extraction,
processing, and transport of the minerals to embarkation points;
GECAMINES-Commerciale, charged with marketing the minerals;
and GECAMINES-Développement, responsible for developing agricultural and livestock units aimed at feeding company workers.
The three legally and financially independent entities were
grouped under GECAMINES-Holding. In 1984, GECAMINES produced 500,000 tons of copper, the seventh largest producer in
the world. It also produced 9,000 metric tons of cobalt, or 60
percent of total production in the non-communist world. Other
minerals it produced that year in raw and semirefined form were
70,000 tons of zinc, 1.2 million ounces of silver, 80,000 ounces

of gold, and 300 tons of cadmium. The company employed
33,500 persons in 1985, of which fewer than 300 were expatriate
technicians. Revenues surpassed $1 billion in 1984. See MIN-
ING.

GENDARMERIE KATANGAISE. A group of well-trained paramilitary
units that helped maintain law and order in Katanga before independence. The Gendarmerie Katangaise, formed primarily of
members of the Lunda ethnic group, supported Tshombe's Katanga
secession in 1961-63. After the end of the secession, it was in-
tegrated into the Zairian army. However, many members became
disillusioned with the Mobutu government and went to live with
family members in Angola. They were implicated in the mutinies
of the Congolese Army in 1966 and were part of a group of mercenaries that occupied Bukavu for 100 days in 1967 in an attempt
to return Tshombe to power. Led by Brigadier-General Nathaniel
Bumba, the group formed the FNLC in 1968 in Paris. The Gendarmerie fought for the Portuguese colonial authorities against
nationalist guerrillas in the early 1970s, and following Angola's
independence, fought with the MPLA government in Luanda against
opposition guerrillas supported by Mobutu, primarily the FNLA.
The Gendarmerie Katangaise came to prominence as the core ele-
ment of the guerrillas involved in the "Shaba incursions" of 1977
and 1978. Some observers said they were supported directly and
controlled by the the Angolan government, which was angry at
Mobutu's support for opposition Angolan movements. Others
felt it was a relatively autonomous group. The rapprochement
between Zaire and Angola following the second Shaba War appar-
ently ended the Gendarmerie's activities, although rumors of
another incursion persisted until the mid-1980s and Bumba ignored the general amnesty and remained in exile. See SHABA.

GENDARMERIE NATIONALE. A paramilitary police force of 20,000
members formed from the colonial Troupes de Service Territorial
in 1959. The Gendarmerie was under the Department of Defense
and its chief-of-staff reported to the FAZ commander. On August
1, 1972, Mobutu decreed the dissolution of the National Police
which was absorbed by the Gendarmerie. The decree essentially
moved police responsibilities from the Interior Department to the
Defense Department and served to make the heads of all the security forces directly answerable to the president.

GENERAL MOTORS--ZAIRE. A company jointly owned by the U.S.
General Motors Corp. and the Zairian government that assembles
cars and trucks. Production began in 1975 at a plant in Kinshasa
with a capacity production of 4,000 vehicles. During the economic recession of 1975-1985, production averaged 10 to 25 percent of capacity.

GERMANY, FEDERAL REPUBLIC OF, RELATIONS WITH. Relations between Zaire and West Germany have been generally good and West

Germany has been an important, though not dominant, donor and trading partner since the mid-1970s. In 1976, a West German rocket manufacturer called Orbital Transport und Raketen Gesell-schaft (OTRAG) signed a contract with the Zairian government, reportedly for $50 million, giving it exclusive access to nearly 100,000 square kms of Zairian territory in a remote part of northern Shaba, near Lake Tanganyika. The purpose of the project was to develop and test commercial rockets designed to place satellites into orbit. However, Tanzania and other nations in the region protested, fearing the operation would be used to spy on them. Zaire cancelled the contract a year later.

GIZENGA, ANTOINE. Vice-Prime Minister in the Lumumba government and chief lieutenant of Lumumba's wing of the MNC, Gizenga was dismissed along with Lumumba by Kasavubu on September 5, 1960. He left for Stanleyville on November 13 to form a secessionist government. Lumumba was captured and subsequently assassinated while trying to join him. The murder caused an outcry among many nations of the "Afro-Arab" bloc and the Soviet bloc. It precipitated the eastern secession and helped Gizenga consolidate his regime, which at its peak received recognition from 13 African and Soviet-bloc countries.

Following negotiations with the Leopoldville government, Gizenga agreed to participate in a federally structured central government. He was made First Vice-Prime Minister of the Adoula government-of-reconciliation, although he remained in Stanleyville. He was arrested on January 16, 1962, with support from the United Nations and was imprisoned on Bula-Bemba Island at the mouth of the Zaire River. When Tshombe became prime minister in July 1964, he freed Gizenga, but placed him under house arrest in October, where he remained until he was liberated by Mobutu following his coup in late 1965. Gizenga was rumored to be involved with the Brazzaville-based Front National de Libération. In the early 1970s, he formed the Forces Démocratiques pour la Libération du Congo (FODELICO) in exile. In 1977, Mobutu invited him to return to Zaire to oppose him in elections. Gizenga, however, declined and Mobutu dismissed him as a tool of the Soviets.

GOLD. The search for gold was one of the main reasons for the arrival and exploration of the interior of Zaire, particularly Shaba, by European traders. However, they found none, and so turned to other pursuits, such as trading in ivory and slaves. However, gold was discovered near Bunia, in the Ituri sub-Region of Haut-Zaire in 1903. Historically, a great deal of Zaire's gold has been smuggled out of the country, most often through east African countries. Official production peaked in the 1930s and 1940s at 16,000 kg. Production fell thereafter, reaching 958 kg of pure gold in 1983. In 1985, the Zairian government launched a large-scale reinvestment program of $142 million, 22 percent of which was to come from mining revenues themselves. The goal was to raise production to 5,000 kg by 1990.

Zaire's known gold reserves are 100 tons. The major gold mining operation is the Office des Mines d'Or de Kilo-Moto, nationalized in 1973, which works alluvial and underground deposits in a 83,000-square-km concession in the Bunia area. Three other companies also have been involved in gold production, primarily in Shaba Region: GECAMINES, SOMINKI, and IKIMO. A fourth, Bureau de Recherches Géologiques et Minières (BRGM), a company of mixed private and state ownership, had completed feasibility studies in 1985 of two sites in Haut-Zaire. However, relatively low prices for gold were hindering a start-up of production. A Brazilian company called Andrade Gutierrez discovered what were believed to be important deposits near Kilo-Moto in 1986; in 1987 the Zairian government granted the company a concession to start up a project estimated to cost $230 million.

GOODYEAR ZAIRE. A subsidiary of the U.S. rubber company, Goodyear Zaire produces tires for automobiles, trucks, and bicycles at two plants in Kinshasa and Kisangani. Like many industries, the production was hindered in the late 1970s and early 1980s by low demand and by a shortage of foreign exchange needed to import equipment and materials not available locally.

GOVERNMENT. Zaire has been ruled by a variety of governmental systems, ranging from a monarchy and a military dictatorship, to parliamentary and highly centralized presidential systems. In virtually all cases, the tendency toward authoritarianism has been a major characteristic. After the partitioning of Africa at the Berlin Conference of 1885, Zaire was recognized as a sovereign territory of King Leopold II and was ruled under the name of the Congo Free State for 23 years. Some argue the king was only continuing trade patterns set centuries earlier by European and Arab traders. Nevertheless, the excesses of his rule caused the Belgian parliament to annex the territory in 1908 and ushered in the formal colonial era, during which the king exercised considerable authority but in conjunction with the executive and the legislative powers. With the advent of independence in 1960, the country adopted a bicameral parliamentary system that considerably diluted executive powers and left unclear how power was to be shared by the president and prime minister. The goal of the system was to provide checks and balances and prevent abuses of power by a single group or individual. However, it led to confusion and a series of confrontations between the president and prime minister. When the authority of the central government broke down following independence, a variety of federal and confederal systems were contemplated and the first constitution, promulgated in 1964, granted considerable autonomy to provincial governments. However, following the coup in 1965, Zaire entered a period during which power was gradually concentrated in the presidency.

Currently, the president benefits from considerable powers of decree and also controls virtually all aspects of security,

law-making, economic policy, and the judicial system. Zaire
has evolved into a party-state, modeled to a large extent on the
Chinese system. However, the African concept of chieftaincy
has also been retained as demonstrated by a considerable cult of
personality centered around the president and his immediate family. The system of government appears to be continuing to evolve
with the introduction of multiple candidates in 1982 for the legislature, although it is weak. A system for political succession in the
case of the president's death exists but has never been tested. Under the constitution, in the absence or incapacitation of the president, the dean of the MPR Central Committee will assume the presidency for a period of 30 to 60 days, during which time the Political Bureau is to organize elections and choose the party's candidate for president. Under the current constitution, there are
seven basic organs of state: the president, who is the "center
for decisions and control of the activities of the MPR" and who
presides over all of the state organs; the Political Bureau of the
party, which is the central policy and decision-making organ; the
Central Committee of the party, which is the major forum for debate and discussion of ideas emanating from the Political Bureau;
the Congress of the Party, which is the broad-based forum for
consultations with party members; the Legislative Council, or
legislature, which is essentially a consultative body; the Executive Council, which is the equivalent of a ministerial cabinet;
and the Council of the Judiciary, which groups the senior judges
and members of the Supreme Court. The party is the supreme
body of state and sole legal party, to which all Zairians automatically belong from birth to death. Administratively, Zaire is
organized into eight regions and the autonomous capital district.
The regions are divided into sub-regions, urban and rural, and
the rural sub-regions are divided into zones. There are five
levels of courts, with a Supreme Court of Justice as the highest
in the land. Independence of the judiciary is guaranteed by the
constitution, but is weakened considerably because of the om-
nipotence of the party and president. See ADMINISTRATION;
CONSTITUTION; ELECTIONS; JUDICIAL SYSTEM; LEGISLATIVE
SYSTEM; MOBUTISM; and MOUVEMENT POPULAIRE DE LA REVO-
LUTION.

GOVERNORS, COLONIAL. The governors of the Belgian Congo were
appointed by the Belgian government. Although they were responsible to the king and the Belgian parliament, they exercised
considerable individual power because of distance and the slow-
ness of communications between Leopoldville and Brussels, which
lasted until the 1950s. The governors carried out the colonial
policy of paternalism, which included isolating Congolese from
other Africans and preventing the formation of political organizations. The policy was well maintained and talk of independence
only began to be heard in the colony in 1957, three years before
it was granted. The last colonial governors were Eugène Jungers
(1946-52), Léon Pétillon (1952-58), and Hendrik Cornelis (1958-
60).

GREAT RIFT VALLEY. A geographical fault separating East Africa from the rest of the continent. The western edge of the rift, characterized by rugged mountain ranges and deep lakes, lies in eastern Zaire, in particular along lakes Tanganyika, Kivu, and Mobutu.

GROSS DOMESTIC PRODUCT (GDP). Zaire's gross domestic product, the total of goods and services produced by the economy, currently is $5 billion per year. Historically, GDP has tended to fluctuate with the world economy and the demand it produces for Zairian exports. GDP rose in the 1920s and 1950s, and declined during the 1930s and part of the 1940s. GDP also declined during the political unrest of the 1960s, but began to climb again at a rate of 6 to 10 percent per year following the return of political stability in 1967. During the mid-1970s, following the drop in copper prices and the world recession caused by the rise in petroleum prices, GDP declined by 4 to 6 percent per year. However, since the 1980s, small but steady growth in the 1 to 3 percent range has been registered. According to Banque du Zaire figures, the mining sector constitutes 25 percent of GDP; agriculture, industry, and transport contribute roughly 10 percent each; trade contributes 15 percent and services, including the government, contribute 31 percent. See ECONOMY.

GUARD, CIVIL. Following the border clashes between Zairian and Zambian soldiers in Shaba region in 1983-84, the Zairian government announced it would create a new corps, called the Garde Civile, which would be responsible for border security, combating smuggling, controlling terrorism, and "re-establishing public order." The government asked West Germany to assist with training, but Bonn initially reacted reluctantly, citing reductions in its foreign assistance program due to austerity measures.

GULF OIL ZAIRE. Part of a consortium, with the Zairian government, Japan Petroleum, and the Belgian Société du Litoral Zairois, engaged in offshore petroleum production near the mouth of the Zaire River. Production averaged 17,000 barrels per day in the 1970s, but has reached 25,000 barrels per day. The Zairian government holds a 15 percent interest in the consortium. Gulf Oil, which was purchased by Chevron in 1984, has more important petroleum concessions in neighboring Angola and Cabinda.

- H -

HAMMARSKJOLD, DAG. Secretary-General of the United Nations from April 11, 1953, until his death on September 18, 1961, in an airplane crash while en route to Ndola, Northern Rhodesia (now Zambia) in an attempt to negotiate an end to the Katanga secession. The cause of the plane crash was never fully determined. It could have been accidental, but anti-U.N. feelings were

running high in the Katangan government, which had a small
air force, and among Belgian supporters who had been angered
by U.N. efforts to end the secession. Furthermore, the Ka-
tangese were bitter over the armed intervention by U.N. troops
in the area and the attempts to expel Belgian advisors and mercenaries from the territory. As a result, many U.N. officials at
the time believed the plane crashed either after being hit or
while being harassed by a fighter plane of the Katangan government, which had been in the air over the region that day.

HASSAN II. King of Morocco who has maintained close relations with
the Mobutu government virtually since it came to power. Morocco sent 1,500 troops to help Zairian forces repel the first Shaba
incursion in 1977. They returned in 1978, following Shaba II,
and remained for several months, forming the backbone of an
OAU peacekeeping force established until Zairian troops could be
retrained and reorganized. The Zairian government has consistently supported Morocco's claim to the Western Sahara. When
the Saharan Republic of the Polisario Front, which was fighting
Morocco for control of the former Spanish territory, was admitted to the OAU in 1984, Morocco left the organization. Zaire,
in a show of support, suspended its participation, the only member to do so.

HAUT-ZAIRE. Zaire's northeastern region, the largest with 503,232
square kms, and most populous with 4,524,467 inhabitants (1982).
Haut-Zaire is rich in timber, rubber, coffee, fish, gold, iron
ore, and hydroelectric and agricultural potential. There is some
herding. However, the region is remote and access to many
areas is difficult if they are not located near one of the several
navigable river networks. The road network is poorly maintained
and supplies, particularly spare parts and fuel, are often difficult to obtain. As a result, industry has been stagnant for
years, except for areas close to the border where trade with
East African nations is possible. Those areas, however, have also been depressed in recent years by political and economic disruption in Uganda, the primary foreign trading partner of the
region. Some parts of the region lie in the Sudanic savanna and
the Great Rift Valley highlands. However, most of the territory
lies in the Congo Basin, where the forest inhibits communication
between communities and causes them to be self-reliant and somewhat independent from the central government. The region was
the scene of three rebellions between 1961 and 1967.

HEALERS, TRADITIONAL. Traditional healing, not to be confused
with sorcery or witchcraft, is a profession that is gaining respect
and legitimacy in Africa and other parts of the world. Zaire supports the scientific study of herbs, plants, and methods used by
traditional healers, often with the backing of international associations and funding. Scientific testing has proven some traditional methods to be effective against malaria, amebic dysentery,

infections, and some parasites. In addition, traditional healers have successfully performed under clinical scrutiny a variety of surgical operations using "primitive" instruments and little or no medication or anesthesia. Growing appreciation of the craft has led members of the international medical community, including the World Health Organization, to support scientific study of healers and their methods which, until only recently, were generally regarded as ritualistic quackery.

HEALTH CARE. Public health care in Zaire is relatively poor and limited primarily to urban centers. The government allocates 3.0 to 3.5 percent of its total budget to health care. There are three hospital beds for every 1,000 persons and one doctor per 15,000 persons. Approximately 20 percent of the population has access to health services, according to UNICEF figures (60 percent of the urban and 17 percent of the rural populations). Approximately one-fifth of children under one year of age receive the four major immunizations (against polio, diphtheria, tuberculosis, and measles). A great deal of health care is supplied by religious missions or by foreign assistance programs during emergencies. Some large commercial concerns provide health care facilities for their employees. Otherwise, private or traditional methods are generally used. Life expectancy is 51 years. Zaire's infant mortality rate is 117 per 1,000 live births during the first five years of life, as opposed to 251 per 1,000 births in 1960. A major health problem is malnutrition caused primarily by protein deficiency. The major diseases include malaria, pneumonia, tuberculosis, measles, gonorrhea, syphilis, leprosy, sleeping sickness, and parasitic diseases. Researchers from Zairian and international health organizations are also studying the relatively high incidence of AIDS in Zaire as well as a disease called Lassa Fever, both deadly mutations reportedly to have originated from central African monkey viruses.

HEMBA. A cluster of ethnic groups, identified by Vansina as living in the savanna area straddling Shaba and the Kasai Regions. A matrilineal group said to be related to the Luba, the Hemba live along the Lualaba River near Kongolo, Kasongo, and Manono. An Hemba kingdom once flourished in the highlands and may have formed part of the Luba empire or an offshoot of it. The kingdom came to an end before the twentieth century.

HUMAN RIGHTS. The Zairian constitution recognizes the International Charter of Human Rights and espouses its ideals. However, human rights organizations over the years have repeatedly accused the government of a variety of human rights abuses. These have included detaining political opponents without charges, holding political prisoners, engaging in torture, allowing poor prison conditions, and maintaining special secret detention camps for opposition leaders and potentially troublesome vagrants. They also accuse the government of failing to guarantee a free and

independent judiciary. Mobutu has denied the charges and at
various times has offered to allow representatives of human rights
organizations to visit Zaire. Few have done so on an official
basis, preferring to rely instead on reports from travellers and
exiles. The U.S. State Department has tended to view Zaire's
human rights record as better than some, but worse than most.
It also has tended to classify the situation as "improving."
Speaking at a public meeting on November 2, 1986, following a
month-long meeting of the MPR's Central Committee, Mobutu acknowledged that some accusations by human rights organizations
had occurred in Zaire. He said steps were being taken to address the problems and announced the creation of the post of
State Commissioner for Citizens' Rights and Liberties. Mobutu
designated a Kinshasa lawyer and former head of the Supreme
Court, Nimy Mayidika Ngimbi, to fill that ministerial-level post.

- I -

IDIOFA. A small town of fewer than 50,000 inhabitants lying about
100 kms east of Kikwit in Bandundu Region between the Kasai
and Kwilu Rivers. The area long has been a center of opposition to the central government. Exiled Zairian dissidents said
an uprising in January 1978 by nearby villagers was harshly put
down by government troops. Human rights groups said several
thousand persons reportedly were killed and 14 local chiefs were
publicly executed. However, a subsequent investigation by international organizations failed to obtain proof of the charges.

ILEBO. A river port town of 40,000 inhabitants, formerly called
Port Francqui, lying on the Kasai River near its confluence with
the Sankuru River. It is the most important port for the Kasai
Regions and an important link to Shaba since goods arriving from
Kinshasa by riverboat are transferred to a railway line that trav-
els through Kamina to the mining centers of Likasi and Lubumbashi.
As such it forms an important link in the National Way by which
a large portion of Zaire's minerals are exported. See NATIONAL
WAY.

ILEO, JOSEPH. A political leader active in the independence movement, Ileo headed the editorial committee of the Conscience Africaine newspaper related to the Catholic Church that in 1956 published the first known public demand by Congolese for political
liberalization. Elected to parliament under the banner of the
MNC/Lumumba party at independence, Ileo was considered a moderate, pro-Belgian leader. Following Lumumba's dismissal on
September 5, 1960, Kasavubu named Ileo to form a new government. However, the government he formed never was installed
because of the constitutional crisis between Kasavubu and Lumumba. Ileo tried a second time, but that government was "neutralized" by Mobutu and the subsequent formation of the College

of Commissioners on September 29. Upon the demise of the College, Ileo became prime minister from February 6, 1961. However, he was unable to attract the major secessionist leaders and stepped down on August 1 of the same year to allow the formation of the Adoula government-of-reconciliation, in which he served as Information Minister and, following the end of the Katanga secession, as Minister in charge of Katangan Affairs.

IMMATRICULES. Congolese who had served in the armed forces, missions, industry or other "colonial" institutions. Under the Colonial Charter, they were recognized as special Africans who would lead future generations of Congolese leaders to an eventual independence. See EVOLUES.

IMPORTS. Zaire's import policy during the first 20 years of independence was often criticized by international financial institutions which said the large amount of imported consumables and luxury goods needlessly aggravated the balance-of-payments deficit and weakened the currency. In the early 1980s, 40 percent of Zairian imports were consumables, 25 percent were raw materials and semi-manufactured goods, 20 percent were capital goods, and 15 percent were energy products. In addition, during those years undeclared imports by the government and state-owned companies often reached 65 percent of the total. Principle imports were such foodstuffs as rice, maize and wheat; consumer goods; raw and semiprocessed material used in the food and clothing industries; and equipment and spare parts. According to government figures published by the IMF, Zairian imports totaled $262 million in 1970, rose to $828 million in 1980, fell to $475 million in 1982, and began rising again, reaching $1,178 million in 1985. In 1985, $260 million worth of imports came from developing countries, of which $41 million came from African nations. Major suppliers in 1985 were Belgium/Luxembourg ($259 million), Brazil ($148 million), France ($134 million), USA ($115 million), West Germany ($97 million), Italy ($62 million), and Netherlands, the United Kingdom, and Japan, each supplying about $50 million worth of imports. Among the developing nations, major suppliers were Brazil, China ($26 million), Zimbabwe ($22 million), Argentina ($6 million), Malawi ($5 million), and Central African Republic ($4 million). See Table No. 7 (page xxxiii).

INCOME. Per capita income in Zaire has varied depending on economic policies and the value of the currency. However, it has tended to average the equivalent of $150 per year, although following the monetary reforms and austerity policies of 1983-85, it fell to $100. The minimum wage historically has been in the range of $20 to $40 per month. Professionals generally earn 10 to 20 times the minimum wage. Senior government officials earn 25 to 50 times the minimum wage in addition to such benefits as food, housing, and entertainment allowances. Economists say distribution of income in Zaire is among the least egalitarian in Africa.

A wide gap separates the incomes of members of the political/ business elite from that of the rest of the population. Recession and austerity measures have virtually eliminated the middle class, and professionals and small businessmen often are unable to afford such "middle class" items as a car or telephone. The situation has led many Zairians to supplement their incomes through parallel activities such as commerce, second jobs, and in some cases graft and corruption. Meanwhile, the elite enjoys imported, luxury automobiles and electronic goods, Swiss bank accounts, and valuable property in Europe and the Americas. See ECONOMY.

INDEPENDENCE. The Belgian Congo became independent on June 30, 1960, after 50 years of colonial rule and following a brief transitional period that saw the emergence of more than 100 primarily regionally and ethnically based political parties and national elections that failed to give a clear mandate to any one party or coalition. At the time, it is said that the most progressive and farsighted Belgian administrators envisioned independence for the territory in 1990 at the earliest. The lack of preparation, the sudden opening of the political system after decades of repression, and the splintered political structure that resulted from interethnic and regional tensions, led to the erosion of central authority and the secessions and rebellions that brought the military coup of 1965 and the authoritarian system that evolved from it. Africanists note that many African nations experienced peaceful and orderly transitions to independence, but few had such wide and remote territories, such diverse populations, and so little time to forge them into a nation-state as did the Congo. See CONGO, BELGIAN; CONGO, REPUBLIC OF; and CONSTITUTION.

INFLATION. Inflation was kept to moderate levels during the colonial period and the first years after independence. However, it began growing at an alarming rate in the mid-1960s, rising to 40 percent in 1973. With the rise in petroleum prices in the mid- and late-1970s, it rose to 60 percent in 1976 and reached 100 percent by 1980. With subsequent austerity measures it was reduced to 50 percent in 1982 and, following the monetary reforms of 1983-84, was reduced to 20 percent in 1985. Inflation led to numerous devaluations and one major monetary exchange exercise. In 1985, the currency, vis-à-vis the U.S. dollar, was worth 1/1,000th of its value at independence. See CURRENCY.

INGA. A village located 40 kms upriver from Matadi which has given its name to a hydroelectrical complex located on a stretch of the Zaire River that drops 100 meters in the distance of 2 kms, creating 40,000 megawatts of hydroelectrical potential. A bend in the river allows for construction of dams in stages without diverting the river. Studies for an electrical power plant were made in the 1950s, but work was not begun until 1968. The first phase of the complex, called Inga I and containing six turbines generating 58 mws each was completed in 1972. Inga II, containing eight turbines generating 175 mws each, was completed in 1982 with participation by U.S., West German, French, and Italian companies. Construction of Inga III was not envisioned in the near future, since a great deal of the capacity of the first two phases, totaling 1,750 mws of potential generating capacity, was not being used. The construction of the Inga-Shaba power line allowed the transmission of up to 560,000 kws to Shaba. The government also hoped to export electricity to Zaire's neighbors, Angola, Congo, Gabon, and Zambia (via the Inga-Shaba line). An agreement was signed in the mid-1980s allowing the sale of small amounts to Brazzaville. Meanwhile, other projects were underway to utilize unused capacity, including electrifying the Kinshasa/Matadi Railway and developing an industrial complex in a nearby trade-free zone. See INGA-SHABA POWER LINE.

INGA-SHABA POWER LINE. One of the world's longest direct-current, high-tension power transmission lines, the Inga-Shaba Power Line can carry 560 megawatts of direct current (with the potential for doubling that amount) across 1,750 kms of Zairian savanna, mountain, and rain forest from the hydroelectrical complex at Inga, near Matadi, to Shaba Region, where it ties into a grid powering the region's mining installations. The line was built at a cost of $1 billion over ten years' time. Construction was hampered, however, by logistical problems, including crossing mountain ranges and dozens of major rivers, a lack of transportation infrastructure, two guerrilla incursions into Shaba, and considerable cost overruns that threatened funding. The construction of two lines, each with three strands of wire, required the building of 8,500 steel pylons every 50 meters along the route, 8,000 kms of permanent and temporary roads, and 2,000 permanent and temporary bridges. It also required the construction of special railroad cars and special river boats, and the maintenance of a fleet of six planes and two helicopters. Built by the Idaho-based Morrison-Knudsen company with large portions of work contracted to French and Italian companies, the line was completed in July 1983 and inaugurated by Mobutu on November 24, 1983. The project was criticized from the beginning as costly and unnecessary, since Zairian studies had revealed that the shortage of electricity in Shaba could be resolved by construction of several medium-sized hydroelectrical plants on rivers in the region. The project was also criticized because it would not deliver electricity to any of the rural areas along the way. Nevertheless, following completion, the Zairian government made plans to increase utilization of the line by seeking financing to build converter stations at Kananga and Kikwit, along the line, and by selling electricity from Inga to mining complexes in Zambia more than halfway across the continent.

INSTITUTE FOR BANTU STUDIES. A concept proposed by Gabon's

Omar Bongo and supported from the beginning by Mobutu to build a center for the study and dissemination of knowledge about Bantu culture. The Institute was inaugurated in 1984 and has its headquarters in Libreville, Gabon.

INTERNATIONAL AFRICAN ASSOCIATION. A European organization created in 1876 ostensibly to encourage the exploration of the African continent and to seek the abolition of slavery. Leopold II began his conquest of central Africa by assuming the presidency of the IAA from 1876 to 1880. During that time, he founded the Committee for the Study of the Upper Congo (Comité d'Etudes pour le Haut Congo) and hired Stanley to explore the Congo River. The Committee became the International Association of the Congo one year later and its work, combined with Stanley's explorations, led the European powers to grant Leopold II sovereignty over the Congo at the Berlin Conference in 1885.

INTERNATIONAL ASSOCIATION OF THE CONGO (ASSOCIATION INTERNATIONALE DU CONGO--AIC). Association established by Leopold II in 1877 as an outgrowth of the Committee for the Study of the Upper Congo, to explore the Congo Basin and encourage trade and the "civilization" of the indigenous people in the area. The association was recognized by the U.S. government and subsequently by 13 European nations that divided Africa at the Berlin Conference in February 1885. The association adopted its own flag and shortly thereafter was disbanded to allow the formation of the Congo Free State. According to historians, the association met only once in its brief history.

INTERNATIONAL BANK FOR RECONSTRUCTION AND DEVELOPMENT (IBRD). More commonly known as the World Bank, the IBRD was set up to assist the reconstruction of Europe following World War II, but it turned increasingly to development financing in the developing world beginning in the 1960s. It has been active in Zaire virtually since independence. The bank has specialized in funding infrastructure projects, such as the building and improvement of roads, railways and maritime networks, telecommunications improvements, and the development of electrical power complexes. Agriculture and rural development projects have also received considerable attention.

INTERNATIONAL DEVELOPMENT ASSOCIATION (IDA). An affiliate of the World Bank that specializes in granting "soft" loans to the world's least developed nations. The IDA grants loans at near-zero interest rates, with long grace periods and long repayment periods for projects such as one in 1978 granting $9 million to Zaire to rehabilitate plantations that deteriorated following Zairianization.

INTERNATIONAL MEMBERSHIPS. Zaire is a member of the United Nations and most of its agencies, the Organization of African

Unity, the Non-Aligned Movement, the Union Douanière des Etats d'Afrique Central (UDEAC), the Communauté Economique des Etats des Grands Lacs (CEEGL), and the African Development Bank. In 1984, Zaire and nine other central African nations signed an agreement in Libreville, Gabon forming the Economic Community of Central African States (ECOCAS), which is aimed initially at harmonizing customs, tariffs, and visa policies with the ultimate goal of establishing a common market in the region. In addition, Zaire signed the Lomé Conventions providing for greater trade and economic cooperation between the European Economic Community and more than 70 nations of Africa, the Caribbean, and the Pacific. It also regularly participates in the annual Franco-African summit meetings.

INTERNATIONAL MONETARY FUND (IMF). Sister institution of the World Bank formed at Bretton Woods, New Hampshire, in 1948 originally to help stabilize the European economies following World War II, the IMF was increasingly called upon to assist governments with serious cash liquidity problems, in particular following the leap in oil prices of the 1970s. In exchange for the implementation of economic stabilization programs that usually included severe austerity measures, the IMF provided infusions of hard currency to governments starved for new capital or experiencing problems repaying their foreign debts. Zaire has been in virtual constant negotiations with the IMF since its debt crisis began in 1975. The programs began as relatively modest "standbys" of $150 million over one year's time to the record, at that time, $1.1 billion standby over three years accorded in 1981. In the early years, Zaire was unable to abide by the programs, which included budget cuts, currency devaluations and regular reimbursements to the IMF. However, in 1983, Zaire instituted drastic economic and monetary reforms, including floating its currency on the free market and removing subsidies on petroleum and agricultural products. The Zairian government also met most of its IMF targets allowing it to draw on a $350 million standby and reschedule a great deal of its debt with the London and Paris Clubs of foreign creditors. However, on October 29, 1986, Zaire signaled a possible change in position on IMF economic programs. After a month-long meeting of the Central Committee of the MPR, the government announced that certain international organizations were "strangling" the Zairian economy, and after several years of budgeting more than half of government revenues for debt servicing, during which it had "regained a certain credibility" with the international community, the "social consequences" had become unacceptable. As a result, the government said it would henceforth limit foreign debt repayments to 10 percent of export revenues and 20 percent of government revenues, or about one-half their previous level.

ISLAM. Although eastern Zaire experienced considerable Islamic influence during the eighteenth and nineteenth centuries, spread

by Arab and eastern African traders, Islam never became entrenched in Zaire as it did in East and West Africa. Muslims
are estimated to compose 1 to 2 percent of the population. Nevertheless, Zairians are free to espouse any belief and there has
been no known repression of Muslims because of their religion.

ISRAEL, RELATIONS WITH. In the early years of the Mobutu government, relations with Israel were friendly and Israelis assisted
in training Zaire's armed forces. Mobutu, in the early 1970s,
even made some attempts to mediate the Middle East dispute. On
October 4, 1973, however, following the Yom Kippur War and
the Arab oil embargo, Mobutu announced before the U.N. General Assembly that Zaire was breaking diplomatic relations with
Israel because of its occupation of the Sinai Peninsula, which
belonged to Egypt--an OAU member. All African nations except
Lesotho, Malawi, Swaziland, and white-ruled South Africa, followed the lead. Relations, however, though clandestine, remained strong and Israeli products could frequently be seen on
the shelves of Zairian stores during the following years. On
May 13, 1982, the Zairian government announced the re-
establishment of relations, saying that Israeli had returned the
Sinai to Egypt as called for in the Camp David accords and as
a result, Africa's quarrel with Israel had ended. Certain internal pressures were also at work. Mobutu hoped to benefit
from Israeli military training once again and make use of the
U.S. Jewish lobby to support Zaire before the U.S. Congress
which had accused his government of mismanagement and human
rights violations and had cut foreign aid appropriations. The
massacre of Palestinians at the refugee camps of Chabra and Shat-
tila that year, reportedly by Israeli-backed, southern Lebanese
Christian militia, embarrassed the Zairian government. Mobutu
said Zaire would not accept military equipment captured from the
Palestine Liberation Organization and it was not until August
1983 that a second African nation, Liberia, followed Zaire's lead.
Mobutu paid an official five-day visit to Israel in May 1985 in
return for the visit to Zaire by Israeli President Chaim Herzog
following the re-establishment of relations.

ITALY, RELATIONS WITH. Italy is a significant though relatively
small trading partner of Zaire. The Italian government has
helped with the training of Zairian armed forces, particularly the
air force, and Zaire has purchased Italian fighter planes. An
Italian oil company has engaged in a joint offshore oil exploration
venture. Another company participates in the SOCIR oil refinery near Moanda. An Italian contractor helped build the Inga-
Shaba power line and an Italian company holds part interest in
the iron and steel works at Maluku.

ITURI FOREST. The Ituri forest is one of the densest and least
explored tropical rain forests in the world. It is named after
the Ituri River that flows from Zaire's border with Uganda north

of Lake Mobutu westward to join the Zaire River below Kisangani.
The Ituri forest covers most of the northeastern corner of Zaire
and is inhabited by Bantu, Pygmy, Nilotic, and Sudanic peoples.
Ranging from the uplands below the Ruwenzori Mountains along
the Ugandan border to the swampy lowlands of the Congo Basin,
the Ituri is rich in timber, gold, and fish and reportedly contains unexploited deposits of iron ore.

ITURI SUB-REGION. One of five sub-regions of the Haut-Zaire Region, the Ituri sub-region covers 65,658 square kms of territory
bordering Uganda. With a population of 1,673,727 (1982), it is
the most populated administrative subdivision of the Region. It
also is one of the most remote and least developed areas, known
mainly for its pygmies, forests, mountains, and gold.

IVORY. The highly valued elephant tusks were one of the riches
that drew foreign, particularly European and Arab, traders to
Zaire as early as the sixteenth century. Ivory continues to be a
major form of commerce, whether in its raw form or cut and
carved, despite official efforts to curb the trade and poaching
that has reduced the Zairian elephant population, which once
numbered in the millions, to one hundredth of its original size.
There are no official estimates of ivory production since for the
most part it is illegal.

- J -

JAGA. A group of warriors of unknown origin that invaded the
Kongo Kingdom from the east in the 1560s. Some historians believe the Jaga were distant Kongo peoples opposed to the Kongo
king who perhaps were joined by non-Kongo peoples in an effort
to capture the coastal slave trade. Others believe that may have
been a European myth. The Jaga were driven away with Portuguese help in 1573 and the debt owed to the Portuguese by the
Kongo contributed to the increased slave trade with Portugal.

JAMAA. A Swahili word meaning "family," Jamaa was the name of a
religious movement established in 1953 in Katanga by the Belgian
Franciscan priest Placide Tempels. The movement combined African mysticism and spiritualism with Catholicism and some of the
priest's own thoughts. Kaplan says the movement involved families in a close relationship with Tempels and his assistants. Doctrine stemmed in part from African roots although the movement
reportedly opposed sorcery and instead emphasized emotionality
and mystical experiences. It also downplayed the importance of
hierarchy and academia. The movement was always linked to the
Catholic Church, but many church leaders became wary of it and
Tempels was ordered back to Belgium in 1962 and required to
break his ties with the movement.

JANSSENS, EMILE. The commander of the Force Publique at independence who according to legend sparked the mutiny of the
force by telling soldiers grumbling over low salaries and the absence of Congolese officers that "After Independence Equals Before Independence," and writing it in the form of a mathematical
equation on a blackboard. The gesture led to a mutiny that
spread to Leopoldville and other regional capitals and brought
the first Belgian paratroop drop in the country's history. The
mutiny also brought about the departure of Commander Janssens
and the other Belgian officers and the appointment of a Congolese
officer corps that would have to face, within weeks, interethnic
rivalry and several rebellions and secessions in the Congo.

JAPAN, RELATIONS WITH. Relations between Zaire and Japan are
based primarily on commercial ties and are strong and growing.
Trade was virtually nonexistent at independence, but by the
early 1980s, Japan had become a major supplier of such Zairian
imports as automobiles, trucks, appliances, and electronic equipment. Japan imported some Zairian minerals but enjoyed a large
trade surplus with Zaire. The Japanese engaged in a modest bilateral development program, building the suspension bridge over
the Zaire River at Matadi in 1982-83 and assisting in the rehabilitation of roads and bridges in the Bas-Zaire and Bandundu regions. On the commercial front, a Japanese company participated
in a mining consortium in Shaba that was liquidated in 1984. And
a company called Japan Petroleum Zaire was involved in a consortium operating offshore oil wells near the mouth of the Zaire
River.

JEUNESE DU MOUVEMENT POPULAIRE DE LA REVOLUTION (JMPR)
(YOUTH OF THE POPULAR REVOLUTIONARY MOVEMENT). The
youth wing of the MPR, Zaire's sole legal party since 1967. All
Zairians are automatically members of the JMPR from birth until
they reach the age of 30 years when they automatically become
members of the MPR. The JMPR was decreed the sole recognized
youth organization in 1968. Other youth-oriented organizations
like the YMCA, scouting and church groups were banned and
many of their assets were taken over by the JMPR. See MOUVE-
MENT POPULAIRE DE LA REVOLUTION.

JOHN PAUL II see POPE JOHN PAUL II

JUDICIAL SYSTEM. During the colonial era, two judicial systems existed. The first applied written law primarily to Europeans, but
on occasion to Congolese. The second applied oral, customary
law (as practiced by traditional ethnic groups) to Africans. Under the system, the findings of each court were subject to review
by the next higher court of the five-tier system. In 1958, a
decree attempted to end distinctions in the laws for Congolese and
Europeans. After independence, the judicial system, like many
other institutions, deteriorated. The United Nations was obliged

to call in jurists from Egypt, Syria, Lebanon, Greece, and Haiti to preside over courts and act as attorneys. They gradually were replaced by Congolese. Under the Fundamental Law, the judiciary was independent of the legislative and executive powers of government. The provision was maintained in the Constitution of 1964 although the president was granted the power to appoint all judges. In 1968, a presidential decree restructured the court system, allowing customary law to be valid and relevant as long as it was "compatible with public order." A decree on February 11, 1972, called for a reform of the civil code in order to make it more authentically Zairian. The reform was implemented on May 5, 1975. The Constitution of 1974 created the Council of the Judiciary, presided over by the president. Magistrates in theory were to remain free and independent. However, they were required to be party members and owed their positions to the president. As Zaire became a party-state and the MPR became the supreme body of government, the party became the source of legality and the Judiciary's role evolved into one of interpreting it. The president of the Supreme Court and the attorney-general were automatically members of the Political Bureau of the party. And the heads of the regional courts belonged to regional committees of the MPR. The court system reflected the administrative and political organization of the country, ascending in importance from urban and rural sub-regional tribunals, to the regional tribunals, to three tribunals of the first instance (appeals) in Kinshasa, Lubumbashi, and Kisangani, to the Supreme Court of Justice based in Kinshasa. Although independence of the judiciary remains guaranteed by the Constitution, international jurists said the application of justice could be influenced by the party and certain influential individuals. There also were reports of judges willing to render favorable verdicts in return for gifts.

JUNE 4, 1969. Date on which a group of university and professional school students in Kinshasa staged a demonstration against the Mobutu government, primarily to protest poor living conditions and delays in payment of their government stipends. The demonstration degenerated into violence and vandalism. The clashes that followed led to more than 100 deaths and the closing of the schools. Dozens of student leaders were arrested and inducted into the army. A group of students and professors formed the Mouvement du 4 Juin (Movement of June Fourth) that later evolved into the MARC opposition group. In following years, June 4 became the date for marches in commemoration of those killed in 1969. These often were harshly repressed by the military. By the mid-1980s, however, the date was no longer being marked.

JUNE 30. June 30 is primarily remembered as the date of Zaire's independence in 1960. However, it also was the date in 1956 of the publication of the Conscience Africaine manifesto demanding greater political freedom for Congolese. And it was the date of publication of a manifesto by former Prime Minister Nguza Karl-I-Bond criticizing what he called the political, economic, and moral bankruptcy of the Mobutu government and calling for free, multiparty elections.

- K -

KABILA, LAURENT. A left-leaning leader from Kivu Region who joined Lumumba's MNC and participated in the Gizenga governments during the eastern rebellions. Kabila later quarreled with Gizenga and left in 1964 to form the Parti de la Révolution Populaire (PRP) (Party of the Popular Revolution) based in Kivu. Since then, the PRP has controlled a remote area west of the Mitumba mountains near Lake Tanganyika. See PARTI DE LA REVOLUTION POPULAIRE.

KALALA ILUNGA. According to legend, Kalala Ilunga was one of the founders of the Luba empire. A nephew of Kongolo, who led the Balopwe into the Kasai area around 1500, Kalala expanded Luba control to a large portion of territory. His relative Kibinda Ilunga moved away in 1600 to found what was to become the Lunda empire.

KALEMIE. A town in northern Shaba Region lying on Lake Tanganyika. Kalemie is linked to Shaba and the Kasais by the CFL railway that joins the KDL system at Kamina. A cement plant, some coal deposits, and textile installations are located near the town which also is a center for trade across the Lake with Tanzania and Burundi.

KALONJI DITUNGA (ALBERT). Early independence leader and president of the secessionist, Independent Mining State of South Kasai from 1960 to 1961. Kalonji was born June 6, 1927, at Kemotinne, in Kasai Province. He was educated by the Scheut Father missionaries and attended the Centre Agronomique de Louvain in Belgium. In 1949 he was named director of the INEAC. He briefly joined the MNC but left and allied with Tshombe to form the main opposition group following independence. However, he also broke with Tshombe following the massacre of the Luba in Katanga and, taking advantage of the disorganization of the central government following independence, declared South Kasai an independent state, and proclaimed himself "mulopwe," or "king." The secession was ended in 1961 and he was stripped of his parliamentary functions and found guilty of sedition. He went into exile in Spain in January 1963, but returned in 1964 to serve as minister of agriculture in the Tshombe government. He was elected a senator on the CONACO ticket in 1965.

KALONJI MUTAMBAYI (ISAAC). Reportedly the dean of the MPR Central Committee and one of the few Zairian politicians to have served without interruption in the government since independence.

Kalonji was born on September 9, 1915, at Lusambo in Kasai Region. He was educated by Protestant missionaries and became an administrator at the Ecole Moyenne de Luebo. He moved to Elisabethville where he became a member of the Conseil de Centre d'Elisabethville and president of the Classes Moyennes du Katanga, two associations of Congolese businessmen and professionals that would become cells for party formation prior to independence. At independence he was elected to the Senate and made State Commissioner for the Kasai in the Lumumba government. He was elected vice-president of the Senate in 1961 and president of the Senate under the Tshombe government. He was a member of the national assembly until 1982 when he joined the Central Committee.

KAMANDA WA KAMANDA. Lawyer and diplomat who was Zaire's first senior official in the OAU Secretariat. Kamanda was born December 10, 1940, in Kikwit, Bandundu Region. After receiving his law degree from Lovanium University, he served on the Kinshasa Court of Appeals, as a professor of law at the Institut National d'Etudes Politiques (INEP) and as legal counsel to the presidency. He was named Assistant Secretary-General of the OAU in 1972 and following the expiration of his term, became Zaire's ambassador to the United Nations in 1981. He became foreign minister on November 5, 1982 for a brief time and on January 3, 1983 was named to the MPR Central Committee.

KAMANYOLA BRIGADE. Named for a battle during the Congo rebellions in which hundreds of ANC soldiers were martyred, the Kamanyola Brigade is one of the prestige divisions of the Zairian army. Trained by the North Koreans, it participated in the paracommando operation to retake Kolwezi during the second Shaba War and was assigned "permanently" to the region following the war. In July 1983, after the Libya-backed forces of Goukouni Oueddai seized portions of northern Chad, the brigade was sent to Chad to bolster the forces of Chadian President Hissen Habre.

KAMINA. A small city in northern Shaba lying on the railway linking Lubumbashi to the Kasai River port of Ilebo that forms part of the National Way. Kamina is also a junction for the railway linking the towns of Kalemie and Kindu in Kivu Region to the Shaba and Kasai transportation networks. A large air base is located nearby that at times has been used for military operations in southern Zaire.

KAMITATU MASSAMBA (CLEOPHAS). An early independence leader who was one of the founders of the Parti Solidaire Africain (PSA) (African Solidarity Party), which participated in the first Congolese governments. Kamitatu was born in June 1931 in Kilamba and educated by the Jesuits. He lead the PSA delegation to the Round Table conferences and was elected a deputy to parliament in June 1960. He was interior minister and subsequently planning and development minister in the Adoula governments in 1962-64 and was foreign minister of the Kimba government that was overthrown by the Mobutu coup in 1965. Following the coup, Kamitatu went into exile where he organized the Front Socialiste Africain (FSA) (African Socialist Front) opposition group and wrote a highly critical biography of Mobutu. He later accepted Mobutu's offer of amnesty and returned to Zaire where he tried unsuccessfully to become a candidate in the 1977 legislative elections. He eventually returned to the government as minister of agriculture in the 1980s and joined the Central Committee.

KANANGA (formerly Luluabourg). The capital of Kasai Occidental Region, Kananga is an administrative urban sub-region with a population of 492,156 (1982) and an area of 378 square kms. From colonial times, Kananga has been the administrative, political, economic, and educational center of the Kasai. However, its influence was diluted somewhat by the establishment of the Kasai Oriental Region. And with the gradual transfer in the 1970s of the diamond marketing industry, and the banking and commercial interests that accompanied it, to the Kasai Oriental capital of Mbuji-Mayi (formerly Bakwanga), Kananga entered into a recession. By the 1980s, infrastructure had decayed severely and the city often was without electricity or running water. Roads were in disrepair and schools lacked such basic equipment as books and desks. However, efforts were underway by 1985 to resolve some of the problems. Kananga remained an important administrative, transportation, and milling center and the installation of a switching station along the Inga-Shaba power line also brought some jobs and capital infusion.

KANDE, DZAMBULATE. Journalist and government official who headed the Congolese Press Agency in 1964 when the United Nations ended its operation in the Congo. Kande was born April 23, 1930, in Kinshasa and studied at Lubumbashi, in Prague, and at the Ecole Supérieure de Journalisme de Paris in the 1950s and 1960s. He served as information minister in the Mulamba government formed after the Mobutu coup and has served in that capacity several times since then.

KANYONGA MOBATELI. Secretary-General of MARC who, along with 18 others, was tried in absentia and received the death sentence in 1978 for conspiring to overthrow the government. He reportedly died shortly thereafter from a gun accident.

KANZA, DANIEL. Known as "Buta Kanza" (meaning the "elder Kanza" in Kikongo), Kanza was vice-president of ABAKO and a member of the ABAKO delegation to the Round Table who served as mayor of Leopoldville from 1960 to June 1962. He was father of Thomas Kanza, who also was an important political figure from the Bas-Zaire and Kinshasa regions.

KANZA, THOMAS. A young intellectual, reportedly the first Congolese to receive a university degree, who participated in early Congolese politics, Thomas Kanza served as ambassador to the United Nations with ministerial rank in the Lumumba and Ileo governments during which the decisions were made that brought the U.N. intervention in the Congo. He was appointed ambassador to London in the Adoula government, but resigned and joined the secessionist Stanleyville government. He served as foreign representative for the Stanleyville government from September 1964 to 1966 when he went into exile in London. Disillusioned with Congolese politics, Kanza wrote a number of books bitterly questioning the future of the Congolese state. He returned for a visit to Zaire for the first time in 1983, following Mobutu's general amnesty.

KASAI REGION(S). Originally one of six colonial provinces, the Kasai was the second richest in minerals after Shaba, producing two-thirds of the non-communist world's industrial diamonds. Kasai also had the highest per capita income after Kinshasa and Shaba. On August 8, 1960, under the leadership of Albert Kalonji, the southern portion of Kasai, encouraged by foreign and local commercial interests, seceded and proclaimed itself the Independent Mining State of South Kasai. However, Kalonji abandoned secessionism in 1961 and joined the central government, but not before a violent internecine war between Luba and Lulua had caused thousands of deaths, the destruction of millions of dollars worth of property, and widespread famine in the region. The South Kasai was represented when parliament reopened July 25, 1961, at Lovanium University under U.N. protection. Partly because of the tensions between the Luba and Lulua, the Kasai was divided into two provinces on December 24, 1966.

Kasai Oriental (East Kasai), with Mbuji-Mayi (formerly Bakwanga) as its capital, had a population of 2,335,951 in 1982 and an area of 168,216 square kms. It is a Luba-dominated region divided into the urban sub-region of Mbuji-Mayi and the three rural sub-regions of Kabinda, Sankuru, and Tshilenge. Mbuji-Mayi (population 334,875) is also the diamond-trading center and has considerable banking and commercial services related primarily to the mining industry.

Kasai Occidental (Western Kasai) is the Lulua and Kete-dominated area with a population of 2,933,528 inhabitants and an area of 156,967 square kms. The capital of the region is Kananga (population 492,156). The region is divided into the urban sub-region of Kananga and the two rural sub-regions of Kasai and Lulua. Primarily economic activity includes transportation, agriculture (primarily subsistence), iron-ore mining, and some of the diamond trade. Like many of the more remote regions, Kasai Occidental suffered from a severe recession in the 1980s and deterioration of infrastructure. The National Way transportation route by which a large portion of Zairian minerals are exported travels through both Kasais, by rail from Kamina to Ilebo and by river boat from Ilebo to Kinshasa.

KASAI RIVER. Zaire's second major river transportation route after
the Zaire River, the Kasai River rises from headwaters in eastern
Angola and flows some 600 kms east to Dilolo in Shaba, then 1,000
kms north to Ilebo, in Kasai Occidental, at which point it turns
to the west and flows an additional 600 kms before joining the
Zaire River 300 kms above Kinshasa. The portion of the river
between Bandundu and the confluence with the Zaire River is
sometimes called the Kwa River. The Kasai River is navigable
from Ilebo to the Zaire River and forms an important part of the
National Way transportation route by which a major portion of
minerals from Shaba are exported. Several other important
tributaries feed into the Kasai River, including the Sankuru,
Lulua, Kwilu, and Kwango rivers.

KASAJI. A small town of about 20,000 in southern Shaba Region,
lying on the road and railway between Dilolo and Kolwezi.
Kasaji was one of several towns captured by FNLC guerrillas
during the first Shaba War in 1977.

KASAVUBU, JOSEPH. First president of Zaire, who governed from
independence on June 30, 1960, until Mobutu's coup d'etat on
November 24, 1965. Kasavubu surprised many observers by his
ability to survive the chaos following independence and the repeated challenges to his position by parliament and prime ministers. Born in 1917 at Kuma-Dizi, a small town near Tshela in
the Mayombe area of Bas-Zaire, Kasavubu received his early education from Catholic missionaries at Kizu. He studied agriculture
at the Institut Philotechnique de Bruxelles and in 1946 became a
member of the Union des Interêts Sociaux Congolais, a "study
group" formed to circumvent the colonial ban on political organizations. In 1950, he joined the Association des Bakongo, an organization formed to defend the interests of the Kongo people
that later became the ABAKO, and was elected its president in
1954. In the late 1950s, Kasavubu became an increasingly outspoken advocate of greater political and personal freedoms for
Congolese. He was elected Bourgemester ("mayor") of the Den-
dale Commune ("township") of Leopoldville in the "Consultations of
1957," the first local elections organized by the colonial authorities. He was imprisoned following the riots for independence in
Leopoldville in January 1959 but was released two months later.
The ABAKO won a number of seats in the elections of 1960.
However, it did not obtain a majority. Following a brief political
standoff, the ABAKO and MNC agreed to a compromise under which
Kasavubu, running against Bolikango, won the presidential vote
in parliament while Lumumba became prime minister at the head of
a broad-based coalition government. Under the Fundamental Law,
the post of president was intended to be largely ceremonial with
governing powers vested primarily in the prime minister. However,
Kasavubu managed to wield considerable power by firing prime
ministers and designating new leaders to replace them. Nevertheless, the prime ministers sometimes retained enough influence in

parliament to block Kasavubu's designated successor, leading to
political standoffs. One such standoff between Kasavubu and
Lumumba led Mobutu to "neutralize" parliament in September
1960 and appoint the College of Commissioners to govern the
country for four months. Another such crisis, between Kasavubu and Tshombe, contributed to the Mobutu coup. Following
his removal, Kasavubu retired to Bas-Zaire where he lived until
his death in 1969.

KASHAMURA, ANICET. A leader with Gizenga of the "radical" faction of the MNC who was minister of information in the Lumumba
government. Kashamura was dismissed along with Lumumba and
Gizenga by Kasavubu on September 5, 1960. In early 1961,
Kashamura took power in Kivu in the name of the Lumumbist
authorities in Stanleyville. He was a minister in the Gizenga
government in 1961, but was driven into exile when the ANC retook the region.

KASONGO. A city on the Lualaba River in southwestern Kivu that
was a center for the Arab trade in slaves and ivory in the nineteenth century. It was considered the capital of the Tippo Tib
empire in the 1870s.

KASONGO NIEMBO. The last of the great African chiefs who held
out in eastern Zaire against the Belgians until 1910.

KATANGA. The name of the mineral-rich province that today is
called Shaba Region. Katanga was also the name of the secessionist state led by Moise Tshombe from 1960 to 1963 that was
recognized by several foreign governments before being ended
by U.N. troops and pressure from the international community.
See SHABA REGION.

KATANGAN GENDARMES. The English translation for the Gendarmerie
Katangaise, the efficient provincial gendarmerie of Katanga Province, the members of which because of their opposition to Mobutu,
became involved in a number of rebellions in the 1960s and 1970s.
See GENDARMERIE KATANGAISE.

KAZEMBE. A group of people related to the Lunda, living in Haut-
Shaba sub-region near the border with Zambia. The Kazembe
had some control of the ivory trade, but their leader, the Mwata
Kazembe, was subordinate to the paramount chief of the Lunda.
Traders from the east eventually bypassed the Kazembe and be-
gan dealing directly with the Lunda and Luba.

KENGO WA DONDO (LUBITSCH). The tough prime minister who was
responsible for enforcing a series of fiscal and economic reforms
in the mid-1980s that brought a measure of economic stability to
Zaire while at the same time plunging the country into a severe
economic recession. Kengo was born May 22, 1935, at Libenge in

Equateur Region. He studied law and received his doctorate
from the Université Libre de Bruxelles in 1962. In April 1968,
he was named Prosecutor-General to the Kinshasa Court of Appeals and in August of the same year, he was promoted to
attorney-general of the Republic. He became president of the
Conseil Judiciaire in December 1977 and a member of the Central
Committee in September 1980. Kengo gained fame as the tough
lawyer who prosecuted Nguza, the 13 parliamentarians, and other
Zairian political dissidents. He was named First State Commissioner (Prime Minister) on November 5, 1982, charged with clean-
ing up corruption in government and enforcing austerity measures
that were part of an IMF package of economic reforms. The reforms were judged successful but also brought on a severe recession in Zaire (see ECONOMY). Kengo became part of the inner
circle of the clan that enjoyed the president's ear and ran the
country. He was not considered a political threat because although born of a Zairian mother, his father, a Pole, was a
foreigner and under the Zairian constitution both parents of a
president of the republic must be Zairian. However, following
a lengthy meeting of the Central Committee in late 1986 in which
some party members argued successfully against the continued
adherence to IMF-imposed austerity measures, Kengo fell out of
favor with the political leadership. The post of prime minister
was abolished in October 1986 and Kengo was named foreign minister. In January 1987, the post was re-established but a young
economist named Mabi Mulumba, who had impressed the Committee
with his arguments against continuing the austerity plan and
who had been named finance minister in the October re-shuffle,
was named prime minister. Kengo lost the Foreign Ministry portfolio and was appointed president of the Court of Auditors.

KENYA, RELATIONS WITH. As fellow members of the "moderate"
group of African nations, relations between Zaire and Kenya generally have been good, although there has been little direct contact between the leaders of the two countries. Kenya sent a
message of support to the Zairian government during the Shaba
Wars.

KHOISAN. Khoisan speakers (sometimes called "Bushmen") spread
into the Congo Basin at one point in history from eastern and
southern Africa, according to some theories. However, to date
there is no evidence they settled in what is now Zaire and no
linguistic traces have been found among the ethnic groups living
in the territory.

KIBINDA ILUNGA. Brother of a reigning Luba king, Kibinda Ilunga
around 1600 led a group of followers from the Luba lands in
southern Kasai and moved southwest to an area near what is
now the Zaire-Angola border to found what became the Lunda
empire.

KIKWIT. A city of 150,000 inhabitants in Bandundu Region, lying on the Kwilu River and on the major road linking Kinshasa to central Zaire. Kikwit prospered during colonial times and following independence, then became the capital of Kwilu Province. However, a series of uprisings beginning with the Mulele rebellion in the mid-1960s that included terrorist bombings in Kinshasa, reportedly caused Kikwit to lose favor in the central government. As a result, a great deal of funds for the region went to build up Bandundu, downriver to the northeast. Bandundu became the capital of Bandundu Region and Kikwit became an urban subregion, albeit an economically important one. Major economic activity in the area includes oil palm and vegetable oil processing, lumbering, some livestock raising, and vegetable farming.

KIMBA, EVARISTE. One of the founders of BALUBAKAT, Kimba was foreign minister in the Tshombe government. Following the dismissal of Tshombe on October 13, 1965, Kimba was asked by Kasavubu to form a government. However, his first attempt was thwarted by Tshombe's parliamentary supporters. His second attempt was thwarted by Mobutu's coup. Five months later, Kimba and three other associates were found guilty of trying to overthrow the Mobutu government in what was called the "Pentecost Plot" and sentenced to death. In June 1966, despite appeals from the international community, the four were publicly hanged.

KIMBANGU, SIMON. Founder of Kimbanguism, the first African Christian church to be recognized by the World Council of Churches. Originally a member of the British Baptist Church, Kimbangu decided to found his own church in the 1920s when he dreamed that he had been appointed by God to heal and preach. He originally worked with Protestant leaders, but split away to form a "sect" when some of them began to express disapproval of certain practices. The colonial authorities attempted to arrest Kimbangu during a religious meeting, but he escaped capture, further enhancing his reputation as a miracle worker. However, he turned himself in to authorities in September 1921. He was tried and sentenced to death on charges of crime against the security of the state, but the sentence was commuted to life imprisonment by Leopold II. Kimbangu, despite pleas from his followers to use his powers to escape, died in prison in 1951. See KIMBANGUISM.

KIMBANGUISM. Formally known as the Church of Christ on Earth by the Prophet Simon Kimbangu, Kimbanguism is considered a "syncretic" sect, that is, one that mixes Christianity with traditional beliefs and practices. The Church was said to have at least two million adherents in the early 1980s, or 5 percent of the Zairian population. It was the first independent African church to be admitted to the World Council of Churches, in August 1969. Kimbanguism was based on the Bible and although it mixed some traditional African practices, it followed the law of Moses and called for the destruction of fetishes and an end to sorcery, fetishism, and polygamy. The church was formed by Simon Kimbangu, an adherent of the British Baptist Church, following a vision in 1921. In the beginning, the church worked with the Protestant Church but came under opposition when some religious leaders objected to its practices, in particular, reports of miracles performed by the Prophet Kimbangu. With Kimbangu's arrest in 1921, the Church was pushed underground, which led to the rise of many apostles also calling themselves prophets and the increased use of animist practices among some of the sects. A church council was organized in 1956 following Kimbangu's death in prison, and it was granted legal recognition by the colonial government in 1959. Like many Zairian churches, Kimbanguism was restricted by the Zairian government in the early 1970s.

KINGS AND KINGDOMS. In traditional society, a king usually was the leader of many clans and chieftaincies, often called a "paramount chief." He usually came into office through one or a combination of several methods: inheritance, designation (usually at death) by the former chief, designation by elders, or by a series of tests. The king, once chosen, usually became wealthy, had many wives and children, and often held the power of life and death over his subjects. Subordinate chiefs paid tribute to the king of money, goods, wives, livestock, slaves, or other wealth, and the king usually ruled until he either died or was deposed by internal or external opponents. See CHIEFS.

KINLAO. Site of Zaire's petroleum refinery, built in 1968, near the mouth of the Zaire River and the town of Moanda.

KINSHASA. The capital of Zaire, formerly called Leopoldville, located on the Zaire River across from Brazzaville. Kinshasa was a small village when Stanley arrived in the 1880s and signed an agreement with the local chief that allowed him to claim the area for Belgium's King Leopold II. It has grown from a city of about 100,000 inhabitants at independence to a megalopolis with an estimated population of three to four million in the 1980s. The political and economic center of Zaire, Kinshasa is the home of one-third of all of Zairian industry, including textiles, milling, shipbuilding, steelmaking, timber, palm oil, chemical and food processing, motor vehicle assembly, tires, footwear and apparel manufacturing. Kinshasa is also an educational center containing the University of Zaire at Kinshasa (formerly Lovanium), the Institut National d'Etudes Politiques, and the Makanda Kabobi party school, among others. Kinshasa is the linchpin of Zairian transportation, being the rail and river port for shipment of goods into the interior and the export of minerals from Shaba (see NATIONAL WAY). The city is linked by paved road to Kikwit to the east, by road and rail to Matadi to the west, and by river to all the eastern regions except Kivu, Shaba, and Kasai Oriental. Zaire's major international airport and telecommunications center are located at Kinshasa and it is the headquarters of the armed forces.

Kinshasa is located in an area traditionally dominated by the Kongo people and Kikongo is one of the languages spoken. However, the use by the army and administration of Lingala predominates. Kinshasa has hosted numerous international meetings, including the OAU summit in 1967, the Franco-African summit in 1982, and the annual FIKIN international fair.

KINSHIP. Kinship can be an important factor in the well-being of an individual and sometimes leads to actions that would be characterized in the western world as nepotism. Within the framework of family solidarity, an individual who is well-off--whether because of a job, political success or financial good fortune--is expected to aid other members of his or her extended family, either by providing jobs, financial opportunities, or outright gifts. Such acts absolve the successful individual to a degree of an obligation to that particular family member who in turn may be besieged by other family members eager to share in his good fortune. To avoid paying the debt is to risk disfavor and even ostracism from the family at large. Likewise, an individual experiencing hardship can draw on well-to-do relatives for assistance during hard times. The custom sometimes leads to offices and plants peopled virtually exclusively by relatives of the boss. It also places considerable financial pressure on the successful individual and often is a major reason for diversion of funds and other corrupt practices.

KISANGANI. Kisangani, formerly Stanleyville, is the capital of Haut-Zaire Region. An urban sub-region with a population of 328,476 inhabitants (1982) and an area of 1,910 square kms, located at the confluence of the Zaire and Tshopo rivers, Kisangani lies at the furthest continuously navigable point upriver from Kinshasa. The city is separated from the navigable portion of the Upper Zaire River (Kindu to Ubundu) by 200 kms of cataracts. Originally a fishing village and minor Arab trading post, Kisangani became a major river port with the arrival of the European traders in the late 1800s. Used as a center for the campaign to drive the Arab traders from Zaire, Kisangani became a sizeable agricultural center during the colonial era, servicing the plantations and timber mills operating in the region. It also was a center for the gold and diamond trade with East Africa. The rebellions following independence and the Zairianization of the large plantations in the early 1970s ruined most private enterprise in the region. Some efforts were made to revive it in the late 1970s but these were hampered by widespread shortages of fuel, electricity and spare parts. Kisangani is the site of a river port, a railway depot linking the region to western Kivu and a network of unpaved roads linking it to the northeastern corner of Zaire, a regional radio station connected by satellite to Kinshasa, a campus of the University of Zaire, and a marketing

center for the surrounding area. By the mid-1980s, the Zairian
government was attempting to revive agriculture and industry in
the area with capital infusions into plantations, the Kilo-Moto
gold mining operation, and several projects to improve infrastructure.

KIVU. One of the most remote of Zaire's eight regions, Kivu is located in central-eastern Zaire bordering the lakes of the Great
Rift Valley. A region characterized for the most part by mountainous and forested terrain, Kivu is one of the most densely
populated regions of Zaire, with a population of 4,361,736 inhabitants (1982) and an area of 256,662 square kms. The region
is divided into the urban sub-region of Bukavu and the three
rural sub-regions of Nord-Kivu, Sud-Kivu, and Maniema. The
terrain is largely inaccessible but rich in tin, tungsten, iron ore,
and some gold. In addition, the high altitude and temperate climate is suitable for growing strawberries, tea, tobacco, sugarcane, and arabica coffee. Plantains, bananas, and vegetables
are also grown by small cultivators. The lakes, except for Lake
Kivu, provide fresh water fish, another staple, and there is
some herding. Tin mines were under operation until the collapse
of tin prices in the 1980s and high transportation costs made
them unprofitable.
    Kivu, which during the colonial era felt largely abandoned by
the authorities in Leopoldville, has always felt somewhat independent from the central government. At independence it sided
with the Gizenga forces in Stanleyville. However, the region's
leaders broke away from the Stanleyville leaders and formed a
separate, highly autonomous group, the Parti de la Révolution
Populaire (PRP), which to this day controls portions of remote
territory in the region near Lake Tanganyika.

KOLWEZI. An urban sub-region in southern Shaba with a population
of 393,702 (1982) that lies on a particularly rich lode of minerals,
including copper and cobalt, along the northwestern edge of the
Zambian Copper Belt between Lubumbashi and Dilolo. The city
of Kolwezi, which contains most of the population of the sub-
region, is primarily a mining town. Its economy is dominated by
GECAMINES, which operates one underground and several open-
pit mines around the town. Kolwezi came to be known to the outside world largely because of the Shaba Wars. In March
1977, FNLC guerrillas advanced to the outskirts of the city after
invading Shaba from Angola, but in the face of a government
counteroffensive, they withdrew without attacking the city. On
May 3, 1978, however, the guerrillas infiltrated the area from the
south and occupied Kolwezi on May 12. Amid reports that the
guerrillas were engaging in widespread looting and killings, the
Zairian government launched a military operation whereby 1,700
Belgian, 700 French, and several thousand Zairian paratroopers
landed in the area. After two weeks of fighting, they drove the
guerrillas out and rescued the population, including 2,000

Europeans. However, 1,000 Zairians and 200 foreigners were
killed during the occupation. Most of the industry in Kolwezi is
related to the mining operations, including a series of hydroelectric installations outside the city and a railroad depot on the
line that links Lubumbashi with the Benguela Railway. A milling
plant is located in the city and there is some herding and vegetable farming on the outskirts. See SHABA.

KONGO. A people living in western Zaire, southern Congo, and
northern Angola, not far from the Atlantic coast. The Kongo
people are one of the best known to Europe because of their
early contact with European explorers, traders, and missionaries.
The Kongo Kingdom was a flourishing empire in 1483 when Diogo
Cao first sailed up the mouth of the Zaire River and landed in
the area near Boma, eight years before Columbus reached America. The Kingdom decayed in the seventeenth century, some say
because of the heavy slave trade that upset the balance of power
among the various tribes and chieftaincies, but the language
and cultural dominance of the group continues to be felt. A matrilineal people with a highly organized judicial and political hierarchy, the Kongo spread as far east as the plains of Kinshasa
and their language, Kikongo, is one of Zaire's four national languages. The Kongo's access to educational opportunities and
their proximity to major cities like Kinshasa and Matadi contributed to their large representation in the colonial civil service
and the urban "évolués." The Kongo were among the earliest
and most influential forces advocating greater liberties for Congolese and, later, independence. They were considered by the
colonial authorities to be one of the more radical independence
groups and one of the most anti-Belgian. They formed the Association des Bakongo in 1950 to protect their culture from influences of the Ngala and Luba who began to arrive in Leopoldville
following World War II. It later became the Alliance des Bakongo
(ABAKO) political party, which was one of the first groups to
press for labor rights, political rights, and finally independence.
ABAKO produced Zaire's first president, Joseph Kasavubu. Following independence the Kongo continued to dominate the government and civil service, occupying more than one-third of the administrative positions. Their large presence in the capital contributed to their influence. Demographic studies reveal that one-
third to one-half of the population of Kinshasa trace their origins
to the Kongo, and one-fifth of that to Kongo of Angolan origin.
Kongo culture transcends political boundaries. All Kongo acknowledge a home village of origin called "Mbanza Kongo," which
represents to a degree a utopic or idyllic capital of Kongo culture.
See KONGO, KINGDOM OF.

KONGO, KINGDOM OF. The Kongo Kingdom was the first Zairian
group to make contact with Europeans and to maintain significant
economic and cultural exchanges with Europe before the end of
the nineteenth century. At its peak from the 1400s to the

1600s, the kingdom stretched from the Kwa and Lefini rivers
in the north and from the Atlantic coast in the west to the
Kwango River in the east. The kingdom primarily was a loose
confederation of sub-kings and hereditary chiefs who paid hom-
age in varying degrees to the central king in the mythical birth-
place of all Kongo, the "Mbanza Kongo dia Ntotila" ("Great City
of the King"). The Portuguese explorer Diogo Cao, encountered
the Kongo in 1483 when he arrived at the mouth of the Zaire
River. He befriended the reigning king, who converted to
Christianity and changed his name to Affonso I.

Affonso I began considerable exchanges with Portugal and
other European powers, sending ambassadors to Lisbon, the Holy
See, and the Netherlands. He asked for missionaries and sought
trade with Europe. Posts were set up to ship ivory and gold to
Europe, but slaving eventually became the dominant trade. In
1570, the kingdom was threatened by Jaga invaders from the
east, but Portuguese troops restored the reigning king, Alvares
I, to the throne. In the early seventeenth century, Dutch and
other European traders and explorers began arriving. The Kongo
allied with the Dutch but were defeated by the Portuguese at the
battle of Ambuila in 1665. The king was assassinated. Christian
practices faded. By the end of the seventeenth century, the
Portuguese presence in the region had been reduced to a few
coastal trading posts. In 1883, as European powers began making territorial claims on Africa, the Kongo kingdom was annexed
to Angola. The territory was later partitioned among Portugal,
France, and Belgium's King Leopold II. See JAGA.

KONGOLO. A chief of the legendary "Balopwe" nobility who migrated into the Congo Basin from the north around 1500 and
founded what became the Luba empire.

KUBA. A Bantu-speaking people driven east, according to some
ethnologists, by the Jaga invasion of the Kongo area in the sixteenth century. The Kuba established themselves between the
Sankuru and Lulua rivers in an area bounded by Luebo and
Mweka to the south and Ilebo to the east. The Kuba were
primarily cultivators and artisans noted for their tapestries and
carvings of angular, diagonal designs. They were ruled by a
king whose successor was chosen from among his nephews. The
kingdom reached its zenith in the eighteenth century and remained
stable until the nineteenth century, when revolts in the east created a near-civil war. The revolt was quelled harshly by the
colonial authorities in the early 1900s. Vansina said Kuba society was the "most complexly organized state with the possible
exception of the Lunda." The Kuba had a hierarchy of higher
and lower chiefs and a high degree of "differentiation" between
them. The Kuba "cluster" included the Lele, Njembe, and a number of groups ruled by the Bashongo.

KUNDA (sometimes KAONDE). A Bantu people living in Haut-Shaba sub-region of Shaba Region south of Kolwezi, identified by Vansina as part of the "Haut-Katanga" cluster.

KUSU. A Bantu-speaking group living along the Lomami River in a remote part of western Kivu Region between Kibombo and Lubao. Official Zairian ethnographers consider the Kusu to be part of the Mongo group, although they have never been reported to identify with that group. Some experts believe the Kusu and the Tetela sprang from the same group but grew apart as the Kusu accepted the cultural influence of the Arab traders while the Tetela rejected it. Tippo Tib used the term "Kusu" to describe the people he met during his trading expeditions in eastern and southern Zaire. The Kusu were unquestionably influenced by the Afro-Arabs. Many adopted their dress, converted to Islam, and adopted Swahili as their lingua franca. The Belgians called them the "Arabisés." After driving the Arab traders from the region at the turn of the century, the Belgian authorities drew a provincial border line between the Kusu and Tetela zones of influence placing the Kusu in Kivu Province and the Tetela in Kasai Province. See TETELA.

KWA RIVER. The name sometimes given to the lower Kasai River between the place where it joins the Lukemie River at Mushie and its confluence with the Zaire River 100 kms downriver.

KWANGO RIVER. A major western Zairian river that rises in central Angola and courses north 1,300 kms before flowing into the Kasai River near Bandundu. It is the domain primarily of the Chokwe and related peoples.

KWESE. A small ethnic group of the Pende cluster living between the Kwilu and Kasai rivers in the southern Kwango and Kasai sub-regions of Bandundu and Kasai Occidental regions.

KWILU SUB-REGION. A sub-region of Bandundu Region located in the central part of the region, Kwilu was a district within the Leopoldville Province during the late colonial and early independence periods. With Kikwit as its main urban center, the Kwilu is a relatively densely populated sub-region of 2,073,692 inhabitants (1982), occupying an area of 78,019 square kms. The people live primarily by fishing and some hunting and subsistence agriculture. There is some lumbering and oil palm cultivation. Other than some vegetable oil processing plants, however, there is little industry, and few attempts have been made to develop an economic infrastructure, according to some officials, because of the local population's resentment toward the central government. In January 1964, a rebellion began under Pierre Mulele, reportedly with Chinese backing, that included acts of sabotage and urban bombings in Leopoldville before it was ended in 1966. In 1978, another uprising was reported near Idiofa. Thousands reportedly were killed and 14 local chiefs were publicly executed,

although the local population, when later contacted by international human rights organizations, would not discuss the matter.

- L -

LABOR. Labor in Zaire historically has been one of the most abused
sectors of society and one of the most compelling proponents of
change. During the Congo Free State, private companies and
government operators were given virtually free rein to obtain
cheap labor. In the late 1800s, the labor tax law allowed operators to require local inhabitants to work or collect rubber and
ivory for the authorities without remuneration. Failure to meet
quotas led to beatings and executions. It also led in some areas
to the cutting off of hands by security agents to prove their
efficiency at punishing uncooperative villages. Outrage in the
European and American communities over these practices led to
reforms in 1906 limiting the labor tax to 40 hours per month, a
practice which was not always observed. In 1910, following the
Belgian parliament's annexation of the Congo, largely because of
the outcry over the abuses, the labor tax was abolished. However, the use of forced labor did not stop. Often workers were
taken or hired from the villages, housed, fed and clothed. These
expenses were then deducted from their earnings. Little was
left. However, in 1925, the Congo's largest company, UMHK,
established a new policy, aimed at building a permanent work
force, that improved working conditions. In 1926, a labor association for whites only, the Association de Fonctionnaires et
Agents de la Colonie (AFAC) was created. In 1946, the colonial
government for the first time authorized unions for Africans, but
they were strictly monitored through a system of councils. In
the 1950s, several trade unions arose in urban areas. In 1957,
they were given true bargaining powers and in the same year,
multiracial unions were legalized. The Social Pact of 1959 recognized full freedom for all unions and the unions subsequently became one of several groups to lead the drive for greater political
freedoms and, eventually, independence. Following independence,
three major labor unions developed: a Christian one, Union des
Travailleurs Congolais (UTC); the socialist-oriented Fédération
Générale du Travail du Kongo (FGTK); and the "liberal" Confédération des Syndicats Libres du Congo (CSLC). Membership ranged
from 50,000 for the CSLC to 10,000 for the UTC in 1966. In addition, a small Communist, Confédération Générale des Travailleurs
Congolais (CGTC) also was formed. In 1967, the unions were
merged into one, the Union Nationale des Travailleurs Congolais
(UNTC), which became the Union Nationale des Travailleurs Zairois
(UNTZa) in 1971. Although some labor leaders protested the loss
of their autonomy, the government argued that the numerous unions
were a divisive force in the labor movement and they should be de-
voting their energies instead to motivating among the workers greater productivity and support for government programs. The senior

leadership of the UNTZa was appointed to policy-making bodies of government like the Political Bureau, and with the growing ascendancy of the party, the lines between labor and government became blurred. Nevertheless, there were occasional labor upheavals, particularly in the transport and banking sectors and there were occasional strikes for better pay and working conditions that often were harshly repressed. In 1983, UNTZa boasted one million registered members, of which two-thirds were in the industrial sectors, 10 percent of which in mining. The government was listed as having one-half million employees, many of which were in the union, while traditional farming was the largest sector of the economy with four million farms averaging 1.5 hectares in size and employing 24 million workers.

LACERDA E ALMEIDA, JOSE. A Portuguese explorer who led the first scientific exploration of the Congo Basin in 1789. He went as far inland as Shaba, where he heard stories of rich deposits of copper and other minerals.

LAKE KIVU. One of Zaire's largest lakes, Lake Kivu is 100 kms long and 60 kms wide and has a large island in its center. Lying in the Great Rift Valley, Lake Kivu drains via tributaries of the Zaire River into the Atlantic Ocean, while the neighboring Mobutu and Edouard lakes drain via the Nile River system into the Mediterranean Sea. The cities of Goma and Gisenyi (Rwanda) lie on its northern shore and Bukavu is on the southern shore. The lake contains a high content of methane gas which prevents the development of virtually any fish or other animal life forms in its waters. Natural gas reserves below the lake are estimated at 60 billion cubic meters. However, the depth of the lake, 250 m, has prevented commercial exploitation.

LAKE MAI-NDOMBE. A relatively shallow lake lying in a marshy area near the center of the Congo Basin between Bandundu and Mbandaka, Lake Maï-Ndombe is 130 kms long and about 40 kms wide, although the boundaries can vary considerably with the level of rainfall. The lake lies in a remote, sparsely populated area of northern Bandundu Region, where the main mode of transportation is the canoe or small power boat.

LAKE MOBUTU SESE SEKO. Formerly Lake Albert, Lake Mobutu lies along the Great Rift Valley on Zaire's border with Uganda, north of the Ruwenzori Mountains, and forms part of the headwaters of the White Nile. Considered Zaire's second largest lake and the 30th largest natural lake in the world, it is 160 kms long and 50 kms wide, covering 5,300 square kms with a maximum depth of 50 m.

LAKE MUWERU (or MOERO). The largest lake in Shaba Region. Lying in northern Shaba along the border with Zambia, Lake Muweru, 130 kms long and 50 kms wide, is fed by the Luapula River and drained by the Luvua River which flows into the Lualaba.

LAKE TANGANYIKA. Considered the seventh largest natural lake in
the world, Lake Tanganyika is 670 kms long and 100 kms wide
at its widest point, covering 32,900 square kms with a maximum
depth of 1,435 m. The lake lies on the Great Rift Valley at an
altitude of 1,500 m. It is connected to Lake Kivu by the Ruzizi
River and is considered to drain via the Zaire River into the
Atlantic Ocean. Lake Tanganyika was first reached by Europeans
in 1858 when British explorers Richard Burton and John Speke
arrived from the East African coast. It enjoys a relatively
temperate climate, good rainfall, and fertile soils, which have contributed to making the area around it one of the most densely
populated in Zaire. Lake Tanganyika forms part of Zaire's
"Eastern Way" transportation route, by which minerals from Shaba
are exported by rail to Kalemie, across the lake by boat to Tanzania
and by rail once again to the port of Dar-es-Salaam. A small group
of antigovernment guerrillas, called the Parti de la Révolution
Populaire (PRP), have controlled some territory near the Lake
virtually since independence. The guerrillas attacked the port
of Moba in 1984 and 1985. The Zairian government accused them
of staging the attacks from refugee camps across the lake in
Tanzania and Burundi. However, it appeared the group was
based in Zaire.

LAKE TUMBA. A small lake, 40 kms long and 40 kms wide located
in a marshy area of the central Congo Basin near the Zaire River
about 80 kms downriver from Mbandaka.

LAKE UPEMBA. A marshy lake lying in a swampy area of northern
Shaba near Bukama. The lake lies near the Lualaba River that
is the headwaters of the Zaire River.

LAKES. Zaire's major lakes lie in the east along the Great Rift
Valley. However, several lakes are in the Congo Basin and
often are linked with a river system. The major Zairian lakes
are listed under their respective names above. See also WATER-
WAYS; TRANSPORTATION; and PORTS.

LAND. Zairian territory covers 2.345 million square kms, or nearly
one million square miles, making it the third largest nation in
Africa after Sudan and Algeria. (Some cartographers say it is
actually larger than Algeria.) Estimated arable land is 25 percent.
However, the U.N. Food and Agriculture Organization has estimated that only 3.3 percent of the land is devoted to crop cultivation. Other organizations estimate less than 2 percent of the
land is under cultivation. One-tenth of Zaire's land is said to
be devoted to pasture, primarily in the west, southeast, and
northeastern regions. Forest and woodlands cover more than 50
percent of the territory. The topsoil of the Congo Basin area
that covers more than half of Zaire is thin and only moderately
fertile. The soils covering territory bordering the basin are
considered better, while the soils of the highland and savanna

areas are considered excellent. Very little was known about soil composition in Zaire until the beginning of satellite surveys, particularly by LANDSAT, in the late 1970s.

LAND TENURE. According to the Zairian Constitution, land belongs to the state which grants or makes it available to individuals, private groups, or publicly owned organizations. The Constitution also guarantees individual and collective rights to property which has been acquired by customary or statutory (written) law. Most land, however, is held by the population under traditional laws of tenure that considerably pre-date colonialism and statutory law. Aspects of ownership may vary, but they generally are communal, that is, ownership by the village, the chiefdom, or a descent group. The one exception is in urban areas where statutory laws have been applied for longer lengths of time and disputed titles have been settled to some degree. Kaplan says land tenure was controlled most often by descent groups, called "lineages," which acted as agents in distributing the land to families. Individuals often have a right to the fruits of the land accorded them and may pass it on to their descendants, but they are not authorized to sell the land or, in other words, transfer it outside the descent group. The lack of outright ownership is said by some to have discouraged farmers from making the investments in land improvement needed to raise profits.

The early colonial authorities did not understand claims by clans and descent groups over land. The Congo Free State initially laid claim to all land not inhabited or under cultivation. A decree in 1906 liberalized the law to allow villages and communities to own three times the land under cultivation, in order to allow for crop rotation. Early CFS legislation allowed Africans to buy and sell land, but the practice never became common. Sales were made to Europeans, but it is likely the Africans saw the sale as more of a lease, that is payment for use of land which would eventually revert back to the traditional owners. In 1938, the colonial government ended sales of land by Africans to private parties, saying land rights could be transferred only to the state and only the state could lease or sell land to private individuals. In 1953, legislation was proposed allowing Africans in urban areas to purchase land, but only three provinces implemented the proposals. The potential did exist for Africans to obtain legal ownership under the "paysannat indigène" system first suggested by Leopold III in 1933, before he became king. The program was aimed at improving agricultural productivity, but it did not begin until the 1950s and was ended following independence. See AGRICULTURE.

LANGUAGES. The languages spoken in Zaire come from four major sources. The dominant root is Bantu, spoken by 80 percent of all Zairians. The Bantu are believed to have moved into the area from the north during the first millennium A.D. and from there expanded across the continent. Most indigenous languages

in Zaire are related to Bantu, which is classified as a branch of
the Benue-Congo group. Sometime during the second millennium
A.D., probably between 1500 and 1600, people speaking languages of the Adamawa-Eastern and Sudanic groups of languages
migrated into northern Zaire, either forcing out the current
residents or assimilating them. Finally in the 1800s, the arrival
of Belgian traders, missionaries and colonial officials brought
French. French is the official language of Zaire, used in all
formal academic, business, diplomatic, legal, political and many
social transactions. Zaire also has four "national" languages--
Kikongo, Lingala, Swahili, and Tshiluba--which in themselves
are regional "lingua francas," that is, languages used by peoples
speaking different mother tongues. Lingala, a trade language
used along the Zaire River, is descendant from the Ngala region
of northwestern Zaire and has long been the language of the
army as well as the primary "national" language of the administration and civil service. Its use by soldiers and civil servants,
who are frequently assigned to regions other than their home
areas, has led to its grudging recognition as at least the second
language of government. Kikongo is the lingua franca of the
residents of Bas-Zaire. Its use extends from the Atlantic Ocean
to Kinshasa and sometimes as far east as Kikwit. Although it is
spoken in a relatively small geographical area, the density of
the population of Kikongo speakers, particularly in Kinshasa,
has contributed to its importance. Tshiluba, the language of the
Luba ethnic group, is the lingua franca of most of the people of
the Kasais and northern Shaba. Swahili, actually a dialectal
version of the Arab/East African tongue currently in use in
Tanzania, is the lingua franca of eastern Zaire. It is liberally
peppered with French words and heard in Haut-Zaire, Kivu, and
parts of Shaba. A fifth language, Lomongo, of the Mongo people, is widely used as a lingua franca in the Equateur Region
of northwestern Zaire. Systematic studies by missionaries seeking to develop local versions of the Bible and hymnals led to the
orthographic representation of a number of languages in the
early 1900s and the adoption of standardized dialects, particularly
of the Kongo, Luba, Mongo, and Ngala tongues. The use of
pidgin forms, particularly of Lingala, has been widely adopted,
and all but those hailing from the most remote villages appear to
be able to communicate with each other, using a combination of
pidgin, the lingua franca from their home region, and sign language.

LEGAL SYSTEM see JUDICIAL SYSTEM

LEGISLATIVE COUNCIL. The official name of Zaire's legislative body
or national assembly, which in the elections of 1982 had 310 seats.
See LEGISLATIVE SYSTEM.

LEGISLATIVE SYSTEM. Since independence, the legislature has
formed one of several branches of the Zairian government.

However, it has steadily been weakened as the presidency and party have assumed greater powers. Under the Fundamental Law that was in effect from 1960-64, the Congo had a bicameral legislature, called the Parliament, similar to Belgium's, with a president elected head-of-state by the body. The prime minister and ministers were also chosen by parliament and could be removed by it. However, the Fundamental Law failed to clarify the degree of power accorded the president and prime minister and as a result, it caused a number of constitutional crises, two of which prompted military interventions in 1960 and 1965. Under the Constitution of August 1964, attempts were made to further define the nature of the balance-of-power. The president was given the power to appoint and dismiss the prime minister with the approval of parliament. Following the coup d'etat that brought Mobutu to power, the president was granted wide powers of decree and the presidency began assuming greater legislative powers. Parliament was reduced to a consultative body and then suspended. The Constitution of June 1967 accorded the president even greater powers, allowing him to govern by executive order, which carried the force of law. The bicameral parliament was replaced by a single chamber called the National Assembly. On July 19, 1972, as part of the authenticity program, the assembly was renamed the Legislative Council. In August 1974, following a meeting of the Political Bureau and Legislative Council, a new constitution was enacted that incorporated all changes and ordinances that followed the 1967 document. Under the new constitution, the Legislative Council became subordinate to the party, the president and his appointed ministers. The Legislative Council remained one of five organs of government. However, the party became the supreme institution of state and the president was automatically president of all five organs. Members of the Legislative Council had the right to initiate laws "concurrently" with the president. Following the Shaba invasions and under pressure from the international community for greater political freedom, a degree of political liberalization was carried out and the Legislative Council regained a measure of its lost power. The post of prime minister, called First Commissioner of State, was reinstated. The Legislative Council was allowed to summon ministers to question them on budgetary matters. And multiple candidates were allowed within the party structure for legislative seats. By the end of 1980, most of these measures had been reversed, except for the provision allowing multiple candidates in legislative elections. However, the influence of the Legislative Council was reduced by the creation on September 2, 1980, of the Central Committee of the MPR, the 120 members of which were chosen by the Political Bureau. The Central Committee eventually assumed most real legislative functions and became the body of "consultation and debate" of the party-state. The Legislative Council's role became one of primarily approving party initiatives. Elections for five-year legislative terms were held in September 1982 during which multiple candidacies, proposed at the local

level with Political Bureau approval, were allowed. More than
three-fourths of the incumbents were turned out and replaced
by a youthful body, the average age of which was 35 years.
See ELECTIONS; GOVERNMENT; and CENTRAL COMMITTEE.

LELE. A small, but independent ethnic group of the Kuba cluster
living in the lower Kasai Region. Organized into groups of relatively autonomous villages, often in conflict with each other, the
Lele are believed to have been moved by war to the less fertile
areas of the Kasai between the Lulua and Loango Rivers. They
were among the tribes that most strongly resisted the Belgian
colonial administration.

LEOPOLD II. The second king of Belgium who financed the first
explorations of the Congo and engineered the territory's exploitation after the partition of Africa in which he was a leading
participant. Leopold II, born in 1835, began seeking a source of
raw materials for his nation soon after acceding to the throne.
He turned his attention to Africa, currently the source of great
tales of mineral wealth, and formed the International African
Association, over which he presided from 1876 to 1880, to encourage exploration of Africa. Following Stanley's highly publicized expedition to "find" David Livingstone, Leopold II recruited
the explorer in 1878 and financed an expedition to explore the
Congo River. Following a second expedition, aimed at obtaining
treaties with as many local chiefs as possible and scouting for
trading stations up the river, Stanley returned in 1884 with 450
treaties which Leopold took to the Berlin Conference to bolster
his claim to be actively engaged in the exploration and "civilization" of central Africa. In 1885, following the Conference, the
13 European powers, and the United States acting as an observer,
recognized the International Association of the Congo as an independent state with Leopold II as its sovereign. In order to pay
for the administration of what in 1886 became the Congo Free
State, Leopold granted large trading concessions to private entrepreneurs and companies which became virtual monopolies. The
king also passed a forced labor tax that allowed companies to require Congolese to work or supply rubber and ivory without pay.
The brutality of some of the companies in collecting the "taxes"
led to a public outcry in Europe and America that forced the
Belgian parliament to annex the CFS in 1908 and take it over as
a colony. Leopold II, who died in 1909, is credited with pioneering the establishment of an administrative and transportation network in the territory. However, he is more frequently remembered as the wily monarch who, because of personal ambitions,
allowed a regime of terror, human rights abuses, and unabashed
exploitation to arise in what one day would become the Republic
of Zaire.

LEOPOLD III. Fourth king of Belgium from February 23, 1934, until
July 16, 1951, Leopold III assumed the throne upon the accidental

death of Albert I. During World War II, he declared Belgium
neutral and refused to join the parliament in a government-in-
exile. He surrendered to the Third Reich and spent most of
World War II under house arrest in Germany and Austria.
Following the war, Leopold III was accused by liberal and socialist members of the Belgian parliament of treason. He lived
in exile in Switzerland for a number of years until he agreed to
abdicate in favor of his son, Baudoin, in order to allow the royal
family to return to Belgium. Leopold III did not possess the
presence or consuming desire for power of his great uncle, Leopold II. In 1933, before becoming king, he first proposed a
system whereby Congolese could obtain legal ownership of land
by cultivating it regularly. The purpose of the proposal was
to counter a law in force at the time by which the state assumed
ownership of virtually all land not under cultivation. Leopold
III's proposal, called "paysannat indigène," eventually was instituted after World War II.

LEOPOLDVILLE. The capital of the Congo during the colonial period
and the first years of independence, the name was changed to
Kinshasa in 1966. See KINSHASA.

LIA. An ethnic sub-group of the Mongo, living between the
Tshuapa and Lomami Rivers in the southeastern corner of Equateur Region. The Lia are said to differ from most of the Mongo
linguistically and culturally in that they are headed by a hierarchy of sacred chiefs and sub-chiefs.

LIBOKO YA BANGALA. Literally translated, the "Arm of the Ngala,"
the Liboko ya Bangala was an association formed in the 1950s to
defend the traditions and interests of the Ngala ethnic group in
the large cities. It was outlawed by Mobutu following his coup
along with all other ethnically based political organizations.

LIKASI. A small city in southern Shaba lying northwest of Lubumbashi on the road to Kolwezi. Likasi is an urban sub-region of
235 square kms with a population of 191,606 (1982). It is the
site of a chemical plant that produces sulphuric acid primarily
for GECAMINES refineries. Milling, cement, and coal mining
operations are located nearby.

LIKULIA, GENERAL. Senior military officer and academic, General
Likulia entered the colonial army in 1958 and following independence studied criminal science in France. He received the French
equivalent of a Ph.D. at the Université d'Aix-Marseilles in 1970.
He has served as auditor-general and commanded several army
divisions, and also is a professor on the law faculty at UNAZA.

LINEAGE see DESCENT GROUPS

LISALA. A small city of 75,000 inhabitants lying in the Equateur

Region of northwestern Zaire between Mbandaka and Kisangani,
Lisala is also known as the city where Mobutu spent his child-
hood and received his early education. Lisala is a river port
that is a transportation and processing center for plantations in
the surrounding area where food crops, palm oil, rubber, coffee,
cocoa, and rice are grown.

LITERACY. Belgian government officials, citing an early emphasis
on primary education for Congolese, say the basic literacy rate
at independence was 60 percent. In 1987, UNICEF reported an
adult literacy rate of 79 percent for males and 45 percent for
females, figures which, if accurate, place Zaire as one of the
countries with the highest literacy rates in Africa. Other
demographers, however, believe the figure was exaggerated and
place functional literacy at 20 percent. Nevertheless, the relatively high literacy rate is believed to be the result of the early
colonial emphasis on primary (though not secondary) schooling
and the participation of many religious groups in education. The
teaching of primary school in Zaire's national languages was instituted in the 1970s as part of the authenticity movement.
Critics say the policy contributed to a decline in literacy, but
others say the decline was due more to deteriorating facilities
and increased absenteeism by teachers obliged because of pay-
roll delays to seek other means of income.

LITHO MOBOTI NZOYOMBO. Uncle of Mobutu and head of the family clan who, until his death on February 25, 1982, was one of
the wealthiest and most powerful men in Zaire. Litho was born
June 22, 1924, at Kawele in Equateur Region. He studied at the
Catholic mission of Molegbe and prior to independence worked as
an agronomist with INEAC. He was a state secretary in charge
of planning at the presidency in 1963-65. From 1965-70 he served
as minister of finance, then minister of agriculture. The owner
of a major group of plantations and food-processing companies,
Litho was also president of the Zairian subsidiaries of a number
of multinational companies. He was elected to the legislature in
1977 and was named to the Central Committee of the MPR in
1980.

LIVESTOCK. Livestock raising is carried out primarily in the savanna and highland areas of Shaba, Haut-Zaire, Kivu, and Bas-
Zaire Regions. The wet areas of the Congo Basin are not conducive to the activity because of the presence of the tsetse fly
and a wide variety of parasites. Cattle numbered one million head
at independence. The population dropped by 20 percent during
the early 1960s but had returned to pre-independence levels by
the mid-1970s. In 1985, the Zairian government said the country
produced 50,000 tons of butchered meat, whereas demand was
110,000 tons. One-fourth of the shortfall was met by imports
and the remainder by substitution, primarily of fish and game
meat. Most traditional herding is in Haut-Zaire and Kivu Regions.

Most commercial herding is in Shaba, Kasai Occidental, Bas-Zaire, Bandundu, and upper Equateur regions. An estimated three million head of sheep and goat are raised, primarily by small herd-owners. Hog production, primarily in Bandundu and Bas-Zaire, reached 800,000 in the 1980s. In addition, there was some commercial raising of chickens and ducks near urban centers, such as at the "model" farm at Nsele outside Kinshasa. Following Zairianization in 1973, foreign-owned ranches were placed under the control of the government agency, Office National pour le Développement de l'Elevage (ONDE) (National Office for the Development of Stock Breeding). Small ranches were leased to Zairians. One year later, however, under Retrocession, some ranches were returned to their previous owners.

LIVINGSTONE, DAVID. Scottish missionary and explorer who was one of the first Europeans to travel through southern and eastern Africa in his search for the source of the Nile River. Livingstone's disappearance for two years in the late 1860s was one of the major reasons for the first expedition by Stanley during which Stanley developed the theory that the Lualaba River, which Livingstone thought to be the headwaters of the Nile, was in fact the headwaters of the Congo River. Stanley met Livingstone at Ujiji on the eastern shore of Lake Tanganyika in 1871 on his way to the Congo River. Livingstone, born in 1813, was one of the first Europeans to reach what is now Zaire. He crossed Lakes Mweru and Bengweulu in 1867-68 and travelled on the Lualaba River, which he thought was the Nile, to reach Nyangwe in 1871. He died in 1873, two years after his meeting with Stanley, without ever leaving Africa.

LOBITO. A port city on Angola's Atlantic coast, 30 kms north of Benguela, which was a major export route for minerals from Shaba until the Benguela Railway was closed by the Angolan civil war in 1975.

LOI FONDAMENTALE (FUNDAMENTAL LAW). A document passed by the Belgian parliament on May 19, 1960, aimed at serving as a temporary constitution for Zaire during its first years of independence. The Fundamental Law, which drew heavily from the Belgian system of government, provided for a chief-of-state and a prime minister elected by the bicameral parliament. However, in its effort to provide adequate checks and balances, the Fundamental Law failed to define adequately the division of power between the executive and legislative branches of government and that, combined with rising ethnic tensions contributed to the political fractiousness following independence. The Fundamental Law was replaced by the first Congolese constitution on August 1, 1964. See CONSTITUTION.

LOMAMI RIVER. A tributary of the Zaire River, the Lomami rises in southern Shaba near Kamina and meanders north, almost parallel to the Lualaba River, for more than 1500 kms before joining the Zaire River some 100 kms downriver from Kisangani.

LOME CONVENTION. An agreement between the European Economic Community and nearly 80 developing nations of Africa, the Caribbean, and the Pacific (called the ACP) to foster greater economic cooperation by lowering tariffs and removing other market restrictions between developing nations and the EEC. It also included provision for development assistance from the European nations. The first "Lomé Convention" was signed in Lomé, Togo, in 1975 and came into force on April 1, 1976, replacing earlier agreements reached in Yaounde (Cameroon) and Arusha (Tanzania). Zaire was an original signatory. The agreement allowed many agricultural products from ACP countries to be exported duty-free to the EEC and an export stabilization program (STABEX) attempted to compensate countries hurt by a fall in commodity prices. A second convention, Lomé II, was implemented on January 1, 1981, and a third convention, Lomé III, came into force May 1, 1986. They expanded the programs to include virtually all imports from ACP countries.

LONDON CLUB. The unofficial name of the group of approximately 100 major commercial and private banks that negotiates requests for debt reschedulings by countries in arrears on their debt repayments. Zaire reportedly owes $400 million to London Club members, an amount considerably lower than the amount owed in the 1970s.

LOVANIUM UNIVERSITY. The original name of Zaire's first university, founded by Catholic missionaries on hills overlooking the outskirts of Kinshasa in the early 1950s. The university was nationalized in 1971 following student unrest and became the Université Nationale du Zaire (UNAZA), Kinshasa Campus. See UNIVERSITIES; UNIVERSITE NATIONALE DU ZAIRE.

LUALABA RIVER. The name often given to the headwaters of the Zaire River, the Lualaba rises in the Shaba plateau at an altitude of 1,500 m above sea level, and courses 1,600 kms north to Kisangani. Although some international cartographers differentiate between the Zaire and Lualaba rivers, official Zairian maps consider the Lualaba River to be the upper extension of the Zaire River. Rice and other food crops are cultivated along the banks of the river and two power plants near Kolwezi furnish 250 megawatts each to the region and its mining installations. The Lualaba is navigable from Bukama to Kasongo near the Shaba-Kivu border, and from Kindu in northern Kivu to Ubundu in Haut-Zaire. Railroads circumvent the unnavigable stretches of the river but most exports from Shaba go by rail to Ilebo and down the Kasai River to Kinshasa, or via Tanzania, Zambia, and Zimbabwe to Indian Ocean ports. See NATIONAL WAY; ZAIRE RIVER.

LUBA. A large ethnic cluster of tribes living in Kasai and Shaba
    regions, the Luba group stretches from the Kasai River around
    Kananga and Mbuji-Mayi, in the west, to the Lualaba and Lufira
    Rivers near Bukavu and Bulundi in the southeast. The Luba are
    primarily patrilineal and speak Tshiluba, one of Zaire's four na-
    tional languages. Vansina divides the Luba into three clusters:
    the Luba-Shaba (which includes the Kanioka, Lakundwe, and
    Lomotwa), the Luba-Kasai (which includes the Lulua, Luntu,
    Binji, Mputu, and North Kete), and Songye (which includes
    Bangu-Bangu and, according to some, the Hemba). Independent,
    proud, and highly ethnocentric, the Luba often resisted out-
    siders, such as the Arabs and Europeans. The colonial author-
    ities were said to have considered them to be a source of dissent
    and as a result to have encouraged the growth of ethnic groups
    opposed to them. During the colonial era, nevertheless, many
    Luba moved to urban and mission centers to take advantage of
    educational opportunities and many rose to positions of responsi-
    bility in business and civil service, particularly in Shaba.

    According to legend, the Luba began organizing under local
    chiefs in the fifteenth century but were invaded by a foreign,
    Bantu-speaking group from the north called the "Balopwe,"
    which, led by Kongolo, founded a Balopwe-dominated empire,
    with its capital at Mwibele. At its peak in the early 1600s, the
    group controlled considerable territory, including most of Shaba
    and southern Kasai. Kaplan says the empire was divided into
    provinces which were divided into chiefdoms, or groups of vil-
    lages. The king retained a great deal of power over appoint-
    ments and tribute. Occasionally, deposed chiefs would leave
    with their followers to form a new state. One such split led to
    the formation of the Lunda empire in the late 1500s. Shifts in
    population and rising trade led to a consolidation of the empire
    in the late 1700s and early 1800s. The Luba empire began to
    decline with the rise of the Chokwe in the late 1800s who raided
    many of their settlements. In the modern Zairian state the Luba,
    like most southern and eastern groups, have tended to be highly
    independent of the central government. They fought Tshombe
    and the Lunda during the Kasai secession and many fled to east-
    ern Kasai following massacres in Katanga in 1960. They also
    fought a bitter land war with the Lulua in 1959-60. Many Luba
    have been critical of the Mobutu government, but many others
    serve in government and high positions of responsibility.

LUBUMBASHI. Formerly Elisabethville, Lubumbashi, the capital of
    Shaba Region and Zaire's copper capital, is the country's second
    most important city. A company town dominated by GECAMINES
    and the mining industry, Lubumbashi is an administrative urban
    sub-region with a population of 800,000 in 1985, lying on the
    Shaba high plateau. Open-pit and underground mines operate
    around the city as well as refineries that produce semirefined,
    and pure copper, rolled and wire copper products, as well as
    by-products of copper ore. As the second largest industrial

center in Zaire with the second highest per capita income after Kinshasa, Lubumbashi is also a manufacturing center for cigarettes, textiles, shoes, metalwork, palm oil, and food processing industries. The city is linked to the Atlantic Ocean by the "National Way" through Zaire, and by the currently closed Benguela Railway through Angola. It also is linked to Indian Ocean ports in Tanzania, Mozambique, and South Africa by rail through Zambia and Zimbabwe. In many ways closer to southern Africa than to central Africa in geography, traditional trade routes, and temperament, Lubumbashi has often felt ignored by the government in Kinshasa which is sometimes perceived as a remote capital that benefits from the region's mineral wealth but provides few services in return. The city was the capital of the secessionist Katanga state in 1961-63.

LUEBO. A major town on the Lulua River in Kasai Occidental that is an important educational, printing and commercial center in the area.

LUFIRA RIVER. A 500-km tributary of the Lualaba River, the Lufira rises in the highlands between Lubumbashi and Likasi, near the Zambian border, and flows north joining the Lualaba River downriver of Bukama. Two hydroelectric complexes are located on the Lufira, near Likasi, that supply electricity to Lubumbashi, Likasi, and the Kolwezi areas.

LULUA. An ethnic group related to the Luba cluster living in Kasai Occidental between the Lulua and Kasai Rivers. The Lulua supplied Angolan slave and ivory traders in the nineteenth century and drove the Luba from western Kasai in the late part of the century. They were courted by the Belgian colonial authorities to counter the independent-minded Luba, who had been victimized by the Afro-Arab slave raiders and were considered more radical.

During the early colonial years, the Lulua were relatively complacent and, until after World War II, did not seek the educational and employment opportunities as actively as did other groups in the region. Politically, the Lulua began to organize themselves following World War II. They formed the Association Lulua Frères (Association of Lulua Brothers) in 1953 to defend their interests primarily in urban centers. Colonial authorities are said to have supported the Lulua prior to independence because they were considered more moderate than the autonomy-minded Luba. The Lulua convened a conference in 1959 during which they called for autonomy rather than independence. Some historians have accused the colonial authorities of aggravating the perennial tensions between the Lulua and Luba. These tensions, centered primarily over historic land disputes, flared into violence in October 1959, resulting in massacres, migrations of refugees, and the destruction of millions of dollars worth of property and crops. The famine that followed in 1960-61 obliged the United Nations to mount a million-dollar relief effort immediately following independence.

LULUA RIVER. A large, but mostly unnavigable river that originates near the Zambian border east of Dilolo and flows 900 kms north and then west, joining the Kasai River between Luebo and Ilebo.

LULUABOURG. The name of the capital of Kasai Province during the colonial era and early years of independence, renamed Kananga in 1966. See KANANGA.

LUMUMBA, PATRICE. Zaire's first prime minister and a principal advocate of pan-Africanism who was assassinated under mysterious circumstances less than one year following independence. Fluent in French, Lingala, and Swahili, Patrice Lumumba was a fiery orator who inspired strong feelings of nationalism in an Africa that still bore the psychological scars of the "colonial yoke." However, his policies and political flirtations with socialist nations caused fear among other groups with vested interests in Zaire, including western governments, commercial interests, and moderate African leaders.

Patrice Lumumba was born on July 2, 1925, in the village of Onalua in Sankuru district of Kasai Province. Of the Tetela ethnic group, he received his primary education from a local Protestant mission and attended secondary school in Leopoldville. He moved to Stanleyville where he became president of the local club of "évolués," provincial president of APIC, and a regular contributor to various magazines. In 1956, he was convicted, reportedly unjustly, of theft and spent one year in prison. He was freed in 1957 with his reputation considerably enhanced. Lumumba worked for a local brewery for two years, rising to the position of commercial director. In December 1958, he attended the first Pan-African Conference in Accra, in newly independent Ghana, where he met Kwame Nkrumah and became further acquainted with the concepts of pan-Africanism and "active neutralism."

Lumumba is said to have been the first Congolese leader to openly call for independence, at a political rally on December 28, 1958. He formed the Mouvement National Congolais (MNC) and attempted to make it a nationally based party by attracting a variety of regional and ethnic leaders. He appeared at first to be succeeding. However, fighting between the Luba and Lulua caused a split in the Kasai-wing of the party and dissatisfaction and personality conflicts caused other leaders to leave to form their own parties. On October 31, 1959, riots erupted in Stanleyville after a MNC meeting. Lumumba was arrested November 1 and accused of having sparked them. However, he was released in January 1960 in order to attend the Round Table Conference in Brussels. The MNC scored significant victories in the elections of May 1960, but did not win an absolute majority. Lumumba succeeded in forging a compromise government in which

Kasavubu of the ABAKO was elected president and he became prime minister and defense minister. However, the agreement lasted only two months, during which time the central government's authority seriously deteriorated.

In late August, Lumumba declared martial law and imprisoned a number of his rivals. He then issued a request for aid from Communist nations to help put down the secessionist groups. That statement caused Kasavubu to order his dismissal. However, Lumumba refused to accept his dismissal. Rather, he and his cabinet accused Kasavubu of treason and voted to dismiss him, precipitating a constitutional crisis. Mobutu announced in mid-September he was "neutralizing" the government for six months and a group of young intellectuals, called the College of Commissioners, was appointed to govern in the interim. When the United Nations voted to seat the Kasavubu delegation, Lumumba, with Gizenga and Kashamura, decided to move the MNC-base to Stanleyville. Gizenga and Kashamura arrived in Stanleyville, but Lumumba never did. He left Leopoldville on the night of November 26-27 and was travelling by road toward the region when he was captured in western Kivu by Congolese forces. He was imprisoned first at Camp Hardy in Thysville, but authorities expressed fear that he would spark an uprising among the soldiers at the camp. In what most historians believe was a calculated move aimed at his elimination, Lumumba was flown to Elisabethville where his arch-enemy Moise Tshombe was based. Furthermore, according to reports compiled by investigatory commissions, he was flown to the Katangan capital under guard by Luba soldiers, who considered him responsible for a massacre of Luba in Katanga by Congolese troops a few months earlier. According to the investigators, Lumumba and his two companions, ex-Senate Vice-President Joseph Okito and ex-Minister of Youth and Sports Maurice Mpolo, were severely beaten during the flight. Most believe he died shortly after his arrival in Elisabethville on January 17, 1961. The Katangan government announced February 13 that he had been killed by "angry tribesmen" following an "escape attempt." Mobutu, in a 1985 interview, said Lumumba was killed on January 17, 1961, in Elisabethville, that he was not killed by soldiers and that a Belgian journalist witnessed the execution. He denied responsibility for the murder saying it occurred in secessionist Katanga. In any case, Lumumba's death caused an international outcry and precipitated the Stanleyville rebellion. It also caused the Soviet Union and many eastern European states to withdraw recognition of the Leopoldville government, refuse to help finance the U.N. operation in the Congo, and begin covert programs supporting various rebellions in the country.

One-quarter century later, Lumumba is still a hero and martyr for many Africans. Although the MNC-Lumumba is a small, exiled opposition group led by his son, François Emery, many Africans still believe in Lumumba's dream of an Africa, off-limits to the East-West ideological confrontation, organized in the pursuit of its own interests and economic development.

LUNDA. A large ethnic group related historically to the Luba living in southern Shaba, northern Zambia, and western Angola.
In Zaire, Lunda-related people also live in an area between the
Lubilash and Kasai Rivers in southwestern Kasai and the southeastern tip of Bandundu Regions. The Lunda empire was formed
by a group led by Kibinda Ilunga, that split from the Luba in the
late 1500s. It flourished during the seventeenth and eighteenth
centuries and expanded south to straddle what has become the
border with Angola and Zambia. Unlike the Luba, the Lunda
sought to expand their empire by absorbing other peoples into
their system. They organized a political structure with related
hierarchies and by the end of the seventeenth century had created the position of paramount king, the Mwanta Yamv, meaning
"King of Vipers." During the eighteenth century the Lunda expanded further in search of copper, salt, slaves, and ivory.
The empire began to decline in the mid-nineteenth century and
was attacked by the Chokwe who at one point took the Lunda
capital. Following World War II, a strong Lunda political organization began to form. It came to be known as the CONAKAT,
headed by Moise Tshombe, and was formed in part to keep Luba
and Chokwe opponents from power. The elections in May 1960
gave the CONAKAT an absolute majority in the Katangan provincial assembly and led to the formation of a one-party state in
Katanga. The Lunda often opposed colonial rule and, during the
first years following independence, the central government.
Part of a group of people living far from Kinshasa that sometimes feel neglected by the national government, the Lunda have
also been a source of opposition to the Mobutu government.
Lunda members led the two Shaba invasions in 1977 and 1978
from bases in Angola. Lunda villages were reported to have suffered reprisals following the Shaba invasions. The Mwanta Yamv
was imprisoned as well as another prominent Lunda, then-Foreign
Minister Nguza Karl-I-Bond. However, both were later freed and
with the rapprochement between Zaire and Angola and greater
government attention to the political situation in Shaba Region,
tensions seemed to subside. See SHABA; LUBA.

LUNDULA, VICTOR. An uncle of Patrice Lumumba, Lundula was a
leader of the MNC who was appointed the Congo's first chief of
the armed forces following the mutiny of the Force Publique five
days after independence. Lundula was dismissed by Mobutu in
September 1960 and placed under house arrest. He broke out of
house arrest with Lumumba and managed to reach Stanleyville
where he was made commander of the armed forces of the Gizenga
government. He later transferred his loyalties back to the central government as part of reconciliation negotiations undertaken
by Adoula. He was an advisor to the Defense Department from
1962-64 and was elected senator from Sankuru district in 1965.
He occupied a number of defense-related posts following the Mobutu coup.

LUNGU. A relatively small ethnic group living near the Bemba and
Kazembe tribes near Lake Tanganyika, the Lungu were dominated
by Tippo Tib and the Afro-Arab traders in the late 1800s.

- M -

MABI MULUMBA. An economics professor who was appointed finance
minister in October 1986 and prime minister on January 22, 1987.
Mabi, the author of a book on banking and Zaire's debt problems,
is a technocrat who is said to have made a case for reducing
payments on Zaire's foreign debt, and made a major impression
on the Central Committee during a meeting in October 1986. Following that meeting, the government announced that IMF economic
stabilization programs were "strangling" the Zairian economy and
thereafter, repayment of Zaire's external debt would be limited
to 10 percent of export earnings and 20 percent of government
revenues. Mabi's appointment signaled the waning of the star
of former Prime Minister Kengo wa Dondo who was the architect
and enforcer of tough austerity measures in the mid-1980s during
which as much as 50 percent of government revenues was set
aside for debt repayment.

MAHDI. The name of the prophet who controlled Sudan in the 1800s.
The Mahdi's supporters controlled trade in northern Zaire until
1890, when they were driven out by European forces fighting to
end the slave trade.

MAIZE. An important staple that is grown throughout Zaire but is
less popular in most regions than manioc, or cassava. Maize
was introduced by Portuguese settlers, along with manioc, in
the 1500s in western Zaire and in central Zaire in 1600. It grows
particularly well in the higher, cooler, climates of Shaba where
it is a major staple.

MAKANDA KABOBI INSTITUTE. The academic center of the party
and repository of many government records, the Makanda Kabobi
Institute was founded in August 1975 to train party cadres and
encouraged study and development of party doctrine and "Mobutism."

MALEBO POOL. Formerly called Stanley Pool, Malebo Pool is a large
body of water 25 kms wide in parts that stretches from Kinshasa's
Mont Ngaliema nearly to Nsele, 80 kms upriver. It is caused by
the backup of water due to the cataracts that begin below Kinshasa.
Brazzaville, the capital of the People's Republic of the Congo,
lies across the pool.

MALULA, JOSEPH (CARDINAL). Archbishop of Zaire and head of
the Zairian Roman Catholic Church, Malula was a former president of Lovanium University, elevated to cardinal by Pope Paul VI

on March 28, 1969. He encouraged the Africanization of church
litany and hierarchy, but suffered reprisals from the government in the 1970s when he opposed some aspects of Zairianization,
in particular the dropping of Christian names and the use by the
government of religious songs with the words altered. He fled
the country after his residence was ransacked by soldiers in
1972 and later decried the corruption and moral decay in Zairian
society. A reconciliation was reached with Pope John Paul II's
visit to Zaire in 1980.

MAMVU. A major ethnic group speaking a language of central Sudanic origin that lives in Haut-Zaire between Isiro and the border
with Sudan and Uganda. Unlike other groups from northern
Zaire, like the Mangbetu and Zande who assimilated other peoples and created states with nobles and commoners, the Mamvu
remained relatively decentralized. Official Zairian ethnographers
classify some of the Mamvu as of the Bantu group.

MANGBETU. A group of Zairians speaking a language of central
Sudanic origin, the Mangbetu migrated into the forest of the
northern and northeastern Congo Basin in the 1600s or 1700s and
currently live between the Ituri and Uelé Rivers near Poko, Isiro,
and Rungu. They assimilated other ethnic groups and established relatively hierarchical societies with aristocracies and com-
moner groups.

MANIEMA SUB-REGION. A relatively sparsely populated sub-region
of western Kivu with a population of 765,017 living in an area of
132,250 square kms, Maniema is rich in iron, gold, and tin, and
its soil is fertile allowing the cultivation of many cash crops.
However, the remoteness of the region and an aging transportation infrastructure has hindered development of the area.

MANIOC. A fast-growing tuburous root that flourishes in relatively
poor soil, manioc was brought to Africa from the Americas by the
Portuguese in the 1500s and introduced in western Zaire. Its
cultivation spread slowly eastward and by the 1800s it had become a major staple crop throughout most of Zaire. After being
harvested, the root is usually soaked for several days, then
dried and pulverized. The resulting flour is then used to make
a paste that is to be eaten with various sauces and dishes. The
high starch and low protein content of manioc can lead to protein
deficiencies, in particular kwashiorkor. In addition, some varieties contain such poisons as strychnine, which over time can
lead to goiter and other diseases if poorly prepared. Researchers
in Zaire and Congo are seeking to develop strains of manioc with
higher protein content and less poison.

MANUFACTURING. Manufacturing is a relatively young economic
sector in Zaire. In the early years of colonialism, few attempts
were made to establish manufacturing industries because of the

focus on extraction of mineral and agricultural products. At the turn of the century, some factories were constructed to produce cement, soap, textiles, and beer. Growth was depressed first by World War I and then by the Great Depression. The greatest expansion began following World War II using capital-intensive methods and expatriate management and technicians. Plants to process flour, sugar, vegetable oil, margarine, fish, leather goods, tobacco, chemicals, paint, palm oil, and timber products were constructed in a number of urban areas. A foundry and shipbuilding enterprise was also constructed in Kinshasa. In the early 1970s, an automobile assembly plant, tire manufacturing plant, and steel works were brought on line. A consortium was formed in the 1970s to construct an aluminum complex, but plans were put on hold "indefinitely" in the 1980s because of continuing depressed prices on the world market.

By independence, Zaire was meeting nearly one-half of its domestic needs for manufactured goods and manufacturing accounted for nearly 10 percent of GDP. Production declined following independence because of political unrest and currency problems, regained pre-independence levels by the late 1960s and continued to expand in the 1970s although at a slower pace. An investment code passed in 1969 provided equal benefits for local and foreign investors. However, the Zairianization in 1973 of all foreign-owned, private enterprises with gross revenues of more than one million zaires caused production to decline and caused the departure of foreign investors. Retrocession, announced one year later, returned partial ownership to private owners, but many foreign investors chose not to return. The fall in prices for copper and debt repayment problems subsequently sent the economy into a recession that caused domestic demand to fall. In addition, shortages of foreign exchange caused production problems. By the early 1980s many plants, with the exception of those in the food processing area, were operating at 10 to 25 percent of capacity, due to shortages of raw materials, spare parts, and fuel. By the mid-1980s, the manufacturing slump appeared to have bottomed out. Although still well below capacity, production was beginning to increase, primarily because of the stabilization of the currency and an infusion of foreign exchange through the World Bank, IMF, and other international lenders.

MARXISM. Although some Zairians, primarily young intellectuals, have espoused Marxist beliefs, most Zairians appear to feel uncomfortable with Marxism's subordination of family and religion to the state. Most left-leaning opposition groups have tended to choose a "nonaligned" or socialistic approach to solving Zaire's problems. However, a few groups have publicly espoused Marxism/Leninism or Maoism, most notably the Stanleyville government in 1964 and the Mulele rebels based in Brazzaville. A few others, like the MNC-Lumumba exiled opposition party, reportedly maintain ties with the Soviet government and its allies.

"MATABISH." A Lingala expression meaning "tip" or in its more usurious forms, "bribe." Similar to "baksheesh" in the Arab world and "dash" in Anglophone Africa, "matabish" is the way many unemployed and underemployed Zairians make ends meet. It can represent the remuneration for small favors, odd jobs, and errands. For the giver, it also can provide a speedier passage through the official bureaucracy.

MATADI. Zaire's major ocean port, lying 200 kms up the Zaire River from the Atlantic Ocean, Matadi is the capital of Bas-Zaire Region and an urban sub-region in Bas-Zaire with a population of 146,930 (1982) and covering an area of 110 square kms. Lying just below the cataracts that render the Zaire River unnavigable to Kinshasa, Matadi is the major shipment point for goods travelling by rail to Kinshasa. As such, it is the linchpin of Zaire's internal transportation network, that includes 14,000 kms of riverways and 5,000 kms of railways. Aside from the port installations, Matadi is the site of ship repairing facilities, a major flour mill, and the only bridge over the Zaire River. Also nearby are a cement factory, sugar processing plant, and the Inga hydroelectric complex. Matadi is the political and economic capital of Bas-Zaire, which after Kinshasa and Shaba, is Zaire's most economically active region. See NATIONAL WAY; TRANSPORTATION; and BAS-ZAIRE.

MAYOMBE FOREST. A forest region located in Bas-Zaire region containing significant reserves of timber and minerals, and soils suitable for agriculture.

MBALA. One of several major groups of the Bantu family living in the western part of southern Zaire between the Kwango and Kasai Rivers that speaks a language related to the Kongo of Bas-Zaire. The Mbala lived primarily along the Kwilu River around Kikwit. Although critical of the Mobutu government, most of the Mbala opposed the Mulele-led Kwilu rebellion of the mid-1960s because of a perception that it was led primarily by the rival Mbun and Pende ethnic groups.

MBANDAKA. The capital of Equateur Region and major city of northwestern Zaire, Mbandaka (formerly Coquilhatville) is an urban sub-region with a population of 153,440 (1982) covering an area of 460 square kms in the southwestern corner of the Region. Lying near the confluence of the Zaire, Ubangi, and Tshuapa rivers, Mbandaka is a major port for the northern Zaire river system. The low-lying land in the area makes farming and herding difficult, although some agricultural activity, particularly upriver has been successful. Petroleum deposits were discovered in the area in the early 1970s. Exploration was carried out by Exxon for a number of years, but it was abandoned in the early 1980s.

MBANZA. Sometimes called "Mbanja" by ethnographers, the Mbanza form one of the larger groups that speak Banda, an Adamawa-Eastern language. They live in Equateur Region, primarily between the Zaire and Ubangi Rivers.

MBANZA KONGO DIA NTOTILA (GREAT CITY OF THE KING). The mythical capital of the Kingdom of the Kongo from which all Kongo people are descended. The capital was located in northwestern Angola around the area that became Sao Salvador in the 1530s. It remains a place for which Kongo people often express nostalgia and longing.

MBANZA-NGUNGU. Formerly Thysville, Mbanza-Ngungu is the capital of the Cataractes sub-region of Bas-Zaire and with 352,273 inhabitants, one of the most densely populated in the region. The city of Mbanza-Ngungu lies on the road and railway linking Matadi to Kinshasa. A farming and herding center, it is a major supplier of food to the Kinshasa area. The city is perhaps most frequently remembered as the site of the army mutiny against the Belgian officers five days after independence. The violence led to the rapid promotion of Congolese into the officers corps and the appointment of Mobutu as Army Chief-of-Staff.

MBOMU. The name given to commoners in Zande society, as opposed to the aristocracy, which were called Vungara. The Mbomu were primarily hunters from Sudan who migrated into northern Zaire in the eighteenth and nineteenth centuries and intermixed with the Bantu inhabitants.

MBUJI-MAYI. The capital of Kasai Oriental Region, Mbuji-Mayi is the commercial center for Zaire's diamond trade. Formerly known as Bakwanga and the capital of the secessionist state of South Kasai, Mbuji-Mayi has been one of Zaire's fastest growing cities since the mid-1970s when a great deal of the banking, marketing, and commercial activities related to the diamond industry were moved there from Kananga. The city also attracted considerable immigration of Luba groups fleeing ethnic tensions in western Kasai and Shaba. An urban sub-region covering an area of 64 square kms, Mbuji-Mayi's population grew from 39,038 in 1959, to 256,154 in 1970, and to 334,875 in 1982.

MBUN. A Bantu people living in the lower Kasai area along the Kwilu River near Idiofa, the Mbun helped stop the Chokwe expansion in 1885. They were among the most ardent supporters of Pierre Mulele, who was from the region, and, with the Pende, helped launch the Kwilu rebellion and wave of terrorist attacks in Leopoldville in the mid-1960s.

MERCENARIES. A term first employed by Léon Roget when sent to organize the Force Publique in 1886, the word "mercenary" has come to represent the foreign professional soldier who, for money,

is willing to participate in invasions and coups against or on behalf of established governments. Moise Tshombe is generally
credited, rightly or wrongly, with being the first African leader
to employ mercenaries, most of them European, to bolster the
forces of his secessionist Katanga state. Upon becoming prime
minister in 1964, Tshombe hired mercenaries to help quash the
eastern rebellions. Mobutu also reportedly hired a small group
of mercenaries to help crush an army mutiny in the east in 1966-
67 that reportedly was aimed at restoring Tshombe to power.
With the return of political stability, the use of mercenaries has
faded in Zaire, although it continues in other parts of Africa.

MERCHANT MARINE. Zaire has a small merchant marine operated by
the state-owned Compagnie Maritime du Zaire (CMZ). The CMZ
operates a number of routes linking Matadi primarily to ports
in West Africa and Europe. However, a lack of funds and deteriorating equipment by the mid-1980s had reduced operations
considerably.

METALLURGIE HOBOKEN-OVERPELT (MHO). A Belgian refining
corporation that, since colonial times, has been a major customer
for raw and semirefined minerals marketed by GECAMINES, in
particular copper, cobalt, and zinc.

MIDDLE CLASS. Zaire, like many developing nations, has a small
middle class that retains nevertheless some influence in the affairs of the nation. Following World War II, Congolese in clerical
and low-level administrative positions, part of the "évolué" group,
began pressing for better wages and working conditions. They
founded a number of study groups and labor organizations. Two
of the most prominent were the Association de Personnel Indigène
de la Colonie (APIC) that grouped civil service workers, and the
Association des Classes Moyennes Africaines (ACMAF) that was
composed primarily of small merchants and farmers and sent representatives to the consultative councils of the colonial government.
Following independence, the middle class grew rapidly as Zairians
took over senior administrative and professional positions vacated
by expatriates. Except for a period in the early 1970s, however,
a deteriorating economy and high inflation consistently eroded
the purchasing power of the middle class. In the 1980s, as a
result, Zaire was a country dominated economically by a wealthy,
political elite. The middle class of salaried workers, professionals,
and small businessmen was living close to the subsistence level.
For example, teachers and professors could not afford telephones
or cars unless they were furnished by the government, and many
were obliged to engage in secondary activities in order to make
ends meet.

MILITANTISM. A term used in many countries to denote active membership in the party. From the early 1970s, however, Mobutu used
the term frequently in his speeches to address the Zairian people.

The major reason was to emphasize the membership of all Zairians in the MPR and the perceived continuing struggle of the Zairian "revolution" to end tribalism, regionalism, and factionalism, and to erect in their stead a new Zairian state, independent, non-alighed, self-sufficient, and authentically Zairian.

MINING. According to Banque du Zaire figures, the mining sector contributes an average of one-third of Zaire's GDP, more than three-fourths of its export revenues and one-half of government revenues. Since the early 1900s, mining has been a source of a great deal of Zaire's wealth. According to historians, Africans knew of copper ore deposits in Shaba long before the arrival of the European explorers in Shaba in the 1890s and in fact the reports reaching the coast of great mineral wealth in the interior are credited with encouraging some of the first explorations. The deposits found in Shaba initially were judged to be too small for commercial exploitation, until 1900, when Leopold II established the Comité Special du Katanga to explore and develop the region. Ore discoveries in 1901 led to the construction of a railway and in 1908 to the formation of Union Minière du Haut-Katanga (UMHK) that later would become GECAMINES. The first smelting plant began operation in 1911, producing 1,000 tons of copper. Production reached 100,000 tons in 1928 and 460,000 tons in 1985, or 7 percent of total world production. Diamond and gold mining began in earnest in the 1920s.

The large mining companies were nationalized beginning with UMHK in 1966. However, private companies were contracted to remain in order to operate the companies in return for a portion of the revenues. In the late 1970s, the Zairian government entered into a number of joint mining ventures with private foreign companies and also allowed private Zairian traders to participate in the commercialization of gold and diamonds. Government participation in the mining sector remains large and production is dominated by a few companies. GECAMINES, the country's largest company, dominates the mining of copper, cobalt, and most minerals in Shaba Region, and the Société Minière de Bakwanga (MIBA), the country's second largest company, dominates the diamond mining industry. In addition to its major mineral products of copper, cobalt, diamonds, uranium, tin, gold, and petroleum, Zaire also produces zinc, manganese, silver, cadmium tungsten, germanium, columbium, tantalum, lithium, monazite, and iron ore. Some economists have criticized the Zairian government for allowing the dependancy on the mining sector to continue and for not working harder to stimulate development in other sectors such as agriculture and transportation. Evacuation of the minerals always has been a problem. The National Way (Voie Nationale) is a tortuous route via rail and river to the port of Matadi, but it lies completely within Zairian territory. The most economic route, the Benguela Railway that links Shaba to the Angolan port of Lobito, has been closed since 1975 by the Angolan civil war. Other routes, to the Tanzanian port of Dar es Salaam, the Mozambican

LEGEND
— International boundary
✳ Capital
• Cities
ⱶⱶⱶⱶⱶ Railroads
Rivers
Tarred roads
Inga-Shaba Power Line
▲ Mines
△ Hydroelectric plants
0   200
Scale, km

Mine listing
1 Adumbi, Yindi-Au, Ag, Cu
2 Moto-Au, Ag, Cu
3 Adidi-Au, Ag, Cu
4 Lueshe-Cb
5 Kalima area mines-Sn, Cb, Ta, W, monazite
6 Mobale-Au, Ag
7 Tshikapa-Diamond
8 Mbuji-Mayi-Diamond
9 Lukuga-Coal
10 Manono-Sn, Cb, Ta
11 Luena-Coal
12 Kisenge-Mn
13 Gecamines Western Group-Cu, Co, Ag
14 Gecamines Central Group-Cu, Co, Ag
15 Kipushi-Cu, Zn, Cd, Ag, Au
16 Musoshi, Kinsenda-Cu

port of Beira, and the South African port of Durban, have been disrupted by port congestion, railway inefficiencies, and political issues. For more details, see specific listings for such major mineral products as COPPER, COBALT, GOLD, DIAMONDS, and URANIUM, and listings for specific companies, for example, GECAMINES, MIBA, and SODIMIZA.

MINISTRIES. In early Zairian governments, the executive branch was divided into ministries, but these were renamed Departments, headed by State Commissioners, on January 5, 1973, as part of a gradual process of introducing an authentic Zairian form of government. See DEPARTMENTS.

MISSIONARIES. Missionaries and missions have played a prominent role in the education of many Zairian leaders and in drawing world attention to human abuses in Zaire, first with the campaign against slavery, later with the campaign against labor abuses in the Congo Free State and the Belgian Congo, and more recently with their reports of abuses of power by the Zairian government. Missionaries have been both praised for introducing Christianity, education, and health facilities to Zaire and castigated for helping colonialists de-Africanize and deculturalize the Zairian individual. Nevertheless, whether good or bad, there is no doubt that the missionaries exerted a significant influence on Zairians and in Zairian history.

Missionaries first arrived in the Kongo area of what is now Bas-Zaire in the 1480s, brought by the Portuguese expeditions. Roman Catholicism flourished for a time in the Kongo Kingdom, but did not spread far, and began a 200-year decline in the 1600s. Organized Roman Catholic and Protestant missionary activity returned in the 1870s and by World War II, the missions had grown to become major providers of education and health services in the colony, sometimes subsidized by the colonial administration. Some of the earliest efforts to standardize Zairian languages and adapt them to written form were made by missionaries seeking to translate the Bible, hymnals, and liturgy into African languages.

At independence, 65 percent of Zairians reportedly identified themselves as Christians and the country's official literacy rate was 60 percent, one of the highest in Africa. The first Congolese priests and pastors were ordained in the 1910s, but in the 1960s considerable efforts were made to increase Zairian leadership and influence in the church, as well as to Africanize litany and ceremony. The first secretary-general of the Eglise du Christ au Congo, which grouped most Protestant denominations in the country, was elected shortly after independence and the first Roman Catholic cardinal was installed on March 28, 1969. The rise of nationalism, authenticity, and party dominance in the early 1970s, however, raised tensions between the Church and State. Zairians were ordered to abandon their Christian names and replace them with "authentic," Zairian ones. The three universities operated by Catholic and Protestant groups were nationalized in 1971. Religious observances were removed from government ceremony and an attempt was made to ban religious teachings in the schools. An exodus began of expatriate missionaries.

By the mid-1980s, however, relations had improved. Missions were still actively engaged in building and running schools, hospitals, printing presses, and some agricultural projects, and had become major distributors of foreign assistance such as food and disaster relief supplies. Furthermore, the deterioration of many government facilities in the social services sector had increased reliance on church-supported institutions. By the 1980s, however, many schools, hospitals, and entire mission stations were being run entirely by Zairian church personnel and the era of the "great white father" missionary who had symbolized the evangelical, colonial, and post-independence eras appeared to have ended.

MITUMBA MOUNTAINS. A mountain range in a remote part of western

Kivu Region that is largely inaccessible except by foot. The
Parti de la Révolution Populaire (PRP) dissident group is said to
control a significant amount of territory in the mountain area
since the early 1960s.

MOBA. A small town of about 50,000 inhabitants on Lake Tanganyika
in northeastern Shaba Region. Moba is the site of an army garrison that was attacked in October 1984 by guerrillas of the Parti
de la Révolution Populaire (PRP). The attack caused an estimated 50 deaths. The Zairian army recaptured the town two days
later and most of the guerrillas disappeared into the surrounding
countryside. The Zairian government accused dissidents living
in refugee camps across the Lake in Tanzania and Burundi of
responsibility. Tanzania acknowledged that a camp of Zairians
existed in its territory but denied they were responsible for the
attack. In June 1985, the PRP launched a second attack, this
one less successful. However, it brought a threat from Mobutu
to use "hot pursuit" raids into neighboring countries if the attacks continued.

MOBUTISM. The official ideology of the MPR party and Zairian state.
Official party documents describe Mobutism as the "thought and
vision of Mobutu." Mobutism encompasses all the policies and
ideological thoughts of Mobutu, whether they be, for example,
the Zairianization of private companies in 1973 or the retrocession
of 1974, whether they be the centralization of political power in
the 1970s, or the decentralization of some aspects of the political leadership in the 1980s. Despite some contradictions, Mobutu
and Mobutism will likely be remembered for several notable trends:
the political unification of the country in the late 1960s; the rise
of authenticity and Zairian nationalism in the early 1970s; the
failure of the economic policies in the late 1970s; the drastic re-
visions of the 1980s aimed at correcting the economic decline; and
the general amnesty of political dissidents in 1983. No student
of Zairian affairs, whether admirer or critic, can deny that Mobutu has dominated Zairian politics during its first quarter-
century; consequently, Mobutism will be an important topic of
study for years to come. See MOBUTU PLAN and MOBUTU SESE
SEKO.

MOBUTU, BOBI LADAWA. Second wife of Mobutu, married since
1980 following the death of his first wife. From Equateur Region,
Mama Bobi, as she is known, has involved herself in work with
women, handicapped persons, and other social services.

MOBUTU, GBIATIBWA GOGBE YETENE. First and much loved wife
of Mobutu. Mama Mobutu, from Equateur Region, married Mobutu
on July 26, 1955. They had ten children before her death due
to poor health on October 22, 1977.

MOBUTU PLAN. A plan announced by Mobutu in November 1977

aimed at revitalizing the Zairian economy. Inspired in part by
the Marshall Plan to reconstruct Europe following World War II,
the Mobutu Plan came after the first Shaba War and amid focused
attention on Zaire's worsening inflation and indebtedness. It
called for new investments to foster agricultural development, improvements in transportation and communications infrastructure,
and some decentralization of economic policymaking. The plan
was to cover the period 1978-82, but became a rhetorical peg on
which to hang subsequent economic proposals. The inability of
the government to revitalize the economy during that period
caused the term to fall into disuse in the early 1980s. See DEBT,
FOREIGN and ECONOMY.

MOBUTU SESE SEKO, PRESIDENT (JOSEPH-DESIRE). One of Africa's
longest ruling heads-of-state, Mobutu was close to power in the
early years following independence and has dominated Zairian political life since the coup d'etat that brought him to power on November 24, 1965. His rule has been characterized by a high
degree of centralization-of-powers that some would call authoritarianism: rewards for those who support him, punishment for
those who oppose him, and forgiveness for dissidents who return
to the fold. He is credited with forging a nation from a territory characterized at independence by administrative collapse,
secessionism, and ethnic and regional rivalry. He has been criticized for allowing a political elite to plunder the public wealth,
centralizing power in the hands of a few cronies, and of ill preparing his political succession. Nevertheless, he has dominated
Zairian political life during Zaire's first 25 years and his influence
will be remembered.

Born October 14, 1930, at Lisala in Equateur Region, Mobutu's
maternal family, of the Ngbandi ethnic group, was originally from
Gbadolite, a town on the Ubangi River across from the Central
African Republic. Mobutu's father reportedly died when he was
eight years old. Young Mobutu attended primary and secondary
school at Mbandaka and entered the Force Publique on February
14, 1950. He began writing articles under the pseudonym of "de
Banzy" for L'Avenir and Actualités Africaines, two periodicals
published in Leopoldville. He left the military on December 31,
1956, and worked as a journalist for L'Avenir Colonial Belge and
Actualités Africaines until he went to Brussels to take courses
at the Institut Supérieur d'Etudes Sociales and work at the Maison de la Presse. Mobutu met Lumumba, joined the MNC in 1958,
and attended the Round Table conference in January 1960. At
independence, he was named a senior aide with the title of "Secrétaire d'Etat" to then-Prime Minister Lumumba. Following the
mutiny of the Force Publique in July 1960, Mobutu was named
army chief-of-staff with the grade of colonel on July 8, 1960,
and undertook a tour of army garrisons around the country in
an effort to pacify the troops. On September 14, 1960, during
a constitutional crisis caused by a political standoff between Kasavubu and Lumumba, he said he was "neutralizing" political

leaders and formed the College of Commissioners, composed of young intellectuals, to govern the country for six months. The College returned power to the constitutional government in February 1961. On November 24, 1965, during a similar crisis between Kasavubu and Tshombe and in the face of a new rebellion in eastern Zaire, Mobutu took power in a coup d'etat. Officially he was "called by the military high command" to assume the leadership of the country. He said he would govern for five years under emergency measures, then hold elections. Over the next few months, the political system was gradually dismantled, parliament was suspended, and Mobutu gained the power to rule by decree.

The Mouvement Populaire de la Révolution party was formed in 1966 and the concept of a Zairian revolution was developed. The MPR became the only legal party, then the supreme organ of state; with the promulgation of Zaire's third constitution in 1974, Zaire became a party-state. Meanwhile, power increasingly was being centralized in the president, who presided over all organs of government, including the legislative and judicial branches, and had the power to appoint and dismiss virtually all leaders of party and government. He ran unopposed in presidential elections in 1970, 1977, and 1984 and each time was re-elected by more than 99 percent of the vote. He was made field marshal on December 11, 1982. At the inauguration of his third term in December 1984, Mobutu said his third seven-year term would be the "social septennial" and outlined specific projects to develop agriculture, industry, transportation, communications, and social services in Zaire over the following seven years.

In 1983, Zaire launched a series of monetary and fiscal reforms that reduced inflation and brought Zaire current on its foreign debt payments. The measures also caused a severe recession in the country, but on October 29, 1986, following a month-long meeting of the MPR Central Committee, the government announced that IMF-sponsored measures were "strangling" the Zairian economy and that the social needs of the country were being overly neglected. As a result, the government announced it would limit payments on its foreign debt to 10 percent of export revenues. The following month, Mobutu acknowledged there had been human rights abuses in Zaire and said he was creating a ministerial-level post for human rights in the government. The moves, coupled with the return of many exiled dissidents under a general amnesty, led some analysts to say the Zairian leadership was showing signs of political maturation, although many expressed cynicism over the possibility of seeing any significant change in the day-to-day lives of the average Zairian.

MOKOLO WA MPOMBO. An official frequently in and out of government during the cabinet shuffles of the 1980s, Mokolo was named state commissioner for foreign affairs in 1985, but was moved to the Department of Higher Education and Science in a reshuffle in April 1986.

MONGO. A major ethnic cluster within the Bantu family that is considered by official Zairian ethnographers to be the largest cluster, although other researchers disagree. Primarily a people of the forest, the Mongo live in most of the Congo Basin and part of the southern uplands in a vast area bordered by the Lulonga River in the north, the Sankuru River in the south, the confluence of the Zaire and Momboyo rivers to the west, and to the confluence of the Lualaba and Lukuga rivers to the east. The Mongo language, a major lingua franca in northwestern Zaire, is remarkably homogeneous, lending credence to the legend that the Mongo are descendant from one man. In the Mongo societies, which can be either matrilineal or patrilineal, chiefs were usually chosen on the basis of wealth, rather than kinship. The village was usually the core group formed around a lineage of which the chief might also be the chief of other, client lineages. Kaplan says only in the southwestern groups were Mongo societies organized into hierarchical systems, divided into provinces and headed by a sacred chief.

MOREL, EDMUND D. A British author who wrote extensively on the atrocities and labor abuses in the Congo Free State. His work led to public reaction that caused the British government in 1897 to instruct its consul-general in Leopoldville to draft a report on the labor practices in the CFS. The report further aroused the public and eventually led to the Belgian Parliament's reluctant annexation of the territory, marking the end of the CFS and the beginning of the Belgian Congo.

MOROCCO, RELATIONS WITH. Relations between Zaire and Morocco have been close virtually since independence, fortified by association in Africa's moderate camp and a similarity of views on a variety of regional and global issues. Morocco sent 1,500 troops to Shaba in April 1977 to help repel an invasion by the FNLC in the first Shaba War. Moroccan troops returned to Shaba in 1978 as part of a peacekeeping force to help maintain order following the Second Shaba War. The troops were gradually withdrawn over the following year. Zaire supports Morocco in the Western Sahara dispute and was the only nation to suspend its participation in the OAU when Morocco withdrew from the Organization in 1984 because of the admission of the Polisario Front's Saharan Republic. However, commercial ties between the two countries remain relatively small. Trade reached $5.2 million dollars in 1981 but declined to $2 million in 1985.

MOTOR VEHICLES. Motor vehicles numbered 300,000 in 1985. More than half were private passenger cars and the remainder commercial vehicles, although such figures can be deceiving since many private vehicles are sometimes used for commercial purposes. Assembly plants by General Motors and British Leyland (Landrover) were capable of producing 3,000 to 5,000 vehicles each per year. However, most vehicles were imported, primarily from Japan, France, Germany, and the United States.

MOUNTAINS. Although most of Zaire is located in the lowlands of
the Congo Basin, the country also contains several mountain
ranges, primarily in the eastern part of the country. The most
spectacular of these is the Ruwenzori in northeastern Zaire. The
highest in Africa, the Ruwenzoris rise primarily between Lake
Mobutu and Lake Edouard and vary from 1,000 to 5,000 m in
altitude. The Virunga Range, north of Lake Kivu, and the Mitumba Range, in southeastern Kivu Region, are less dramatic but
more fertile. In western Zaire, the Crystal Mountains, lying between Kinshasa and Matadi, are relatively low, but are noted for
causing the cataracts that render the Zaire River unnavigable
for 200 kms and hinder transportation between the Atlantic Ocean
and most of Zaire east of Matadi.

MOUVEMENT D'ACTION POUR LA RESURRECTION DU CONGO (MARC)
(ACTION MOVEMENT FOR THE RESURRECTION OF THE CONGO).
A Brussels-based opposition group headed by Munguya Nbege,
a former commissioner in Shaba. MARC evolved out of the
"Mouvement du 4 Juin" that was formed following the student unrest of the late 1960s. MARC was accused of fomenting uprisings
and in March 1978, a military tribunal sentenced 19 alleged plotters to death, five of them in absentia. Thirteen of those found
guilty were executed on March 17.

MOUVEMENT NATIONAL CONGOLAIS (MNC) (NATIONAL CONGOLESE
MOVEMENT). One of the major political parties at independence,
the MNC was formed by Zairian "évolués" in Leopoldville in October 1958. The founders included Lumumba, Ileo, Ngalula, Diomi,
Pinzi, and Adoula. One of the few parties at independence that
eschewed regionalism and attempted to develop a national base of
support, the MNC tried to elaborate a cogent ideology that took
its inspiration from African nationalists like Ghana's Nkrumah and
Guinea's Sekou Toure. It sought to establish a nationalistic program of economic, political, and cultural development and supported the concept of Pan-Africanism. By 1959, however, the
MNC had begun to splinter. Albert Kalonji left following the massacres of Luba in Katanga and other leaders left to form their
own parties. During elections prior to independence, the MNC
and ABAKO parties received the largest number of votes, but neither received an absolute majority. Lumumba eventually succeeded
in striking a compromise whereby he became prime minister and
Kasavubu, of the ABAKO, became president. The MNC, which
expressed nationalistic and anticolonial sentiments that were applauded by eastern governments and viewed with anxiety by
western governments, was radicalized following the assassination
of Lumumba in early 1961. It became the major force behind the
eastern rebellions from 1961 to 1964, and although it was splintered and weakened by the end of the decade, it remained a
prominent exiled opposition group until the 1980s.

MOUVEMENT POPULAIRE DE LA REVOLUTION (MPR) (POPULAR

REVOLUTIONARY MOVEMENT). Zaire's sole legal party, the MPR has grown in power and prestige since it was established six months after the Mobutu coup d'etat and has become the supreme organ of state. The party's early roots lie in the Corps de Volontaires de la République, a group of idealistic, primarily young intellectuals called to service by Mobutu in January 1966. The MPR was formally constituted on April 17, 1966. The party's ideology was outlined following a meeting at Nsele, which eventually became party headquarters, outside Kinshasa. The Nsele Manifesto, issued on May 20, 1967, proclaimed an official ideology of authenticity and Mobutism, which was defined as "authentic Zairian nationalism" and which condemned regionalism and tribalism. The Manifesto proclaimed a policy of "positive neutralism" in world politics and espoused a path between capitalism and communism, characterized by the phrase "neither to the right nor to the left, but forward." The Manifesto also established the national objectives of economic independence, strengthening the authority of the central government throughout the country, building the Congo's international prestige and working for the social and economic development of the Congolese people. The rise of the party was rapid. The MPR was declared the supreme organ of state and sole legal party on December 23, 1970, and was fused with the government beginning in 1972. The Constitution of 1974 formally established the Zairian "party-state." It codified the concentration of power in the president and the "unity" of party, people, and government (and the absence of separation-of-powers). By law, all Zairians from birth are automatically members of the party's youth wing, the Jeunesse du Mouvement Populaire de la Révolution (JMPR) (Youth of the Popular Revolutionary Movement). At 30 years of age, every Zairian becomes a member of the party and remains a member until death.

The organization of the system gives an indication of the rise of the party to a position of dominance over government. The MPR Political Bureau, a body of several dozen senior leaders, is the senior policymaking body. The Congress of the Party is a larger forum for discussion and debate that meets every five years. The Legislative Council of 310 members originally ratified the laws proposed by the Political Bureau. The Executive Council composed of heads of departments (ministries) and the first state commissioner (prime minister) oversaw the administration. And the Judicial Council, composed of presidents of the highest courts, interpreted the law. In 1980, the MPR Central Committee, composed of 120 senior party members, was created and began to emerge as the de facto parliament with a mandate to review and carry out the initiatives of the Political Bureau. As a result, the Legislative Council lost most of its power. The president presides over all of the organs. As noted, party congresses are held every five years. However, extraordinary congresses were held in 1970, 1977, and 1984 to nominate Mobutu as the sole candidate for presidential elections in those years.

The avowed purpose of the MPR was to mobilize and politically

educate the masses and to encourage their support for government policies and actions. Another major goal was to foster
unity, which after the fragmentation of the early 1960s remained
a major concern among many citizens. Political analysts note,
however, that the MPR, like the parties of most one-party African
states, did not arise from popular roots, but was created and imposed from the top. And critics have said the main result has
been to institutionalize a political system that receives little input
from the masses, and concentrates political and economic power
in the hands of an elite clique. Originally, all members of the
Political Bureau were nominated by the president. The Political
Bureau then selected members of the other institutions and nominated the sole candidates for the Legislative Council. The
president, as chief executive, chose the state commissioners,
state governors, and other senior members of the executive.
However, in 1978 a degree of liberalization was introduced. A
portion of the members of the Political Bureau were chosen by
party members. And multiple candidates within the party were
allowed in the legislative elections. However, the size of the
Political Bureau was changed to maintain the majority of presidential appointees, and the legislative candidates, although chosen
by local party cells, were subject to review by senior party officials. The election of part of the members of the Political
Bureau was later abolished and the Central Committee, whose
members were appointed by the Political Bureau, assumed most of
the lawmaking duties formerly held by the Legislative Council.
In January 1985, in a move aimed at eliminating "conflicts of interest," a by-law was adopted forbidding members of the Political
Bureau and Central Committee to hold office in the executive or
legislative bodies. Most officials chose to retain their party
posts. See CONSTITUTION; DISSIDENTS; JEUNESSE DU MOUVE-
MENT POPULAIRE DE LA REVOLUTION; LEGISLATIVE SYSTEM;
and PRESIDENCY.

MOVIMENTO POPULAR DE LIBERTAÇAO DE ANGOLA (MPLA) (POPU-
LAR MOVEMENT FOR THE LIBERATION OF ANGOLA). One of
three major guerrilla groups that fought for Angola's independence and, following independence, fought a civil war for control of the country. The MPLA, headed by Agostinho Neto and
backed by Cuba and the Soviet Union, took control of the capital
of Luanda, but was subsequently faced with guerrilla attacks from
opposition UNITA and FNLA groups, as well as incursions by
South African forces fighting SWAPO guerrillas in Namibia. José
Eduardo dos Santos became head of the MPLA and president of
Angola following Neto's death on September 10, 1979. FNLA activity diminished in the 1980s but UNITA continued to threaten
the MPLA government. UNITA controlled large portions of territory in the eastern and southern parts of the country and disrupted the economy by halting diamond mining and agricultural
activities in the region and by sabotaging the Benguela Railway
that provides the most efficient transportation link between the
Zairian mines in Shaba Region and the Atlantic Ocean.

MPINGA KASENDA.   Former prime minister and senior party official, Mpinga was born on August 30, 1937, at Tshilomba in Kasai Oriental Region.   He received a degree and later a doctorate in Political Sciences from Lovanium University and studied at the Institut Technique Supérieur d'Etudes Sociales at Lubumbashi. A professor at UNAZA's Kinshasa campus during the early 1970s, he became a member of the Political Bureau in 1972 and director of the Makanda Kabobi party institute, the MPR party school, in 1974.   He served as first state commissioner from 1977 to 1979 and became Permanent Secretary of the Political Bureau in 1979 and member of the Central Committee on September 2, 1980.

MULAMBA NYUNY WA KADIMA, COLONEL (LEONARD).   Mulamba was named prime minister on November 28, 1965, following Mobutu's coup d'etat.   The post was eliminated on October 26, 1966, and the duties of head-of-government were assumed by the president.

MULELE, PIERRE.   The Beijing-trained guerrilla who led the Kwilu revolt and brought urban guerrilla terrorism to Zaire for the first, and to date, only time.   At independence, Mulele was the head of the Parti Solidaire Africain (PSA) (African Solidarity Party) and a minister of education in the Lumumba government. He left the country following Lumumba's death and went to China where he received military training.   Mulele and his supporters, espousing a Maoist form of peasant revolution, began their operations in January 1964.   They destroyed many administrative and missionary institutions and set off bombs that terrorized Leopoldville for a number of months.   When the rebellion was put down in 1965, Mulele went into exile in Brazzaville which, it was believed, had been his base of operations.   Mulele was offered amnesty by the Mobutu government and returned to Zaire where he was summarily tried for treason and executed on October 8, 1968.   Congo/Brazzaville broke relations with Zaire following the execution.

MUNGUL DIAKA (BERNADIN).   Former education minister and ambassador to Belgium who sought asylum in Brussels in the mid-1970s and led a group of exiled dissidents until he returned to Zaire under the general amnesty of 1983.   Mungul was a Lumumba supporter at independence who became Gizenga's ambassador to Beijing during the eastern rebellion.   He was provincial minister of Kwilu in 1962-63, minister of the middle classes in the Mulamba government, and ambassador to Brussels in 1966-67.   He was education minister when in July 1968 he resigned and went into exile.

MUNGUYA MBENGE.   Commissioner (governor) of Shaba Region during the 1977 invasion by FNLC guerrillas, Munguya fled into exile. He was tried and convicted in absentia of collaborating with the FNLC.

MUNONGO, MWENDA M'SIRI SHYOMBEKA (GODEFROID). Tshombe's interior minister in the secessionist Katanga government and in the Congolese government when Tshombe was prime minister, Munongo was head of security and one of the most feared members of the Katangan regime. The son of a traditional chief of the Bayeke ethnic group, Munongo was born November 20, 1925, in Benkeya and received his education at mission schools in Katanga. He was a provincial judge in 1954-59 and was elected the first president of CONAKAT in 1959. He was interior minister in the Katanga government and in the Tshombe central government of 1964-65. He was dismissed in a cabinet reshuffle on July 9, 1964, a few months before Mobutu's coup. He was arrested as part of a general crackdown on December 26, 1966, and subsequently spent several years in prison and, later, under house arrest.

MUSIC. One of Zaire's greatest contributions to contemporary African culture has been its music, particularly the orchestra music that developed in the 1960s. The first authentic Zairian musicians were troubadors of the 1940s and 1950s, who travelled and performed primarily in the more remote provinces. Among the early troubadors was Antoine Wendo, born in 1925, who gained recognition with his recording of "Liwa ya Paul Kamba." He travelled as a soloist in the Kasai, Oriental, and Mai-Ndombe areas. Other soloists included Paul Kamba, Tête Rossignol, Polidor, Jean Bosco, and Colon Gentil. As the music developed, the solo acts became groups, adding African drums and acoustic guitars. Antoine Kasongo, Tekele Monkango (perhaps the first female music star), and Odéon Kinois were among the first leaders of groups. The second generation left traditional music for new forms and added more instruments.

   The first recordings of Congolese music were reportedly made beginning in 1947 by colonial museums. Joseph Kabasele, another founding father, formed the African Jazz Orchestra around 1953 and made a few records. Franco Luambo, born in 1938, formed the O.K. Jazz Orchestra and was one of the first to begin playing cha-chas. Beginning in the late 1950s, the influence of Cuban and Latin music began to be felt, and a number of Latin American records were adapted and recorded by Congolese groups. These included "Kay-Kay," "Son," "Tremendo," "L'Amor," and "Lolita." The Latin influence led to the composition of songs with Latin rhythms and Congolese lyrics, including such classics as "Indépendance Cha-cha" by Rochéreau to commemorate independence, and "Cha-cha-cha de Amor" by Franco. Congolese musicians eventually adopted the term "jazz" to describe their music. Musicologist Michel Lonoh writes that the first instance of use of the term "Congo Jazz" occurred in the song called "Pasi ya mokili et Congo Jazz akei" (roughly translated: "Heartache for the homeland and Congo Jazz took off"). By the mid-1960s, the term "Congo Jazz" was generally used to describe Congolese orchestral music, with Franco's O.K.

Jazz, Rochéreau, and Docteur Nico among the most popular musicians. By the late 1960s, the term "soukouma" (Lingala for "shake") had entered the lexicon and gradually became the dominant form of music. By this time, Zairian music was one of the most popular in Africa. By the late 1970s, the number of bands had multiplied and the music had become considerably pluralized. Some leaders incorporated disco, jazz, and blues harmonies into their compositions. Others favored ballads and more traditional musical forms. Many languages were used in the lyrics, but Lingala remained the most common.

Zairian music is primarily dance music, most often favored in the large, open-air dance clubs where the orchestra plays and the beer often flows until dawn. Kinshasa was one of the earliest recording centers in Africa. However, economic difficulties and shortages of foreign exchange led to a decline in the late 1970s, while other West African cities like Abidjan and Lagos became popular recording sites. Zairian orchestras also frequently perform and record in Paris and Brussels. A few of the better known orchestras have toured the United States.

MUTSHATSHA. A small town in western Shaba Region lying on the railway connecting the Shaba mining centers to Angola's Benguela Railway. Mutshatsha gained international renown in 1977 as one of the most important conquests of the FNLC during the first Shaba invasion.

MVUBA. An ethnic group of central Sudanic origin living in Haut-Zaire Region north of the Uelé River. The Mvuba were said to be primarily a group of decentralized, small-scale political entities, lacking chiefs and dominated by the Mamvu and Mangbetu.

MWANTA YANVU. Sometimes written as "Mwaant Yaav," the Mwanta Yanvu (meaning "King of Vipers") is the traditional paramount chief of the Lunda, the political and religious ruler of the people, and a strong political force in Shaba politics. See LUNDA.

- N -

NAME CHANGES. A number of name changes have been carried out during the history of Zaire that have affected the name of the country, regions, cities, and even the citizens themselves. In 1908, the Congo Free State became the Belgian Congo. At independence, the country was named the République du Congo, but with the promulgation of the first constitution in 1964, it was renamed the République Démocratique du Congo. The country became the République du Zaire on October 27, 1971. Meanwhile, as part of authenticity, cities with Belgian names were Zairianized in 1966. Leopoldville became Kinshasa; Elisabethville became Lubumbashi; and Stanleyville became Kisangani, among others (see Guide to Former and Current Names, page xxi). In addition, countless streets, bridges, and buildings were renamed to honor Zairian heros and respected persons. Finally, in May 1972, Zairians were ordered to drop their Christian names and adopt Zairian ones instead. For example, Joseph-Désiré Mobutu became Mobutu Sese Seko Kuku Ngbendu wa za Banga. See AUTHENTICITY.

NATIONAL WAY. The name given to the only transportation route entirely through Zairian territory that links Zaire's mining areas in Shaba Region to the Atlantic Ocean. Established in 1928, the National Way was intended to replace the route for Shaba exports through Tanzania and Mozambique to the ports of Dar es Salaam and Beira. A tortuous route, 2,750 kms long, the National Way required transporting mineral products by rail from Shaba to the port of Ilebo (formerly Port Francqui) on the Kasai River, by river to Kinshasa, by rail once again to Matadi, and from Matadi by ocean liner to the foreign ports of destination. The route required two to six months' time but it became vital to Zaire's mineral exports after 1975 when the Angolan civil war closed the Benguela Railway. The Benguela, which opened in 1931, had been the most direct way from Shaba to the Atlantic Ocean. Although more costly and time consuming than the "Southern Way" through Zimbabwe and South Africa, the National Way was politically more favorable because it was entirely within Zaire. According to government figures, 45 percent of Shaba's minerals were exported via the National Way in 1985.

NATIONALISM. Following independence, "nationalism" remained an elusive ideal, as Zaire was wracked by ethnic and regional divisions. Colonial policies had restricted political activity in the colony until a few years before independence. As a result, the development of a sense of nationhood had been suppressed and political parties, once they were allowed to form, grew primarily out of the associations formed to defend the interests of the major ethnic groups. One of the major reasons for the military coup in 1965 was the weakness of the multiparty political system that had been modeled on the checks-and-balances concept of the Belgian government. And one of the major goals during the early years of the Mobutu government was to unify Zairians and instill in them a sense of nationhood. Tribalism and regionalism were seen as the major causes of the chaos following independence, and so it was not surprising that government efforts following the Mobutu coup concentrated on eliminating these impediments to national unity. The N'Sele Manifesto, the magna carta of the MPR party, specifically mentioned the need to eliminate tribalism and regionalism and the early years of the Mobutu government were characterized by an increase in nationalism that resulted in the mid-1970s in the establishment of the party-state and the development of the ideologies of "authenticity" and "Mobutism." The feelings of national strength and pride were also aided by the rise in Zaire's economic fortunes in the early 1970s. In the late 1970s, however, the decline of the Zairian economy, the Shaba invasions, the rise of a number of dissident groups and growing resentment by the people against the political oligarchy contributed to a creeping disillusionment with the ideals of the early Mobutu years and the rise of an attitude of self-preservation among many Zairians. Nevertheless, the concept of nationhood continued to mature and by the 1980s, talk of secessions and regional autonomy was rarely heard, even in the areas that felt most neglected by the government in Kinshasa.

NATIONALIZATION. Nationalization of Zairian industry began in 1966 with the government takeover of the Union Minière du Haut-Katanga (now called GECAMINES) mining company. It reached its peak in November 1973 with the "Zairianization" of large and medium-sized businesses. The deterioration of the commercial sector, combined with falling economic fortunes due to the drop in copper prices, led to a partial privatization called "Retrocession" in 1975. Further privatization of certain sectors, like agriculture, diamond and gold trading and transportation, was announced during the 1980s. See ECONOMY and ZAIRIANIZATION.

NAVY. The Zairian government maintains a small navy of 500 persons engaged primarily in coastal, border patrols along the Atlantic Ocean in the west and the great lakes in the east. The largest ship, the Zaire, is a 70-ton vessel based at Matadi. The remainder of the fleet is comprised of one dozen lighter patrol vessels of U.S. and North Korean manufacture. The U.S. government has maintained a bilateral aid program with the Zairian navy since 1977 that includes the supply of patrol boats, spare parts, and some training.

NDEMBO. An ethnic group in western Shaba Region related in language and descent patterns to the Lunda, but which has tended to side with the Chokwe in opposing the Lunda in modern-day politics.

NDJILI AIRPORT. Zaire's largest airport located near the suburb of Ndjili on the northern outskirts of Kinshasa, Ndjili airport has one of the longest runways in Africa and is home-base for a significant portion of the Zairian air force. It is the headquarters of the national carrier Air Zaire and several private Zairian carriers. It also is serviced by a number of international carriers, including Air Afrique, Sabena, TAP, Cameroon Airlines, Ethiopian Airlines, UTA, and Alitalia. For years the airport was one of the stops on Pan Am's West African coastal route from New York to Johannesburg. However, Kinshasa was one of several stops eliminated from the route in the 1980s as part of cost-cutting measures by the U.S. carrier.

NDOLA. A mining town in Zambia's copper belt that has considerable

commercial ties with Lubumbashi. Ndola was the destination of
U.N. Secretary-General Dag Hammarskjöld's plane when it crashed
over Katanga in 1961, killing all of its occupants.

NDOLO AIRPORT. Kinshasa's first commercial airfield located in the
heart of the city in Ndolo commune, less than 15 minutes from
downtown Kinshasa. Since the opening of Njili airport in 1960,
Ndolo has become a domestic airfield used primarily by small, private, and government aircraft and for some military cargo shipments.

NENDAKA, VICTOR. An influential figure in the early Congolese
governments, Nendaka was vice-president of the Lumumba wing
of the MNC and head of the Sûreté secret police from September
1960 until 1965, when he became interior minister in the Tshombe
and Kimba governments. He was finance minister from August
1968 until August 1969 and subsequently ambassador to Bonn.
He was disgraced and sent into internal exile in the early 1970s.
Rehabilitated in the late 1970s, he since has remained on the
periphery of Zairian politics.

NETO, AGOSTINHO. The first president of Angola, Neto was the
poet-liberation leader of the MPLA faction in Angola's war for
independence and subsequent civil war. A socialist with close
ties to the Soviet Union, Neto was disliked by Mobutu, who supported the FNLA faction. However, following the Shaba invasions
by FNLC guerrillas based in Angola, Mobutu, and Neto met in
Brazzaville and agreed to cease hostilities and support for each
other's opposition groups. Diplomatic relations were subsequently
established although tensions and suspicions remained. Neto
died of cancer in the Soviet Union on September 10, 1979.

NGALA. One of the major ethnic groups of northwestern Zaire, living between the Zaire and Ubangi Rivers, whose language, Lingala, is one of Zaire's four national languages. Zairian ethnographers consider the Ngala to be of the Bantu cluster. However, others say they belong primarily to the Sudanic group.
Both clusters settled in the area and there was considerable in-
termingling among the groups, but the Ngala language appears
to be related more to the Bantu tongues than to any others.
Originally, a relatively small tribe, the Ngala has gained importance in the minds of many Zairians for two reasons. Lingala,
based on the traditional Ngala tongue came into increasing use
beginning in the mid-1800s as the trade language of the lower
Zaire River and the lingua franca of the military. It became the
lingua franca in Leopoldville during the colonial era and, following independence, was adopted as the conversational idiom of the
civil service and administration (as opposed to the official, written idiom which continued to be French). Secondly, Mobutu
traditionally has used Lingala (as opposed to other national languages) to address Zairians.

NGALULA MPANDAJILA (JOSEPH). One of the founding fathers of the MNC who, with Lumumba, attended the Pan-African Congress in Accra in December 1958 and upon his return addressed a rally at which the first calls for independence were heard. When the MNC split, Ngalula joined the Kalonji wing and became vice-president and prime minister of the secessionist Mining State of South Kasai. Following the end of the South Kasai secession, he returned to Leopoldville and was appointed minister of education in the first and second Adoula governments. He was dropped from the government in 1963. However, Ngalula remained in Zairian politics and came to attention once again in the 1980s as one of the founders of the UDPS. He was tried, imprisoned, banished and pardoned several times during the mid-1980s for advocating the creation of a second political party, which is against Zairian law.

NGBAKA. A significant sub-group of the Banda, a central-Sudanic group living in the northwestern corner of Zaire along the Ubangi River near Zongo.

NGBANDI. A Sudanic people, according to some ethnographers, related to the Ngala, living in northwestern Zaire between the Zaire and Ubangi Rivers east of Busingu. The most famous Ngbandi son is Mobutu, who traces his parental and ancestral origins to the group living around Gbadolite. Mobutu, however, was born in Lisala and grew up among the Ngombe and Ngala people.

NGOMBE. A sub-group of the Mongo people living along the Zaire River north of Mbandaka and Basankusu.

NGONGO LUTETE. A Congolese leader who fought in the campaign to drive the Arab traders from eastern Zaire in the 1890s and, with the help of the Sambala people, pacified and occupied the Maniema area of western Kivu Region.

NGOUABI, MARIEN. Founder of the Marxist state of Congo/Brazzaville who headed the National Council of the Revolution that took power in a military coup d'etat in the Congo in September 1968. President of Congo from January 1, 1969, until his assassination on March 18, 1977, Ngouabi was born in 1938 at Ombélé and was a member of the Congolese armed forces who, following independence, became an admirer of Marxism. His arrest in 1968 led to the military coup d'etat that overthrew Massamba-Debat. Ngouabi, along with Marx and Lenin, is considered one of the heroes of the official Congolese revolution. He led the Congo during some of the periods of worst relations with Zaire, but was also responsible for organizing the meetings between Mobutu and Neto in 1976 that later brought diplomatic relations between Zaire and Angola.

NGUZA KARL-I-BOND. A former prime minister who became a leading Zairian dissident before returning to Zaire under the Amnesty
of 1983. Nguza was born August 4, 1938, in Musumba, near
Kapanga in western Shaba Region. At an early age, he moved
to Likasi where he attended primary school with the Xavier
Brothers. He attended secondary school at Lubumbashi under
the Benedictine Fathers. He was graduated from Lovanium University in July 1965 with a degree in international relations and
entered the diplomatic corps. Nguza was of the Lunda ethnic
group and related to Moise Tshombe and the Lunda paramount
chief. He was also a well-spoken technocrat and rose quickly
through the diplomatic corps. He served as the second ranking
diplomat at the Zairian mission to the United Nations. He was
appointed foreign minister on February 24, 1972, replaced in a
cabinet reshuffle on March 8, 1974, and returned to the post on
February 4, 1976, during a period when he was highly touted in
western Europe and the United States as a possible successor
to Mobutu. However, he was accused of having prior knowledge
of the first Shaba invasion and was arrested on August 13, 1977,
and dismissed as foreign minister six days later. He was sentenced to death for treason but the sentence was commuted to life
imprisonment by Mobutu. He was freed one year later, appointed
foreign minister once again on March 6, 1979, and promoted to
prime minister shortly thereafter. In April 1981, Nguza resigned
and went into exile accusing the Zairian government of corruption,
authoritarianism, and abuses of power in virtually every aspect
of Zairian life. He published a book in mid-1982 that documented
some of his charges, detailed his trial and torture in 1979, and
advocated a return to multiparty democracy in Zaire. He launched
a promotional tour of Europe and North America during which he
testified before the U.S. House of Representatives' Africa Subcommittee. He continued to be an outspoken leader of the exiled
Zairian opposition until he was muzzled by the Belgian government, along with other Zairian dissidents, in a move to improve
relations with the Zairian government. In June 1985, Nguza accepted the general amnesty of 1983 and returned to Zaire, where
he appeared at the festivities marking the 25th anniversary of
Zaire's independence. He was appointed ambassador to the United
States in September 1986. He was appointed foreign minister
once again on March 7, 1988.

NKRUMAH, KWAME. First president of Ghana and one of the leaders
of the Pan-Africanist movement, who organized the Union of African States with Guinea and Mali in 1961. Lumumba met Nkrumah
at the All-African People's Congress in Accra in December 1958.
He is said to have greatly influenced Lumumba's thinking on such
topics as African solidarity, the need for African nations to distance themselves from the colonial powers, and the need to forge
a pan-African nation by integrating political and economic systems. Nkrumah was deposed in a military coup d'etat in 1966
and lived in exile in Guinea until his death.

NKUTSHU. Sometimes written "Kuntshu," the Nkutshu are an ethnic group of the Bantu cluster related to the Mongo. They live in the central portion of eastern Zaire between the Lukenie and Sankuru Rivers and are sometimes identified with the Tetela and to a lesser degree with the Kusu people of the same region.

NORD-KIVU. A sub-region of Kivu containing some of Zaire's most fertile soil and most temperate climate. With a population of 1,861,960 (1982), living in an area of 59,563 square kms, Nord-Kivu is one of Zaire's most densely populated areas. It produces vegetables, palm oil, timber, and some gold.

NOVEMBER 24, 1965. The day the military took power in a bloodless coup and asked then Lt. Colonel Joseph-Désiré Mobutu to assume presidential powers. The coup ended a fractious and disorganized, multiparty democracy and brought to power a man who has become one of Africa's longest governing leaders. The takeover was decided on Wednesday, November 24, at an all-night meeting of the armed forces high command which had gathered in Leopoldville ostensibly to commemorate Congolese soldiers who had died fighting the rebellions. However, in the face of an upsurge of rebel activity in the east and yet another constitutional crisis and political paralysis caused by a dispute between the president and prime minister, the 14 senior officers who made up the high command were called from their respective garrisons by armed forces chief-of-staff Mobutu to discuss a military takeover. The 14 who signed the proclamation of the coup and became known as the companions of the revolution were Generals Mobutu, Bobozo Salelo Ndembo Aduluma, Colonels Masiala Kinkela Kulu Kangala, Mulamba Nyunya Wa Kadima, Nzyoyigbe Yeu Ngoli, Itambo Munkina Wa-Kambala, Bangala Oto Wa Ngama and Lieutenant-Colonels Ingila Grima, Tshatshi Ohano, Moyango Bikoko Ebatamungama, Singa Boyenge Mosambayi, Basuki Belenge, Malila Ma-Kende, and Tukuzu Gusu-Wo Angbanduruka. Among other things, the proclamation dismissed Kasavubu and prime minister-designate Kimba and underscored that the military's actions were not aimed at creating a military dictatorship.

November 24 is currently Zaire's National Day and is celebrated with greater pomp than any other day, including Independence Day. Because it is the national holiday, it is also often the date for the inauguration of important development projects like the Voix du Zaire telecommunications facility in 1976, the Inga-Shaba power line in 1983, and the bridge over the Zaire River at Matadi in 1984.

November 24, 1964 is also the day that Belgian paratroopers, using U.S. planes, dropped on Stanleyville to free 10,000 Zairians and 1,000 foreigners being held hostage by secessionist forces during the eastern rebellion.

NSELE MANIFESTO. The Nsele Manifesto was issued on May 20, 1967, following a lengthy meeting of the Binza Group, the Corps des

Volontaires de la République, and other intellectuals at Nsele,
the model farm 60 kms up river from Kinshasa which was to become the MPR retreat and headquarters. The manifesto became
the basis for the gradual emergence of Mobutism and the one-
party state. It was aimed at ending the bickering and political
in-fighting that had characterized the post-independence era.
The Nsele Manifesto attempted to chart a new course for the
Congo. It called for "positive neutralism" in world affairs and
set as national objectives economic independence, stronger government authority throughout the territory, actions to increase the
nation's prestige abroad, and the promotion of economic and social
development for the Congolese people. The subsequent policies
of authenticity, Zairianization and, to a degree, Mobutism, were
outgrowths of the Manifesto. See MOUVEMENT POPULAIRE DE
LA REVOLUTION.

N'SINGA UDJUU ONGWAKEBI UNTUBE (JOSEPH). A party technocrat who was former first state commissioner and member of the
Political Bureau, N'Singa was born September 29, 1934, at Nson-
tin in Bandundu Region. He studied theology for one year but
received a law degree from Lovanium University in 1963. A provincial official in the Lac Leopold II administrative district from
1963 until 1966, he was named to the central government in
1966 and was justice minister from 1967-68 and subsequently
served in ministerial-level positions in the Interior Ministry and
the Presidency. A technocrat, he was named first state commissioner on April 22, 1981, but left the government on November
5, 1982, and was named to the Political Bureau of the party on
January 3, 1983.

NTOMBA. A relatively large sub-group of the Mongo ethnic cluster
living along the Maringa River between Basankusu and Djolu in
northwestern Zaire. Zairian ethnographers have also identified
a Ntomba-related group living southeast of Mai-Ndombe Lake.
Kaplan says the Ntomba differ from most Mongo peoples in language and hierarchical system. Their chiefs are considered
sacred and administratively their territory is divided into provinces.

NYAMWEZI. A group of east African traders from Tanzania that entered Zaire in the sixteenth or seventeenth century and established the Yeke Kingdom. The kingdom flourished for 30 years
before declining into smaller groups which live in Shaba Region
around Kolwezi and Kasanga.

NYANGWE. A small trading city on the Lualaba River in southern
Kivu Region, now called Kibombo, that was a major base for Afro-
Arab traders in the nineteenth century. Livingstone, searching
for the headwaters of the Nile, was the first European to reach
Nyangwe, in 1871. Verney Lovett Cameron reached the town in
1874, two years before Stanley and, by measuring the flow of

water, deduced that the Lualaba was one of the headwaters of the Congo River and not of the Nile, as Livingstone had supposed. The Arab influence diminished following the anti-slavery campaign by Commander Francis Dhanis in the 1890s. The Arab traders were driven away in 1893 and the city taken over by the colonial authorities.

NZONDOMIO A DOKPEDINGO. Politician from Equateur Region, born December 30, 1931, at Libenge Kete, who served as justice minister from 1972-74, President of the Legislative Council thereafter, and member of the Central Committee since 1980.

- O -

OFFICE DE GESTION DE LA DETTE PUBLIQUE (OGEDEP) (OFFICE FOR THE MANAGEMENT OF THE PUBLIC DEBT). A government agency formed in January 1977 after Zaire fell seriously behind in its debt repayments. The agency's purpose was to oversee Zaire's foreign debt repayments. Its representatives also participated in government negotiations with foreign creditors.

OFFICE DES MINES D'OR DE KILO-MOTO (OKIMO) (OFFICE OF THE GOLD MINES OF KILO-MOTO). Known more commonly as "Kilo-Moto," OKIMO is the major gold mining company in Zaire, with 5,900 employees of which fewer than ten are expatriate. It has been state-owned since Zairianization in 1973. The company is located in Haut-Zaire Region where it works both subterranean and alluvial deposits in a 83,000 square km concession around Bunia and Isiro. An additional mine, called Adidi, began operating in 1973 at Mongbwalu and a Brazilian company reportedly discovered sizeable deposits in the area in 1986. See GOLD.

OFFICE DES ROUTES (HIGHWAY OFFICE). A government agency established in 1972 to build and maintain Zaire's roads. The Office des Routes began a three-year program in 1985 to rehabilitate existing roads, in particular the highway linking Kinshasa and Matadi, and to construct new roads, including a new highway from Kisangani to Bukavu. At a donor's meeting in Paris in March 1984, pledges totaling $105 million of the $134 million sought were made by donors that included the African Development Bank, the World Bank, the EEC, United States, West Germany, France, Belgium, the United Kingdom, and Japan. See ROADS.

OFFICE NATIONAL DE CAFE (ONC) (NATIONAL COFFEE BOARD). The Zairian government's national coffee marketing board, the ONC exported 80,000 tons of coffee in 1985, making it Zaire's largest agricultural exporter.

OFFICE NATIONAL DE PECHE (ONP) (NATIONAL FISHING BOARD).

The Zairian government's agency that promotes fishing in the country and, in some cases, markets the products of state and privately owned fisheries and fish processing plants. See FISHING.

OFFICE NATIONAL DES TRANSPORTS DU ZAIRE (ONATRA) (NATIONAL TRANSPORT OFFICE OF ZAIRE). The state-owned company that dominates river transport in Zaire, ONATRA was known as the Office d'Exploitation des Transports Coloniaux during colonial times. It was created in 1935 as a government-sponsored agency to operate river and seaport facilities and to control all water transport in the colony except that of the Upper Zaire River and Lake Tanganyika. It was renamed OTRACO (Office des Transports du Congo) at independence and became ONATRA upon its nationalization in the early 1970s. ONATRA operated 700 barges, 100 tugboats, and 40 other vessels on Zaire's principle waterways at its peak in 1972. However, economic recession and a shortage of foreign exchange and operating capital caused operational problems in the 1980s. A relatively efficient parastatal company, however, ONATRA was able to keep most of its fleet in operation, but shipping times were generally long and pilferage made shipment of valuable cargo hazardous. ONATRA also operated passenger service along the Zaire, Kasai, and Ubangi rivers. ONATRA's monopoly of river transport was abolished by government decree in 1977. See TRANSPORT.

OFFICE NATIONAL DU SUCRE (ONS) (NATIONAL SUGAR BOARD). Government agency established by decree on January 1, 1974, grouping all sugar refineries and most of the large cane plantations as part of Zairianization. The ONS was disbanded on May 8, 1978, and a sugar development board called Projets Sucriers au Zaire (PSZ) was established. See SUGAR.

OFFICE NATIONAL POUR LE DEVELOPPEMENT DE L'ELEVAGE (ONDE) (NATIONAL LIVESTOCK DEVELOPMENT BOARD). A government agency that took over ownership and operation of many large ranches following Zairianization in 1973. Under Retrocession, some of the ranches were returned to their former owners. Others were turned over to private operators while the government retained ownership. See LIVESTOCK.

OIL see PETROLEUM

OPPOSITION. Opposition parties were numerous during the first five years of Zaire's independence, but they were suspended along with all political activity following the coup that brought Mobutu to power in 1965 and have been outlawed since 1967 when the MPR was declared the sole legal party. Indeed, according to Zairian law, attempting to form a second party is considered treason. As a result, most opposition to the Zairian government has come from exiles. In the early 1980s, however, a group of

13 former parliamentarians attempted to form a second party, the UDPS. They were tried in 1983 and sentenced to prison terms ranging from 15 years to life, but were later pardoned. See DISSIDENTS.

ORBITAL TRANSPORT UND RAKETEN GESELLSCHAFT (OTRAG). A West German company that signed a contract with the Zairian government, reportedly for $50 million, giving the company virtually complete control over 100,000 square kms of a remote northeastern corner of Shaba Region. The avowed purpose of the lease was to allow the company to develop and test commercial rockets. However, the secrecy that surrounded the project raised suspicions in the international community and the news media. In addition, some of Zaire's neighbors expressed strong disapproval of such a project near their borders. The contract was cancelled the following year. OTRAG reportedly eventually negotiated a similar contract with a South American nation but little has been heard of the company since.

ORDRE NATIONAL DE LEOPARD (NATIONAL ORDER OF THE LEOPARD). The major national order of merit with varying degrees of elevation, established by Mobutu in the late 1960s to honor esteemed national and foreign leaders. The order is named for the national animal of Zaire, the leopard, which is highly respected in many traditional Zairian societies for its speed and hunting prowess.

ORGANISATION COMMUNE AFRICAINE ET MALGACHE (OCAM) (AFRO-MALASY COMMON ORGANIZATION). One of the first pan-African organizations created following the wave of independences in the early 1960s to press for economic integration and development on the continent. With the development of more regionalized economic organizations, however, OCAM gradually outgrew its usefulness and declined in membership and influence. Zaire, which was a founding member, withdrew in 1972. The organization was dissolved in 1984.

ORGANIZATION OF AFRICAN UNITY (OAU). The pan-African organization founded in 1963 in Addis Ababa, Ethiopia, to unite Africa in its struggle to end colonialism and racial discrimination. Other purposes that gained prominence as the colonial era began to wane were to further economic development and to provide a forum for the peaceful settlement of African disputes and the drafting of joint African positions on international issues. Zaire has remained for the most part a member of the "moderate" camp of the OAU. It has supported independence movements and the struggle against apartheid, but opposed membership for the Soviet-backed MPLA faction that took power in Angola and "suspended" its participation in the organization in 1984 when the Polisario Front was admitted as the (Western) Saharan Republic over the protests by Zaire's long-time ally, Morocco. Mobutu

served as OAU chairman in 1967-68 and Zaire hosted the OAU
summit of 1967. For the event a multimillion dollar "OAU Village"
was constructed in Kinshasa that now is used as an exclusive
resort and guest quarters for other major international gatherings
like the Franco-African summit of October 1982.

ORIENTALE PROVINCE. The former name for the northeastern part
of Zaire, Orientale was renamed "Haut-Zaire" as part of the administrative reforms of 1966 and the capital of Stanleyville became Kisangani. See HAUT-ZAIRE.

- P -

PALM OIL. At independence, Zaire was Africa's second largest exporter of palm oil, after Nigeria. The country produced 245,000
tons in 1959, of which 75 percent was exported, accounting for
12 percent of total export revenues. However, by 1976 production had fallen to 136,000 tons, of which one-fourth was exported,
accounting for 2 percent of total export revenues. By 1982 production had fallen to 100,000 tons of which little was exported.
The fall in production was due largely to a shortage of laborers
and the absence of replanting programs. However, the government announced ambitious plans to expand production in the mid-
1980s.

PALU. The site of the first Belgian settlement on Lake Tanganyika,
established in May 1883. It was used primarily as a base to
drive the Arab traders from the territory, to establish Belgian
sovereignty over the eastern Congo and to explore the mineral
riches of Katanga.

PAN-AFRICAN CONFERENCE. Officially called the All-African Peo-
ple's Conference, the meeting came to be more commonly known
as the Pan-African Conference because of the concept of Pan-
Africanism that it helped to launch. The conference was held
in December 1958 in Accra, the capital of newly independent
Ghana. Lumumba, Joseph Ngalula, and Gaston Diomi attended
(Kasavubu was prevented from going by the colonial authorities).
There they came into contact with the nationalist ideas of such
African leaders as Ghana's Kwame Nkrumah, Egypt's Gamal Abdel
Nasser, and Guinea's Ahmed Sekou Toure. They also became
aware of the growing demands for independence by Africans of
the French colonies, de Gaulle's offer of autonomy to France's
African colonies, and the Congo's relative isolation. The Congolese representatives, particularly Lumumba, returned home fired
by the passion for independence. He first called for independence during a speech at a rally on December 28, 1958. A rally
on January 3, 1959, led to calls for independence and some attacks on white-owned properties. That demonstration was harshly
put down by the colonial authorities. It is said to have been a

major cause of the two weeks of rioting that began the following
day and led within a year to the Belgian government's decision
to grant independence to the Congo.

PARIS CLUB. The unofficial name given the group of government
creditors that works in conjunction with the IMF and the London
Club (private creditors) to reschedule the foreign debts of
financially strapped governments. Zaire's debt to Paris Club
members varied during the 1970s and 1980s between 15 and 20
percent of its total foreign debt. In 1978, debt service to
foreign government lenders was $68 million whereas service to
private creditors was $392 million. Debt service for bilateral
public debt had risen to $105 million in 1983, while service on
the private foreign debt had fallen to $213 million.

PARLIAMENTARIANS, THIRTEEN. The group known as the Thirteen
Parliamentarians has become Zaire's primary group of internally
based dissidents. They have been convicted of conspiracy, jailed,
banished to their home villages, and pardoned several times since
1982 when they created an opposition party, the UDPS, which is
illegal under Zairian law. The parliamentarians, mostly from
Shaba and Kasai Regions, have also lost their positions in party
and government as a result of their activities. They were most
recently amnestied in 1985, but by 1986 had reportedly been sent
into internal exile once again for refusing to cease their activities. See DISSIDENTS.

PARTI DE LA REVOLUTION POPULAIRE (PRP) (PEOPLE'S REVOLU-
TIONARY PARTY). Currently the only known armed resistance
to the Zairian government that is based inside the country. The
PRP, originally headed by Laurent Kabila, was linked to the
MNC-Lumumba and the first Stanleyville secession of the early
1960s, but it broke away in 1964 and established guerrilla bases
in the remote forests of Kivu Region west of the Mitumba mountain range. In 1975, PRP guerrillas kidnapped four foreign students from a Tanzanian wildlife refuge. They were later released. A reporter for New African magazine visited the area
and wrote in 1982 that the guerrillas had established some social
and economic infrastructure and provided indoctrination along
communalist/socialist lines to people living in the areas under
their control. However, the guerrillas were said to be unable
to control villages near Lake Tanganyika because of the presence
of government troops. In November 1984, PRP guerrillas attacked and briefly occupied the garrison at the port town of
Moba, calling for Zairians to rise up and overthrow the Mobutu
government. The Zairian army retook Moba two days later. Official casualty figures were never released but were estimated at
between 10 and 50 dead. The government accused Zairian exiles
living in neighboring Tanzania and Burundi of responsibility.
However the PRP denied the charge, saying it was based entirely
within Zaire. The guerrillas staged a second attack on Moba in

June 1985 in an effort to underscore opposition to the Mobutu government as Zaire was celebrating the 25th anniversary of its independence. The second attack, however, was quickly repelled and brought threats of hot pursuit from the Zairian government against neighboring governments if they "continued to seek to destabilize" Zaire. Mobutu invited the guerrillas to take advantage of the general amnesty but the PRP maintained it would accept nothing less than the end of the Mobutu regime.

PARTI SOLIDAIRE AFRICAIN (PSA) (AFRICAN SOLIDARITY PARTY). A left-leaning party founded by Gizenga and Kamitatu in the late 1950s which sent delegates to the Round Table Conference in 1960. At independence, the PSA joined with the MNC to form the first Congolese government and received three portfolios including that of vice-prime minister. Its ministers were dismissed with Lumumba on September 5 and left Leopoldville to form a rival government in Stanleyville following the U.N. recognition of the Kasavubu government and the assassination of Lumumba. The PSA was included in the reconciliation government of Adoula, with first Gizenga, then Kamitatu holding the most senior portfolio. With the election of the Tshombe government, the PSA left the government and many of its leaders went into exile. Gizenga later resurfaced in Stanleyville to form the FODELICO and lead the second eastern rebellion. Mulele, another PSA leader and former secretary-general, had already left for military training in China. He went to Congo/Brazzaville where he joined the Brazzaville-based Conseil de Libération du Congo and launched the Kwilu rebellion and terrorist attacks on Leopoldville. The PSA was banned along with all political parties following the Mobutu coup.

PATERNALISM. The term often used to characterize Belgium's policy toward its African colonies, and in particular the Congo. According to the concept, Africans were considered like children, well intentioned but easily frightened, prone to excesses and not to be trusted with too much authority or responsibility. They were to be taught moral and Christian values and the need to face up to responsibility. They were to be "civilized" and taught basic literacy and health care. The brighter ones could aspire to positions such as office clerk, teaching assistant, or assistant nurse. In 1959, however, political independence and the assumption of leadership and policy-making roles in the professions was seen by colonial leaders to be at least one generation away. As a result, at independence, few Belgians with experience in the colony believed the Congolese would be able to run the country.

PENAL CODE. Before the colonial era, traditional law was the basis for punishment for most crimes among the various ethnic groups and foreigners did not tamper with it. With the creation of the Congo Free State, however, traditional law came under criticism as savage and brutal. As a result, a penal Code was adopted in

1888. Based on the Belgian penal code, it remained in force
until a new code was enacted in 1940. The code permitted the
death penalty for premeditated murder and certain crimes against
the state. Lengthy prison terms were given to those convicted
of serious crimes such as involuntary murder, kidnapping, rape,
and aggravated assault that caused disability. Theft, arson,
fraud, and embezzlement also could draw serious prison terms
and fines. However, considerable latitude was given to judges
to take into account the extent of damages, mitigating circumstances, the age of the offender, and the offender's previous
record. Historians note that traditional or "customary" law continued to be used in many cases where the crime did not involve
a European. In the 1970s and 1980s, some changes were enacted
that reduced penalties for certain offenses and increased emphasis on rehabilitation. However, the death penalty was accorded
in many cases to those convicted of treason or subversion and
conviction on charges such as plotting against the state could
draw penalties more severe than all but the worst of crimes.

PENAL SYSTEM. Mobutu has stated, in response to questions concerning Zairian criminality, that his government has built no
new prisons since he came to power. However, human rights
organizations like Amnesty International have repeatedly criticized the Zairian penal system for being poorly funded, corrupt,
and harsh. Maltreatment of prisoners and malnutrition are reportedly widespread. Beatings are common. The U.S. State
Department has echoed a number of these findings while noting
that similar conditions exist in most prisons in the developing
world. Most of Zaire's prisons are in the urban areas and three
of the largest are located in the Kinshasa area: Makala, Ndolo,
and Linguela. Zairian dissidents have also accused the government of building several secret prisons and "re-education camps"
in remote areas of Zaire for habitual offenders and political dissidents. Dissidents, for example, have reported the existence of
a detention center called Kota-Koli near Gbadolite in northern
Zaire. Some efforts are made to isolate juvenile offenders from
adults, but a common practice has been to induct youthful,
chronic offenders into the army. Most observers say the harsh-
ness of the penal system in the case of all but political dissidents
is due more to poor management, corruption, and a lack of funds
than to malice. Most inmates, however, in order to survive for
any length of time, depend on food, clothing, and medicine provided by their families that is transmitted through the prison
guards usually for a fee.

PENDE. A cluster of Bantu-speaking people living between the
Kwilu and Kasai Rivers south of Gungu in southern portions of
Bandundu and Kasai Regions. One of four diverse ethnic groups
living in the area, the Pende joined the Mbun and Njembe in the
1880s to stop the expansion of the Chokwe nation. Closely related to the Mbun, the Pende supported the Mulele rebellion in
the Kwilu area in 1964-65.

PETROLEUM. Zaire's heavy dependence on imported petroleum (combined with a drop in export revenues for copper and cobalt) helped precipitate the economic crisis in the mid-1970s from which the country has yet to completely recover. Despite exploration that began during the colonial era, there was no petroleum production until 1975, when significant deposits discovered offshore in 1970 and 1972 began to be exploited. Production increased steadily, reaching the rate of 20,000 barrels per day in the late 1970s. By the end of 1983, six fields had been discovered, of which four were in production. By 1985, total production had reached 30,000 barrels per day, of which more than one-half was exported. Total proven reserves were estimated at 60 million barrels. Production was carried out by U.S., Japanese, and Belgian companies in partnership with the Zairian government. Gulf Oil, bought out by Chevron in 1984, operated 38 wells in Zaire, of which 16 were wildcat operations. Ninety percent of Zaire's petroleum to date has been offshore in the rich central African basin that has made Angola, Cabinda, Congo, and Gabon major producers. However, Zairian offshore reserves appeared to be limited because of its small, 37-km-long, coastline. Nevertheless a field was also discovered on an island at the mouth of the Zaire River and was in production in the mid-1980s. In addition to the offshore explorations, positive seismic tests led to exploratory drilling near Mbandaka in Equateur Region in the early 1980s, but no commercially exploitable fields were found and drilling was halted in 1984. Seismic explorations were also undertaken in the lakes of the Great Rift Valley, leading to the discovery of considerable deposits of natural gas in Lake Kivu. However, these have yet to be exploited because of the great depth of the lake.

A refinery, built with Italian participation in 1968 to process imported oil, refines some Zairian crude. Called the Société Zairo-Italienne de Raffinage (SOZIR), the plant has a refining capacity of 17,000 barrels per day. However, because of the high wax content of Zairian petroleum, very little Zairian crude can be refined by SOZIR. As a result, locally produced crude is traded for imported oil that can be processed. Two aboveground pipelines, the first built in the 1920s and the second completed in the 1950s, carry oil from Matadi to Kinshasa. The government agency Petro-Zaire distributes the refined petroleum products through private dealers.

PINZI, ARTHUR. Zairian politician prominent in the independence years, Pinzi participated in the drafting of the Conscience Africaine manifesto in 1956. He helped found the MNC in 1958 but split away before independence to form his own small party. Elected mayor of Kalamu commune in 1958, Pinzi was elected to parliament in 1960. He later joined ABAKO and served as finance minister in the Adoula government from August 2, 1961, to July 10, 1962.

PIPELINES. Two above-ground pipelines carry petroleum 350 kms
from Matadi to Kinshasa and were both built long before petroleum was discovered near the mouth of the Zaire River. The first,
10 cm (four inches) in diameter, was built in the 1920s. The
second, 15 cm (six inches) in diameter, was built in the 1950s.
In addition, a 40 cm- (16 inch-) diameter pipeline carries petroleum from an offshore terminal to the Zairian coast near Moanda
and slurry pipelines are used in Shaba to transport unrefined
minerals. See PETROLEUM.

PLANTATIONS. Large commercial plantations were begun in the
1800s in Zaire and were considered to be the primary source of
Zaire's wealth after the end of the slave trade and before the
beginning of the mining operations in Shaba. During the colonial period, hundreds of plantations were established, usually on
land grants, for the cultivation of rubber, timber, sugarcane,
oil palm, coffee, tea, cocoa, and for the raising of livestock.
Following independence, however, many of them fell into disuse.
Others slowly declined because of transportation problems, the
lack of government incentives and a shortage of foreign exchange
for inputs. Zairian government statistics indicated more than
1,500 single-crop plantations of 100 to 1,000 hectares were operating in Zaire in 1970. By 1980 the number of those operating
commercially had been reduced by half. However, in 1983, new
government policies and a liberalization of domestic prices for
agricultural products had encouraged a modest upturn, particularly in western Zaire and Shaba Region.

POLICE SYSTEM. During the early colonial years, policing of the territory was carried out by the Force Publique. Following World
War I, a sub-unit of the Force was established for police activities, called the Troupes en Service Territorial (Territorial Service Troups). Following independence the police force, at the
time of about 3,000 officers, largely disintegrated. Under a
U.N. program with equipment and funds supplied by the United
States, Nigerian police were brought in to train a new Zairian
police force, the Gendarmerie Nationale. In 1966, the government enacted a series of laws combining all police operations under
a national system within the Interior Ministry. The force was
charged with crime prevention, the apprehension of offenders,
the protection of citizens, and the maintenance of law and order.
During the late 1970s, the force grew to 20,000 men and women.
It was divided into regional units responsible to the local authorities. Training centers were established with Belgian and U.S.
assistance in Kinshasa and Lubumbashi. On August 1, 1972,
however, in a move reflecting the growing trend toward centralization of political and security powers, the force was dissolved by decree and its functions were absorbed by the Gendarmerie Nationale. The move brought policing activities under
the Defense Department and diluted the influence of local authorities over regional garrisons. In 1976, the head of the Gendarmerie

gained the same rank as the chiefs-of-staff of the army, navy, and air force and was answerable only to Mobutu, who held the defense portfolio and was armed forces chief-of-staff.

POLITICAL BUREAU (OF THE MPR). The most powerful organ of state, ranking immediately below the president, the Political Bureau is a highly restricted group of veteran political leaders close to the president and appointed by him, who control most of the political process in Zaire. According to the MPR Manifesto, the Political Bureau "creates policy initiatives which are examined by the Congress of the Party" and, since 1980, by the party's Central Committee. During a period of political liberalization in the late 1970s, the composition of the Political Bureau was altered to allow some of the members to be elected by party members, instead of appointed by the president. Mobutu announced on July 1, 1977, that 12 members would be appointed and 18, two from each region, would be elected. However, the number of appointees was soon increased to 18 with the head-of-state, as president of the Bureau, holding the tie-breaking vote. By 1980 when the size of the Bureau was reduced to 20, the president once again was appointing all the members of the Bureau. Originally, the Political Bureau chose all candidates for the Legislative Council. However, following the liberalization, local party cells were allowed to propose a number of candidates for each given seat in the respective districts. The Political Bureau then "vetted" the candidates. In the legislative elections of 1982, approximately one-half of the candidates proposed by the local cells were rejected.

The Political Bureau sits at the highest level of the political pyramid, under the president. The Central Committee, established in 1980 toward the end of the "liberalization" period, is composed of 120 appointed members, all party stalwarts. Most political debate and consultations now are carried out in the Central Committee. The role of the Legislative Council is primarily to approve the "initiatives" emanating from the party structure. The Congress of the Party, which meets once every five years, plays an even more limited role. According to the constitution, the Political Bureau can dismiss the president for "deviation from the doctrine" (of Mobutism). However, the Founder of the MPR (Mobutu) may not be dismissed. The president has the power to dismiss members of the Bureau, but no more than one-third of the total membership during any one term. The Bureau also controls the succession process. Should the office of the presidency become vacant, the oldest political commissioner assumes the office temporarily. The Bureau schedules an election within 30-60 days and nominates the candidate for the presidency. See CENTRAL COMMITTEE; CONSTITUTION; MOBUTISM; and MOUVEMENT POPULAIRE DE LA REVOLUTION.

POLITICS. Under colonial rule, political activity was strictly prohibited, although following World War II, it began to grow through trade unions, alumni organizations, ethnic associations and "study" groups. The ban on politics was lifted in preparation for local elections in 1959 and political parties proliferated. Many of the parties grew out of the ethnic associations. Some attempts were made to form nationally based parties, but policy disputes and personal rivalries led to many splinterings. At independence, an estimated 125 parties had been created. During the legislative elections of 1965, a number of attempts were made to form broad coalitions, such as Rassemblement des Démocrates Congolais (RADECO), Comité Démocratique Africain (CDA), Front Commun National (FCN), and Confédération Nationale des Associations Congolaises (CONACO). CONACO won a majority of the seats in the 1965 elections and succeeded in forming a government. However, the trend toward political consolidation, if indeed it was a trend, was cut short by yet another political standoff between the president and prime minister and the subsequent military coup. In December 1966, the Corps des Volontaires de la République (CVR) called for an end to all political parties, in order to allow the formation of a single party. All parties except the recently formed MPR were banned by presidential decree in January 1967. Subsequently, politics were tightly controlled by the president and a few close collaborators. In 1977, a degree of liberalization was allowed by permitting multiple candidates within the MPR party for legislative seats and the election of some members of the Political Bureau. The measures led to the infusion of some new blood into the political hierarchy and the elimination of some of the old guard. By 1980, however, most of the measures had been discarded or circumvented. In 1982, a group of parliamentarians announced the formation of a second political party, which is against Zairian law. They were convicted of treason and sentenced to lengthy prison terms.

Most political analysts agree Zairian politics have evolved from the fractious, chaotic scramble at independence into a highly centralized, hierarchical system where some criticism of government is allowed, particularly of the lower and middle levels, but where senior-most officials may not be attacked as long as they are in favor.

POPE JOHN PAUL II. Pope John Paul II visited Zaire in May 1980, the first pontiff ever to do so, and officially ended eight years of strained relations between the Roman Catholic Church and the Zairian government that were due primarily to the authenticity policies. Mobutu, a widower, married for the second time shortly before the visit and asked for a papal blessing for the union. The Pope reportedly was dismayed by the degree to which he found African traditions had been incorporated into church services and litany. However, Zaire statistically has the largest Catholic population in Africa and both sides appeared anxious to make the visit a success. Pope John Paul II visited Zaire a second time in August 1985, during which he canonized a Zairian nun who was killed in the mid-1960s by Simba rebels during the eastern rebellion. See CATHOLIC CHURCH, ROMAN.

POPULATION. A nationwide census used for the 1982 elections revealed a total population of 29,198,334 in Zaire. However, the
Zairian government estimated population had risen to 31 million
by 1985. The population growth rate from 1965-84 was estimated
by UNICEF to be 3.0 percent per year. The ratio of males to
females is 95 to 100, except in urban areas where males outnum-
ber females. More than one-half of the population is believed to
be under 16 years of age despite a rise in life expectancy from
42 years in 1960 to 51 years in 1985. One-fifth of the population
lives in urban areas. Kinshasa, with a population of at least
three million, is the largest city. The fastest growing cities since
independence have been Kinshasa, Mbuji-Mayi, Bandundu, and
Kikwit. Average population density, according to 1985 estimates,
was 12.2 persons per square km, up from 9.2 persons per square
km in 1970. Population density is considered low from a global
perspective, but high in comparison to most central and southern
African nations. Rural population density varies considerably,
from 1-2 persons per square km in the Congo Basin to more than
30 persons per square km in parts of the eastern highlands and
western Bas-Zaire Region. The higher population densities tend
to be located in areas where soil fertility, rainfall and climate are
conducive to farming. The less sparsely populated areas tend to
be in the low wetlands where the soils are unable to support intensive farming. Eighty percent of the Zairian population is of
the Bantu cluster of ethnic groups. The remainder is divided
between peoples of Sudanese, Nilotic, and Pygmy origins. More
than 250 languages and 400 dialects have been identified among
the population living in the national territory. See ETHNIC
GROUPS and BANTU.

PORTS. Zaire has three ports for ocean-going vessels: Matadi,
Boma, and Banana, all lying on the lower part of the Zaire
River. Banana, nearest the Atlantic Ocean, is linked to Boma
and Matadi by road. Matadi is linked to the rest of Zaire by rail
and river networks. The major river ports are Kinshasa, Mbandaka, Bumba, Kisangani, Ubundu, and Kindu on the Zaire River;
Bandundu and Ilebo on the Kasai River; Zongo on the Ubangi
River; and Kongolo and Bukama on the Lualaba (Upper Zaire)
River. The major lake ports are Kalemie on Lake Tanganyika
and Goma on Lake Kivu. See TRANSPORTATION; RAILWAYS;
and RIVERS.

PORTUGAL, RELATIONS WITH. Zairian relations with Portugal are
500 years old, dating to the 1480s when Diogo Cao and other
Portuguese explorers sailed up the mouth of the Zaire River and
came to know the people of the Kongo Kingdom. Initially, relations were close. The Kongo kings asked for missionaries, technical advisors, and occasionally military assistance in exchange
for trade concessions, ivory, and slaves. Zairians went to Portugal to study and represent the Kingdom at the Portuguese royal
court. The relationship became primarily a commercial one in the

early-1600s, as the Kongo Kingdom began to decay and other European maritime powers began to compete for the region's resources. The arrival of the Belgian colonial presence following the Berlin Conference of 1885 completed the displacement of the Portuguese as the primary European power in Zaire. However, relations continued to be close because of the proximity of Angola and Cabinda and the large number of Portuguese traders and merchants who had established themselves in Zaire. Following Zaire's independence, the Zairian government began to openly support the Angolan struggle for independence and the population of Angolan refugees in Zaire grew steadily. These factors strained relations with Portugal. In a speech before the United Nations in 1973, Mobutu condemned Portugal for blocking independence in Angola and its other African colonies. Later that year, the Portuguese embassy in Kinshasa was besieged by an angry mob. The embassy was closed and the Portuguese diplomats went home. The Zairianization policies that began that year also obliged many Portuguese traders, farmers, and businessmen to leave the country, further straining relations. Following Angola's independence, relations began to improve and the return of properties nationalized under Zairianization brought some Portuguese back to Zaire. In the mid-1980s, relations were considered excellent. Mobutu paid a visit to Portugal in 1984 and President Ramalho Eanes also visited Zaire to sign new agreements aimed at encouraging small and medium-size Portuguese businessmen to invest in Zaire.

POVERTY. Although Zaire is considered one of the wealthiest sub-Saharan nations in mineral and human resources, poverty is widespread in the country and affects all but a small, primarily urban elite. Per capita income, which rose to nearly $200 per year in the early 1970s fell to $140 by the mid-1980s, according to U.N. figures. The figures place Zaire at the level of many of the impoverished nations of the Sahel, and below some West African nations (Cameroon, Ivory Coast and Togo) and East African nations (Kenya, Tanzania, and Mozambique). Subsistence agriculture is a way of life for most rural dwellers, who constitute 80 percent of the population, and it often is used by urban dwellers to supplement their incomes. The poverty of most Zairians sharply contrasts with the conspicuous consumption of luxury imports by the elite which, although it represents less than one percent of the population, controls most of the wealth in the country.

PRESIDENCY. The presidency, as envisioned at independence by the Fundamental Law, was meant to be a largely ceremonial office. The power of government was to rest largely with the prime minister and parliament. However, Zaire's first president, Kasavubu, repeatedly used the powers of the presidency to dismiss the prime minister and on several occasions caused a constitutional crisis when parliament refused to accept the dismissal. Following the

coup that brought Mobutu to power, the president gained the
power to issue decrees and ordinances with the power of law.
Since then, with each successive constitution, the presidency
has assimilated political power until it has become the predominant
force in Zairian politics and government. The Bureau du Président (Bureau of the President) is a well-funded branch of government that reportedly has virtually no budget limitations and is
staffed with the best and brightest administrators and cadres.
Mobutu has said that Zaire, in order to be governable, requires
a strong, individual leader, and the Zairian presidency fulfills
that role. The president of Zaire is the president of the MPR
party, which is the supreme institution of state, as well as head
of the six organs of state. Under the current constitution, the
president is elected by direct vote and may serve an unlimited
number of seven-year terms. Mobutu ran unopposed in 1970,
1977, and 1984 and was elected each time by more than 99 percent of the vote.

PRESS. Despite the gradual dominance of party and government
over most aspects of the information process, the Zairian press
on occasions has shown an independence that has caused problems
for journalists and editors. Some reporters have sought to report on cases of corruption and inefficiency in government, but
the focus usually has been limited to lower echelons of the bureaucracy. Journalists have been harassed, arrested, and beaten
for some of their reports. As a result, a great deal of self-
censorship is exercised and criticism is usually limited to targets
that are currently politically acceptable. Daily newspapers include
Elima and Salongo in Kinshasa, Mjumbe in Lubumbashi, and
Boyoma in Kisangani. Zaire, a monthly magazine, is also published and a variety of specialized periodicals are published by
church, academic, and social groups.

PRESSES UNIVERSITAIRES DU ZAIRE (PUZ). The official printing
and publishing house of UNAZA, established in October 1972 to
foster the dissemination of monographs, textbooks, and other
studies of Zaire by Zairian authors and researchers. During its
early years, PUZ published hundreds of titles a year. Following
the economic crisis of the mid-1970s, however, the number of
titles was reduced considerably, due primarily to budget constraints and the rising cost of materials.

PRICE CONTROLS. Like many nations, Zaire has long used a system
of price controls on goods produced within the country. However, the controls have been dictated more by political than
market concerns. Prices paid for agricultural products traditionally have been set low to favor the urban populations and maintain political stability. Prices paid by government marketing
boards to miners for gold, diamonds, and other minerals have
also tended to be low, while petroleum prices at the pump have
been subsidized. These policies, experts argued, tended to

encourage the consumption of products of which Zaire is a net
importer. They also were considered to have discouraged farming
and the legal marketing of minerals and agricultural produce and
as a result, to have contributed to an increase in smuggling, a
decrease in official exports, and a shrinking of the tax base.
In mid-1983, the Zairian government liberalized many of these
policies. Agricultural and mineral prices were still set, but at
levels which removed overall subsidies. In the case of fuel, for
example, high octane gasoline, that is used primarily for personal cars, was set high enough to pay for a continued subsidy
of diesel fuel which is used primarily for commercial transportation. A similar pattern was adopted for agricultural products.
In addition, restrictions were lifted on farming and mineral trading by private individuals, leading to significant increases in
productivity in these sectors.

PRIME MINISTER. The office of prime minister has changed considerably since Zaire became independent 25 years ago. At independence, under the Fundamental Law, the office was considered to be the most powerful position in government, balanced
by parliament and the power of overview of the largely ceremonial presidency. Lumumba, Adoula, and Tshombe were some
of the more notable prime ministers during that period. However,
the lack of definition of the division of power and the absence of
precedence caused a series of constitutional crises. These were
caused by political standoffs between the president and prime
minister when the president tried to dismiss the prime minister,
but parliament refused to support the dismissal. The paralysis of
government that accompanied the crises led to a loss of faith in
the system; as a result, the Constitution of 1964 gave the president unquestioned power to dismiss the prime minister and cabinet and, with parliamentary approval, appoint a new government.
Following the coup that brought Mobutu to power in 1965, the
post was first suspended, then eliminated by decree on October
26, 1966. The Constitution of 1967 institutionalized the move,
making the president head-of-government. In July 1977, however,
following the first Shaba War, as part of a series of liberalization
moves aimed at countering international criticism, the post of
head-of-government was resurrected and named "First State Commissioner" in keeping with a set of new names instituted earlier.
The first state commissioner currently coordinates the activities
of the executive and is considered the second-ranking official in
government. However, the visibility of the position belies its
power, for it has been diluted considerably by the pre-eminence
of the party and Political Bureau, headed by the president, and
by the president's position as president of the Executive Council
(cabinet). Mpinga, Nguza, Umba, and Kengo were some of the
most notable Zairian leaders to serve in the post. However, they
tended to be technocrats and administrators rather than leaders
with their own political bases, and none of them remained long
enough to become a fixture or assimilate enough power to guarantee their longevity.

PRIVATIZATION. A term given in the mid-1980s to the program of reducing state dominance in certain sectors of the Zairian economy, in particular agriculture, transportation, and diamond and gold trading. It is not to be confused with Retrocession, which was the term used in 1974-75 to return enterprises nationalized under Zairianization to private and mixed, private/public ownership. See RETROCESSION and ZAIRIANIZATION.

PROJETS SUCRIERS AU ZAIRE (PSZ). State organ formed on May 8, 1978, to market Zairian sugar and to develop the country's sugar industry. See SUGAR.

PROPHETS. The name given to African religious leaders who developed their own teachings, often based on Christian principles. Over time they developed their own group of followers who accepted their vision of life and the after-life. Prophets were numerous in early Zairian history and although many played small roles, others developed followings large enough to be considered a danger by the authorities. One of the most famous of early Zairian prophets was Dona Beatrice, who lived in the 1700s and came to be called the "Black Joan-of-Arc." She was burned at the stake by Portuguese religious and civilian authorities after she developed a strong following and proclaimed to have delivered a child of virgin birth. Her sect died out. On the other hand, a twentieth century prophet, Simon Kimbangu, developed a following that grew into a major Zairian church. Kimbangu was imprisoned in 1921 after reports of his "miracles" began to disturb the colonial authorities. Kimbangu's death in prison in 1951 led to the rise of Kimbanguism which was formally admitted to the World Council of Churches in 1969, the first of several "synchretist" African churches to be recognized by western church groups. Although prophets have been viewed with some suspicion, since independence their activities are usually tolerated by the government if they do not violate the law and social taboos.

PROTESTANTISM. Protestant missionaries arrived in Zaire after their Roman Catholic counterparts, founding the first Protestant mission among the Kongo in 1878. However, their work expanded quickly and they were responsible for the standardization of and implementation of orthography for numerous Zairian languages in order to publish and disseminate the Bible and hymnals in local tongues. The Belgian colonial authorities, while in some cases favoring Catholic missions, were nevertheless supportive and at independence, 46 Protestant missionary groups were working in Zaire, primarily in the areas of health, education, and the training of African church leaders. The Protestant churches formed the Congo Continuation Committee in 1911 to encourage contact and cooperation and minimize competition among themselves. The CCC became the Congo Protestant Council in 1924. The members formally renamed their group the Church of

Christ in the Congo in 1934 and it became the Church of Christ
in Zaire (Eglise du Christ au Zaire--ECZ) in 1971. It claimed
83 members in 1982 (the Anglicans and Plymouth Brethren were
the only Protestant churches not to join) and seven million members throughout Zaire. With the advent of independence, efforts
intensified to Africanize the church hierarchy. Rev. Pierre
Shaumba became the first Zairian secretary-general of the ECZ
at independence and, following his retirement, Rev. (later Archbishop) Jean Bokeleale was elected. During the authenticity
period of the early 1970s the church came under pressure from
the Zairian government and many foreign missionaries left. However the church continued to grow and by the 1980s, many missions, hospitals, and schools were flourishing entirely under the
leadership of Zairian religious leaders.

PROVINCES. During the colonial era, Zaire was divided administratively into six provinces which were retained for a time following
independence. In June 1963, however, they were subdivided into 21 provinces in an attempt to reduce regional tensions and
strengthen the central government. Their number was reduced
to 12 in April 1966 and under the administrative reorganization
of December 24, 1966, further consolidated into eight provinces
with a separate capital district surrounding Kinshasa. The
provinces were renamed "regions" on July 19, 1972. See RE-
GIONS.

PYGMIES. The earliest known inhabitants of the Congo Basin, the
pygmies are forest dwellers who are best known for their small
size and hunting prowess. Adults usually grow to only about one
meter (3 to 4 feet) in height. Pygmies are thought to be of
Bantu origin, but some anthropologists believe they are more
closely related to Khoisian speakers of southern and eastern
Africa. Seminomadic hunters and gatherers, they traditionally
lived in houses of branches and leaves that allowed them to move
easily. The reasons for and frequency of their displacements
have been a source of much speculation. Some say they avoided
other groups which historically often took them as slaves. They
are also known to have adopted the languages and customs of
their neighbors. Others say the migratory patterns were related
to changes in the source of food. The largest known group in
Zaire inhabits the forest and swamps above Lac Mai-Ndombe in
northwestern Zaire. This group is part of a larger pygmy group
inhabiting parts of northern Congo, Gabon, and Cameroon. Another major group lives in northeastern Zaire's Ituri Forest and
parts of Kivu northeast of the Lualaba and Lomami Rivers.

- R -

"RADIO TROTTOIRE." Literally translated, "sidewalk radio," Radio
Trottoire is the overactive rumor-mill that even Mobutu has

acknowledged is so influential as to occasionally oblige reaction on the part of the government.

RAILWAYS. Five separate railway systems totalling 5,169 kms operate in Zaire. They were owned and operated jointly by government agencies and private companies until 1974 when they were nationalized under Zairianization and taken over by the newly established Société Nationale des Chemins de Fer Zairois (SNCZ) (National Zairian Railway Company). Railways connecting river ports were the main means by which the colonial administration sought to evacuate raw materials from the territory and bring in manufactured goods. The railways were built at great human and material cost, primarily between the 1890s and 1930s. Thousands of laborers, local and foreign, as well as hundreds of European technicians died from disease, malnutrition, and accidents during the construction. Since the mid-1970s deteriorating track and rolling stock and a shortage of spare parts and fuel have been constant problems for most of the lines.

The oldest line is the Chemin de Fer Matadi-Kinshasa (CFMK), which links the ocean port of Matadi to Kinshasa and the river and rail network that services most of the country. Construction began in 1889 on the line to Thysville and was completed in 1898. Construction on the extension to Leopoldville was begun in the 1920s and completed in 1932. The CFMK provides the only national land link between the Atlantic Ocean and 95 percent of the territory which, because of the cataracts on the Zaire River between Kinshasa and Matadi, is essentially landlocked.

The longest system, the Chemin de Fer Kinshasa-Dilolo-Lubumbashi (KDL), connects the mining area of southern Shaba Region to the port of Ilebo on the Kasai River and ultimately to Kinshasa by the Kasai and Zaire rivers. The 1,645-km railway actually does not reach Kinshasa, although plans have existed since the 1920s for an Ilebo-Kinshasa leg. The first section of the line, from Elisabethville to Bukama, which lies on the upper end of the navigable part of the Lualaba, was begun in 1911 and completed in 1918. In 1923, construction of a 1,123-km line connecting Bukama to Ilebo was begun and completed in 1928. The final 522-km leg of the system from Tenke to Dilolo was completed in 1931 in order to connect the KDL system to the Benguela Railway through Angola. The Dilolo-Benguela route was widely used to export minerals from Shaba to the Atlantic port of Lobito in Angola until the Angolan civil war closed the Benguela Railway in 1975.

In eastern Zaire, the Chemin de Fer des Grands Lacs (CFL) is a 960-km truncated system that connects the navigable portion of the Lualaba River to the navigable portion of the upper Zaire River. The Lualaba flows into the Zaire River but commercial navigation is impeded by cataracts between Kongolo and Kindu and between Ubundu and Kisangani. The first 125-km section of the line from Kisangani to Ubundu was opened in 1906. The second, 355-km section from Kindu to Kongolo was opened in 1911

and extended to Kabalo in 1938. A 275-km branch was later
added to extend the system eastward to Kalemie on Lake Tanganyika, where goods may be shipped across the lake by steamer to
Tanzania and transported by rail to Dar es Salaam. In 1956, the
CFL system was linked to the KDL system by a 201-km branch
from Kabalo to Kamina.

The fourth system, the Chemin de Fer de Mayumbe (CFM) is
a 140-km line linking the ocean port of Boma in Bas-Zaire Region to the agricultural area of Tshela near Cabinda.

The fifth system, the Chemins de Fer Vicinaux du Zaire
(CVZ) is a 1,025-km narrow-gauge railway in northeastern Zaire
that links agricultural areas in Mugbere and Isiro in the east
and Bondo to the north to the port of Aketi on the Itumbiri
River, a tributary of the Zaire River. The line was extended
to Bumba on the Zaire River in 1973.

A multimillion dollar plan was announced by the Zairian government in 1984 to rehabilitate and modernize the railways. It
was part of a $135 million dollar project to improve transportation infrastructure to be financed by the African Development
Bank, the World Bank, and a number of governments in Western
Europe and North America. See NATIONAL WAY and TRANSPORTATION.

RAIN FOREST. A dense, triple-canopy, tropical forest that covers
most of the Congo Basin and the northern third of Zairian territory.
Heavy rainfall, combined with a thin layer of topsoil that has been
leached of many nutrients, makes the rain forest a delicate ecological entity that is poorly suited to intensive farming. Timbering and rubber collection have been widely carried out in the
forest, but the large number of natural barriers have prevented
the widespread deforestation that has occurred in other parts of
the world. The Zairian rain forest is one of the least explored
regions on earth. The presence of many diseases makes farming
and animal husbandry difficult. As a result, it is one of the
most sparsely populated regions in Zaire. The forest is believed
to hide interesting archeological artifacts and possibly important
mineral reserves; however, the dense canopy makes aerial surveys
difficult. The area is known to contain millions of species of
flora and fauna that have yet to be studied by science and important hydroelectrical and piscatorial potential. Environmentalists
say intense commercial farming is not possible in the area without serious damage to the ecology, but controlled exploitation of
such goods as pharmaceutical products, fisheries, nuts, and rubber
is possible. See CONGO BASIN.

RAINFALL. Rainfall in Zaire ranges from 100 to 220 centimeters (40
to 88 inches) per year. The zones of heaviest rainfall are in
the Congo Basin, the rain forest of northern Zaire, and the eastern highlands. Zones of least rainfall lie in the savannas of
Shaba and Kivu Regions and westernmost Bas-Zaire. No region
of Zaire suffers from chronic drought. In addition, the fact that

Zaire straddles the Equator means northern Zaire's dry season
(November through March) occurs during southern Zaire's rainy
season, and vice-versa. As a result, Zaire's main rivers (unlike
the Niger and Nile rivers, which are susceptible to drastic seasonal fluctuations that sometimes prevent navigation) are navigable the entire year. The one notable exception is the Ubangi
River, which lies entirely north of the Equator and is only navigable six months of the year.

RAMZANI BAYA. A former director of the Zairian News Agency, AZAP,
Ramzani was named high commissioner for information in February 1985 and added the posts and telecommunications portfolio
to his responsibilities when the two departments were merged in
mid-1986.

REBELLIONS. Since independence, Zaire has experienced a number
of rebellions, several of them secessions and the most serious of
which occurred immediately after independence. The first, more
accurately described as a mutiny, occurred five days after independence when the Force Publique mutinied because of frustra-
tion over low pay and the lack of advancement opportunities.
The mutiny led to a more rapid Africanization of the officer
corps. The first major rebellion occurred on July 11, 1960, when
Tshombe, angered by the lack of CONAKAT representation in the
central government and encouraged by private mining interests,
declared the secession of Katanga Province and formed an independent state. The secession was declared at an end on January
14, 1963. On August 8, 1960, Albert Kalonji, angered by the
massacre of Luba allegedly by government troops and taking advantage of the disorganization in the central government, declared the secession of the diamond-rich portion of southern
Kasai and formed the Independent Mining State of South Kasai.
That secession ended in early 1961 and Kalonji joined the Adoula
government-of-reconciliation. The third major secession was declared in eastern Zaire on November 10, 1960, following the dismissal of the Lumumba government by Kasavubu and the vote by
the United Nations to seat the Kasavubu delegation instead of the
rival Lumumba delegation. The assassination of Lumumba, announced February 13, 1961, helped Gizenga consolidate the regime. Several members of the Gizenga government in Stanleyville
were named to the Adoula government in 1961. Gizenga was arrested by Adoula in 1962 and was freed by Tshombe in 1964.
He returned to Stanleyville where, on September 7, 1964, he declared the People's Republic of the Congo (not to be confused
with the People's Republic declared in Congo/Brazzaville in 1973).
At its peak the PRC was recognized by 13 foreign governments,
but its excesses led to the Belgo-American airdrop on Stanleyville and an operation by the Congolese army backed by foreign
mercenaries that retook control of most of the eastern region by
1965. In April 1964, meanwhile, a former lieutenant of Gizenga,
Mulele, launched a rebellion in Kwilu Province, a region bordering

Leopoldville, that included bombing attacks in the capital. That
rebellion was ended in 1965. Following the Mobutu coup, there
were other, smaller rebellions, in particular a third eastern rebellion sparked by an army mutiny in 1966 and followed by the
occupation of Bukavu in Kivu Province by mercenaries and Katangan Gendarmes for three months in 1967, and an uprising in
Idiofa in Kwilu sub-region in 1978. All were put down with relative ease. The most noted in recent history, however, were the
two rebellions (called invasions by the Zairian government) of
Shaba Region in 1977 and 1978 by the FNLC led by former Katangan Gendarme Bumba. These were put down with the help
of foreign troops, including an air assault in 1978 on the mining
center of Kolwezi by Zairian, French, and Belgian troops. Currently, only one rebellion can be said to be still active on Zairian
territory. It is that of the PRP which has controlled a small
portion of remote territory in southern Kivu since 1964 and refuses to acknowledge the authority of the central government.
The PRP kidnapped a group of foreign students from Tanzania in
the mid-1970s and staged relatively minor attacks on the town of
Moba on Lake Tanganyika in 1984 and 1985. However, the PRP
has never posed a threat to the central government, which maintains it is based and financed from neighboring countries.

REGIE DE DISTRIBUTION D'EAU ET D'ELECTRICITE (REGIDESO).
A government agency responsible for water and electric utility
administration and development. REGIDESO is responsible for
the water works in Zaire. In 1985, REGIDESO administered 7
million meters of pipe to 202,828 registered clients. It employed
4,180 agents and pumped 1.75 mil. cubic meters of water during
the year. It also furnished electricity provided by small petroleum-
powered complexes to about 23,000 clients in 40 towns in the interior until 1979 when these operations were turned over to the
Société Nationale d'Electricité (SNEL), the national electrical
power agency.

REGIONS. Administrative sub-division of Zairian territory, called
provinces until the administrative reforms of July 19, 1972.
Zaire is divided into eight regions and the capital district of
Kinshasa. The regions include Bas-Zaire, Bandundu, Equateur,
Haut-Zaire, Kasai Occidental, Kasai Oriental, Kivu, and Shaba.
The regions are divided into 43 urban and rural sub-regions.
Rural sub-regions are further divided into zones. Under the
Constitution of 1964, which replaced the Fundamental Law of
post-independence, the provinces were granted considerable autonomy including their own assemblies and executive branches.
With the advent of the Mobutu government and the trend toward
centralization of power, however, the regions lost most of their
powers. Under the Constitution of 1974 the regional assemblies
became consultative rather than legislative and laws were passed
in Kinshasa that applied equally to all regions. The rise of the
party to the position of supreme institution of state further

weakened regional autonomy. Currently, the party, the administrative and legislative branches of government, and the military are subdivided along regional lines. The regions are administered by commissioners, formerly governors, who hold considerable power over the local administration. However, regional party officials and local military commanders also wield considerable power. Under the Mobutu government, commissioners and military commanders traditionally have been assigned to regions other than their home areas. The purpose has been to combat tribalism and regionalism. However, critics note the system also has encouraged the rise of regional officials who may be less interested in the well-being of their region and its people than in pleasing the central authorities. See ADMINISTRATION and CONSTITUTIONS.

RELIGIONS. Although Zaire officially is a secular state and Mobutism, the MPR, and country officially are placed above God, most Zairians are deeply religious and are free to practice any religion as long as it is not subversive or abusive to others. The influence of Christian missions has been strong since the 1970s and two-thirds of all Zairians are estimated to avow some sort of ties with Christianity, although their faith may be mixed with traditional practices and beliefs. The remaining one-third are considered to have been relatively untouched by outside religious influences and adhere to traditional, sometimes called animist, beliefs. An estimated 40 percent of the population practice some form of Roman Catholicism, 15 percent are said to be Protestant, and 10 percent adhere to smaller Christian-related groups, such as Kimbanguism, Rosicrucian, Celeste, etc. About one percent of the population is considered Muslim. Figures reported by the churches tend to be higher. See CHURCH; CATHOLIC CHURCH, ROMAN; ISLAM; KIMBANGUISM; MISSIONS; and PROTESTANTISM.

REPUBLIQUE POPULAIRE DU CONGO (RPC) (PEOPLE'S REPUBLIC OF THE CONGO). Short-lived people's republic proclaimed on September 7, 1964, during the rebellion in eastern Congo. The RPC dissolved following the Belgo-American mission to free Stanleyville and Paulis and the ANC and mercenary offensive to retake control of the territory during 1965. At its peak, however, it was recognized by 13 foreign governments and its delegations were seated at some international conferences. Not to be confused with the People's Republic of the Congo (Brazzaville) declared in the former French Congo by Marien Ngouabi on June 24, 1973. See MOUVEMENT NATIONAL CONGOLAIS; GIZENGA; GBENYE; REBELLIONS; and SIMBAS.

RETROCESSION. The official name given to the policy, announced December 30, 1974, of reversing Zairianization and returning nationalized foreign-owned enterprises, primarily farms and businesses, to their former owners. Under Retrocession partial ownership, up to 40 percent, of large enterprises and those operating in certain "strategic" sectors also was returned to the private sector. The degree of private ownership allowed in these ventures was later expanded to 60 percent.

RHODES, CECIL. British explorer and empire builder who extended British influence over parts of southern Africa and competed against the agents of Leopold II for control of the copper belt that traverses Zambia and Zaire's Shaba Region.

RICE. The second most important cereal in cultivation in Zaire, rice is Zaire's fifth largest crop, after manioc, sugarcane, bananas, and maize. The country produced 165,000 metric tons per year at independence, primarily from small landholdings often of less than one hectare. Production fell drastically, however, following independence and in 1965 only 56,000 tons were produced. Production began to rise in the 1970s, reaching 135,000 tons in 1975 and 145,000 tons in 1982, according to Banque du Zaire figures. Because of the popularity of rice as a staple among urban dwellers, the Zairian government is obliged to continue to import significant amounts and rice is often included among foreign aid food shipments.

RIVERS. Zaire has more than 12,000 kms of navigable rivers that were largely responsible for the early exploration and development of the territory. Aside from a few rivers that form part of the hydro-system of the Great Rift Valley lakes in eastern Zaire, most of Zaire's rivers are part of the Congo Basin system, of which the backbone is the Zaire River, the world's second largest river, after the Amazon, in terms of volume of water (120,000 cubic m/second). The system straddles the Equator and drains regions in both the northern and southern hemispheres, which have opposite rainy seasons. As a result, the system for the most part is navigable during the entire year. However, it is truncated by three sets of cataracts that prevent commercial navigation between Kinshasa and Matadi, Ubundu and Kisangani, and Kongolo and Kindu. Were it not for the cataracts, the Zaire River would provide a direct shipping route between the mines of Shaba Region, bordering southern Africa, and the West African Atlantic coast. To circumvent the cataracts, a system of railways was constructed between 1890 and 1932 that remains today. See RAILWAYS and NATIONAL WAY.

The headwaters of the Zaire River are formed by the Lualaba River that rises near the border with Zambia. Tributaries of the Lualaba, or Upper Zaire River as it is called by the Zairian government, include the Lufira, Luvua, Luama, Elila rivers in Shaba and Kivu Regions, and the Lomami, Aruwimi, and Itimbiri rivers below Kisangani. One of the major tributary systems of the Zaire River is the Kasai River system which extends into northern Shaba, the two Kasai, and southern Bandundu regions. The port of Ilebo on the Kasai River is a major shipment point

for Shaba minerals being exported via the National Way. The
Kasai's major tributaries are the Kwango, Kwilu, Lukenie, and
Sankuru rivers. A second tributary system drains the southern
part of Equateur Region via the Tshuapa, Lomela, and Songela
rivers, which join the Zaire River at Mbandaka. A third tributary system is the Ubangi River system that drains the Equateur
region via the Lua and Giri rivers, which are navigable only
during the rainy season. See WATERWAYS; PORTS; TRANS-
PORTATION; ZAIRE RIVER; and individual river listings.

ROADS. Zaire is estimated to have 145,000 kms of roads, most of
them built before independence. In 1985, the government said
2,600 kms of asphalted roads existed in the country and 40,000
kms of treated roads were being maintained. About one-half of
the system consisted of dirt tracks. The rural road system was
built primarily to connect agricultural and mineral producing
areas to the river and rail systems. Major asphalted highways
in western Zaire link Kinshasa to Boma via Matadi and Kinshasa
to Kikwit, and in the southeast link the mining centers of Kolwezi
and Lubumbashi in Shaba to northern Zambia. Most other highways are either dirt or gravel and required frequent maintenance
during the rainy seasons. Most roads in Zaire were considered
to have deteriorated considerably during the years following independence and many of the roads through lowlands were impassable
during heavy rains. The paving of the Boma-Matadi and
Kinshasa-Kikwit roads were the notable exceptions. A series of
construction and improvement projects were begun in the late
1970s and intensified in the 1980s. The U.S. and Japanese governments launched bridge building and road improvement programs
as part of their bilateral aid programs. The Japanese helped
build the first bridge across the Zaire River. Built at Matadi
and completed in 1983, the suspension bridge improved transportation links between the western part of Bas-Zaire and the
rest of the country. In the 1980s, USAID began a program to
build bridges in the Bandundu area aimed at replacing the ferries and log-crossings that were considered the weakest links in
the system. Another program was launched to repair and refurbish the 300 river ferries in operation in the country. The
government agency Office des Routes was created in 1972 to oversee road maintenance and construction. Like most agencies, the
OR suffered from a lack of funds. In many cases, the agency
concentrated its maintenance efforts on the larger public highways
and allowed private companies or local residents to take responsibility for the smaller, less travelled roads. See TRANSPORTA-
TION and RAILWAYS.

ROBERTO, HOLDEN. The leader of the Frente Nacional de Libertaçao de Angola (FNLA) that fought against the Portuguese during
the struggle for Angolan independence and fought against the
MPLA and UNITA factions during the civil war that followed independence. Roberto, who was related by marriage to Mobutu,

received considerable logistical support from the Zairian government during the early years of the civil war and reportedly received covert U.S. assistance through the Zairian government. However, he began to fade from the international scene following an agreement between the Zairian and Angolan government in 1978 to end hostilities and cease support for each other's opposition movements. FNLA activities resumed on a smaller scale in the early 1980s, but Roberto did not reappear until U.S. President Reagan's administration announced its intention to resume covert aid to UNITA guerrillas in mid-1986. During that year, Roberto visited Washington and was promised $200,000 of "nonlethal" equipment and supplies by a group of retired U.S. military officers. See FRENTE NACIONAL DE LIBERTAÇAO DE ANGOLA.

ROGET, LEON (CAPTAIN). The first commander of the Force Publique, Roget was appointed by Leopold II in 1886 to form an army for the Congo Free State. He forged the Force in two years using a core of European officers and African soldiers hired from West and East African territories.

ROUND TABLE CONFERENCES. The first and most famous Round Table Conference was held in January 1960 following the riots and political unrest that began on January 4, 1959, and the inconclusive elections of December 1959. Hastily organized (the Belgian government only announced its intention to "form a democracy" in the Congo on January 13, 1960), the conference from the Belgian point-of-view was held to resolve differences with some of the African parties primarily over the timetable of independence. These differences had led to the boycott of the elections by some of the most important parties and a threat of renewed violence. The conference was to open January 20, but the 45 Congolese delegates, led by Kasavubu and Lumumba, demanded that two preconditions be granted: first, that a date be set for independence and secondly, that the resolutions of the conference be binding. In a move that was widely interpreted as a victory for the Congolese, the Belgian government agreed. As a result, the date for independence was set for June 30, 1960, and the conference opened January 25.

A second Round Table Conference began on April 26, 1960, and continued into May, aimed at examining the financial affairs of the soon-to-be-independent nation and establishing the framework for self-government. The Fundamental Law, drafted to act as a constitution during the initial years of independence, was passed by the Belgian Parliament on May 19, 1960. The Law repealed the Colonial Charter and set up a political system modeled on Belgium's. See COLONIAL CHARTER and FUNDAMENTAL LAW.

RUBBER. One of the principal commercial crops of Zaire, rubber was one of the first exports of the Congo Free State, and the harsh labor practices used in its extraction were the main cause of the public outcry that led to the end of the CFS and the beginning of the Belgian colonial era. Rubber is grown throughout the tropical forest area of northern Zaire, but is a major crop primarily in the Kisangani area. At independence, Zaire produced 40,000 metric tons per year, of which virtually all was exported. Production declined during the political instability of the early 1960s, reaching 20,000 in 1965. It began to rise again and peaked in 1973 at 45,000 tons, of which 30,000 tons were exported. With Zairianization and the economic crisis beginning in the mid-1970s, rubber production began a sharp decline and according to the Banque du Zaire, Zaire produced only 17,000 tons in 1982.

RUWENZORI MOUNTAINS. The Ruwenzori mountain range, known as the "Mountains of the Moon" because of its stark, desolate landscape, is considered Africa's highest. Located on the Zaire-Uganda border south of Lake Mobutu, the range lies in one of the most remote and sparsely populated regions of Africa. It is inhabited primarily by Pygmies and Nilotic peoples.

RUZIZI RIVER. A medium-sized river, 120 kms in length, unnavigable because of cataracts, the Ruzizi flows from Lake Tanganyika into Lake Kivu in eastern Kivu Region. Because of the difference in altitudes of the two lakes, the river generates considerable hydroelectrical potential and a 12,600-kilowatt installation near Kamanyola supplies electricity to Bukavu.

RWANDA, RELATIONS WITH. One of three former Belgian colonies, Rwanda's ties with Zaire have been generally strong. A small, densely populated country of 4.5 million inhabitants lying on the Great Rift Valley across Lake Kivu from eastern Zaire, Rwanda and Burundi were originally German colonies that were placed under Belgian trusteeship following World War I. Relations were good at independence, but were strained in 1967 when Congolese army units mutinied over the lack of pay and, joined by foreign mercenaries and former members of the Gendarmerie Katangaise, tried to bring down the central government. Loyal Zairian troops succeeded in driving the rebels first to Bukavu, then into Rwanda. The Zairian government's request for extradition was denied, leading to a break in diplomatic relations on January 11, 1968. An OAU committee was able to negotiate a compromise and the mercenaries were evacuated by the Red Cross in April 1968. Relations were re-established in February 1969 and strengthened by the establishment in September 1976 of the Communauté Economique des Pays des Grands Lacs (CEPGL) with its seat in Gisenye, Rwanda. Ties remained strong through the early 1980s with Presidents Mobutu and Juvenal Habyarimana exchanging many vists.

- S -

SALARIES see WAGES AND SALARIES

"SALONGO." Meaning "work" in Lingala, "Salongo" was a term coined in the early 1970s to denote labor holidays set aside for community clean-up activities. Local party leaders were entrusted with organizing this activity and prominent leaders were expected to make an appearance. Enthusiasm for the practice, however, waned in the late 1970s and by the 1980s it was primarily party cadres, students, and other groups organized by the government that were the primary participants.

SAMBALA. A people of the Tetela ethnic group that, through association with the Afro-Arabs and Belgians, eventually became identified as a separate group. Sambala was the name given to the people of the Tetela and Kusu groups who joined Ngongo Lutete to pacify and occupy the Maniema area of what is now western Kivu toward the end of the nineteenth century. Following the end of the war to drive the Arabs from Congolese territory, they were placed in charge of the area. They led the other ethnic groups in the region in access to education and economic advancement. See KUSU and TETELA.

SAMPASSA KAWETA MILOMBE. An economist and government official long associated with youth and education, Sampassa was born January 23, 1942, at Likasi in Shaba Region. He was educated in Shaba and received a degree in Economic and Financial Sciences from the Université Officielle du Congo (now UNAZA/ Lubumbashi). He served as minister of youth and sports on a number of occasions from July 12, 1970, until June 1, 1975, when he was appointed secretary-general of the JMPR, the youth wing of the party. He was appointed state commissioner for culture and the arts on February 18, 1981, and state commissioner for secondary and university education on May 7, 1982.

SAO SALVADOR. The Portuguese name for the capital of the Kongo Kingdom, located in what is now northern Angola. The name was changed from Mbanza Kongo by Affonso I, after his conversion to Christianity. See MBANZA KONGO.

SATELLITES. Zaire uses satellites for telephone, telex, and telegraph communications, relying on a land station at N'sele outside Kinshasa for links to most of the regional capitals and for international connections to Europe and the Americas. Automatic dialing service was inaugurated to Belgium in 1984, to France in 1985 and to the United States in 1986. Zairian interregional telecommunications are heavily reliant on satellites because of the decaying network of overland, long-lines. Some satellite service is also used to transmit radio and television programs to regional broadcasting stations. The Etudes des Ressources Terrestres par

Satellite agency works on mapping Zaire's mineral and agricultural resources using data furnished by LANDSAT and other services. See COMMUNICATIONS and TELECOMMUNICATIONS.

SCHOOLS see EDUCATION

SCHRAMME, JEAN. A Belgian former mercenary who participated in the Katanga secession of 1960-63, and in 1967 led a group of former Katangan Gendarmes in an invasion of northeastern Zaire in an attempt to topple the central government. When the rebellion was crushed, Schramme disappeared for a time, but resurfaced later in Brazil. In April 1986, a Belgian court at Mons convicted Schramme in absentia of murdering a Belgian diamond dealer, Maurice Quintin, in Yumbi in 1967. Schramme was sentenced to 20 years at hard labor. However, Brazil refused to extradite him because he was married to a Brazilian citizen. Schramme said he ordered the killing of Quintin because the businessman had been spying for the Mobutu government.

SECRET POLICE see AGENCE NATIONALE DE DOCUMENTATION

SECURITY. Zairian internal security under the Mobutu government is considered efficient, relying on a large network of informants and foreign technical advisers at different times from Belgium, France, the United States, Morocco, North Korea, and, most recently, Israel. The security network, which operates independently of all other organs, reports directly to the president and is well endowed with its own communications system. It has been credited with unmasking several attempted coups and, reportedly, dozens of assassination plots. Security is weakest in the remote rural areas of northern, eastern and southern Zaire, primarily because of a lack of communications facilities, personnel, and material resources in those areas. As a result, some of these areas have been the scenes of the most successful attempts to undermine the authority of the government. See AGENCE NATIONALE DE DOCUMENTATION.

SENDWE, JASON. An early political leader who founded BALUBAKAT to represent the Luba in Katanga Province. He tried to mediate the conflict between Lunda and Luba in Katanga in 1960-61. He was assassinated in Albertville (now Kalemie) in June 1964 during an internal dispute in the BALUBAKAT.

SENGELE. An ethnic group living west of Lake Mai-Ndombe in Bandundu Region. Part of the Mongo language group, the Sengele differed from many Mongo groups because of a more complex and hierarchical social structure.

SHABA REGION. Shaba, meaning "copper" in Swahili, is the name of the mineral-rich southeastern Region of Zaire that, after Kinshasa, is the wealthiest and most developed in Zaire. Called

Katanga until 1971, Shaba has an area of 496,965 square kms and
a population of 3,762,806 (1982). Shaba is rich in copper, cobalt, tin, tungsten, gold, and other by-products of copper ores,
and its exports supply more than one-half of the government's
revenues and two-thirds of its foreign exchange. Yet, Shaba is
more closely linked historically, ethnically, and economically to
southern Africa than to the societies of the West African coast.
When Leopold II's agents managed to lay claim to the region in
the 1890s, beating out the British explorer Cecil Rhodes, they
found local residents already hostile to outside powers. During
the early years of the Congo Free State, the region was run at
first by the privately owned Comité Special du Katanga. In
1910, however, Leopold II placed the territory under a vice
governor-general, separate from the rest of the CFS. It was
brought under the central colonial administration in 1933 in a
move that was widely criticized by local and foreign residents
of the region alike. Periodic uprisings during the colonial era
were harshly put down. At independence, Tshombe's CONAKAT
party swept the local elections, leading to the formation of a one-
party provincial government. Unhappy with CONAKAT's representation in the central government, polarized along ethnic lines
and encouraged by private commercial interests and an organization of European residents called the Union Katangaise, Katanga
seceded on July 11, 1960, 12 days after independence. The
Katanga secession held world attention during the following two
years as Tshombe stalled mediation efforts and the United Nations attempted carrot-and-stick approaches to reunification.
Congo's first prime minister, Patrice Lumumba, and U.N. Secretary-
General Dag Hammarskjöld died in Katanga, and thousands of Luba
and Lunda were killed during the secession in internecine fighting. Only after two military actions by U.N. forces that were
widely condemned by some members of the international community
was the Katanga secession declared ended on January 14, 1963.

Shaba returned to the front pages of the international press
on March 8, 1977, when a group of dissidents, based in Angola,
attacked and successively occupied a series of towns along the
railway that links Shaba's mining centers to Angola's Benguela
Railway. The guerrillas, called the Front National pour la
Libération du Congo (FNLC), were primarily of the Lunda ethnic
group and were led by Nathaniel Bumba, a former officer in the
Gendarmerie Katangaise that supported the Katangan secession
and invaded Kivu in 1967 in an attempt to overthrow the Mobutu
government. Sometimes called the "Eighty Day War," the first
Shaba invasion was launched not as a secession attempt but in
the hope of sparking a general uprising in Zaire. However, the
FNLC stopped before it reached the important mining town of
Kolwezi and was eventually driven back into Angola by the Zairian
army, backed by 1,400 Moroccan troops with French support.
In 1978, the FNLC attacked again. This time, however, it infiltrated the area around Kolwezi and in a lightning attack on
May 3 seized the city and halted work at the mines and other

industrial installations in another effort to bring down the central government. The guerrillas then went on a week-long looting and killing spree in which 1,000 Zairians and 200 foreigners were eventually killed. Zairian armed forces, backed by 700 French Foreign Legionnaires, were parachuted into Kolwezi and retook the city after several days of bloody fighting. More than 1,000 Belgian paratroopers were also dropped on the city of Kamina to the north. The U.S. government supplied equipment and transport that included 18 C-141 planes. The guerrillas filtered out of the territory in stolen vehicles, primarily into Zambia. A peacekeeping force composed of Moroccan, Senegalese, and Togolese troops was deployed while Zairian army units were reorganized, reequipped, and retrained. Charges of Angolan and Cuban support for the rebels brought condemnation in international forums, but the two attacks also focused attention on the inability of the armed forces to defend the national territory and the high degree of political and military centralization of the Mobutu government. The invasions led to a measure of liberalization in Zairian politics and to diplomatic initiatives to resolve the differences between the Zairian and Angolan governments. Zaire had supported the FNLA faction in the Angolan civil war and reportedly was supplying arms to the FNLA for attacks on Angolan installations. After Shaba II, however, Zaire and Angola agreed to cease hostilities and stop supporting each other's opposition guerrillas, and the FNLC leadership went into exile in Europe. Zaire and Angola established diplomatic relations later that year.

In the early 1980s, a series of clashes and cross-border raids by Zairian and Zambian troops raised tensions in the region. However, Presidents Mobutu and Kenneth Kaunda expressed a desire for negotiated solutions to the conflicts and a joint commission was established to resolve disputes. In 1984 and 1985, PRP guerrillas based in the mountains of northern Shaba, near Kivu Region, attacked the town of Moba in an attempt to embarrass the Zairian government, but government troops quickly regained control of the town.

SHI. A group of Bantu related people living in the highlands of Kivu Region near Bukavu between Lake Tanganyika and Lake Kivu.

SILVER. A relatively small amount of silver is produced as a by-product of gold mining by SOMINKI and GECAMINES in Shaba Region. Zaire produced four million ounces of silver at independence, but production had declined to 1.2 million ounces by 1984.

SIMBAS. Simba (Swahili for "lion") was the name taken by rebels during the eastern rebellions of the early 1960s. The Simbas gained fame by using potions and incantations that they believed rendered them invulnerable, turned bullets into water, and incapacitated the enemy. The Simbas were primarily young recruits,

average age 15 years, who were often drugged and who fought
with a ferocious fearlessness that in many of the initial battles
routed government troops. Accounts from local residents following the liberation of the region revealed that the Simbas also engaged in gruesome torture and atrocities against the local population. The "Simba" rebellion was ended in 1965. See REBEL-
LIONS.

SINGA BOYEMBE MOSAMBAYI. One of the sponsors of the coup
d'etat that brought Mobutu to power, Singa has remained at the
senior political and military levels virtually since independence.
Born on October 10, 1932, in Ibembo, Haut-Zaire Region, Singa
was educated in Haut-Zaire and Kasai Regions and received military training at the Ecole Royale de Gendarmerie Belge in Belgium,
and in the United States and Israel. He was made commissioner
(governor) of Shaba Region in 1978 following the Shaba invasions
and became army chief-of-staff on January 1, 1980. He was
named to the Central Committee on September 2, 1980.

SLAVERY. Slavery was practiced to a certain degree by traditional
Zairian societies, usually as part of the spoils of war, but it
reached mass proportions in the sixteenth and seventeenth centuries because of the demand for cheap labor in the Americas.
Between 1500 and 1900, when slavery was ended, as many as 30
million Africans may have been shipped against their will from
ports on the central Atlantic coast to "markets" primarily in Brazil, Central America, and the Caribbean. An estimated three
million persons were shipped from what is now Zaire and during
the height of the trade, 50,000 were shipped annually. Meanwhile, in eastern Zaire, Arab and African slave traders exported
an estimated 50,000 to 70,000 slaves per year to markets in
Arabia and the Middle East. Territorial wars and the battles
fought to capture slaves destroyed a large portion of the region's
population. Entire villages were often wiped out in order to
capture a few dozen "exportable" slaves. In the late eighteenth
century, Denmark, Sweden, and the Netherlands abolished slavery. England abolished the trade in 1807 and slavery itself in
1833. Portugal followed in 1835 and Franch in 1848. By the mid-
nineteenth century, all European countries had abolished the
practice, although it continued unofficially for decades afterwards.
The importation of slaves was prohibited by the U.S. Congress
in 1808 and the United States abolished slavery with the Emanci-
pation Proclamation of January 1, 1863, although it was not until
the Civil War was ended in 1865 that abolition came into force
throughout the nation. The social implications of slavery in
African society have been examined in great detail by academicians.
Most agree slavery in the traditional African context did not carry
the degree of social and economic dispossession that it assumed
when it was converted into an export industry. In traditional
African society, slaves had rights, a heritage, and could improve
their lot within certain constraints, unlike the non-African

system, in which slaves were owned by the master, had no legal rights, and could expect nothing better for their descendants.

SMUGGLING. Smuggling of certain Zairian agricultural and mineral products traditionally has been high. Banque du Zaire officials estimated in the early 1980s that one-half of Zaire's diamonds were being marketed outside official channels. Gold, ivory, coffee, and tea are other commodities cited as heavily smuggled items. A primary reason for smuggling was the low prices paid by government marketing boards, taxes, and restrictions on private participation in the exploitation of minerals in particular. However, another reason was said to be the weakness of the Zairian currency and shortages of consumer goods in the remote regions where many of the commodities were produced. Because of domestic shortages, smugglers in Kasai Oriental, Shaba, and Haut-Zaire regions often traded illegally across the border for fuel, food, cloth, and manufactured goods. In 1983, the Zairian government liberalized the commercialization of gold and diamonds and raised domestic prices for many commodities. In the six months following the move, revenue from diamonds alone reportedly doubled.

SOCIAL SERVICE. A system of welfare and social service was set up at independence much along the lines of the colonial system. However, as in many African nations, the effectiveness of the system declined over the years because of inflation, austerity measures, corruption, and inefficiency. Today, a pensioner, veteran, or in some cases, a disabled person is entitled to a nominal stipend. However, when the individual is able to collect it, it rarely provides more than a few days' sustenance. As a result, Zairians requiring social assistance depend for the most part on family and the strained services provided by churches and charitable organizations.

SOCIALISM. Socialism, like communism and capitalism, has been officially condemned by party ideologists who call it a foreign ideology and advocate instead an "authentic Zairian nationalism" that is "neither to the right nor the left but forward." However, some aspects of socialism can be discerned in government policies that call, for instance, for universal health care, an end to hunger, and a heavy degree of government involvement in the economy. Since the economic crisis of the mid-1970s, however, Zairian economic policies have been drifting away from the centralization common to many socialist-oriented governments and toward privatization, with increasing private participation in the mining, agriculture, and transportation sectors. Nevertheless, Zairian society appears unlikely to be comfortable with doctrinaire forms, or labels, of either socialism or capitalism.

SOCIETE BELGO-AFRICAINE DU KIVU (SOBAKI). A mining consortium

of mixed public and private ownership, which until 1965 was
called the Comité National du Kivu. The company was established in 1908, one of the large, privately owned consortiums
licensed to operate by Leopold II and given a virtual monopoly
over large tracts of land with the ostensible goal of helping to
develop the territory. The company was nationalized under
Zairianization but was returned to mixed ownership under Retrocession.

SOCIETE DE DEVELOPPEMENT INDUSTRIEL ET MINIER (SODIMIZA).
The second largest copper mining company in Zaire, SODIMIZA
was formed in 1969 and given mining rights to a 93,000 square
km tract of land in southeastern Shaba Region. Copper production from two underground mines at Musoshi and Kinsenda began
in 1972 and reached 80,000 tons in 1984, but low copper prices
and the closure of the Benguela Railway prevented a large-scale
expansion of production. The ore from the mines is processed
through a crusher and blender at Musoshi and the semirefined
copper is then shipped by rail to Zambia for smelting and refining. SODIMIZA is owned by the Zairian government but
operated by the Philip Barrett Kaiser Co. of Canada.

SOCIETE DES CIMENTS DU ZAIRE (CIZA). Owner-operator of one
of two major cement plants in Bas-Zaire Region, CIZA produced
630,000 tons of cement per year in the early 1980s despite production problems caused primarily by shortages of spare parts
and occasional disruptions in the supply of raw materials.

SOCIETE DU LITTORAL ZAIROIS. Belgian company, 15 percent of
which is owned by the Zairian government, engaged in offshore
oil production along the Zairian coast.

SOCIETE GENERALE DE BELGIQUE (SGB). A large Belgian capital
investment and holding company chartered in 1891 and granted
large territorial concessions in Zaire, particularly in Shaba.
The SGB's parent company, the Société Générale, was founded
in 1822 by the king of Netherlands and private members of the
aristocracy. The SGB began a massive growth program in 1919-
25 and was an influential stockholder in UMHK until its nationalization in 1966. Nevertheless, SGB's refining subsidiaries,
based primarily in Belgium, continue to be major purchasers of
Shaba minerals, particularly from GECAMINES.

SOCIETE GENERALE DES MINERAIS (SGM). The former agent for
UMHK, SGM is a Belgian mineral company that processes semirefined copper from Shaba. It began operating GECAMINES (at
the time called GECOMINES) under an agreement with the Zairian
government, after GECOMINES was nationalized, with responsibility for mining, processing, marketing, procurement, and
staffing. In 1969, a 25-year extension was signed, aimed at
eventually compensating SGM for the Zairianization of UMHK and

for operating costs. A revised agreement in 1974 settled the compensation issue and in return SGM agreed to aid with a projected expansion of copper refining in Shaba and the establishment of a casting operation in Bas-Zaire Region. However, the agreement was abrogated by Zaire later that same year, paving the way for the creation of a government-owned minerals marketing entity called the Société Zairoise de Commercialization des Minerais (SOZACOM), which nevertheless continued to market a great deal of copper through SGM. SOZACOM was dissolved in 1984 and GECAMINES assumed responsibility for marketing its own minerals.

SOCIETE MINIERE DE BAKWANGA (MIBA). Zaire's second largest company and major diamond-mining entity, MIBA was formed in December 1961 by combining three private companies: the Société Minière du Beceka (MIBEKA), founded in 1919; the Société d'Entreprise et d'Investissements S.A. (SIBEKA), owned by SGB; and the Anglo-American Corporation. MIBA was nationalized in 1973, although 20 percent ownership was returned to SIBEKA in 1978. MIBA produces most of Zaire's industrial and gem-stone diamonds, primarily from alluvial deposits on a concession of 43,000 square kms in the southern parts of the Kasai Regions. MIBA production accounts for two-thirds of the non-communist world's supply of industrial diamonds. In 1984 MIBA reversed a slow decline following independence and nearly doubled production in one year. It produced 13.6 million carats of industrial diamonds and 4.8 million carats of gem-quality stones. The figures represented a return to production levels of industrial stones at independence and a more than tenfold increase in the production of gem-quality stones over the same period. A great deal of the increase, particularly in gem-stone production, was attributed to new government policies announced in 1983 that allowed private traders to deal in diamonds and to the floating of the Zairian currency that allowed dealers a realistic return on their transactions. See DIAMONDS.

SOCIETE MINIERE DE KISENGE (SMK). Zaire's major producer of manganese, operating at Kisenge in southwestern Shaba Region near the Angolan border. The SMK was originally the Société Beceka Manganèse, a holding of the Société Générale founded in 1950. SMK was nationalized in 1973. Manganese production peaked in 1960 at 381,000 tons per year and remained above 300,000 tons per year until the closure of the Benguela Railway in 1975 and the Shaba invasions of 1977-78 caused a considerable decline in production. Operations virtually halted in 1983. However, considerable stockpiles remain and 15,000 tons of ore were processed in 1984.

SOCIETE MINIERE DE TENKE-FUNGURUME (SMTF). A copper mining company formed in 1970 with 20 percent state participation and the remainder owned by a consortium of U.S., European, and

Japanese companies. It was granted a concession of 1,425 square kms in southern Shaba Region to exploit estimated copper ore reserves of 55 million metric tons. However, the operation depended heavily on the reopening of the Benguela Railway and the company was liquidated in October 1984.

SOCIETE MINIERE ET INDUSTRIELLE DU KIVU (SOMINKI). A company of mixed ownership formed March 25, 1976, by merging eight companies, some of them in existence since 1928, engaged primarily in tin mining in Kivu Region. The company is 28 percent owned by the Zairian government and 78 percent owned by a Franco-Belgian company, Empain-Schneider. It was granted a concession area of 9,800 square kms lying in a 90,000 square kms part of the Kindu area of western Kivu Region. Known tin reserves in the area were 29,000 metric tons and estimated resources were 43,700 tons. Output in 1983 was 2,582 tons cassiterite. Production and the possible exploitation of known deposits in another area at Twangiza were hampered by transportation problems and low tin prices. SOMINKI also operates a 50-year-old gold mine at Mobale with an output of 1,000 troy ounces per month. Total known reserves of gold in the area were 899,700 ounces and estimated reserves were 1,545,000 ounces. See GOLD and TIN.

SOCIETE NATIONALE D'ELECTRICITE (SNEL). The government-owned agency charged with the development and administration of electrical power generation in Zaire. SNEL operates all of Zaire's electricity generating complexes. The agency's largest projects in the 1970s were supervising the construction of the Inga hydroelectric complex in Bas-Zaire and the Inga-Shaba power transmission line linking the complex to the Shaba power grid. Refurbishment of smaller hydroelectric complexes in Shaba and other parts of Zaire was begun in the late 1970s and plans were inaugurated for a rural electrification program in the early 1980s. See ELECTRICAL POWER.

SOCIETE NATIONALE DES CHEMINS DE FER ZAIROIS (SNCZ). Zaire's national railroad authority formed in 1974 by combining a number of railway lines and charged with operating the five major railway systems in the country. See RAILWAYS.

SOCIETE ZAIROISE DE COMMERCIALISATION DES MINERAIS (SOZA-COM). A government agency established in June 1974 to market Zairian minerals, primarily those produced by GECAMINES. SOZA-COM also took over the marketing of MIBA diamonds in 1983 following a dispute with de Beers, which had been the marketing agent. However, SOZACOM was judged to be inefficient and was dissolved in 1984. GECAMINES and MIBA subsequently assumed responsibility for marketing their own minerals.

SOCIETE ZAIRO-ITALIENNE DE RAFFINAGE (SOZIR). A company

jointly owned by the Zairian government and private Italian interests that operates Zaire's sole petroleum refinery, completed in 1968 at Kinlao near Moanda on the Zairian coast. The installation has a capacity to refine 17,000 barrels per day of primarily low-grade crude. The refinery cannot process most Zairian crude because of its high wax content. As a result, locally produced crude is traded for imported oil that can be processed. Production at the refinery has rarely exceeded one-half of capacity. SOZIR refined 183,730 tons of crude in 1984. See PETROLEUM.

SOCIETY. Zairian society is complex, variegated, and undergoing considerable change. Societal structures varied considerably among different ethnic groups and were altered by colonial and post-independence events and policies. In particular, differences between rural and urban societies have led many Zairians to lament what they feel is the shredding of the fabric of family and communal lifestyles. Many urban dwellers express a sense of loss of roots. Meanwhile, rural dwellers express despair over falling ever further behind their urban brethren in education and income levels.

In the rural areas, some traditional structures remain. They vary considerably (matrilineal vs. patrilineal, methods of choosing and roles of chiefs, etc.) but general similarities can be discerned. Local communities are often centered around a descent group, clan or extended family. They usually are headed by a chief, chosen through a variety of methods, who often represents the gods or ancestors to the group. In societies with more complex hierarchical systems, a number of chieftaincies may be grouped under a king who has authority over and receives tribute from the lesser chiefs, if such exist. The chief often performs religious or ritual functions. The major purpose of these is to better the lives of his followers, whether by increasing fertility and harvests, or by directing war strategy and mediating disputes. However, the chief, despite the considerable deference accorded him, rarely acts without consulting advisors, such as village elders or senior relatives. It is to be noted that colonialism considerably affected the chieftaincy structure in Zaire. Authorities granted administrative powers to some of the traditionally chosen chiefs, but most of the Africans chosen to represent the authorities at the village level were selected on the basis of their willingness to cooperate. Since independence, government administrators have been more accommodating of traditional chiefs and customs. However, the tendency has been the same: to encourage the rise of chiefs willing to cooperate with officials in implementing government policies and objectives.

In modern as well as traditional Zairian society, members may be distinguished on a scale of worthiness or merit. Age is generally respected as are the holding of political or religious office, wealth, and prowess in certain endeavors such as hunting, warrioring, and storytelling. Males are generally accorded higher status than females, although notable exceptions exist. "Slaves" and indentured servants in general have less access to the rights and privileges of "free" individuals. However, processes usually exist whereby they may aspire to gain "freedom."

In urban centers, the extended family and ethnic group remain the pillars of societal structure, but have been weakened by the stresses of urban life. During the colonial era, a working class began to develop in the 1920s and 1930s, but its influence remained low until the trade union movement was allowed to grow following World War II. The late 1940s and 1950s brought the development of a petite bourgeoisie, sometimes called "évolués," the members of which were primarily salaried, low-level, white-collar workers in the colonial bureaucracy (clerks, secretaries, etc.). Small traders operating low-capital businesses also began to flourish. Most large businesses were foreign owned. The lowest urban class, the unemployed, also began to form, although the authorities tried to restrict the growth of this group by limiting travel to the cities by Africans without jobs. Independence, and the exodus of expatriate technicians and administrators that accompanied it, altered societal structures and created new classes among the Congolese virtually overnight when Congolese began to occupy white-collar and management jobs vacated by Europeans.

A quarter-century after independence, the new structures have been established and although sociologists differ on their classification, several levels in general have been agreed upon. At the highest level in current Zairian society is the ruling, political elite, which Nzongola called the state bourgeoisie. Many of its original members came from the pre-independence, petite bourgeoisie: clerks and assistants who became ministers and directors. Members of the elite have since been joined by educated young Zairians, "cadres," and political appointees. They usually owe their position in society to political patronage or a close relative in a high position. They usually have applied their income, acquired officially or unofficially, to build a business that sometimes is strong enough to safeguard their position in society if they fall out of political favor. Some sociologists differentiate between the political elite and the large merchants. However, individuals in one group are usually related to someone in the other. (It is quite common for a high political appointee to launch his wife or son in business.) Lower in status but still respected is the professional class: professors, military officers, physicians, intellectuals and, to a lesser degree, university students. They enjoy a degree of wealth but recent economic hardships, including high inflation and frozen salaries, have forced many of them from the "middle class" income levels. Often called the "sous-bourgeoisie" ("under-bourgeoisie"), many of them survive financially by placing relatives in small trading or farming activities. Indeed, small traders could be placed in this category although they command less respect. Blue collar wage earners, including journeymen and semiskilled workers, are usually classified in the next category. Some analysts group them with small farmers, particularly in income level. However, they usually enjoy a higher status than their rural compatriots because of their proximity to urban centers and the amenities of health and education. Cash crop and subsistence farmers are often grouped together in a "peasant" class. And lastly, the urban unemployed are viewed as the underclass and considered to be the breeding ground for the thievery and spontaneous violence that tends to threaten those in the ruling classes. The growth of this group is viewed with apprehension by the authorities and frequent round-ups of the unemployed and indigent are carried out in the major cities and those detained are sent to their villages or, if they are young, into the armed forces. Zaire's economic ills and, some argue, the government's policies have created a small class of "haves" and a predominant class of "have-nots," some of whom are highly resentful of inequities, but many of whom appear too busy trying to survive to bear a grudge.

SONGYE. A Bantu-speaking people living near Kabinda, in southern Kasai Oriental Region between the Lubufu and Lomami rivers in Shaba Region.

SOUTH AFRICA, RELATIONS WITH. Zaire's relations with the white-minority government of South Africa, like those of many African governments, are dichotomous. They reflect political and moral repulsion for the apartheid system of racial separateness and white domination, yet acknowledge a pragmatic economic reliance on the greater economic development of the South African nation. During the early years of independence, Zaire was not in the forefront of the growing movement to ostracize South Africa from the international community. It often abstained on U.N. resolutions condemning the Pretoria government. Zaire did not support the move to expel South Africa from the United Nations in 1975 or the U.N. General Assembly resolution equating zionism with racism. The Zairian and South African governments have also been united in their opposition to the Cuban and Soviet presence in Africa, particularly in Angola where during the civil war, they backed factions opposed to the MPLA that eventually took power in Luanda. However, Mobutu violently condemned the apartheid regime before the United Nations in 1973 and since the late 1970s, Zaire has voted with the African bloc on most anti-South African resolutions at the UN and the OAU.

Despite political opposition to the South African government, however, economic ties have been longstanding. As much as one-half of Zaire's mineral exports travelled through Zimbabwe to the South African port of Durban (see SOUTHERN WAY), particularly following the closing of the Benguela Railway and the deterioration of the road and railway system within Zaire (see NATIONAL WAY). In addition, South African products, primarily food, arrived by air on a regular basis in Zaire and could often be seen in local stores. In October 1986, however, amid the rising tide of support for economic sanctions against South Africa in the international community, Mobutu attended a meeting in Lusaka, Zambia, of the leaders of southern Africa's frontline states aimed at finding ways to compensate for South African trade restrictions that were expected following a new set of international trade sanctions against South Africa. Mobutu also hosted a frontline meeting in Gbadolite in November 1986.

SOUTH KASAI. The southern region of the former province of Kasai. At independence, ethnic rivalry between the Luba and Lulua in Kasai and between the Luba and Lunda in Katanga (now Shaba) drove many Luba into South Kasai, tripling its population between 1958 and 1963, according the United Nations. The presence of large mineral deposits, including two-thirds of the non-communist world's industrial diamond deposits, contributed to the pressures that led to the secession of the region and the proclamation of the Independent Mining State of South Kasai by Kalonji on August 8, 1960. The secession was ended on February 2, 1961, when Kalonji joined the Adoula government of reconciliation. Ethnic tensions remained in the Kasai Region, and the government responded to these pressures in the 1970s by creating two regions, Kasai Occidental dominated by the Lulua, and Kasai Oriental dominated by the Luba. See KASAI OCCIDENTAL; KASAI ORIENTAL; and REBELLIONS.

SOUTHERN WAY. The second most economic way to export Zaire's minerals from Shaba Region, after the Benguela Railway. The 3,500-km route carries Shaba minerals by rail through Zambia, Zimbabwe, and South Africa to the ports of Durban, East London, and Port Elizabeth. Although longer than the more politically favored National Way, the route takes less than one-half of the time: 30 days. The Southern Way was used to transport 43 percent of Shaba's minerals in 1985, according to government figures.

SOVIET UNION, RELATIONS WITH. Relations between Zaire and the Soviet Union generally have been cool since independence, and occasionally hostile. Zaire has regarded the Soviet government as backing a number of opposition groups and the Soviet government views the Zairian government as a western puppet. Diplomatic relations were established at independence and at one point Lumumba threatened to ask for Soviet military assistance to help put down the Congo secessions. That threat was one of the reasons for his dismissal by Kasavubu in 1960. When Mobutu "neutralized" the Kasavubu-Lumumba government on September 5, 1960, he gave the Soviet embassy 48 hours to leave the country. A low-level mission returned a few years later, only to be expelled by the Tshombe government. After Mobutu took power, he re-established relations in December 1965.

Ambassadors were exchanged in 1968. However, relations were strained in the 1970s by Soviet support for the MPLA faction in

Angola and suspicion of Soviet responsibility for the Shaba invasions of 1977 and 1978. In the early 1980s relations remained cool. For example, no Soviet representative was invited to the extensive inauguration ceremonies of Mobutu's third presidential term in December 1984 and no mention was made of the Soviet Union in the publication on Zaire's foreign relations issued on the occasion. However, a Soviet trade delegation paid a ten-day visit to Kinshasa in March 1985 and Soviet officials announced their desire to increase cooperation in the areas of mining, health, energy and fish processing. They said during the visit that Soviet exports to Zaire reached $10 million in 1984, four times the level of trade the year before. The figures were not confirmed by the Zairian government. Zairian exports to the Soviet Union historically have been negligible.

SPEKE, JOHN. English explorer who travelled with John Burton in East Africa and reached Lake Tanganyika in 1858. Speke is credited with being the first European to reach the source of the "Victoria" Nile on Lake Mobutu (formerly Lake Albert) near Jinja in 1862.

SPIRITUALISM (FETISHISM, SORCERY, and WITCHCRAFT). Many Zairians, like many Africans, are deeply mystical and some of their traditional rites and beliefs, or "superstitions," have been born by the diaspora to Europe, the Middle East and the Americas. The beliefs, often called witchcraft in the industrialized world but which would perhaps better be characterized as spiritualism, frequently co-exist with equally deep, religious beliefs in Catholicism, Protestantism, Islam, or African adaptations of monotheological religions, such as Kimbanguism. The beliefs range from the honoring and consulting of one's ancestors for advice, to the wearing of talismans for protection and the consultation of practitioners to obtain one's wishes or protect one from opponents. As with most forms of spiritualism, the intentions of the individual often govern the malignity or benignity of the acts and rituals carried out. Ethnographers have observed that beliefs tend to vary from tribe to tribe and even from clan to clan within specific ethnic groups. In most of the societies of Zaire, however, the spiritual system is often based on one supreme god with lesser and subordinate gods, or spirits and ancestors. The lesser spiritual beings sometimes may communicate with the living, thus providing a link between those in what is considered to be the temporary existence that is life, and those in the eternal existence that precedes and follows life. The spirits may be contacted at times by individuals, sometimes with the help of diviners or intermediaries. Practitioners who invoke the spirits for malevolent purposes, or in some cases to deflect evil or hardship from a client to another person, are often called witches or sorcerers. Others who seek the help of the spirits for benign purposes are often called healers or physicians. The terms, however, are often interchangeable and since many of the practitioners use tangible items such as fetishes or talismans as part of their rituals, they often are called fetishists.

SPORTS. As in most countries, sports are popular in Zaire and closely followed by a large segment of the population. In addition, the government encourages the development of sports activities and often provides funds for teams and sporting events. Soccer, or football, is considered the national sport with numerous professional and amateur groups competing at the national and regional level. Boxing, track and field, and, to a lesser degree, basketball, handball and volleyball are also popular. Other activities primarily for the wealthy include motorcycle racing and auto rallying. Zaire sends a relatively large contingent of athletes to the Olympics although it has yet to win a medal. Zaire was one of a dozen African nations that boycotted the 1980 Olympics in Moscow because of the Soviet presence in Afghanistan. It has no sporting ties with South Africa because of its apartheid policies. The sporting event in Zaire that drew perhaps the most international attention was the world heavyweight boxing championship fight between Muhammad Ali and George Foreman in Kinshasa on October 30, 1974.

STANLEY, HENRY MORTON. Journalist-explorer who, as a star reporter for the New York Herald, led an expedition into central Africa to find missionary/explorer David Livingstone and later explored the Congo River for Belgium's King Leopold II. Stanley was born in Denbigh, Wales, in 1841. He went to America at an early age, was naturalized a U.S. citizen, and later went to work for James Gordon Bennet, Jr. at the Herald. He was sent to central Africa in October 1869 on an unlimited budget to find Livingstone, who had not been heard from in two years. Stanley began his trip in January 1871, starting from Zanzibar. He arrived at the shores of Lake Tanganyika in November 1871 and met Livingstone at Ujiji with the famous words, "Dr. Livingstone, I presume." During the trip, he became interested in proving that the Lualaba, which many thought to be the headwaters of the Nile, was in fact the headwaters of the Congo River, of which little was known. Following Livingstone's death, Stanley set out again to discover the source of the Congo River, the mouth of which had been known to Europeans since the late fifteenth century. He began in Zanzibar in September 1874. After mapping Lake Victoria and Lake Tanganyika and marching across the Maniema forest, he reached the headwaters of the Congo River at the confluence of the Luama and Lualaba rivers on October 17, 1876. He sailed down the river to prove the headwaters were indeed those of the Congo River and reached Kinshasa on March 9, 1877. After a grueling crossing of the Crystal Mountains, he reached Boma on August 9, 1877, 999 days after having left Zanzibar. In 1878, Stanley was hired by Leopold II to charter and open up the Congo for trade. He left in January 1879 and arrived on August 14, 1879, at Vivi, across the river from what today is Matadi., From the base at Vivi, he worked his way up the river, building a road and establishing trading stations along the way. He reached Stanley Pool (now Pool Malebo) at Kinshasa in mid-1881 and negotiated a treaty with the King of Ngaliema on the pool's southern bank. Count Pierre Savorgnan de Brazza would beat Stanley to the northern bank and sign a treaty for France with the local chief on that side of the river, leading the French to claim what would become Congo/ Brazzaville. The road to Vivi was completed by the end of 1881 and Stanley returned to Europe. He returned in December 1882 and sailed up the Congo River to what is now Kisangani, signing more than 450 treaties with local chiefs in the name of Leopold II. Stanley made a final voyage in 1887 ostensibly to rescue a British garrison under siege at Juba, southern Sudan, by the forces of the Mahdi. The trip lasted three years, but the expedition never reached Juba. Stanley is credited with opening up the Congo River, from Kinshasa to Kisangani, to European trade and for establishing the treaties with local tribes that Leopold used to take control of most of the Congo Basin when Africa was partitioned among the European powers at the Berlin Conference in 1885. Stanley died in 1904.

STANLEY FALLS. The name given during the colonial era to the cataracts on the Zaire River between Ubundu and Kisangani, where Stanley began his voyage down the Congo River.

STANLEYVILLE. The name for the trading station and later capital of Orientale Province, established by Stanley at the point furthest up the navigable portion of the lower Zaire River. The city was renamed Kisangani in 1966. See KISANGANI.

STEEL. Zaire's only steel mill is located at Maluku, about 100 kms upriver from Kinshasa. Construction was begun in 1972 with financing largely from German and Italian investors. Production began in 1974 with a capacity of 250,000 metric tons per year using a labor force of 1,250 at full production. However, the mill has been besieged with problems and has tended to operate at 10 to 25 percent of capacity.

STUDENTS. Students, particularly university students, often have played a political role in Zaire, whether by supporting the government during the "revolutionary" days following the Mobutu coup or by criticizing the government in the years that followed. Students exerted little influence during the early years following independence, but by the mid-1960s they had organized into associations and were said to form major blocs in certain liberal and progressive parties. Many had supported Lumumba and were angered by his assassination. By 1968, two major organizations had emerged: the Union Générale des Etudiants Congolais (General Union of Congolese Students), with branches on all three Congolese campuses and in Belgium; and the Association Générale des Etudiants de Lovanium (General Association of Lovanium Students), based at Lovanium University in Kinshasa. Both were disbanded by the government in 1968 and the JMPR youth wing of the party was proclaimed the only recognized youth organization. One of the major responsibilities of the JMPR was student mobilization. The students originally supported Mobutu, out of opposition to Tshombe whom they linked with the Katanga secession, mercenaries, and the assassination of Lumumba. They also agreed with Mobutu's policies of eliminating tribalism and regionalism and strengthening the central government. In subsequent years, however, disenchantment grew with the Mobutu government because of inefficiencies, the president's growing personal fortune, and his close ties to the U.S. government. Students demonstrated against the visit to Zaire by Hubert Humphrey in January 1968. On June 4, 1969, students at Lovanium demonstrated against low stipends and what they considered to be extravagant government spending. Hundreds of them marched from the campus into the city, breaking through several police and army roadblocks. Soldiers opened fire. Estimates of the number of students killed vary between 40 and 100, although official figures were never published. Thirty-four students were arrested and charged with subversive activities. A number of them fled the country and were given asylum in Bulgaria. However, many were tried and given sentences of up to 20 years in prison. They were amnestied on October 14. On June 4, 1971, students demonstrated at Lovanium and Lubumbashi campuses in memory of the 1969 victims and clashed with the army. The universities were closed and students were inducted into the army, an event that was to be repeated in 1977, 1981, and 1982. Following the protests of 1971, a single, national university was created from the three private universities at Lovanium, Lubumbashi, and Kisangani. See MOUVEMENT D'ACTION POUR LA RESURRECTION DU CONGO.

SUCCESSION. As in many African nations, the question of political succession is a topic that rarely is discussed in public, although it hangs heavy in the political atmosphere. Mobutu is still relatively young but his 20 years in power and the unstated policy of removing any potential successor has kept the question alive, particularly for foreign businessmen thinking of investing in Zaire. Under the Constitution of 1974, if the presidency falls vacant the oldest political commissioner (usually a member of the Political Bureau) assumes the office temporarily. The Political Bureau then meets, sets a date for elections to be held within 30 to 60 days and nominates the sole candidate. In essence, then, the task of choosing a successor falls to the handful of senior party officials and close collaborators of the president who fill the Political Bureau. The second-ranking official in government, though not necessarily in the party, is the prime minister and consequently the foreign media have tended to look to that position for possible successors. However, the prime ministers tend to be technocrats and administrators with little or no political base of support. In addition, they tend more to inspire animosity and jealousy among their colleagues than political support and they rarely serve more than a few uninterrupted years in the post. As a result, the political succession remains open in Zaire with what analysts say is a strong possibility, in the face of a political vacuum following a vacancy in the presidency, of continued military dominance.

SUGAR. Sugarcane is grown commercially in central Bas-Zaire and Ruzizi River valley in Kivu Region, an industry that employs 2,500 persons. Production of raw sugar cane, one of Zaire's major cash crops, peaked in 1975 at 614,000 metric tons, declined in subsequent years, but began to rise again in the 1980s, reaching 550,000 tons in 1985. Production of refined sugar reached 80,000 tons in 1985. However, imports were still required to meet 150,000-ton annual consumption. Production began on a commercial scale in 1925 and the first sugar refinery, Moerbek, was built in 1929 in Bas-Zaire with a capacity of 7,000 tons in 1930 and rising to 40,000 tons in the 1980s. In 1956, a second sugar refinery called Sucrerie et Raffinerie de l'Afrique Centrale (SUCRAF) was created at Klibi, in southern Kivu, that produced 15,000 tons in 1985. With Zairianization, both refineries were grouped under the Office National du Sucre (National Sugar Board). However, they were returned to their private owners under Retrocession and the ONS was liquidated on May 5, 1978. A sugar development board called "Projets Sucriers au Zaire (PSZ), was established on May 8 to oversee the industry and promote the development of new projects. A third refinery was established under a joint Zairian-Chinese venture in 1984 in Yawenda, Haut-Zaire Region, with a planned capacity of 15,000 tons per year. It produced 3,000 tons in 1985. The PSZ announced plans in 1985 to construct four additional refineries: at Mushie-Pentane near Bandundu; at Lubilashi in Shaba Region; at Luiza in Bas-Zaire; and at Businga in Equateur Region. Each refinery was to have an annual production capacity of 15,000 tons.

SUKU. A sub-group of the Yaka living in southwestern Zaire north of Feshi between the Inzia and Kwilu Rivers.

SWITZERLAND, RELATIONS WITH. Relations between Zaire and Switzerland have been primarily commercial. However, they were strained in November 1985 when 53 Zairians and 6 Angolans were deported from Switzerland after Swiss authorities discovered they had applied for political asylum under false identities. Upon their arrival in Zaire, many of the deportees were hospitalized and a number of them reportedly died. Swiss newspapers said the deportees were beaten by Zairian authorities. However, the Zairian government said they were mistreated by Swiss police.

- T -

TANANARIVE CONFERENCE. Conference between various Congolese factions in March 1961 in the capital of Madagascar. The conference adopted a resolution calling for a confederal system of government in the Congo. Opposition by the central government in Leopoldville led to the Coquilhatville conference in Equateur Province in April and May. The Coquilhatville Conference renounced confederalism and called for a federal system of government. Neither conference, however, came up with a system of government that was acceptable to the various secessionist groups.

TANZANIA, RELATIONS WITH. Relations between Zaire and Tanzania officially are good. However, they repeatedly have been strained by Zairian accusations that Tanzania is harboring Zairian dissident guerrillas of the PRP on its side of Lake Tanganyika. In mid-1975, PRP guerrillas kidnapped a group of foreign students from a game preserve and held them in eastern Zaire for a number of weeks. In November 1984, the guerrillas attacked the Zairian port city of Moba on Lake Tanganyika and held it for two days before government troops arrived to retake it. The guerrillas attacked Moba again in June 1985 in a less successful action. Zairian authorities said the guerrillas were based in Tanzania and Burundi and threatened to carry out "hot pursuit" raids into Tanzania if they attacked again. Tanzania and Burundi denied the charges and the guerrillas said they were based entirely within Zaire. See PARTI DE LA REVOLUTION POPULAIRE.

TEACHERS see EDUCATION

TEKE. A Bantu-speaking people living on both sides of the Zaire River between Kinshasa and the confluence of the Kasai and Zaire Rivers. Widely believed to have entered the Kinshasa area as early as the 1600s, the Teke were one of the groups that made early contact with the Europeans, beginning with the arrival of Father de Montesarchio in 1652. They traded in tobacco, and some agricultural goods but became heavily dependent on the slave trade in the eighteenth century. Kaplan describes the Teke's political structure as a group of chiefdoms, each with several villages. The villages tended to be small and unstable and had no centralized defense system. Chieftaincy was hereditary and one of the chief's major duties was to collect tribute for the king, who was elected by the village elders and acted as the judicial authority.

TELECOMMUNICATIONS. There were an estimated 8,000 television sets in Zaire, 150,000 radios, 30,000 telephones, and 200 telegraph offices in 1982. A satellite station at N'sele, linked by microwave towers to Kinshasa and the Voix Du Zaire complex provided telecommunications links with the outside world and allowed the Voix du Zaire to receive television and radio feeds

primarily from French networks and to transmit television and
radio feeds to eight regional stations in Matadi, Mbandaka, Kisangani, Lubumbashi, Bandundu, Kananga, Mbuji-Mayi, and Bukavu.
The Voix du Zaire complex, inaugurated on November 24, 1976,
broadcast in French and the four national languages (Kikongo,
Lingala, Swahili, and Tshiluba). The regional stations broadcast
in other local languages as well. Reception was possible of television and radio broadcasts from Brazzaville but the absence of
any nongovernment stations on local frequencies contributed to a
high rate of listenership to international shortwave broadcasters.
See COMMUNICATIONS.

TENKE. A small town in Shaba, east of Likasi, near an area where
significant deposits of copper and cobalt have been found.

TERRITORIAL POLICE. A colonial police force, consisting in 1960
of 6,000 men, armed and uniformed, that guarded prisons and
public buildings and provided reinforcements to police when called
upon. The group was disbanded following the Mobutu coup.

TERRITORIAL WATERS. Zaire claims territorial waters extending 12
nautical miles from its 37-km coastline and an economic zone extending 200 kms from the coast. There are offshore petroleum deposits and some fishing, but otherwise little commercial activity.

TETELA. A Bantu-speaking group living between Lusambo and the
Upper Zaire River in Sankuru and Maniema districts of Kasai
Oriental and Kivu regions respectively. Ethnologists view the
Tetela and Kusu as closely related to each other and as distant
members of the Mongo cluster. The Tetela began to be viewed
as a distinct group in the late 1800s with the arrival of the Afro-
Arabs from the east and the Belgians from the west and south.
The Tetela, living in Kasai, had less contact with the Afro-Arabs
than the Kusu, who in some cases adopted Muslim religion and
dress. In addition, the Belgian colonial authorities separated
the two groups when they divided the area into Kasai and Kivu
provinces. Lumumba was a Tetela who tried to unite his people
with the Kusu. He was unsuccessful. The Tetela reportedly
were the object of a major purge within the army in 1975.

THEATER. Theatrical arts are vibrant in Zaire, particularly in
Kinshasa where more than a dozen theater groups flourished even
during the recession of the 1970s and 1980s. Schools, universities, religious and social organizations were major sponsors of
acting troups. However, neighborhoods and friends in the artistic community have been known to occasionally sponsor plays.
Some plays from the international theater are produced but many
are written by local playwrights. Production is "authentic,"
using African storytelling techniques, like the "griot" or narra-
tor, dream and fantasy sequences, and singing and dancing to
the background of drums and musical instruments. The

government-sponsored Théâtre National (National Theater) sponsors plays that tour nationally and internationally.

THIRTEEN PARLIAMENTARIANS see PARLIAMENTARIANS, THIR-
TEEN

TIN. Tin in deposits of cassiterite is found primarily along the
southern side of the Lualaba River in southern Shaba and in
Kivu east of Bukavu. In the 1940s, Zaire was the second largest
producer of tin in the world after Bolivia and produced 14,000
metric tons of the mineral in 1942. However, production has declined steadily due to low prices and the exhaustion of easily
mined deposits. Output of tin contained in ore and concentrate
was 3,000 tons in 1983. Smelter production was 150 tons. In
Shaba Region, tin is mined by ZAIRETAIN, which is 50 percent
owned by the Zairian government and 50 percent by the Belgian
GEOMINES company that operates the mine. Other companies
with operations in Shaba include GECAMINES (government owned)
and the Entreprises Minières du Zaire (EMZ) of mixed ownership.
In Kivu, tin deposits are mined by EMZ, Société Minière de Ka-
tando (SOMIDO), Société Minière et Industrielle du Kivu (SO-
MINKI), and the Société Minière du Goma, all of mixed public
and private ownership. The major deposits in Kivu are located at Manono, Kalimbi, and Katondo. Although production
has declined, interest in tin mining remains strong. A survey
of Zaire's mineral reserves conducted by the Bureau de Recherches Géologiques et Minières (BRGM) under a 1969 agreement with the government revealed tin reserves estimated at
600,000 metric tons.

TIO KINGDOM. A relatively small kingdom established along both
sides of the Malebo Pool as early as the sixteenth century.
Relatively friendly and anxious to trade, the Tio kings signed
agreements with Stanley and Count de Brazza that led to the
rapid development of the capitals of the Belgian and French
colonial empires in central Africa: Leopoldville and Brazzaville.
See TEKE.

TIPPO TIB. The most famous and perhaps most powerful of the
Afro-Arab traders, whose kingdom at its peak in the late 1800s
stretched from Lake Tanganyika to central Zaire and reputedly
employed more than 4,000 agents. Tippo Tib traded primarily
in slaves and ivory taken in raids or purchased from marauding
tribes in exchange for cloth, guns, and manufactured goods.
Tippo Tib came to be regarded as the virtual ruler of eastern
Zaire and for a brief time was appointed governor of Orientale
Province by Leopold II. Harassment by the colonial authorities
seeking to combat slavery and extend their control into eastern
Zaire caused Tippo Tib's influence to wane. A protracted war
beginning in the 1880s gradually drove him and his agents from
the region by 1894.

TOGO, RELATIONS WITH. Relations between Zaire and Togo have
been close since General Gnassingbe Eyadema came to power in
a coup d'etat in 1967. Eyadema was one of the first African
leaders to embrace Mobutu's authenticity program and also imitated in many ways the Zairian president's cult-of-personality.
Togo under Eyadema has traditionally sided with Zaire, Ivory
Coast, Cameroon, Senegal, and other "moderates" on regional
and international issues. Togo contributed troops to the Pan-
African Peacekeeping Force sent to Shaba in 1978 following the
Shaba invasions.

TOPOGRAPHY. Zaire covers a vast territory of 2,344,895 square
kilometers (905,365 square miles), the largest nation by territory in sub-Saharan Africa, and 80 times the size of Belgium.
Zaire shares 9,165 kms of border with nine other countries:
Angola on the southwest; Zambia to the south; Tanzania, Burundi, Rwanda, and Uganda on the east; Sudan to the northeast;
Central African Republic to the north; and Congo on the west
and northwest. In addition, Zaire borders the Angolan enclave
of Cabinda to the west near the mouth of the Zaire River. Zaire
is considered a semienclaved country since it has only 37 kms of
coastline on the Atlantic Ocean, north of the mouth of the Zaire
River. Indeed, the 4,300-km Zaire River and its tributaries
form the backbone of the national infrastructure, providing the
major surface transportation route, despite unnavigable cataracts
above Kisangani and between Kinshasa and the deepwater port
of Matadi. Zaire straddles the Equator and the dry and wet seasons in the northern hemisphere (about one-third of the territory)
are virtually opposite the seasons in the southern hemisphere.
As a result, the Zaire River maintains a relatively constant flow
of water of 30,000 to 80,000 cubic meters per second, making it
the second largest flowing body of water in the world after the
Amazon. Two-thirds of Zairian territory lie in the low, sometimes
marshy, tropical rain forest called the Congo Basin. Rainfall in
the basin is heavy, 180-220 cms per year. The topsoil of the
basin is relatively poor for farming and the population is relatively sparse (as low as one person per square km). To the north
and south lie high plains covered by savanna and woodlands.
The southern, high plains, primarily in Shaba Region, constitute
about one-fourth of the total territory. The weather there is
drier and cooler with some semblance of seasons (cool months in
June-August). The climate permits the cultivation of crops like
maize and millet and the raising of cattle, which is difficult in
the lowlands because of the presence of the tsetse fly and various parasites. To the east lie highlands bordering the Great
Rift Valley, with ranges of mountains rising as high as 5,000
meters. The lakes of the Great Rift Valley form part of Zaire's
eastern border. The eastern highlands for the most part are
covered with thick forest, but enjoy arable land and high rainfall, leading to a relatively dense population. In western Zaire,
between Kinshasa and Boma lies the Crystal Mountain range and

low-level plains containing land suitable for most farming and some livestock raising. From Boma to the Atlantic Ocean are low-lying grasslands and woodlands.

TRADE. Trade was the major reason for the early European exploration and exploitation of Zaire, although social concerns were the primary motivation of the missionaries in the Kongo Kingdom. When the territory became the Belgian Congo, however, following the public outcry over the cruelties of the agents of the crown and private monopolies during the CFS era, trade ceded some of its preeminence to the social effort of "civilizing" Congolese (see PATERNALISM). Nevertheless, the Belgian government, which only reluctantly accepted its colonial charge, exerted considerable pressure on colonial administrators to balance expenditures with revenues. As a result, large corporations were given incentives to invest in mineral and agricultural enterprises, and small and medium-sized entrepreneurs were allowed to operate with few restrictions.

As in most of colonial Africa, formal trade patterns until independence were primarily with nations in Europe and the Americas (and later with Japan), which bought copper, cobalt, industrial diamonds, uranium, and some agricultural products, and in exchange marketed manufactured goods in the territory. Considerable informal trade, however, also developed in such items as cloth, food, and construction materials with Zaire's neighbors. With the "authenticity" period, awareness began to grow of the need to promote trade with other African nations. The move toward intra-African trade was encouraged by the U.N. Economic Commission for Africa and the OAU, which promoted the creation of regional trade organizations like the Communauté Economique des Pays des Grands Lacs (CEPGL), the Union Douanière et Economique de l'Afrique Centrale (UDEAC), and more recently, the Economic Community of Central African States (ECOCAS). As a result, trade has been increasing with other nations of Africa and the developing world, in particular, Morocco, Congo, and Brazil. Zaire subscribes to the nonaligned nations' agreement to trade with any nation. However, trade with developing nations remains a fraction of that with Belgium, France, the United States, United Kingdom, and Japan. See EXPORTS; IMPORTS; and tables.

TRANSPORTATION. The size and terrain of Zaire, combined with its status as a virtually enclaved country, have made the development of efficient transportation routes difficult. Most of the current system was built during the colonial era. The 14,000 kms of navigable waterways form the backbone of the system. Five thousand kms of railways (five separate systems), circumvent unnavigable portions of the rivers and also link urban, mining, and agricultural centers to the river and rail systems. Most of the railways were built between 1900 and 1932 and most of the roads were constructed in the decade following World War II. The system deteriorated following independence and only two paved roads were constructed: between Boma and Matadi and between Kikwit and Kinshasa. In 1983, the Japanese government provided assistance in building a suspension bridge over the Zaire River at Matadi that improved road links between the breadbasket, Bas-Fleuve sub-region, and the Kinshasa market. A second level of the bridge to carry rail traffic was to be constructed eventually. The transport sector was one of several nationalized under Zairianization in 1973 and liberalized following Retrocession in 1975. In the 1980s, the Japanese and U.S. governments were engaged in bilateral programs to develop transportation in Bandundu and Bas-Zaire regions. Initial stages of the project included building hundreds of concrete bridges to replace small ferries and log crossings. Ferries on larger rivers were to be refurbished. Grading and paving projects were to come later. In a speech on December 5, 1984, marking the inauguration of his third term, Mobutu announced an ambitious seven-year plan to improve roads in Zaire's interior. He also promised to replace 200 of Zaire's 300 ferries with bridges by 1991 and in particular to improve roads in the neglected Ituri, Ubangi, and Kivu areas. There were 300,000 motor vehicles in Zaire in 1985, of which 150,000 were commercial vehicles. Passenger-kms traveled totaled 389 million in 1981 and cargo transported totaled 1.7 billion ton-kms. In 1982, civil aviation registered 683 million passenger-kms and air freight totaled 31.5 million ton-kms. See AIR TRANSPORTATION; MOTOR VEHICLES; NATIONAL WAY; RAILWAYS; ROADS; and WATERWAYS.

TSETSE FLY. A fly common to the wet, low-lying forest areas of Zaire that is a major carrier of sleeping sickness. Because of the tsetse fly, commercial cattle herding in Zaire is limited primarily to the high plains of Shaba, Bas-Zaire, and Haut-Zaire.

TSHIKAPA. A city of about 50,000 inhabitants lying on the Kasai River in the heart of the diamond-mining area of southern Kasai Occidental Region. Many residents of Tshikapa dig and pan for diamonds in the alluvial deposits on the Kasai, Tshikapa, Lovua, Lonaishinie, and Lubembe rivers of the region. In the past, competition for the diamonds has led to clashes between local residents and soldiers who also sometimes work the area.

TSHISEKEDI WA MALUMBA (ETIENNE). Former minister, parliamentarian, and ambassador who was one of the most prominent of the "13 parliamentarians" who have been repeatedly sent into internal exile, imprisoned, and pardoned since 1982 for denouncing Zaire's single-party system and seeking to form a second party. See PARLIAMENTARIANS, THIRTEEN.

TSHOMBE DITENJ (JEAN). Son of former Prime Minister Moise Tshombe, who was an exiled dissident for a number of years until 1984 when he returned to Zaire under the 1983 general amnesty.

He was named state secretary (the equivalent of deputy-minister) for mines and energy in the cabinet reshuffle of January 25, 1985.

TSHOMBE, MOISE KAPENDA. A controversial Congolese leader who epitomized for some the fractiousness of early Congolese politics and the subservience of some leaders to foreign interests. For others, however, he was a pragmatic leader who, as prime minister, attempted to unify the country. Tshombe was born on November 10, 1919, at Musamba, the traditional capital of the Lunda Empire. He was of noble Lunda family, related to the Lunda king, and the son of a prominent businessman. He received his primary education from Methodist missionaries at Sandoa, obtained a teaching diploma at Kanene lez-Kinda and later received an accounting diploma. In the 1950s, Tshombe helped found the CONAKAT party and became its president-general. He led the CONAKAT delegation to the two Round Tables of 1960. In the elections of 1960, he was elected to the national assembly as a delegate from Katanga, but his southern-based supporters failed to obtain enough seats elsewhere in the country to form a majority. As fighting broke out in the south between Luba and Lunda, the CONAKAT gradually edged the BALUBAKAT out of influence in Katangan politics. Angered by what he felt was the lack of Katangan representation in the Lu-mumba cabinet and encouraged by Belgian commercial interests in Katanga, Tshombe declared the secession of Katanga on July 11, 1960. The Katanga secession brought the first mercenaries to independent Africa and prompted the United Nations' first and only police action on the continent. The secession was ended in February 1963 and Tshombe went into exile in Spain. The following year, Kasavubu named him prime minister with a mandate to end the rebellions in Kwilu and the eastern provinces. The Tshombe government, with a core of leaders from his CONACO coalition, was installed on July 6, 1964. Tshombe held five port-folios. Tshombe subsequently infuriated Africanist circles by hiring mercenaries, many of them veterans of the Katanga seces-sion, to end the rebellions, and by authorizing the Belgian air-drop on Stanleyville. Under the Constitution of 1964, the prime minister assumed greater powers and his party, the CONACO, scored sizeable gains in elections in 1965. Kasavubu, however, dismissed him on October 13, 1965, and appointed Evariste Kimba to form a government. Kimba's attempt was blocked by Tshombe's supporters, leading to a stalemate that was one of the major rea-sons for the military coup d'etat on November 24, 1965. Tshombe fled into exile in Spain once again. He was condemned to death in absentia for high treason on March 13, 1967, by a high court in Kinshasa. On June 30, 1967, he was kidnapped while on a flight over the Mediterranean and placed under house arrest in Algeria. The Algerian government announced he died of a heart attack on June 30, 1969.

TSHOPO RIVER. A small river in northeastern Zaire that flows into the Zaire River near Kisangani. A 12,000-kw hydroelectrical complex on the river supplies electricity to the area.

TSHUAPA RIVER. A 800-km river that rises in northern Kasai Oriental near Kataka-Kombe and flows north, then west. It merges with the Lomela River at Boende to become the Busira, which subsequently flows into the Zaire River at Mbandaka. It is navigable by shallow-draft boats from Mbandaka to Ikela.

TUCKEY, JAMES (CAPTAIN). A British explorer who led an expedition up the Congo River, reaching Isangila near what is now Matadi in 1816. He is credited with making the first detailed mappings of the Bas-Zaire region.

- U -

UBANGI RIVER. A 1,000-km-long river that is the demarcation line for Zaire's border with the northern Congo and southwestern Central African Republic. The Ubangi forms where the Boma and Uele Rivers join together near Yakoma. It flows past Mobutu's home town of Gbadolite and the Central African capital of Bangui before joining the Zaire River about 100 kms downriver from Mbandaka. The Ubangi is navigable only during the rainy season, usually from June through October.

UELE, UPPER AND LOWER SUB-REGIONS. Two remote sub-regions of Haut-Zaire Region in the northeastern corner of Zaire, the Uele's main economic activities include farming and some mining of iron ore and gold. They are linked to the rest of Zaire only by an intermittently navigable river and a small-gauge railway. As a result, traditional trading patterns have been with southern Sudan and southeastern Central African Republic. One of the most sparsely populated regions in Zaire, the Haut-Uele, lying to the north of the Uele River, had 1,063,202 inhabitants in 1982 and the Bas-Uele, lying to the south of the Uele River, had 567,040.

UELE RIVER. Small, commercially unnavigable river in northeastern Zaire that rises near Zaire's border with southern Sudan (called the Dungu River at that point) and flows 750 kms west into the Ubangi River near Yakoma.

UJIJI. A small port city on the eastern shore of Lake Tanganyika that was the departure point for many exploring expeditions into eastern Zaire. Stanley met Livingstone there in 1871.

UMBA DI LUTETE. Lawyer, diplomat and on several occasions foreign minister, Umba was a technocrat who rose primarily through the executive branch. Born on June 30, 1939, at Kangu, in Bas-Zaire

Region, he received a law degree from Lovanium University in
1965 and other law certificates in Belgium and the United States
during the early 1960s. He served in senior staff positions in
the foreign ministry and at the Presidency from 1965-67. He
was vice-foreign minister from 1967-69, minister of energy from
1970-71, state commissioner (after ministers were renamed state
commissioners) of mines in 1971-74, state commissioner for foreign
affairs in 1974-75, ambassador to the United Nations in 1976-77,
and state commissioner for foreign affairs again in 1977-79 and
1984-85.

UNEMPLOYMENT. The Zairian government issues no figures for unemployment rates, but economists estimate unemployment in urban centers, if they were calculated on bases similar to those used
in the industrialized world, would average 20 percent. However,
sociologists say that fewer than one-half of working-age males
in the cities participate in the formal economy.

UNIAO NACIONAL PARA A INDEPENDENCIA TOTAL DE ANGOLA
(UNITA) (NATIONAL UNION FOR THE TOTAL INDEPENDENCE
OF ANGOLA). A nationalist Angolan guerrilla group, headed by
Jonas Savimbi and reportedly backed by South Africa, that fought
a war for independence against the Portuguese colonial authorities
in the 1960s and 1970s and, in the civil war that followed Angola's
independence, fought two rival factions for control of the country.
The Soviet-backed MPLA faction gained control of Luanda in 1975
and was recognized by the United Nations in 1976. However,
UNITA has continued its guerrilla war and controls significant portions of territory in eastern and southern Angola. UNITA also
has prevented the operation of the Benguela Railway, the most
economical route for mineral exports from Zaire's Shaba Region,
although it reportedly agreed in 1987 to allow nonmilitary transport
on the line. See BENGUELA RAILWAY and SHABA REGION.

UNION DES ETATS DE L'AFRIQUE CENTRALE (UEAC) (UNION OF
CENTRAL AFRICAN STATES) see UNION DOUANIERE ET
ECONOMIQUE DE L'AFRIQUE CENTRALE

UNION DOUANIERE ET ECONOMIQUE DE L'AFRIQUE CENTRALE
(UDEAC) (CENTRAL AFRICAN CUSTOMS AND ECONOMIC
UNION). French-sponsored customs and tariffs union of former
French Equatorial African states. Mobutu tried to form a similar
organization in 1968, called the Union des Etats de l'Afrique Cen-
trale (UEAC) with Chad and Central African Republic. Chad
agreed to join, but the CAR declined. Cameroon, Congo, and
Gabon, backed by France, actively opposed the UEAC and it
never reached the operational stage. Zaire eventually joined
UDEAC in the early 1980s and Chad, which had dropped out of
UDEAC after it joined the UEAC, was readmitted in 1984.

UNION KATANGAISE. A group of primarily Belgian expatriates living in Katanga that pressed for autonomy for Katanga Province in the 1950s. Part of the Union pour la Colonisation, founded in 1944, the Union Katangaise was accepted into CONAKAT in 1959 and was one of the strongest advocates of an autonomous Katanga within a federal Congolese state. During the Katanga secession, the Union became a shadow group advising officials and occasionally recruiting abroad for it.

UNION MINIERE DU HAUT-KATANGA (UMHK). A mining consortium of primarily Belgian ownership formed in 1906 to exploit recently discovered deposits of copper ores in Katanga (now called Shaba). Historically the largest company in Zaire, UMHK was nationalized in 1966 and its name was changed to "GEOMINES." In 1971 the name was changed to "GECAMINES." See GECAMINES.

UNION MONGO (UNIMO). A group organized in the 1950s to represent the interests of the Mongo people, particularly prior to the elections for local councils in 1957. UNIMO sent a delegation-- headed by founder Justin Bomboko--to the Round Table conferences in 1960 and was represented in the early Congolese governments.

UNION NATIONALE DES INTERETS SOCIAUX CONGOLAIS (UNISCO) (NATIONAL UNION OF CONGOLESE SOCIAL INTERESTS). One of Zaire's first nationalist organizations, UNISCO was founded in 1946 as an association, because of the ban on political activity, to "coordinate activities" of alumni groups such as those of the Scheut Fathers, the Christian Brothers, the Jesuits, and the Marists.

UNION NATIONALE DES TRAVAILLEURS ZAIROIS (UNTZa) (NATIONAL UNION OF ZAIRIAN WORKERS). Zaire's only trade union, it was originally formed as the Union Nationale des Travailleurs Congolais in 1967 by bringing together all of the trade unions existing at that time. The merger drew protests from some labor leaders who feared the union would become too closely aligned with the party and government. In subsequent years, through decrees and constitutions, that fear was born out. The Zairian government believed trade unions should serve to mobilize workers behind government policies. However, UNTZa continued to demonstrate occasional independence at the grass roots level and, despite opposition from its senior leaders (many of whom held senior party positions), it organized demonstrations and strikes on a number of occasions to protest low salaries and government austerity measures. In 1983, UNTZa had one million registered members, of which 677,000 were in the industrial sectors. Of that group, 71,000 were in the mining sector and 500,000 were employees of government or state-owned enterprises. See LABOR.

UNION POUR LA COLONISATION (UNION FOR COLONIZATION). A

group of primarily Belgian inhabitants of Katanga, founded in
1944 to promote the European colonial presence in Zaire. The
group advocated Katangan autonomy and portions of its leadership
belonged to the militant Union Katangaise that was accepted into
the CONAKAT in June 1959. The group strongly influenced
CONAKAT's subsequent positions regarding Katangan autonomy,
a federal Congo and, following independence, the decision to
secede.

UNION POUR LA DEMOCRACIE ET LE PROGRES SOCIAL (UDPS)
(UNION FOR DEMOCRACY AND SOCIAL PROGRESS). A political
"party" founded in early 1982 by 13 parliamentarians, many of
whom had been in government since independence and some of
whom had served as ministers. The MPR is the only legal party
in Zaire and forming a second party is illegal under the Constitution of 1974. The parliamentarians were arrested, convicted of
sedition, and in June 1982, sentenced to prison terms ranging up
to 15 years. They were amnestied on May 21, 1983, but their
leaders were arrested and banished to their home villages on several occasions afterwards, including following a meeting on August
12, 1983 with a delegation of U.S. Congressmen visiting Kinshasa.
They were amnestied again but, according to reports from human
rights organizations in 1986, many of them had been placed under
house arrest or banished to their home regions once again.

UNITA see UNIAO NACIONAL PARA A INDEPENDENCIA TOTAL DE
ANGOLA

UNITED KINGDOM, RELATIONS WITH. Britain was one of the first
European nations in the 1800s to become interested in central
Africa, the Congo River, and the commercial possibilities of the
region. The British government and British associations financed
numerous exploration expeditions, particularly in eastern Zaire
(see BURTON; SPEKE; BAKER; and LIVINGSTONE) and of the
Congo River (see STANLEY). British firms traded for a time
with merchants in Zaire, but following the Berlin Conference,
focused increasingly on the British colonies. Britain was in the
forefront of the antislavery movement and led the international
outcry against the harsh labor practices of the Congo Free State.
Today, the United Kingdom has less economic and social ties with
Zaire than most of the other industrialized nations, such as
Belgium, France, the United States, Japan, West Germany, and
Italy. However, relations are considered good despite British concern over mismanagement, authoritarianism, and human rights
abuses in Zaire.

UNITED NATIONS. Zaire was the venue for the United Nations'
first and to-date only police action in Africa. Faced with the
deterioration of security and collapse of government services following independence, and the perceived threat of a Belgian re-
occupation of the territory following Belgian troop landings in

Matadi, Elisabethville, and Luluabourg, the Kasavubu government asked for U.N. military assistance on July 12, 1960, 13 days after independence. The United Nations passed a resolution on July 14 agreeing to send U.N. troops to Zaire, but it limited their responsibilities to "internal" Congolese affairs, namely the Katanga secession. However, it soon became evident that assistance was needed in other areas and the size of the U.N. contingent in the Congo grew to 20,000 before the operation was ended in July 1964. The U.N. helped set up the Zairian civil service and staffed the police and judiciary which had been devastated by the sudden departure of Belgian technicians and professionals. Some U.N. officials also served for a number of months as a "shadow cabinet" for the Congolese government. Nevertheless, the U.N.'s role in Katanga was the most controversial and received the most attention. Faced with the continued inability of the Kasavubu government to end the secession, the U.N. on February 21, 1961, passed a resolution more strongly worded than the one following independence, giving the U.N. forces the authority to "prevent civil war." U.N. officials, in a move that was severely criticized by some U.N. members, used the resolution to try to expel foreign mercenaries from Katanga in September 1961, causing an outbreak of fighting. The fighting was stopped following the death of Dag Hammarskjöld in a plane crash while on a trip to northern Rhodesia to meet Tshombe. However, fighting resumed in December when U.N. troops moved again to remove the mercenaries. That action was more successful and led Tshombe to resume unification negotiations. The controversy caused by the U.N. role in the Congo (the Soviet Union, for example, refused to contribute funds to the operation) led to a reluctance on the part of the world body to engage in other police actions on the continent and to concentrate its efforts, instead, on diplomatic mediation in armed disputes, economic development, and the struggle against drought, disease, and hunger.

UNITED STATES, RELATIONS WITH. The United States has been interested in Zaire since the New York Herald newspaper sent Stanley to find Livingstone in 1871. The U.S. government initially supported Leopold II's pledge to "civilize" the peoples of the Congo and was the first nation to recognize his Congo Free State following the Berlin Conference. However, public outcry in the United States and Europe over reports of harsh labor practices and atrocities committed against Congolese by agents of the CFS and private companies operating there led to the takeover of the territory by the Belgian government in 1908. Although U.S. economic interests in the Belgian Congo remained smaller than those of Belgium during the colonial period, U.S. churches sent large numbers of missionaries to the Congo from 1930-1960 to establish and staff schools, churches, and hospitals. Uranium from the Congo was used to make the first atomic bomb in the 1940s and following World War II appreciation grew for the fact that the territory was one of the largest sources of industrial diamonds, cobalt, and other strategic minerals in the non-communist world.

The U.S. government was one of the first to establish diplomatic relations with the Congo following independence and many programs of the U.S. Agency for International Development and the Peace Corps were established in the country during the 1960s. The U.S. supported the central government in Leopoldville and opposed the Katanga secession and the various rebellions during the early 1960s. U.S. planes transported Belgian paratroopers that landed in Stanleyville on November 24, 1964, to rescue several hundred European and American hostages being held by the Simba rebels. U.S. investment increased during the 1960s. However, relations cooled somewhat when Mobutu began moving the country toward a one-party state in the late 1960s. They deteriorated further following Zairianization and Zaire's diplomatic rupture with Israel in 1973. In June 1975, Mobutu accused the U.S. government of supporting an attempted coup d'etat. The U.S. government denied the charges and recalled its ambassador from Kinshasa. Despite the strain in relations, both governments opposed the MPLA faction in Angola's civil war and provided aid to the opposing FNLA and UNITA factions. The U.S. government provided transport planes, arms, and food to Zairian troops to repel the first Shaba invasion in 1977. It sent additional aid following the second Shaba war in 1978 and accused Cuba and the Soviet Union of complicity in the attack on Kolwezi in which one U.S. citizen was killed.

Following the Shaba wars, Mobutu began a rapprochement with the United States and other western nations where increased criticism was being heard of corruption and human rights abuses by the Zairian government. Relations were cool during the late 1970s because of President Carter's administration's emphasis on human rights. However, relations and bilateral aid programs improved markedly under President Reagan's administration, which expressed greater appreciation than its predecessor for Zaire's strategic location, mineral wealth, and support for U.S. policies in the region. Military assistance, which had been reduced to less than $8 million per year under Carter, increased to more than $30 million. A group of liberal Congressmen continued to criticize authoritarianism and economic mismanagement in Zaire. However, the U.S. government expressed support for and pleasure over the economic reforms enacted by the Zairian government and the re-establishment of diplomatic ties with Israel in the mid-1980s. Vice-President George Bush visited Zaire in November 1982, Secretary-of-State George Schultz visited in February of 1987, and Mobutu visited the United States regularly in private and official capacities. A bilateral investment treaty was signed in 1984 aimed at encouraging U.S. private investment in Zaire. The treaty guaranteed that companies would be able to transfer profits abroad and repatriate capital. Some major U.S. investments in Zaire include General Motors Zaire, Firestone Zaire, construction of the Inga-Shaba power transmission line and participation in mining, cement, and petroleum exploration ventures.

UNIVERSITE NATIONALE DU ZAIRE (UNAZA) (NATIONAL UNIVERSITY OF ZAIRE). The sole institution of higher learning other than professional schools in Zaire, UNAZA was created by decree in August 1971 following several years of student protests against the government. It was created from three church-run universities: the Université de Lovanium in Kinshasa, the Université Officielle du Congo in Lubumbashi, and the Université Libre du Congo in Kisangani. Lovanium, the oldest and perhaps most prestigious, was founded in 1954 by the Catholic Church. The Lubumbashi University was first established in 1956 by Protestant groups as the Université Officielle du Congo Belge et du Ruanda-Urundi. It became the Université de l'Etat du Congo in 1960, the Université d'Elisabethville in 1963, and the Université Officielle du Congo in 1964. The Kisangani university was founded in 1963 by Protestant missions groups, but classes were disrupted for a number of years because of the eastern rebellions. Following the creation of UNAZA, the three campuses were maintained in the regional capitals but the administration was centralized in Kinshasa. Although there were some degrees offered by two or more of the campuses, there was a certain degree of specialization: medicine at Kinshasa campus, for example, philosophy and letters at Kisangani, and natural and social sciences at Lubumbashi. The creation of a fourth campus at Kananga was announced in 1984 and work on the facility had begun by 1985. Most educators agree the quality of education of the universities was seriously eroded during the late-1970s and early 1980s by a lack of funds, low salaries, and frequent closings due to student protests, usually over poor living and study conditions. However, UNAZA continues to increase Zaire's population of university graduates, from 12 at independence, to 167 in 1968, to an estimated 2,000 in 1985. Graduates of professional and technical schools numbered roughly twice those of the universities.

UNIVERSITIES. Since 1971, Zaire has had a single, national university, the Université National du Zaire (UNAZA), with campuses in Kinshasa, Lubumbashi, Kisangani, and, since 1985, Kananga. Prior to 1971, the campuses were private universities, run primarily by church groups with financial support from some lay organizations and philanthropic foundations. Total enrollment ranged from 15,000 to 20,000 students. The Institut Makanda Kabobi, of the MPR party, provides post-secondary school training to party cadres, and the Ecole National d'Administration (National School of Administration) trains civil servants. See EDUCATION and UNIVERSITE NATIONAL DU ZAIRE.

URANIUM. Uranium deposits are known to exist in a number of copper-mining areas of Shaba Region. However, actual mining of the mineral to date has been only at one location, the Shinkolobwe

gold mine in southern Shaba, 40 kms south of Likasi, and at
that location only between 1944 and 1960 by UMHK (now called
GECAMINES). Radium was discovered in gold ore there as early
as 1922. The first concentrates were produced from tailings in
1944 and sold to the Combined Development Agency (CDA) of the
U.S. and British governments. A 1985 report by the U.S. Bureau
of Mines states uranium bought by the U.S. government was used
in the Manhattan Project that produced the atomic bombs dropped
on Japan. The report adds the CDA purchases from 1944 to 1960
totaled 32,500 metric tons of (U308) concentrate. The Shinkolobwe
mine was closed in April 1960, prior to independence. In 1982,
Zaire signed an agreement with the French government to under-
take surveys and production of uranium. The survey of the
Shinkolobwe mine showed remaining reserves were too deep to
justify reopening the mine. However, surveys of other GECA-
MINES concessions showed commercially exploitable deposits in
copper ore.

URBANIZATION. Zaire has experienced the same rapid urban growth
as most of the developing world since the 1960s. Urban populations are estimated to have doubled from 1960 to 1970 and more
than doubled again from 1970 to 1980. UNICEF estimated in its
1987 report that more than one-fourth of Zaire's population has
become urban dwelling. Although there are indications that the
severe economic recession of the early 1980s may have reduced
the rate of migration to the cities, the prospect of jobs, participation in the cash economy and a desire for access to health and
social facilities has continued to attract rural inhabitants to the
urban centers. The migration strained social services and tended
to aggravate unemployment and crime. The Zairian government
at times was reported to have forcefully taken homeless, unemployed persons from the cities and returned them to their home
regions. It also has been reported to have inducted jobless young
persons into the army.

- V -

VIRUNGA MOUNTAINS. A chain of mountains lying in eastern Zaire
north of Lake Kivu with altitudes as high as 5,000 meters above
sea level. Remote and dense, the Virungas have been a haven
for antigovernment guerrillas since the early 1960s. The inhabitants of the region are said to remain still largely outside
the sphere-of-influence of the government. See PARTI DE LA
REVOLUTION POPULAIRE.

VIVI. First "capital" of King Leopold II's Congo, founded by Stanley in 1880. Vivi was a small fishing village lying across the
Zaire River from what has become Matadi. It was used by Stanley as a base for the arduous overland trek to Leopoldville.
However, Leopoldville, with its strategic position as the main

river port for the interior of the territory, quickly became the
political and economic center of the territory.

VOIE NATIONALE see NATIONAL WAY

VOLCANOS. There are a number of active volcanos in remote parts
of eastern and northeastern Zaire. Two notable eruptions occurred when the Nyirangongo Volcano, altitude 3,500 m, erupted
in 1977 and the Nyamuragira, altitude 3,000 m, erupted in 1984.

VOTING see ELECTIONS

VUNGARA. One of two major groups of the Zande peoples living in
northernmost Zaire and speaking a language related to the
Adamawara-Eastern cluster. The Vungara lived primarily in the
eastern part of Zande land near Ango and Faradje between the
Uele and Ubangi Rivers. They began to emerge in Zaire in the
eighteenth and nineteenth centuries when groups of hunters,
divided into the Vungara aristocracy and the Mbomu commoners,
entered northern Zaire and conquered the local peoples, some of
whom spoke Sudanic languages, others of whom spoke languages
of the Bantu cluster. Chieftaincy among the Vungara was handed
down from father to son. However, the son was obliged to vanquish any of his brothers who chose to contest the succession.
The vanquished brothers were then expected to leave in order
to conquer their own people and found their own lineages. This
pattern of succession is said to be one of the major reasons for
the mosaic mixture of Sudanic and Bantu cultures in northern
Zaire. The Vungara in some cases maintained ties with tribes
to the north and fiercely resisted the Belgian colonial authorities
until the followers of the Mahdi of southern Sudan were defeated
in the late 1890s.

- W -

WAGES AND SALARIES. Wage and salary earners in Zaire have always been near the bottom of the organized economy, while successful businessmen and entrepreneurs have usually occupied the
upper levels and senior political officials constitute the elite,
state bourgeoisie. Minimum wage has varied between $30 and
$60 per month. In 1985, the minimum wage was $50 per month,
professionals earned two to six times that amount, while ministerial-
level, government and party officials earned 25 times the minimum
wage, not including benefits like subsidized housing, cars, educational expenses, and entertainment allowances. Zaire's per capita
income has always been low in comparison to equally endowed
African countries. The fact is due in part to the large Zairian
population that lives outside the formal economy (70 percent of
the total population in 1985) and also due to the active parallel,
or informal economy. Per capita income peaked at $200 per year

in the mid-1970s but fell to $140 by 1985. Banque du Zaire
figures have shown that traditionally, income levels are highest
in Kinshasa and Lubumbashi, having reached $280 per year in
the mid-1970s. Shaba, Bas-Zaire, and Kasai Oriental regions follow in that order with per capita income levels averaging one-
half to one-fourth of those in Zaire's two major cities. Real
earning power was considerably eroded by inflation in the late
1970s and early 1980s due in part to the fact that indexation-for-
inflation was abolished in 1976. The fiscal reforms of September
1983, whereby the currency was floated on the open market, sent
the official currency exchange rate to one-fifth of its previous
level, while wages were frozen. Officially prices were also
frozen, but controls were difficult to enforce and most prices in
a matter of days doubled or in some cases tripled. Workers
eventually were given a 50 percent wage increase. However,
wages remained frozen during the next two years while annual
inflation reached 100 percent. The government allowed a 25 percent wage increase in early 1985 and promised another, while
annual inflation that year dropped to 50 percent. The increases
somewhat eased the crisis for workers, many of whom had been
driven into parallel commercial activities in order to survive.
See ECONOMY and INFLATION.

WATERWAYS. Zaire's 14,000 kms of navigable waterways provide a
unique natural transportation system. However, parts of the
major rivers are not navigable and the road and railway systems
designed to circumvent them are plagued by swamps, mountain
ranges, and dense rain forest. The disparity explains why
Zaire's regions have such widely divergent population densities,
per capita incomes, and levels of economic development. Only
those remote regions with sizeable deposits of commercially exploitable minerals or agricultural potential have been considered
worthy of capital investment programs in transportation infrastructure. The Zaire River forms the backbone of the water-
way system with 4,300 kms of navigable waters, which unfor-
tunately are truncated in three places by unnavigable cataracts:
between Kongolo and Kindu and between Ubundu and Kisangani
on the upper Zaire River, and between Kinshasa and Matadi on
the lower portion of the river. The Kasai, Tshuapa, and Ubangi
rivers are major, navigable tributaries. Five railway systems connect the navigable rivers to areas of mineral and agricultural
production and circumvent unnavigable portions of the rivers
(see RAILWAYS). In eastern Zaire, the lakes of the Great Rift
Valley, Tanganyika, Kivu, Mobutu and Edouard, provide major
transportation links with East Africa and points along the eastern
Zairian border. See NATIONAL WAY; LAKES; PORTS; RIVERS;
and TRANSPORTATION.

"WAX." The name, derived from the method of making patterned
cloth using wax and dyes, that has come to denote the brightly
colored cloth that in Zaire is used for everything from table cloths

and curtains to clothes for men and women. Wax originated in
the Dutch-influenced areas of Malaysia and Indonesia and was
brought to Africa by Dutch traders returning from Asia. The
cloth is widely used throughout Africa and most nations have
textile industries that manufacture the cloth, although the use of
the authentic "wax" method has been abandoned. See CLOTH
and DRESS.

WELFARE see SOCIAL SERVICE

WITCHCRAFT see SPIRITUALISM

WOMEN. In most traditional Zairian societies, women played an important role in lineage (many ethnic groups are matrilineal) and
family. An elderly woman could rise to the position of village elder
and, in some societies, chief. However, male pastimes and voca-
tions like hunting, fishing, and warring tended to be regarded
as more noble and valorous than the traditional female occupations
of cultivating, collecting firewood, and cooking. Like most African states, Zaire has enacted laws guaranteeing women equal rights,
the vote, and property and custodial rights in divorce. Zairian
law also outlaws in principle the practice of polygamy. The civil
service and armed forces are open to women (the latter has had
its own battalion since 1976), and as many as three ministerial
portfolios at one time have been occupied by women. Since independence, a number of women have risen to prominence as bar-
risters, professors, functionaries, and physicians. Observers
note, however, that full equality has yet to be achieved. Sig-
nificantly fewer women attend and graduate from high schools
and universities than males. According to government statistics,
literacy rate for women was 45 percent in 1985, while it was 79
percent for males. Fewer still rise in the professional ranks and
their salaries often are lower than males fulfilling similar or less
responsible functions. Others note, however, that with the high
incidence of unemployment, job openings tend to go to heads-of-
family, who usually are considered to be male, despite an increasing number of families in urban areas headed by women. In
addition, sociologists say, given the tendency in family disputes
toward recourse to traditional law and custom, rare indeed is the
women who can draw satisfactory compensation from a divorce if
the husband decides to take the children and belongings. Although African and Zairian feminism is young and certainly not
as militant as its European and American counterparts, observers
note it has grown since the 1960s and has achieved some progress
in the quest for equality.

WORLD BANK see INTERNATIONAL BANK FOR RECONSTRUCTION
AND DEVELOPMENT

WORLD WARS. The Belgian Congo provided important human and
material resources to Belgium and the Allies during the World

Wars. Troops of the Force Publique fought German forces in
Cameroon and Tanganyika during World War I and Nazi and
Fascist forces in Ethiopia and Nigeria in World War II. In both
wars the heroism of the Congolese contingents was praised by
the allied command. In addition, mines in Katanga supplied copper, tin, cobalt, and other minerals to the war industry. They
also furnished the raw uranium used to make the atomic bombs
dropped on Japan that ended World War II and launched the
nuclear age. Revenues from Zairian exports were largely responsible for keeping the treasury of the Belgian governments-
in-exile afloat during the wars and helped finance the post-
World War II reconstruction effort.

- Y -

YAKA. A group of Bantu-speaking people that originally lived between the Kwango and Wamba rivers in southwestern Zaire.
Some ethnologists say the Jaga invasion that severely weakened
the Kongo Kingdom in the 1600s was actually mounted by the
Yaka. A fierce, independent people, the Yaka during the colonial era tended to avoid the Belgian authorities for geographical and political reasons. Yaka residents of Leopoldville clashed
with the Kongo following independence and occasionally engaged
in armed resistance during the 1960s against attempts by the
central government to assume control of their lands.

YEKE. A people of the Bantu cluster with some Arab influence who
live in southern Shaba Region between Kolwezi and Kazanga near
the Zambian border. According to Kaplan, the Yeke are descendants of a kingdom established in the 1800s by Tanzania-
based traders called the Nyamwezi. Some Yeke joined the Lunda
in forming the CONAKAT party in the late 1950s.

YEMO, MAMA. Mobutu's mother, who was the model for the "Black
Madonna" African motherhood theme that was prominent in the
early stages of the authenticity movement. Following her death
on May 18, 1971, Kinshasa's main hospital was named after her.

YOUTH. More than one-half of Zaire's population is below the age
of 16 years and two-thirds are younger than 25 years of age.
The growth of the country's youth population has been the result
of continued high birth rates and lower infant mortality due
largely to improved health and nutrition in the country. In the
mid-1960s Zairian cities experienced a dramatic increase in their
youth population, due not only to demographic factors, but also
to migration to the cities by young people seeking jobs and the
modern life. High unemployment and the decay of the traditional
extended family that provided support systems led to severe
problems of homeless youth and juvenile crime. The Zairian government, aware of the potentially destabilizing threat of its youth,

sought to channel its energy through the youth wing of the MPR, called the Jeunesse du Mouvement Populaire de la Révolution (JMPR). However, the zeal of the early JMPR organizers in taking over all church and lay youth movements and property, and in denouncing individuals considered against the movement, created considerable popular resentment during the late 1960s. The feelings waned as the movement became institutionalized and more mature. However, the lack of educational facilities and job prospects, combined with natural youthful idealism, later made some of Zaire's youth, particularly university students, the most persistent critics of the government. Protests organized by university students and supported by secondary students in 1969 led to clashes with the army in which dozens were killed. Continued protests by university students to commemorate the first clashes led to the nationalization of the universities in 1971 and a centralization of curricula in 1972-73. Other protests were organized in subsequent years leading to frequent closings of the universities and secondary schools. Many of the protests were for better living and study conditions and, sometimes, against what was viewed as wasteful government spending. The protests also occasionally led to vandalism and looting. They usually prompted a stern response from the authorities including arrests, suspensions, and induction of the leaders into the army. Many of the antigovernment student leaders later rose to senior positions in party and government. Others went into exile to become political dissidents. See JEUNESSE DU MOUVEMENT POPULAIRE DE LA REVOLUTION and STUDENTS.

- Z -

ZAIRE, REPUBLIQUE DU. The formal name of the nation since October 27, 1971, when it was changed by decree from the République Démocratique du Congo. Zaire was the name first given by Portuguese explorers to the Congo River. Legend has it that the local inhabitants, asked by the newly arrived explorers what was the name of the great river, responded saying "Nzadi," which meant "river" in their dialect. The river and the territory were subsequently given the name "Congo" after the Kongo people living near the mouth of the river who were the first to enter into contact with the Europeans. During the authenticity movement, however, the desire arose to change the name in order to find an authentic African name that did not evoke one sole Zairian ethnic group, and to remove a painful reminder of the brutality of colonialism and the chaos following independence. The name change was also aimed at eliminating confusion with neighboring Congo/Brazzaville, the former French colony. The word "zaire" had been adopted in 1967 for a new currency to replace the Congolese franc. It was also adopted as the name for the Republic and for the river that constituted its main transportation artery. It should be noted that the Brazzaville government has

never accepted the renaming of the river and continues to call
it the Congo River. Although most of the river lies within
Zairian territory, part of it lies along the Congolese border.
Because of a lack of agreement between the two parties, most
international cartographers continue to use the name Congo River.
See AUTHENTICITY; CONGO, BELGIAN; CONGO FREE STATE;
CONGO, REPUBLIQUE DU; CONGO, REPUBLIQUE DEMOCRATIQUE;
and NAME CHANGES.

ZAIRE COMMITTEE. A group of intellectuals, consisting primarily
of Belgian former teachers in Zaire and exiled Zairian dissidents,
that opposes the Mobutu government and publishes an occasional
newsletter denouncing corruption, authoritarianism and human
rights violations in Zaire. Exiled Zairian politicians at times have
allied themselves with this committee and contributed to its work
by providing documents and verbal accounts of the excesses of
the regime, but most have preferred to form and lead their own
dissident groups.

"ZAIRE" CURRENCY. The major unit of currency since 1967 when it
replaced the Congolese franc that had been closely associated with
the Belgian franc. One zaire equals 100 makuta (likuta in the
singular) and one likuta equals 100 sengi. In 1987, one U.S.
dollar was worth 80 zaires. See CURRENCY.

ZAIRE RIVER. The Zaire River, often called the Congo River, is
the second largest body of flowing water in terms of volume in
the world after the Amazon River, and the second longest river
in Africa after the Nile. It is the major artery of the drainage
system for the Congo Basin, which experiences some of the heaviest rainfall in the world. Portuguese explorers first arrived at
its mouth in 1483 and the quest for its headwaters sent a number
of European explorers on expeditions from Eastern Zaire in the
second half of the nineteenth century. The backbone of Zairian
transportation, the Zaire River rises in the highlands of Shaba
at an altitude of 1,500 meters above sea level about 1,500 kms
from both the Atlantic and Indian Ocean in a region bordering
southern Africa. It traces a wide arc across central Africa,
first flowing north across the Equator, then west through the
heart of the Congo Basin before turning southwest to cross the
Equator a second time and flow into the Atlantic Ocean. With
an official length of 4,300 kms, the Zaire begins with the headwaters of the Luapula and Lualaba rivers in southern Africa and
by the time it reaches the Atlantic it is flowing at a rate of
70,000 cubic meters per second, a rate strong enough to make
its waters distinguishable from as far as 50 kms out to sea.
Because the river drains areas in both the northern and southern
hemispheres, its rate of flow varies far less with the seasons than
other rivers. Its ratio of high flow to low flow is only 3:1,
whereas it is 20:1 for the Mississippi River and 48:1 for the Nile.
The river is navigable for 3,000 kms of its length and with its

tributaries provides more than 11,000 kms of navigable waterways within the Zairian borders. However, it is not navigable
at three points, between Kongolo and Kindu in western Kivu Region, between Ubundu and Kisangani in southern Haut-Zaire
region above Kisangani, and between Kinshasa and Matadi in
Bas-Zaire Region. As a result, rail systems were built between
1900 and 1932 to ship goods past these points. Although it is a
major transportation artery, the river's size and its cataracts
have also proven to be a barrier to transportation. It was only
in 1983 that the first bridge was completed across the river, at
Matadi. In 1986, the Zairian and Congolese governments signed
an agreement to build a second, 17-km bridge over the river
linking the capitals of the two countries. See RIVERS and
TRANSPORTATION.

ZAIRETAIN. A tin mining company established in 1968, 50 percent
owned by the Zairian government and 50 percent owned by the
Belgian company GEOMINES. See TIN.

ZAIRIANIZATION. The term used to describe the policy of nationalizing foreign-owned companies in strategic sectors of the
economy between 1973 and 1975. On November 30, 1973, amid
rising mineral prices and at the peak of the authenticity movement, Mobutu announced a program aimed at transferring a great
deal of Zaire's wealth still in foreign hands to Zairians. The
large mineral companies had been nationalized in the late 1960s.
Zairianization transferred most large and medium-sized companies
in the agricultural and transport sectors and all companies with
gross annual revenues of more than one million zaires (at the time
equal to one million dollars) to public ownership. The program
most affected Zaire's medium-size merchants and small business-
owners, most of whom were foreign individuals of Asian, Arab,
and southern European nationalities who were perceived as
profiteering middlemen. Their companies were turned over to
Zairian citizens chosen by the government.
    In many of the more than 100 large enterprises that were
Zairianized, the government appointed representatives, called
"délégués," but retained the original owners as operators or
partners. In the smaller businesses, however, there were fewer
controls and the new owners often merely sold off the existing
stock and assets and abandoned the business. Zairianization also
seriously hurt the agricultural sector because the new owners
failed to maintain transportation, distribution, and marketing infrastructures. In addition, the lack of guidelines for compensation
and the favoring of political and party loyalists brought criticism
at the domestic and international levels.
    On December 30, 1974, in the face of falling production figures
and criticism from the international financial community, the
Zairian government granted a partial retrocession, allowing up
to 40 percent of ownership of the Zairianized properties to be

returned to the foreign owners. The proportion was increased
to 60 percent nine months later. However, the government did
retain ownership of what were considered vital industries, namely in the energy, timber, and large-scale transportation sectors.
By the mid-1980s, Zairianization was officially remembered as a
noble but flawed experiment as the Zairian government adopted
increasingly liberal, domestic economic, and foreign investment
policies. See ECONOMY and RETROCESSION.

ZAMBIA, RELATIONS WITH. Relations between Zaire and Zambia for
the most part have been good, in large part because of the longstanding friendship between Mobutu and Zambian President Kenneth Kaunda. However, border problems and competition for
markets for the principal exports of both countries (copper and
cobalt) have caused occasional strains. Relations were strained
during the Shaba invasions of 1977 and 1978 when FNLC guerrillas used Zambian territory to travel from bases in Angola to
Shaba Region. However, tensions eased when it became evident
that they did so without the consent of the Zambian government.
Relations were also strained in 1983 and 1984 by a series of
border clashes in southern Shaba. In one incident, Zairian soldiers raised the Zairian flag over several small villages claimed
by both countries. In another incident Zairian passengers were
abducted from a train in Zambian territory. These and other incidents and subsequent acts of retaliation were often characterized as acts of banditry by hungry soldiers or attributed to disputes between smugglers. The two governments responded by
reaffirming their political will to retain good relations and formed
a joint commission to settle disputes. The Zairian and Zambian
governments in 1985 also announced their intention to observe an
agreement to prevent prices for cobalt from falling below certain
levels. The two countries contain most of the known cobalt
reserves of the non-communist world.

ZANDE. A large cluster of ethnic groups of Sudanic origin, speak-
king languages of Adamawa-Eastern origin, that live in northern
Zaire along the Ubangi and Uele Rivers bordering the Central
African Republic and Sudan. A warrior-like tribe, they are believed to have arrived in the rain forests of the Congo Basin in
the 1700s and 1800s, although ethnologists are not certain why.
They resisted the colonial administration until the early 1920s.
A hierarchical society, the Zande were sometimes divided into an
aristocracy called the Vungara and commoners called the Mbomu.
Chieftaincy, generally within the Vungara group, was passed from
father to a designated son who was obliged to vanquish any of his
brothers who opposed his ascendancy. Vanquished brothers were
obliged to leave the society and find new peoples to conquer.
The practice is believed to have been a major cause of the inter-
mingling of Zande and Bantu-related groups in northern Zaire.

ZINC. Zinc in Zaire is produced solely by GECAMINES at a single

mine at Kipushi, west of Lubumbashi. Ore with zinc graded as
high as 19 percent is extracted from depths of up to 1,280 meters.
A plant at Kipushi produces concentrates that are shipped to
Likasi for roasting and then to the Uzine de Zinc de Kolwezi, at
Kolwezi, where 25 kg ingots of 99.995 percent pure zinc are produced through the electrolytical process. Zaire's zinc reserves
are estimated at 2.2 million metric tons. Production of concentrate reached 109,182 tons in 1960 but began a steady decline
that bottomed at 67,000 tons in 1980. Production had returned
to 80,000 tons by 1984. Zinc ingots were produced beginning in
the late 1950s and production reached 66,000 tons in 1984, most
of which was exported.

ZONGO RIVER. A river located in Bas-Zaire Region east of Matadi
that flows into the Zaire River, the Zongo is the site of a dramatic waterfall where a 60,000-kw hydroelectrical complex, built
in 1928, supplies power to Bas-Zaire. The station became less
important following the completion of the Inga hydroelectrical
complex, but remains in operation, the oldest such complex in
Zaire.

THE BIBLIOGRAPHY

TABLE OF CONTENTS

INTRODUCTION

The literature available on Zaire is abundant as the length of this bibliography will testify. In addition, interest in Great Britain and the United States in the affairs of Zaire since the years of the Congo Free State has contributed to a significant body of literature in the English language. However, a student seeking an advanced or specialized knowledge of the country will find the absence of at least a working knowledge of French to be a serious handicap. This bibliography is devoted primarily to works in English and French. In addition, a few works in Flemish, German, Italian, and Portuguese that present new material or a different point of view also have been included.

For the student seeking a general overview of Zaire in English, several works exist. One that is relatively complete, succinct, and unopinionated is the Zaire Area Handbook, edited by Irving Kaplan as part of the series of country handbooks published by American University in Washington, D.C. This edition, published in 1979, follows events in Zaire through the two Shaba wars. However, research was ended in 1978 and consequently the work does not deal with the liberalization attempts following the Shaba wars or the attempted economic reforms and the dissident movements and general amnesty of the mid-1980s. Mention should also be made of the two earlier editions: the U.S. Army's Area Handbook for the Republic of the Congo (Leopoldville), published in 1962, which provides

considerably more detail on events leading up to and including independence, and the Area Handbook for the Democratic Republic
of the Congo (Congo-Kinshasa), published in 1971, which provides
additional detail on the years following independence and the beginnings of Mobutism. In French, Du Congo au Zaire. 1960-1980,
edited by J. Vanderlinden, takes a similar, long view of political,
economic, and cultural developments in Zaire.

Other, more recent works in English that tend to focus primarily on the Mobutu government include The Rise and Decline of
the Zairian State by Crawford Young and Thomas Turner, published
in 1985; The Crisis in Zaire: Myths and Realities, edited by
Nzongola-Ntalaja, published in 1986; and The State-Society Struggle:
Zaire in Comparative Perspective by Thomas M. Callaghy, published
in 1984. In varying degrees these works focus on problems such as
authoritarianism, centralization, the lack of political freedoms, corruption, and declining standards-of-living that have been among the
most recurrent indictments of Mobutism. The Nzongola book, a collection of papers presented at a conference sponsored by Howard
University at Washington, D.C., contains a revealing segment on how
Zairians survive the economic hardships of low wages or unemployment.

Several other specialized works also bear mention. Among
the bibliographies, the seminal A Study Guide for Congo-Kinshasa
by Edouard Bustin, published in 1970, is a well-organized collection
of virtually all the major material on Zaire through 1968. The listings of the Cataloging Distribution Service of the Library of Congress
provide a relatively comprehensive record of monographs published
since 1967. Articles in periodicals tend to provide recent, although
often slanted, material on current Zairian affairs. For recent articles,
readers should examine Africa Report magazine, which annually publishes a listing of the articles published in its pages in its final issue of the year. Other periodicals with frequent articles on Zaire
include Africa, Africa Confidential, Africa News, and West Africa.
Zairian publications include Elima and Salongo daily newspapers and
Zaire magazine.

Work on ethnic groups in Zaire has been extensive. Some of
the broader publications include Kingdoms of the Savanna by Jan
Vansina, published in 1966, and in French, Carte Ethnique du Congo.
Quart sud-est and Carte Ethnique de la République du Congo.
Quart sud-ouest by Olga Boone, published in 1961 and 1973 respectively. In addition, the series, Ethnographic Survey of Africa
by the International Africa Institute in the early 1950s provides a
broad though dated overview. Finally, the monographs published by
the Centre d'Etudes Ethnographiques de Bandundu (CEEBA) bear
mention as an example of Zairian efforts to collect, preserve, and
analyze information on their traditional societies.

Because of the size of the body of work and the difficulty with which articles in older periodicals are retrieved, this bibliography focuses primarily on monographs. Articles are mentioned when monographs are lacking on a certain subject.

Most scholars agree that the literature on Zaire needs more contributions from Zairian and African scholars. Nevertheless, it should be noted that contributions by Zairians have increased since the 1970s due in large part to the efforts of certain university presses in Zaire, Belgium, Britain, and the United States. It is hoped this trend will continue. In addition, Zairian scholars have tended to focus on the arts, ethnological, and social studies. These are valuable, but also needed are historical assessments of colonialism and independence by Zairian authors, as well as objective analyses of Mobutism and the post-independence period.

List of Abbreviations and Acronyms
Used in Bibliography

ARSOM	Académie Royale des Sciences d'Outre-Mer
CEDAF	Centre d'Etude et de Documentation Africaines
CEEBA	Centre d'Etudes Ethnographiques de Bandundu
CEMUBAC	Centre Scientifique et Médicale de l'Université Libre de Belgique en Afrique Centrale
CEPSI	Centre d'Etudes de Problèmes Sociaux Indigènes
CRISP	Centre de Recherche et d'Information Socio-politiques
I.A.I.	International Africa Institute
INEAC	Institut pour l'Etude Agronomique du Congo
INMZ	Institut des Musées Nationaux du Zaire
IRCB	Institut Royal Colonial Belge
IRES	Institut de Recherches Economiques et Sociales
JPRS	Joint Publications Research Service
SRBG	Société Royale Belge de Géographie
MRAC	Musée Royal de l'Afrique
UNAZA	Université Nationale du Zaire

I. GENERAL

1. Bibliographies

Belgium. Office de la Coopération au Développement. Belgium and Cooperation in Development: A Bibliographical Survey. Brussels: Belgian Information and Documentation Institute, n.d. (1963?).

Boogaerts, M. "L'enseignement au Congo: Bibliographie," Cahiers Economiques et Sociaux, IRES, vol. V, no. 2 (1967), pp. 237-265.

Boone, Olga. Bibliographie ethnographique de l'Afrique subsaharienne. Tervuren: MRAC, 1960- , (annual, continues
work below).

Boone, Olga. Bibliographie ethnographique du Congo Belge et des
regions avoisinantes. Tervuren: MRAC, 1931-60 (31 vols.).

Bustin, Edouard. A Study Guide for Congo-Kinshasa. Boston:
African Studies Center, Boston University, 1970.

Dargitz, Robert E. A Selected Bibliography of Books and Articles
in the Disciples of Christ Research Library in Mbandaka, Democratic Republic of the Congo. Indianapolis: Department of
Africa and Jamaica, United Christian Missionary Society, 1967.

Gaskin, L. J. P. A Bibliography of African Art. London: International African Institute, 1965.

_____. A Select Bibliography of Music in Africa. London: Inter-
national African Institute, 1965.

Heyse, Théodore. "Bibliographie du Congo Belge et du Ruanda-
Urundi, 1939-51," in Cahiers Belges et Congolais, nos. 4-22
(Brussels, 1953).

_____. Index bibliographique coloniale. Brussels: Falk, Fils,
G. Van Campenhout, 1937.

_____. "Le Travail bibliographique colonial belge de 1876 à 1933,"
in Zaire (June 1948), pp. 639-656.

Huisman, M., and Jacquet, P. Bibliographie de l'histoire coloniale
1900-1930: Belgique. Paris: Société de l'Histoire des Colonies,
1932.

Institut de Recherches Economiques et Sociales (IRES). Université
de Lovanium. Catalogue des Archives du Centre d'Etudes Politiques. Série: Les Provinces du Congo. Léopoldville, 1966.

Institut Royal Colonial Belge. Biographie Coloniale Belge. Brussels:
Van Campenhout, 1948. 5 vols.

International African Institute. Africa Bibliography Series: West
Central Africa. London: 1966.

_____. African Urbanization: A Reading List of Selected Books,
Articles and Reports. London: 1965.

Kadima Nzuji Mukala. "Bibliographie Littéraire de la République du
Zaire, 1931-72," in Celria, Lubumbashi, August 1973. (Also
published in Zaire-Afrique no. 87, August-September 1974.)

238 / The Bibliography

Lemarchand, René. "Selective Bibliographical Survey for the Study
of Politics in the former Belgian Congo," American Political Science
Review, vol. LVI, no. 3 (1960), pp. 715-728.

Liniger-Goumaz, Max. Préhistoire et protohistoire de la République
Démocratique du Congo: Bibliographie. Geneva: Editions du
Temps, 1969.

_____. République du Zaire, Kivu-Maniema: bibliographie.
Geneva: Editions du Temps, 1977.

Mitchel, Robert C.; Turner, Harold W.; and Greschat, Hans J. A
Comprehensive Bibliography of Modern African Religious Movements. Evanston, IL: Northwestern University Press, 1966.

Musée Royal de l'Afrique Centrale. Bibliographie géologique du
Congo et du Rwanda. Tervuren: 1952-1961.

Rossie, Jean Pierre. Bibliographie commentée de la communauté
musulmane au Zaire des origines à 1975. Brussels: CEDAF,
1976.

Ryelandt, Dominique (ed.). "Bibliographie générale des articles
et ouvrages politiques sur la République du Congo (Léopoldville),"
Etudes Congolaises (special issue, March 1963).

Santos Hernandez, Angel. Bibliografia Missional. I: Parte doctrinal.
II: Parte historical. 2 vols. Santander: Editorial "Sal Terrae,"
1965, pp. 944, 1299.

Smet, A. J. La Philosophie africaine. Bibliographie sélective. Kinshasa and Lubumbashi: UNAZA, 1974.

Vriens, Livinus. Critical Bibliography of Missiology. Nijmegen:
Bestelcentrale del V.S.K.B., 1960.

Walraet, Michel. Bibliographie du Katanga. I: 1824-1899. II:
1900-1924. III: 1925-1949. (3 vols.) Brussels: ARSOM, 1954-
60.

Wauters, Alphonse-Jules. Bibliographie du Congo 1880-85. Brussels:
Administration du Mouvement Géographique, 1895.

Zaretsky, Irving I. Bibliography on Spirit Possession and Spirit
Mediumship on the African Continent. Berkeley: University of
California, Department of Anthropology, 1967.

2. Demographic Statistics

Boute, Joseph. Demographic trends in the Republic of Zaire.

Pasadena: Munger Africana Library, California Institute of Technology, 1973.

_____, with Léon de Saint Moulin. Perspectives démographiques régionales, 1975-1985. Kinshasa: République du Zaire, Département du Plan, 1978.

Congo, République Démocratique du. Ministère du Plan et de la Coordination Economique. Service des Statistiques. Bureau Démographie. Etude par sondages de la main d'oeuvre à Léopoldville, 1958. Léopoldville: 1961.

_____, Institut National de la Statistique. Receuil des rapports et totaux. Recensement en 1970. Kinshasa: n.d.

_____, with Institut de Recherches Economiques et Sociales, Lovanium University. Enquête démographique par sondage 1955-57: Analyse générale des résultats statistiques. Léopoldville, 1961.

De Smets, R. E. Carte de la densité et de la localisation de la population de l'ancienne Province de Léopoldville (République Démocratique du Congo). Brussels: CEMUBAC, 1966.

_____. Carte de la densité et de la localisation de la population de la Province Orientale (Congo). Brussels: CEMUBAC, 1962.

Fortems, G. La densité de la population dans le Bas Fleuve et le Mayombe. Brussels: ARSOM, 1960.

Gourou, Pierre. "Carte de la densité des populations," Atlas Général du Congo Belge. Brussels: IRCB, 1951.

_____. La densité de la population rurale au Congo Belge. Brussels: ARSC, 1955.

Huysecom-Wolter, Claudine. La démographie en Equateur. Brussels: CEMUBAC, 1964.

Knoop, H. "Some Demographic Characters of a Suburban Squatting Community of Léopoldville: A Preliminary Analysis," Cahiers Economiques et Sociaux IRES, vol. 4, no. 2 (1966), pp. 119-149.

Lamal, F. Essai d'étude démographique d'une population du Kwango: Les Basuku du territoire de Feshi. Brussels: IRCB, 1949.

Neven, M.; De Potter, J.; and Danakpali, H. Enquête démographique en milieu azande, Uelé, Congo. Brussels: ARSOM, 1962.

Pauwels, Jacques. "La répartition de la population dans le territoire de Gungu (Congo)," Bulletin de la Société Royale Belge de Géographie (1962), pp. 89-129.

Romaniuk, Anatole. La fécondité des populations congolaises. Paris and The Hague: Mouton, 1967.

_____. Tableau général de la démographie congolaise. Enquête démographique par sondage, 1955-1957: Analyse générale des résultats statistiques. Léopoldville: Bureau de la Démographie and IRES, 1961.

Saint Moulin, Léon de. Atlas des collectivités du Zaire. Kinshasa: Presses Universitaires du Zaire, 1976.

Smet, Roger E. de. Cartes de la densité et de la localisation de la population de la province du Katanga (République du Zaire). Brussels: CEMUBAC, 1971.

U.S. Agency for International Development, Office of Development Information and Utilization. Africa, Zaire: selected statistical data by sex. Washington, D.C.: 1981.

Verheust, Thérèse. Enquête démographique par sondage, 1955-1957: Province Orientale, district de Stanleyville, district du Haut-Uelé. Brussels: CEDAF, 1978.

Zaire, République du. Planification du Développement, with Institut National de la Statistique. Perspectives démographiques provisoires pour la République du Zaire, 1970-1980. Kinshasa: 1972.

3. General Information and Interdisciplinary Works

American University. Foreign Areas Studies. Area Handbook for the Democratic Republic of the Congo (Congo-Kinshasa). McDonald, Gordon C., ed. 2nd edition. Washington: 1971.

_____. Area Handbook for the Republic of the Congo (Leopoldville). MacGaffey, Wyatt, ed. Washington: 1962.

_____. Zaire, a Country Study. Kaplan, Irving, ed. 3rd edition. Washington: 1979.

Archer, Jules. Congo, the Birth of a New Nation. (Juvenile) New York: J. Messner, 1979.

Belgium. Office de l'Information et des Relations Publiques pour le Congo Belge et le Ruanda-Urundi. Belgian Congo. (Translated from the French by Heldt, F. H. and Heldt, C.) Brussels: 1959-60.

British Overseas Trade Board. Republic of Zaire. London: 1976.

Bustin, Edouard. "The Congo," in Five African States: Responses to Diversity. Carter, G. M., ed. Ithaca, NY: Cornell University Press, 1963.

Cambridge History of Africa. Vols. 6-8, 1979-80.

Carpenter, John Allen. Zaire. (Juvenile) Chicago: Childrens Press, 1974.

Chapelier, A. Elisabethville: Essai de géographie humaine. Brussels: ARSC, 1957.

Comeliau, Christian. Fonctions économiques et pouvoir politique; la Province de l'Uelé en 1963-1964. Léopoldville: IRES, 1966.

Congo. 9 vols. (Published annually, various editors) Brussels: CRISP, 1959-67.

Congo, République Démocratique du. Bilan, 1965-1970. Kinshasa: 1970.

_____. Armée Nationale. Service d'Education et d'Information. Le Sixième anniversaire de la République Démocratique du Congo, 30 juin 1966. Kinshasa: 1966.

_____. Haut Commissariat à l'Information. Le Congo en bref. Kinshasa: 1966.

Crane, Louise. The Land and People of the Congo. (Juvenile) Philadelphia: Lippincott, 1971.

Diallo, Siradiou. Zaire Today. Paris: Editions J.A., 1977.

Dictionary of African Biography. 2 vols. Algonac, MI: Reference Publications for Encyclopedia Africana, 1979.

Encyclopédie du Congo Belge. 3 vols. Brussels: Bieleveld, 1950-1953.

First, Ruth. Power in Africa. New York: Pantheon, 1970.

Frank, Louis. Le Congo Belge. Brussels: La Renaissance du Livre, 1930.

Gann, L. H., and Duignan, P. White Settlers in Tropical Africa. Baltimore: Penguin, 1962.

Gappert, Gary, and Thomas, Garry, eds. The Congo, Africa and America. Syracuse: Syracuse University Press, n.d. (1965?).

Gott, Richard. Mobutu's Congo. London: Fabian Society, 1968.

242 / The Bibliography

Hailey, Lord. An African Survey. (revised ed.) London: Oxford
University Press, 1959.

Henderson, Faye. Zaire: A Country Profile. Washington: U.S.
Agency for International Development, Office for Foreign Disaster
Assistance, 1981.

Heyse, Théodore, and Berlage, Jean. Documentation générale sur
le Congo et le Ruanda-Urundi, 1953-1960. 3 vols. (Cahiers
Belges et Congolais, nos. 26, 31 and 34.) Brussels: Van Campenhout, 1956, 1958 and 1960.

Jewsiewicki, B. Etat Indépendant du Congo, Congo Belge, République du Zaire? Québec: SAFI Press, 1984.

Laman, Karl E. The Kongo. Vols. I, II, III and IV. Uppsala:
Studia Ethnographica Upsaliensia, 1953, 1957, 1962, and 1968.

McKowan, Robin. The Congo: River of Mystery. (Juvenile) New
York: McGraw-Hill, 1968.

_____. The Republic of Zaire. (Juvenile) New York: F.
Watts, 1972.

Michiels, A., and Laude, N. Congo Belge et Ruanda-Urundi.
(18th ed.) Brussels: Editions Universelles, 1958.

Newbury, David S. Vers le passé du Zaire: Quelques méthodes de
recherche historique. Bukavu: Institut pour la Recherche Scientifique en Afrique Centrale, 1973.

Nzongola-Ntalaja, ed. The Crisis in Zaire: Myths and Realities.
Trenton, NJ: Africa World Press, 1986.

Stefoff, Rebecca. Republic of Zaire. Edgemont, PA: Chelsea
House Publishers, 1986.

Ziegler, Jean. La Contre-révolution en Afrique. Paris: Payot,
1963.

4. Periodicals, Newspapers, and Mass Media

Berlage, Jean. Répertoire de la presse du Congo Belge et du
Ruanda-Urundi (1920-1958). Brussels: Commission Belge de
Bibliographie, 1959.

Boyoma. Newspaper published in Kisangani.

Centre d'Etude et de Documentation Africaine. Les Périodiques
zairois (1970-1977). Brussels: CEDAF, 1978.

Congo, Belgian. Nsango ya Bisu; nos nouvelles. (Semi-monthly periodical for the Force Publique.) Léopoldville: 1943-60.

Congo, République du. La Voix de l'Armée Congolaise: Lolaka ya Armée Congolaise. (Semi-monthly periodical for the armed forces, replaced by Nsango ya Bisu.) Léopoldville: 1960.

Congo, République du. Bibliothèque Centrale du Congo. Répertoire des périodiques congolais se trouvant à la Bibliothèque Centrale du Congo. Léopoldville-Kalina: 1961.

Congo, République Démocratique du. Ministère de la Culture et des Arts. Direction des Archives et Bibliothèques. Répertoire alphabétique des périodiques de la Bibliothèque Nationale. Kinshasa: 1969.

_____, Ministère de l'Education Nationale. Répertoire des périodiques congolais. Léopoldville: n.d.

_____. Moniteur Congolais. semi-monthly. Leopoldville: 1960-67.

Courier Africain. (Irregular series of monographs) Brussels: CRISP, 1960- .

Elima. Daily newspaper published in Kinshasa.

Kitchen, Helen, ed. The Press in Africa. Washington: Ruth Sloan Associates, 1956.

Lonoh, Malangi Bokelenge. Agences de presse et information au Zaire. Paris: Université de Droit, d'Economie et de Sciences Sociales de Paris, Institut Français de Presse et des Sciences de l'Information, 1982.

Mjumbe. Daily newspaper published in Lubumbashi.

Mukamba, Longesha. La Cible manquée: une Etude de la pratique des média dans une ville africaine, Lubumbashi. Louvain-la-Neuve: Cabay, 1983.

Salongo. Daily newspaper published in Kinshasa.

Simons, Edwine and Kerremans, Marie Louise. Les Périodiques zairois, 1970-1977: bibliographies. Brussels: CEDAF, 1978.

Van Bol, Jean Marie. La Presse quotidienne au Congo Belge. Brussels: Pensée Catholique and Paris: Office Général du Livre, 1959.

5. Description, Travel, Guides, Maps, and Statistical Abstracts

Adamson, Joy. Queen of Shaba: The Story of an African Leopard. New York: Harcourt Brace Jovanovich, 1980.

Atlas Général du Congo. Brussels: IRCB, 1948.

Atlas de la République du Zaire. Laclavère, Georges, ed. Paris: Editions J.A., 1978.

Augouard, P. Vingt-huit années au Congo. Potiers: private publisher, 1905.

Belgium. Académie Royale des Sciences d'Outre-Mer. Atlas Général du Congo et du Ruanda-Urundi. Brussels: 1948-63.

_____. Institut Belge d'Information et de Documentation. Répertoire de l'Information en 1972 en République du Zaire. Brussels: 1972.

_____. Institut National de la Statistique. Annuaire Statistique, 1968-1978. Kinshasa: 1979.

_____. Office de l'Information et des Relations Publiques pour le Congo Belge et le Ruanda-Urundi (INFORCONGO). Congo Belge et Ruanda-Urundi: Guide du Voyageur. 4th ed. Brussels: 1958.

Burrows, Guy. The Curse of Central Africa. London: Everett, 1903.

_____. The Land of the Pygmies. New York: Thomas Crowell, 1898.

Burton, R. F. Two Trips to Gorilla Land and the Cataracts of the Congo. 2 vols. London: Low, Marston and Searle, 1876.

Cameron, Vernay L. Across Africa. London: George Philip, 1885.

Capello, H. De Angola à contra-costa. Lisbon: 1886.

_____, and Ivens, R. From Benguella to the Territory of Yacca. 2 vols. London: Low, 1882.

Coart, Emile Jean Baptiste. Vannerie et tissage. Brussels: Renaissance d'Occident, 1926.

Cole, Mary. Dirt Roads. Dublin: Gill and Macmillan, 1975.

Congo, Belgian. Institut Géographique. Various maps published from 1946 to 1960. Léopoldville: 1946-60.

Congo, République Démocratique du. Foire Internationale de Kinshasa. (International trade fair, June 24 to July 12, 1970.) Kinshasa: 1970.

_____. Institut Géographique. Various maps published intermittently. Léopoldville/Kinshasa: 1960– .

Conrad, Joseph. Heart of Darkness. London: 1902 (first publication).

Contact-Kinshasa (association). Contact Kinshasa: le guide de la République du Zaire. 3rd ed. Kinshasa: 1975.

Coquilhat, Camille. Sur le Haut-Congo. Paris: Lebègue, 1888.

Crawford, Daniel. Thinking Black: Twenty-two Years without a Break in the Long Grass of Central Africa. London: Morgan and Scott, 1912.

Crokaert, Jacques. Boula matari; au Congo belge avec le Roi Albert. Brussels: Collection Nationale, 1929.

Dennet, R. E. Seven Years among the Fjort. London: Sampson Low, 1887.

Derkindren, Gaston. Atlas du Congo Belge et du Ruanda-Urundi. Brussels: 1955.

Donegan, George J. Katanga Philatelist: a Specialized catalogue of the "Etat du Katanga" Postal Issues. Springfield, MO: 1964.

Dorman, Marcus Roberts Phipps. A Journal of a Tour in the Congo Free State. Westport, CT: Negro Universities Press, 1970.

Douville, Jean Baptiste. Voyage au Congo et dans l'interieur de l'Afrique equinoxiale fait dans les années 1828 et 1830. Stuttgart: Bureau des Nouveautés de la Littérature Française, 1832.

Elisofon, Eliot. Zaire: a Week in Joseph's World. New York: Crowell-Collier Press, 1973.

Guinness, Fanny Emma (Fitz Gerald). Congo Recollections. Edited from Notes and Conversations of Missionaries. London: Hodder and Stoughton, 1890.

Hilton-Simpson, Melville William. Land and Peoples of the Kasai. New York: Negro Universities Press, 1969.

Hoare, Michael. Congo Mercenary. London: Hale, 1967.

Idoti. With God in the Congo Forests during the Persecution under

Rebel Occupation, as Told by an African Pastor to David M. Davies. Bulstrode: Gerrards Cross, Worldwide Evangelization Crusade, 1971.

Isy-Schwart, Marcel. Congo Safari. Paris: Editions G.P., 1973.

Janssens, Emile. J'étais le Général Janssens. Brussels: Dessart, 1961.

Jean-Aubry, Georges. Joseph Conrad in the Congo. Norwood, PA: Norwood Editions, 1976.

Jeannest, Charles. Quatre années au Congo. Paris: G. Charpentier, 1884.

Kabanda, Aloys. Ali/Forman: le Combat du siècle à Kinshasa, 29-30 octobre, 1974. Sherbrooke, Québec: Naaman, 1977.

Kenney, Lona B. Mboka: A Congo Memoir. New York: Crown Publishers, 1973.

Lederer, André. Atlas Général de la République du Zaire: Carte des transports de surface. Brussels: ARSOM, 1976.

Livingstone, David. The Last Journals of David Livingstone in Africa. Waller, Horace, ed. London: John Murray, 1874.

_____. Missionary Travels and Researches in South Africa. London: John Murray, 1857.

_____. The Zambezi Expedition of David Livingstone, 1858-1863, vol. 1, The Journals. vol. 2, The Journals Continued, with Letters and Dispatches Therefrom, vol. 3. Wallis, J. P. R., ed. Oppenheimer Series. London: Chatto and Windus, 1956.

Lopez, Duarte. A Report of the Kingdom of the Congo and of the Surrounding Countries, drawn out of the writings and discourses of the Portuguese Duarte Lopez, by Filippo Figafetta. (Translated from Italian by Hutchinson, Margarite.) London: F. Cass, 1970.

McKinnon, Arch C. Kipitene of the Congo Steamship Lapsley, and with McKinnon, Fannie W. Treasures of Darkness. (published together) Boston: Christopher, 1968.

Michaux, O. Au Congo. Carnets de campagne; episodes et impressions de 1889 à 1897. Namur: Dupagne-Counet, 1913.

Moloney, Joseph A. With Captain Stairs to Katanga. London: S. Low, Marston, 1893.

Mopila, Francisco José. L'Enfance /Mopila; traduit de l'Espagnol par Jaime Castro-Segovia avec la collaboration de Jacques Lanotte. Kinshasa: Editions du Mont Noir, 1972.

Nagy, Lazlo. Katanga. (travel atlas) Lausanne: Editions Rencontre, 1965.

Newman, Gerald. Zaire, Gabon, and the Congo. New York: F. Watts, 1981.

Nouveau guide illustré de la ville de Kinshasa. Kinshasa: EDICA, 1973.

Oxford Regional Economic Atlas for Africa. Oxford: Clarendon Press, 1965.

Pirlot, Paul. Le Pays entre l'eau et le feu, et autres beautés de l'Afrique; récits congolais. Montréal: Beauchemin, 1969.

Prémorel, Raoul de. Kassai: the Story of Raoul de Premorel, African Trader. (as told to Reginald Ray Stuart.) Stockton, CA: Pacific Center for Western Historical Studies, University of the Pacific, 1975.

Roome, W. J. W. Tramping through Africa. London: 1930.

Vass, Winifred Kellersberger. Thirty-one Banana Leaves. Atlanta: John Knox Press, 1975.

Willaert, Maurice. Kivu redécouvert. Brussels: W. Arnold, 1973.

Zaire, République du. Institut Géographique du Zaire. Bureau d'Etudes d'Aménagements Urbains. Atlas de Kinshasa. Paris: Institut Géographique National, 1976.

_____. Bureau du Président. Profiles of Zaire. Kinshasa: 1971.

II. CULTURE

1. Fine Arts

African-American Institute. Art in Zaire. New York: AAI, 1975.

Les Arts au Congo Belge et au Rwanda-Urundi. Brussels: C.I.D., 1950.

Association Internationale des Critiques d'Arts. Trésors de l'Art Traditionnel. Kinshasa: AICA-Zaire, 1973.

248 / The Bibliography

Bantje, Han. Kaonde Song and Ritual. And Gansemans, Jos. La Musique et son rôle dans la vie sociale et rituelle Luba. (Published together.) Tervuren: MRAC, 1978.

Biebuyck, Daniel P. The Arts of Zaire. Berkeley: University of California Press, 1985.

Bokonga Ekanga Botombele, ed. Cultural Policy in the Republic of Zaire: A Study. Paris: UNESCO Press, 1976.

Brandel, Rose. The Music of Central Africa: An Ethnomusicological Study: Former A.E.F., Former Belgian Congo, Ruanda-Urundi, Uganda, Tanganyika. The Hague: Nijhoff, 1961.

Brueil, Henri. Les Figures incisées et ponctuées de la grotte de Kiantapo (Katanga). And Mortelmans, G. Les Dessins rupestres gravés, ponctués et peints du Katanga: Essai de synthèse. (published together.) Tervuren: MRAC, 1952.

Bustin, Marie-Louise. Art Décoratif Tschokwe. 2 vols. Lisbon: Subsidios Para a Historia, Arqueologia Ethnografia Dos Povos Da Lunda, 1961.

Centre d'Etudes Ethnologiques de Bandundu. Les Masques pende. Bandundu: CEEBA, n.d.

Cornet, Joseph. Art of Africa; Treasures from the Congo. (Translated from French by Thompson, Barbara.) London: Phaidon, 1971.

_____. Art From Zaire - L'Art du Zaire: 100 Masterworks from the National Collection. (Exhibition of traditional art from the Institut des Musées Nationaux du Zaire.) New York: African-American Institute, 1975.

_____. "Pictographies Woyo," Quaderni Poro. Milan, 1980, pp. 7-141.

_____. Pierres sculptées du Bas-Zaire. Kinshasa: Institut des Musées Nationaux du Zaire, 1978.

_____. A Survey of Zairian Art: The Bronson Collection. (Translated by McGaughey, Matt.) Raleigh: North Carolina Museum of Art, 1978.

Duvelle, Charles. Musique Kongo: Ba-Bembe, Ba-Kongo, Ba-Kongo Nseke, Ba-Lari. (LP record with annotations.) Ocora LP OCR 35k, 1967.

Elisofon, Eliot. The Sculpture of Africa. New York: Hacker Art Books, 1978.

Enquête sur la vie musicale au Congo Belge, 1934-1935. Question-
naire Knosp. Tervuren: MRAC, 1968.

Fagg, William. African Tribal Sculpture: Vol. II. The Congo Basin
Tribes. New York: Tudor, 1966.

Galerie Kamer. Congo. (Exhibition catalogue) New York: 1969.

Harris, Elizabeth. Late Beads in the African Trade. Lancaster, PA:
Center for Books on Beads, 1984.

Institut des Musées Nationaux du Zaire. Trésors de l'art traditionnel. (Catalogue for an exhibition in Kinshasa from September 13
to October 18, 1973.) Kinshasa: IMNZ, 1973.

Janzen, John M. Lemba, 1650-1930: A Drum of Affliction in Africa
and the New World. New York: Garland, 1982.

Kanza Matondo ne Mansangaza. Musique zairoise moderne. (Ex-
cerpts from a seminar delivered at Kinshasa campus of UNAZA in
1969.) Kinshasa: CNMA, 1972.

Lonoh, Malangi Bokelenge (Michel). Essai de commentaire de la
musique congolaise moderne. Kinshasa: Imprimerie St. Paul,
1969.

_____. Négritude et musique; regards sur les origines et l'évo-
lution de la musique négro-africaine de conception congolaise.
Kinshasa: République Démocratique Congolaise, 1971.

Low, John. Shaba Diary: A trip to Rediscover the "Katanga" Gui-
tar Styles and Songs of the 1950s and '60s. Wien-Föhrenau: E.
Stiglmayr, 1982.

Maquet, J. N. Note sur les instruments de musique congolaise.
Brussels: ARSC, 1956.

Mobyem, M. K.-Mikanza. Je fais du théatre. Paris: L'Harmattan,
1984.

Neyt, Françcois. Approche des arts Hemba. Villiers-le-Bel: Arts
d'Afrique noire, 1975.

_____. Arts traditionnels et histoire au Zaire: Cultures for-
estières et royaumes de la savane. (Translated into English by
Bryson, Scott.) Brussels: Société d'Arts Primitifs, 1981.

Nicolaisen, Johannes. Art of Central Africa: Selected Works of Art
from Central Africa in the Ethnographical Department of the Dan-
ish National Museum. Copenhagen: National Museum of Denmark,
1972.

Olbrechts, Frans M. Les Arts plastiques au Congo Belge. Brussels: Erasme, 1959.

_____. Congolese Sculpture. New Haven, CT: Human Relations Area Files, 1982.

Ortolani, Sante. Initiation esthétique à l'art zairois contemporain. Kinshasa: Institut des Sciences et Techniques de l'Information, 1976.

Otten, Rik. Le Cinema dans les pays des grands lacs: Zaire, Rwanda, Burundi. Paris: L'Harmattan, 1984.

Sidoff, Phillip G. Art of the Congo. Milwaukee, WI: Milwaukee Public Museum, 1974.

Söderberg, R. Les Instruments de musique au Bas-Congo et dans les regions avoisinantes. Stockholm: Ethnographical Museum of Sweden, 1956.

Sousberghe, Léon de. L'Art pende. Brussels: Palais des Académies, 1959.

Syra Dji, visages et racines du Zaire. (Exhibit organized in Paris from May 7 to August 30 (1982?) under the auspices of the Zairian government's Département de la Culture et des Arts.) Paris: Musée des Arts Décoratifs, 1982.

Thieme, Darius L. African Music: A Briefly Annotated Bibliography. Washington: Library of Congress, Reference Department, Music Division, 1964.

Thompson, Robert Farris. African Art in Motion. Los Angeles: University of California, 1974.

_____, and Cornet, Joseph. The Four Moments of the Sun. (Catalogue of an exhibition of Kongo sculpture at the National Gallery of Art, Washington, D.C. in 1981.) Washington: National Gallery of Art, 1981.

Wannyn, Rob L. L'Art ancien du métal au Bas-Congo. Champles par Wavre, Belgium: Editions du Vieux Planquesaule, 1961.

Wingert, Paul S. The Sculpture of Negro Africa. New York: Columbia University Press, 1961.

2. Languages and Linguistics

Ayibite, P. Initiation à l'enseignement des langues zairoises: 1e et 2e années secondaires. Lubumbashi: Centre de Linguistique Théorique et Appliquée, 1982.

Bentley, William Holman. Dictionary of the Kongo Language. London: Baptist Missionary Society, 1887.

Bryan, M. A. The Bantu Languages of Africa. (Handbook of African Languages.) London: International African Institute, 1959.

Burssens, A. Introduction à l'étude des langues bantoues congolaises. Antwerp: Kongo-Overzee, 1955.

Carrington, J. F. "The Drum Language of the Lokele Tribe," African Studies, vol. 3, no. 2 (June 1944).

_____. Talking Drums of Africa. London: Carey Kinsgate Press, 1949.

Clarke, R. T. "The Drum Language of the Tumba Tribe," American Journal of Sociology, vol. 40 (1934).

Dalby, David, ed. Language and History in Africa. New York: Africana, 1970.

De Rop, Albert J. Introduction à la linguistique bantoue congolaise. Brussels: Mimosa, 1963.

Fabian, Johannes. Languages and Colonial Power: The Appropriations of Swahili in the Former Belgian Congo, 1880-1938. Cambridge: Cambridge University Press, 1986.

Gouala, Pierre Macaire. Problems of Learning English in the Congo Due to Mother-tongue Interference. Nairobi: African Curriculum Organisation Project, 1981.

Gusimana. Dictionnaire Pende-Français. Bandundu: CEEBA, 1972.

Guthrie, Malcolm. Comparative Bantu: An Introduction to the Comparative Linguistics and Prehistory of the Bantu Languages. 4 vols. Farnborough: Gregg Press, 1967-72.

Haddad, Adnan. L'Arabe et le swahili dans la République du Zaire: Etudes islamiques. Paris: Société d'Edition d'Enseignement Superieur, 1983.

Hulstaert, G. Carte linguistique du Congo Belge. Brussels: publisher unknown, 1950.

_____. Au Sujet de deux cartes linguistiques du Congo Belge. Brussels: IRCB, 1954.

Kaji, Shigeki. Deux mille phrases de Swahili tel qu'il se parle au Zaire. Tokyo: Institute for the Study of Languages and Cultures of Asia and Africa, 1985.

Lubadika Botha Mak'ekebende. Le Style dans la correspondance administrative: Approche théorique. Kinshasa: Presses Universitaires du Zaire, 1983.

Matumele Maliya Mata Bonkoba. La Recherche en lexicologie politique au Zaire. Lubumbashi: Centre de Linguistique Théorique et Appliquée, UNAZA, 1975.

Mayaka. Quelques belgicismes en République du Zaire. Kinshasa and Lubumbashi: Société Nationale des Linguistes du Zaire, 1974.

Muyunga, Yacioko Kasengulu. Lingala and Ciluba Audiometry. Kinshasa: Presses Universitaires du Zaire, 1979.

Ndolo, Pius. Vocabulaire mbala. Tervuren: MRAC, 1972.

Ndomba Kanyinda. Structure syllabique du vocabulaire élémentaire du Français et du Ciluba: Etude comparative. Lubumbashi: Centre de Linguistique Théorique et Appliquée, UNAZA, 1973.

Polomé, E. "Cultural Languages and Contact Vernaculars in the Republic of the Congo," University of Texas Studies in Literature and Language. Vol. 4, no. 4 (Winter 1963), pp. 499-51.

Schicho, Walter. Syntax des Swahili von Lubumbashi: Kreolislertes Swahili vs. Standardvarietät. Wien: Afro-Pub, 1982.

Sumaili, N'gaye Lussa. Documents pour une étude des particularités lexico-sémantiques du Français au Zaire. Lubumbashi: Centre de Linguistique Théorique et Appliquée, UNAZA, 1974.

United States. Department of Defense. Lingala-English Dictionary. Washington: 1962.

_____. Department of State. Foreign Service Institute. Lingala: Basic Course. Washington: 1963.

Université Nationale du Zaire. Centre de Linguistique Théorique et Appliquée. Kusoma na kwandika Kiswahili: 1ère année primaire. (Teachers guidebook for teaching Swahili in elementary school.) Lubumbashi: CELTA, 1975.

_____. Swahilismes lexico-syntaxiques relevés dans les copies d'élèves: méchanisme et approche méthodologique de correction. Lubumbashi: CELTA, 1974.

Van Buick, G. Les Deux cartes linguistiques du Congo Belge. Brussels: IRCB, 1952.

_____. Manuel de linguistique bantoue. Brussels: IRCB, 1949.

_____. Les Recherches linguistiques au Congo Belge. Brussels: IRCB, 1948.

Vass, Winifred Kellersberger. The Bantu Speaking Heritage of the United States. Los Angeles: Center for Afro-American Studies, 1979.

Verbeke, Ronald. Etudes psychométriques en milieu africain: La compréhension du vocabulaire dans l'apprentissage d'une langue étrangère. Kinshasa: UNAZA, 1970.

Verbeken, Auguste. "Le Tambour-téléphone chez les indigènes de l'Afrique centrale," Congo, (1920).

Wtterwulghe, Georges-François. Vocabulaire à l'usage des fonctionnaires se rendant dans les territoires du district de l'Uelé et de l'enclave Redjai-Lado. Brussels: Etat Indépendant du Congo, 1903.

Le Zaire, deuxième pays francophone du monde? Québec: Centre International de Recherche sur le Bilinguisme, 1977.

3. Literature and Oral Folklore

Biebuyck, Daniel. Hero and Chief: Epic Literature from the Banyanga (Zaire Republic). (Publisher unknown.)

Bokoko, Elolo, ed. Anthologie de poésie de Bandundu. Bandundu: CEEBA, 1983.

Bol, V. P., and Allary, J. Littérateurs et poètes noirs. Léopoldville: Bibliothèque de l'Etoile, 1964.

Colldén, Lisa, ed. Trésors de la tradition orale Sakata: Proverbes, mythes, légendes, fables, chansons et devinettes de Sakata. Uppsala: University of Stockholm, 1979.

Comhaire-Sylvain, Suzanne, ed. Jetons nos couteaux: Contes des garçonnets de Kinshasa et quelques parallèles haïtiens. Bandundu: CEEBA, 1974.

De Decker, J. M. Les Clans Ambuun (Bambunda) d'après leur littérature orale. Brussels: IRCB, 1950.

De Rop, Albert Jozef. La Littérature orale: Synthèse et bibliographie. (Mongo tales) Brussels: CEDAF, 1974.

_____, ed. Versions et fragments de l'épopée mongo. Brussels: ARSOM, 1978.

254 / The Bibliography

_____, and Ecelaert, E., eds. Versions et fragments de l'épopée mongo, Nsong'a Lianja. Partie II. (Companion to Versions et fragments de l'épopée mongo.) Mbandaka, Zaire: Annales Aequatoria, 1983.

Djungu-Simba Kamatenda, ed. Autour du feu: Contes d'inspiration lega. Kinshasa: Editions Saint Paul, 1984.

Dzokanga, A., ed. Chansons et proverbes lingala. Paris: Conseil International de la Langue Française, EDICEF, 1978.

Frobenius, Leo, ed. Mythes et contes populaires des riverains du Kasai. (Translated into French from German by Murat, Claude.) Wiesbaden: Franz Steiner Verlag GMEB, 1983.

Gakondi. Anthologie des écrivains congolais. Kinshasa: SNEC (Lokole), Département de la Culture et des Arts, 1969.

Gisaangi, Sona, ed. Dieu nous a tout confié excepté cette forêt. Bandundu: CEEBA, 1974.

Hochegger, Herman. Allons, tuons la mort: Mythes sakata. Bandundu: CEEBA, 1974.

_____. Femme, pourquoi pleures-tu?: Mythes buma. Bandundu: CEEBA, 1972.

Hulstaert, G. Contes Mongo. Brussels: ARSOM, 1965.

Ilunga Bamuyeja. Deux Griots de Kamina: Chants et poèmes. Kinshasa: Centre Africain de Littérature, 1974.

Jones, A. M. Studies in African Music. London: Oxford University Press, 1959.

Kadima Nzuji Mukala. La Littérature zairoise de langue française: 1945-1965. Paris: Editions Karthala, 1984.

Katende, Cyovo, ed. Voilà la nouvelle lune! Dansons! Chansons populaires de la zone de Gandajika. Bandundu: CEEBA, 1977.

Kavutirwaki, Kambale. Contes folkloriques nande. Tervuren: MRAC, 1975.

Kinzanza. Mon Manuel de musique congolaise moderne. Kinshasa: Institut National des Arts, 1971.

Kishwe. Anthologie des écrivains congolais moderne. Kinshasa: SNEC (Lokole), 1969.

Knappert, Jan. Myths and Legends of the Congo. Nairobi: Heinemann Educational Books, 1971.

Jadot, J. M. Les Ecrivains africains du Congo Belge et du Ruanda-Urundi: Une Histoire, un bilan, des problèmes. Brussels: ARSC, 1959.

Labi Tawaba and Tamundel Mubele, eds. Qui la sortira de cette pierre?: Mythes yansi. Bandundu: CEEBA, 1974.

Lumbwe Mudindaambi, ed. Mythes mbala. Bandundu: CEEBA, n.d.

_____, ed. Mange ces dents! (Mbala tales) Bandundu: CEEBA, 1972.

_____, ed. Pourquoi le coq ne chante plus?. Bandundu: CEEBA, 1973.

_____, and Kimbungu, eds. My Femme n'est pas ton gibier. (Mbala tales) Bandundu: CEEBA, 1977.

Maalu-bungi, C. Contes populaires du Kasai. Kinshasa: Editions du Mont noir, 1974.

Manzanga Kaladi and Makumar Mpang Brick. Ne me tue pas, épouse-moi!: Mythes dinga. Bandundu: CEEBA, 1977.

Mbuya Bangu. Le Père dans la peau du lion. (Pelende tales) Bandundu: CEEBA, 1977.

Monsengo Osantwene and Ipasso Lokope, eds. Le Père qui ne voulait pas de fille: Mythes nkundu et tere. Bandundu: CEEBA, 1974.

Mulyumba wa Mamba, Itongwa. Les Proverbes, un langage didactique dans les sociétés africaines traditionnelles: Le Cas des Balega-Bashile. Brussels: CEDAF, 1973.

Munongo, A. (Mwenda II). "Chants historiques des Bayeke, traduits en Français et expliqués," Bulletins Juridictions Indigènes et du Droit Coutumier Congolais, vol. 16 (1948), pp. 280-294 and vol. 20 (1952), pp. 305-316.

N'Sanda Wamenka. Contes du Zaire: Contes des montagnes, de la savane et de la forêt au pays du fleuve Zaire. Paris: Conseil International de la Langue Française EDICEF, 1975.

Nziata Mulenge. Pour la guérir, il faut ton coeur!: Mythes pende. Bandundu: CEEBA, 1974.

Nzuji Madija, C. Devinettes tonales--Tusumwinu. Paris: SELAF, 1976.

_____. Kasala: Chant héroïque luba. Lubumbashi: Presses Universitaires du Zaire, 1974.

Nzungu Mavinga Lelo di Kimbi Kiaku. Santé et tradition: Proverbes et coutumes relatifs à la santé. Kangu-Mayombe, Zaire: Bureau d'Etudes et de Recherches pour la Promotion de la Santé, 1975.

Périer, Gaston Denys. Petite histoire des lettres coloniales de Belgique. Brussels: Office de Publicité, 1944.

Roland, Hadelin. Quarante contes de la région des Basanga. Brussels: Artes Africanae, 1937.

Ross, Mabel and Walter, Barbara, eds. "On Another Day...": Tales Told among the Nkundo of Zaire. Hamden, CT: Archon Books, 1979.

Schicho, Walter and Mbayabo Ndala. Le Groupe Mufwankolo. Wien: Afro-Pub, 1981.

Stappers, Léonard and Vinke, Jacques. Textes Luba. Contes d'animaux. Tervuren: MRAC, 1962.

Sumaili N'gaye-Lussa. Chronologie des oeuvres littéraires zairoises. Kinshasa, Gombe: Comité Directeur de l'Union des Ecrivains Zairois, 1981.

Tito Yisuku Gafudzi. Négritude et tendances de la poèsie zairoise contemporaine. Kinshasa: Editions La Grue Couronnée, 1976.

Van Coppenolle, Renée. Contes de Muakudi l'Africaine. Waterloo: Fichermont, 1975.

Wannyn, Rob. L. Les Proverbes anciens du Bas-Congo. Brussels: Editions du Vieux Planquesaule, 1983.

III. ECONOMY

1. General

Belgium. Direction Etudes Economiques, Statistique et Documentation. Statistique des mouvements de capitaux au Congo Belge et au Ruanda-Urundi de 1887-1956. Brussels: 1958.

_____. Ministère des Colonies. La Situation économique du Congo Belge et du Ruanda-Urundi. (Yearly reports 1950-1959.) Brussels: 1951-60.

Bézy, Fernand. Problèmes stucturels de l'économie congolaise. Paris and Louvain: Nauwelaerts, 1957.

Bongoma. Indépendance économique et révolution. Kinshasa: Léopard-Okapi, 1969.

British National Export Council. New Light on the Congo. (Report on the B.N.E.C. Africa Seminar held in London on April 23, 1969.) London: BNEC, 1969.

Carael, M. Le Kivu montagneux: Surpopulation, sousnutrition, érosion du sol. Brussels: CEDAF, 1979.

Carrol, Douglas F. Basic Data on the Economy of the Democratic Republic of the Congo (Kinshasa). Washington: U.S. Bureau of International Commerce, 1968.

Centre de Recherches Economiques et Sociales. Morphologie des groupes financiers. Brussels: CRISP, 1962.

Diambomba, Miala. Analyse exploratoire des effets de la dépendance sur l'évolution des économies africaines: l'example du Zaire. Québec: Université Layal, Faculté des Sciences de l'Education, 1981.

Fédération des Entreprises Congolaises. The Congolese Economy on the Eve of Independence. Brussels: 1960.

Gran, Guy. "Zaire 1978: The Ethical and Intellectual Bankruptcy of the World System," Africa Today, vol. 25, no. 4 (1978), pp. 5-24.

Gran, Guy, and Hull, Galen, eds. Zaire, the Political Economy of Underdevelopment. New York: Praeger, 1979.

Houyoux, Joseph. Budgets ménagers, nutrition et mode de vie à Kinshasa (République du Zaire). Kinshasa: Presses Universitaires du Zaire, 1973.

International Bank for Reconstruction and Development (World Bank). "The Economy of Zaire," World Economy 1975. Report no. 821-ZR, July. Washington: 1975.

_____. Zaire: Current Economic Situation and Constraints. Washington: 1980.

Jewsiewicki, Bogumil. "The Great Depression and the Making of the Colonial Economic System in the Belgian Congo," African Economic History, vol. 4 (1977), pp. 153-176.

_____. Histoire économique d'une ville coloniale, Kisangani: 1877-1960. Brussels: CEDAF, 1978.

Kalele-Ka-Eila. Le F.M.I. et la situation sociale au Zaire: Basusu na bisengo, basusu na mawa. Lubumbashi: Laboratoire des Sciences Sociales Appliquées, 1984.

Kankwenda Mbaya. Sur les conditions du décollage économique au Zaire. Kinshasa-Gombe: Presses de l'Institut de Recherche Scientifique, 1981.

Klein, Carolyn K. Basic Data on the Economy of the Republic of Zaire. Washington: U.S. Bureau of International Commerce, 1972.

Le Fèvre, Jacques. Structures économiques du Congo Belge et du Ruanda-Urundi. Brussels: Editions du Treurenberg, 1955.

Leclercq, Hughes. Conjoncture financière et monétaire au Congo. 2 vols. Léopoldville: IRES Lovanium, 1960-61.

Lutumba-Lu-Vilu na Wundu. De la Zairianization à la rétrocession et au dialogue nord-sud: Une Tentative de libération intégrale du peuple zairois, 1973-1975. Brussels: Office International de Librairie, 1976.

Muteba-Tshitenge. Zaire: Combat pour la deuxième indépendance. Paris: Editions l'Harmattan, 1985.

Palmer, Robin, and Parsons, Neil, eds. The Roots of Rural Poverty in Central and Southern Africa. London: Heinemann, 1977.

Peemans, Jean-Philippe. Diffusion du progrès économique et convergence des prix: Le cas Congo-Belgique, 1900-1960; la formation de système des prix et salaires dans une économie dualiste. Louvain: Editions Nauwelaerts, 1968.

Stolper, Wolfgang F. Report to Ambassador Vance and Acting Director Kelly on Certain Problems of the Zairian Economy. Washington: Agency for International Development, 1972.

Van der Mark, D. F. W. Zaire. Zutphen: Terra, 1984.

Zaire, République du. Département des Finances. Conjoncture Economique. Kinshasa: 1983.

_____. Département du Plan. Syntèse économique, 1976. Kinshasa: 1977.

2. Agriculture and Livestock

Belgium. Ministère des Colonies. Aperçu sur l'économie agricole de la province de Léopoldville. Brussels: 1955.

_____. Ministère du Congo Belge et du Ruanda-Urundi. Direction Agriculture, Forêts et Elevage. Promotion de la société rurale du Congo Belge et du Ruanda-Urundi. Rapport générale des Journées d'Etudes Coloniales tenues à l'INUTOM à Anvers, les 23, 24 et 25 avril, 1957. Brussels: 1958.

Biebuyck, Daniel, ed. African Agrarian Systems. London: Oxford University Press, 1963.

Brixhe, A. Le Coton au Congo Belge. Brussels: Ministère des Colonies, 1958.

_____. Les Parasites du cotonnier en Afrique centrale. Tableaux de détermination. Brussels: Ministère des Affaires Etrangères et du Commerce Exterieur, Service des Publications de l'Assistance Technique, 1961.

Bruens, F. La Culture maraîchère dans la Province du Kivu. Brussels: Ministère du Congo Belge et du Ruanda-Urundi, Direction de l'Agriculture, Forêts et Elevage, 1960.

Bulletin Agricole du Congo Belge. (Note especially "L'Agriculture, les forêts, l'élevage, la chasse et la pêche de 1885 à 1958" in Jubilee Volume, 1960.) Brussels: Periodical published four times per year from 1910 until 1953 and six times per year from 1954 until 1961.

Cardwell, Lucy. Transport Cost and Other Determinants of the Intensity of Cultivation in Rural Zaire. New Haven: Economic Growth Center, Yale University, 1975.

Chambon, R., and Alofs, M. Le District agricole du Tanganyika. Brussels: Ministère des Colonies, 1958.

Collart, A. Pêche artisanale et pêche industrielle au Lac Tanganyika. Brussels: Ministère du Congo Belge et du Ruanda-Urundi, 1958.

Cornet, René Jules. Les Phares verts. Brussels: L. Cuypers, 1965.

De Halleux, B.; Ergo, A. B.; De Haes, W.; and Bal, G. Bibliographie analytique pour l'agronomie tropicale, Zaire, Rwanda, Burundi. Tervuren: Centre d'Informatique Appliquée au Développement et à l'Agriculture Tropicale, MRAC, 1972.

De Schlippe, Pierre. Shifting Cultivation in Africa. The Zande System of Agriculture. London: Routledge & Kegan Paul, 1956.

De Wildeman, Emile. Les Caféiers: Etude publiée sous les auspices de l'Etat Indépendant du Congo. Brussels: Veuve Monnom, 1901.

Deramée, O. L'Elevage du mouton en Afrique centrale. Brussels: CEDESA, 1967.

Devred, R. Récolte, collection et conservation des végétaux au Congo Belge et au Ruanda-Urundi. Brussels: Ministère du Congo Belge et du Ruanda-Urundi, 1958.

D'Hendencourt, Roger. L'Elevage au Katanga. Bruges: Desclée De Brouwer, 1953.

Diamond, R. B., et al. Supplying Fertilizers for Zaire's Agricultural Development. (Prepared for the U.S. Agency for International Development.) Muscle Shoals, AL: Tennessee Valley Authority, 1975.

Drachoussolf, V. "Agricultural Change in the Belgian Congo," Stanford University Food Research Institute Studies, vol. 5, no. 2 (1965), pp. 137-201.

Goorts, P.; Magis, N.; and Wilmet, J. Les Aspects biologiques, humains et économiques de la pêche dans le lac de retenue de la Lufira (Katanga). Liège: FULREAC, 1961.

Guldentorps, R. E., and Scuvie, L. Recherche de la densité optimale du palmier à huile planté en allées. Brussels: INEAC, 1968.

Hall, Gordon E., et al. An Evaluation of Proposed USAID Project for Improvement of Lake Tanganyika's Fishery Resources in Zaire. (publisher unknown): 1975.

Harms, Robert. Land Tenure and Agricultural Development in Zaire, 1895-1961. Madison: Land Tenure Center, University of Wisconsin, 1974.

Hathcock, J. S. A Study of Agricultural Conditions in the Belgian Congo and Ruanda-Urundi. Paris: Office of the U.S. Special Representative in Europe, Food and Agriculture Division, 1952.

Hecq, J.; Lefèbre, A.; et al. Agriculture et structures économiques d'une société traditionnelle au Kivu (Congo). Brussels: INEAC, 1963.

Institut pour l'Etude Agronomique du Congo Belge (INEAC). Division de Phytopathologie et d'Entomologie Agricole. Normes de main d'oeuvre pour les travaux agricoles au Congo Belge. Brussels: 1958.

_____. Précis des maladies et des insectes nuisible recontrés sur les plantes cultivées au Congo, au Rwanda et au Burundi. Brussels, 1962.

Jewsiewicki, Bogumil. Agriculture nomade et économie capitaliste: Histoire des essais de modernisation de l'agriculture africaine au Zaïre à l'époque coloniale. 2 vols. Lubumbashi: UNAZA, 1975.

_____. "Contributions to a History of Agriculture and Fishing in Central Africa," African Economic History, special issue, 1979.

Jones, William. Manioc in Africa. Stanford: Stanford University Press, 1959.

Jurion, F. and Henry, J. Can Primitive Farming be Modernized? Brussels: INEAC, Imprimerie Wellens-Pay, 1969.

Kazadi-Tshamala. La Formation du capital dans l'agriculture du Zaïre post-colonial: Situation et perspectives. Brussels: CEDAF, 1983.

Leplae, Edmond. La Crise agricole coloniale et les phases du développement de l'agriculture dans le Congo central. Brussels: IRCB, 1932.

Lumumba, Tolenga Emery. Le rôle de l'agriculture dans les pays du tiers monde, particulièrement au Zaïre. Budapest: Institut d'Economie Mondiale de l'Académie des Sciences de Hongrie, 1976.

Malengreau, Guy. Vers un paysannat indigène: Les lotissements agricoles au Congo Belge. Brussels: IRC, 1949.

Mbuki Mwamufiya and Fitch, James B. "Maize Marketing and Distribution in Southern Zaïre." Occasional paper. Mexico City: International Maize and Wheat Improvement Center, 1976.

Miracle, Marvin P. Agriculture in the Congo Basin: Tradition and Change in African Rural Economies. Madison: University of Wisconsin Press, 1967.

_____. Maize in Tropical Africa. Madison: University of Wisconsin Press, 1966.

Mulambu-Mvuluya, Faustin. Cultures obligatoires et colonisation dans l'ex-Congo Belge. Brussels: CEDAF, 1974.

Mwamufilya, V. "Choix économique de modes de production des protéines animales en République Démocratique du Congo," Etudes Congolaises, vol. 12, no. 2 (1969), pp. 54-80.

Ochse, J. J.; Soule, M. J.; et al. Tropical and Subtropical Agriculture. 2 vols. New York: Macmillan, 1961.

Peeters, Gérard. Essai sur l'économie de l'élevage du bovidé au Congo. Léopoldville: Editions de l'Université, 1960.

Popelier, G. H. Nature et évolution de l'agriculture zairoise (1958–1975). Brussels: CEDAF, 1977.

Schmitz, Jean-Louis. L'Eleveur et son bétail: l'élevage bovin villageois dans l'ouest du Zaire. Brussels: Coopération Technique Belge, and Kinshasa: INADES-Formation-Zaire, 1985.

Sorenson, L. Orlo. Maize Marketing in Zaire. (Prepared for the U.S. Agency for International Development.) Manhattan, KN: Food and Grain Institute, Kansas State University, 1975.

Tollens, Eric F. Problems of Micro-Economic Data Collection on Farms in Northern Zaire. East Lansing, MI: Department of Agricultural Economics, Michigan State University, 1975.

Tondeur, G. L'Agriculture nomade au Congo Belge. Brussels: Ministère des Colonies, 1957.

United States Department of Agriculture. Foreign Agriculture Service. "The Agricultural Economy of the Belgian Congo and Rwanda-Urundi." (Unpublished report.) Washington: June, 1960.

Vallaeys, G. Les Caféiers au Congo Belge, la pratique de la taille du caféier Robusta. Brussels: Ministère du Congo Belge et du Ruanda-Urundi, 1959.

Wilmet, Jules. Systèmes agraires et techniques agricoles au Katanga. Brussels: ARSOM, 1963.

Zaire, République du. Centre de Documentation Agricole. Index: Agriculture, 1960–1976. Kinshasa: 1977.

_____. Département de l'Agriculture et du Développement Rural. Plan de relance agricole: 1982–1984. Kinshasa: 1982.

_____. Présidence de la République, Commissariat Général au Plan. Production vivrière face aux besoins alimentaires de la région de l'Equateur: Evaluation et types d'actions. Mbandaka: 1981.

3. Business, Commerce, Finance, and Money

Belliveau, Nancy. "Heading off Zaire's Default," Institutional Investor, March 1977, pp. 23–28.

Bézy, Fernand. Accumulation et sous-développement au Zaire, 1960–1980. Louvain-la-Neuve: Presses Universitaires de Louvain, 1981.

Bouët-Willaumez, L. E. Commerce et traite des Noirs aux côtes occidentales d'Afrique. Paris: Imprimerie Nationale, 1848.

Centre de Recherche et d'Information Socio-Politiques. L'Investissement privé étranger et national du Zaire. Brussels: CRISP, April 25, 1972.

Congo, République Démocratique du. Banque nationale du Congo. Rapport Annuel. (Annual reports of the central bank, issued until the bank was renamed Banque du Zaire.) Kinshasa: 1967-1970.

Delahaye, Pierre. Petites et moyennes entreprises de production de Kinshasa, 1er semestre, 1973. Kinshasa: Office de Promotion des Petites et Moyennes Entreprises Zairoises, 1973.

Duban, Marie Paule. Un Instrument de développement: le mouvement coopératif de crédit au Kivu: ses activités en milieu rural et urbain. Sherbrooke, Québec: Centre d'Etudes en Economie Coopérative, Université de Sherbrooke, 1976.

Dupriez, Pierre. Contrôle des changes et structures économiques, Congo: 1960-1967. The Hague: Mouton, 1970.

Gray, Richard, and Birmingham, David, eds. Pre-Colonial African Trade: Essays on Trade in Central and Eastern Africa before 1900. London: Oxford University Press, 1970.

Louwers, O. Le Problème financier et le problème économique au Congo Belge en 1932. Brussels: IRCB, 1933.

Lukama Nkunzi. Service de la dette publique du Zaire, 1908-1975: Considérations théoriques, analyse et discussion des modes et procédés techniques de réduction et/ou extinction de la dette publique. Kinshasa: UNAZA, IRES, 1978.

Mabi Mulumba. Les banques commerciales face aux mutations structurelles de l'économie zairoise. Kinshasa: Centre de Recherches Pédagogiques, UNAZA, 1983.

Mbakar Ayingol. Budgetprobleme des Zaire: eine Analyse der Probleme der Budgetpolitik in der wirtschaftlichen und sozialen Entwicklung. Zurich: Juris Verlag, 1976.

Michelini, Philip. Marketing in Zaire. Washington: Overseas Business Reports of the U.S. Department of Commerce, 1977.

Mulumba Lukoji. Le Service de la dette publique de l'ex-Congo Belge: le Cas des dettes financières. Brussels: CEDAF, 1973.

Mutwale-Muyimbwe. Les Sources publiques de financement de l'Etat

Indépendant du Congo. 1885-1907. Essai d'analyse économique. Brussels: CEDAF, 1973.

Nguyen Chanh Tam et al. Guide juridique de l'entreprise. Kinshasa: Faculté de Droit, UNAZA, 1973.

Nzeza zi Nkanga. Les enquêtes sur les budgets des ménages en milieu urbain en République du Zaire. Kinshasa: Institut National de la Statistique, 1972.

Parisis, Albert. Les Finances communales et urbaines au Congo Belge. Brussels: ARSOM, 1960.

Place et rôle du capital zairois dans le développement national: actes du colloque tenu à Kinshasa du 16 au 21 juin 1980. Kinshasa: Département de Recherches en Sciences Economiques et Financières, Centre de Kinshasa, 1981.

Roberts, A. "Nyamwezi Trade," in Pre-Colonial African Trade, Gray, R. and Birmingham, D., eds. London: 1970.

Ryelandt, Bernard. L'Inflation en pays sous-développé: Origines, mécanismes de propagation, et effets des pressions inflatoires au Congo, 1960-1969; interactions entre phénomènes monétaires et réels. Paris: Mouton, 1970.

Simonis, Raymond. Une Banque centrale éphémère: la Banque Centrale du Congo Belge et du Ruanda-Urundi, 1951-1961. Brussels: Centre d'Etudes Financières, 1981.

Société Congolaise de Financement du Développement. Textes Constitutifs. Kinshasa: 1970.

Tshiunza Mbiye. Le Zaire face à l'indépendance monétaire. Kinshasa: Imprimerie Sodimca, 1973.

_____. Le Zaire-monnaie, de l'étalon-dollar à l'étalon D.T.S. Kinshasa: Presses Universitaires du Zaire, 1975.

Zaire, République du. Ordonnance-loi régissant la protection de l'épargne et le contrôle des intermédiaires financières. (Banking law.) Kinshasa: 1972.

_____. Banque du Zaire. Rapport Annuel. (Annual reports of Zaire's central bank, formerly the Banque Nationale du Congo, issued from 1971 until the present.) Kinshasa: 1973- , (continuing).

_____. Institut National de la Statistique. Direction des Statistiques Economiques et Financières. Kinshasa: 1982.

4. Development

Belgium. Académie Royale des Sciences d'Outre-Mer. L'Apport scientifique de la Belgique au développement de l'Afrique centrale (Livre Blanc). 3 vols. Brussels: 1962-63.

_____. Ministère des Colonies. Le Plan décennal pour le développement économique et social du Congo. 2 vols. Brussels: Editions De Visscher, 1949.

Bézy, Fernand. Principes pour l'orientation du développement économique au Congo. Léopoldville: Université Lovanium, 1959.

Breitengross, J. P., ed. Planification et développement économique au Zaire. Hamburg: Deutsches Institut für Afrika Forschung, n.d.

Centre de Recherches Universitaires du Kivu (CERUKI). Le Problématique du développement au Kivu: Actes du troisième Colloque au CERUKI, Bukavu, 17-21 avril 1978. Bukavu: CERUKI, 1983.

Ciamala Kanda. "Eléments de blocage du développement rural au Zaire (cas Luba du Kasai)," Cahiers Economiques et Sociaux, vol. 16, no. 3 (Sept. 1978), pp. 334-371.

Ciparisse, Gérard. "An Anthropological Approach to Socioeconomic Factors of Development: The Case of Zaire," Current Anthropology, vol. 19, no. 1 (March 1978), pp. 34-41.

Coméliau, Christian. Conditions de la planification du développement: L'Example du Congo. The Hague: Mouton, 1969.

Congo, Belgian. Commissariat au Plan Décennal. Plan décennal pour le développement économique et social du Congo Belge; rapport annuel 1955. Léopoldville: 1956.

Congo, République Démocratique du. Haut Commissariat du Plan et à la Réconstruction Nationale. Plan intérimaire de relance agricole. Kinshasa: 1967.

Dethine, P. Aspects économiques et sociaux de l'industrialisation en Afrique. Brussels: CEDESA, 1961.

Diambomba, Miala. Hypotheses for a Training Program for Local Administrators in Zaire and Proposals for Its Realisation. Québec: Faculté des Sciences de l'Education, Université Laval, 1981.

Etude du développement intègre de la zone d'influence du complèxe hydroelectrique d'Inga. Rome: Società di Ingegneria e Consulenza Attività Industriali, 1964.

Fleischle-Jaudas, Waltraud. Répertoire de développement: Zaire
1985. Kinshasa: Centre d'Etudes pour l'Action Sociale, 1985.

Gouverneur, Jacques. Productivity and Factor Proportions in Less
Developed Countries: The Case of Industrial Firms in the Congo.
Oxford: Clarendon Press, 1971.

Institut de Recherches Economiques et Sociales. Etude d'orientation
pour la relance agricole. Kinshasa: Haut Commissariat au Plan
et à la Reconstruction Nationale, July 1966.

_____. Etudes d'orientation pour le plan de développement et de
diversification industriels. 2 vols. Kinshasa: Haut Commissariat
au Plan et à la Reconstruction Nationale, July 1966.

_____. Indépendance, inflation et développement: L'Economie
congolaise de 1960 à 1965. Paris and The Hague: Mouton, 1968.

Kankuenda M'baya. Les Industries du pôle de Kinshasa: Réflexion
sur la stratégie des pôles de croissance en pays africains.
Brussels: CEDAF, 1977.

Lacroix, Jean-Louis. Industrialisation au Congo: La Transformation
des structures économiques. Paris and The Hague: Mouton, 1967.

Lukomo. Change et développement au Congo. Kinshasa: Congolia
(Lokole), Département de la Culture et des Arts, 1971.

Lwamba Katansi. Le Plan de développement économique, social, et
culturel du Zaire: Que sera-t-il, impératif ou indicatif? Kinshasa:
publisher unknown, 1977.

Mitchnik, David A. The Role of Women in Rural Zaire and Upper
Volta: Improving Methods of Skill Acquisition. Oxford: OXFAM,
1978.

Peemans, Jean-Philippe. "L'Etat fort et la croissance économique,"
Revue Nouvelle (Brussels), vol. 62, no. 12 (1975), pp. 515-527.

_____. The Political Economy of Zaire in the Seventies. Document
7406. Louvain: Institut d'Etude des Pays en Voie de Développement, Université Catholique de Louvain, 1974.

_____. "The Social and Economic Development of Zaire since In-
dependence: An Historical Outline," African Affairs, no. 295
(1975), pp. 148-179.

Piret, Baudoin. "L'Aide Belge du Congo et le développement inégal
du capitalisme monopoliste d'état," Contradictions, no. 1 (1972),
pp. 111-137.

_____. "Le Sous-développement du Zaire vu à travers la balance des paiements Belgique-Zaire," Contradictions, no. 15-16 (1978), pp. 187-205.

Recherches sur le développement rural en Afrique centrale. Liège: FULREAC, 1968.

Segers, Joseph. Actions pour le développement en République du Zaire. Kinshasa-Gombe: Centre d'Etudes pour l'Action Sociale, 1971.

Tiker-Tiker. "Le Concept du 'Développement Rural' dans le processus du développement économique du Zaire," Cahiers Economiques et Sociaux, vol. 16, no. 3 (Sept. 1978), pp. 243-257.

United Nations Educational, Scientific and Cultural Organization (UNESCO). The Role of the Human Factor in the Development of Newly Independent Countries. Paris: 1967.

Vianda-Kioto Luzolo. Tradition et développement en milieu rural au Bas-Zaire. Ottawa: Institut de Coopération Internationale, Université d'Ottowa, n.d.

Zaire, République du. Département du Plan. Rapport relatif au Séminaire National d'Information et de Sensibilisation sur l'Elaboration du Plan Quinquennal 1986-1990, du 13 août au 3 novembre 1984. Kinshasa: 1984.

5. Mining Industry

Bézy, Fernand. Changements de structure et conjoncture de l'industrie minière au Congo, 1938-1960. Léopoldville: IRES, Lovanium University, 1961.

De Kun, Nicolas. The Mineral Resources of Africa. Amsterdam: Elsevier, 1965.

Deliens, Michel. Les Minéraux secondaires d'uranium du Zaire. Tervuren: MRAC, 1981.

_____. Les Oxydes hydratés de cobalt du Shaba méridional, République du Zaire. Tervuren: MRAC, 1974.

Derriks, J. J. Le Gîte d'uranium de Shinkolobwe: Etat actuel des connaissances du point de vue géologie et métallogénie. (publisher unknown): 1955.

D'Ydewalle, Charles. L'Union Minière du Haut Katanga: de l'âge colonial à l'indépendance. Paris: Plon, 1960.

268 / The Bibliography

Financial Times. Mining Yearbook. London: annual.

Générale des Carrières et des Mines (GECAMINES). Rapport Annuel. (Annual report) Lubumbashi: annual.

Groupe Wajingaji. Industrie minière et développement au Zaire. Vol. I. Kinshasa: Presses Universitaires du Zaire, 1973.

Ilunga Ilunkamba. Propriété publique et conventions de gestion dans l'industrie du cuivre au Zaire. Brussels: CEDAF, 1984.

International Bank for Reconstruction and Development (World Bank). Appraisal of GECAMINES Expansion Project, Zaire. Report nos. 576-aCK and P-1551-CK, Dec. and Jan. 1974.

Katzenellenbogen, Simon E. Railways and the Copper Mines of Katanga. Oxford: Clarendon Press, 1973.

Lukieni Lu Nyimi. Etude générale sur le cuivre. Louvain-la-Neuve: Université Catholique de Louvain, Faculté de Droit, 1982.

Marthoz, A. L'Industrie minière et métallurgique au Congo Belge. Brussels: ARSC, 1955.

Morgan, George A. Zaire. Washington: U.S. Department of the Interior, Bureau of Mines, 1985.

Motoulle, L. Politique sociale de l'Union Minière du Haut Katanga pour sa main d'oeuvre indigène et ses résultats au cours de vingt années d'application. Brussels: IRCB, 1946.

Mulumba Lukoji, et al. Industrie minière et développement au Zaire. Kinshasa: Presses Universitaires du Zaire, 1973.

Panou, G. Le Gisement de Bukena: Un Cas particulier d'estimation des réserves. Brussels: ARSOM, 1974.

Prigogine, A. Accroissement de la production du cuivre dans la République du Zaire: rôle joué par les concentrateurs. Brussels: ARSOM, 1973.

Radmann, Wolf. "The Nationalization of Zaire's Copper: From Union Minière to GECAMINES," Africa Today, vol. 25, no. 4 (1978), pp. 25-47.

Schaar, Georges. Les Mines d'or du 5ème parallèle. Brussels: ARSC, 1959.

Union Minière du Haut-Katanga. L'Union Minière du Haut Katanga, 1906-1956. Brussels: Cuypers, 1956.

_____. Union Minière du Haut Katanga, 1950. Elisabethville: 1950.

_____. Union Minière du Haut Katanga: 1964. Brussels: 1964.

United Nations Economic Commission for Africa (ECA). Le Role des sociétés transnationales dans l'industrie du cuivre au Zaire. Addis Ababa: 1982.

United States Department of the Interior. Bureau of Mines. Mineral Industries of Africa. Washington: 1976.

_____. Minerals Yearbook. Washington: annual.

6. Other Industry

Bézy, Fernand. L'Industrie manufacturière à Léopoldville et dans le Bas-Congo et ses problèmes d'approvisionnement. 1960-1961. Léopoldville: IRES, Lovanium University, 1962.

Colloque national sur le développement industriel, Kinshasa, Zaire, 1971. (Conference held June 14-17, 1971.) Kinshasa: Kinshasa Chamber of Commerce, 1971.

Gamela Nginu Diamuan Gana. Performances de l'entreprise dans les P.V.D.: Le Rôle de la fonction approvisionnement dans la stratégie de l'entreprise (cas des entreprises manufacturières du Zaire). Louvain-la-Neuve: Cabay, 1982.

Kayitenkore wa Sangano. L'Industrie de la construction et le développement. Kinshasa: Presses Universitaires du Zaire, 1978.

M'Baya, Kankuenda. Les Industries du pôle de Kinshasa: Réflexions sur la stratégie des pôles de croissance en pays africains. Brussels: CEDAF, 1977.

Michel, Herbert. Wirtschaftesstruktur und Industrialisierungsprobleme Zaires: e. Regionale Analyse. Munich: Weltforum-Verlag, 1976.

Mutombo, Pierre Sylvain. Les Fibres de coton en République Démocratique du Congo et l'industrie textile. Kinshasa: Office National de la Recherche et du Développement, 1970.

Zaire, République du. Présidence. Commissariat Général au Plan. Séminaire national sur l'importance et les possibilités de développement de l'industrie chimique au Zaire. Kinshasa: 1981.

7. Labor

CADICEC. Gérants d'entreprise, ce que vous devez savoir ... du cheque en droit congolais. Kinshasa: Editions CADICEC, 1971.

_____. La Représentation des travailleurs dans l'entreprise: Code congolais du travail. Kinshasa: Editions CADICEC, 1971.

Doucy, Arthur, and Feldheim, Pierre. Problèmes du travail et politique sociale au Congo Belge. Brussels: Librairie Encyclopédique, 1952.

_____. Travailleurs indigènes et productivité du travail au Congo Belge. Brussels: Institut de Sociologie, Université Libre de Belgique, 1958.

Friedland, William H. Unions, Labor and Industrial Relations in Africa. An Annotated Bibliography. Ithaca, NY: Cornell University Press, 1965.

Gassana Muhirwa. Le Syndicalisme et ses incidences socio-politiques en Afrique: Le Cas de l'UNTZa. Kinshasa: Presses Universitaires du Zaire, 1982.

International Labor Organization. Formation, recyclage et perfectionnement du personnel de la REGIDESO. Geneva: 1981.

_____. Rapport au gouvernement de la République du Zaire sur l'administration de la sécurité sociale. Geneva: 1972.

_____. Rapport sur les salaires dans la République du Congo. Geneva: 1960.

_____. Réflexions pour une politique de l'emploi au Zaire: Alternatives pour les secteurs rural et non-structuré. (Report by a special commission of the Programme des Emplois et des Compétences Techniques pour l'Afrique, May-June 1984.) Addis Ababa: 1984.

_____. Renforcement de la Direction générale de l'Institut National de Préparation Professionelle, Kinshasa. Geneva: 1981.

Kazadi wa Dile, Jacques S. Politiques et techniques de rémunération dans l'entreprise au Congo: Leurs implications quant au développement économique. Kinshasa: IRES, 1970.

Lux, André. Le Marché du travail en Afrique noire. Louvain and Paris: Nauwelaerts, 1963.

McCabe, James L. Distribution of Labor Income in Urban Zaire. (Report for USAID.) New Haven, CT: Economic Growth Center, Yale University, 1973.

Perin-Hockers, Maryse. L'Absentéisme des travailleurs africains et l'instabilité dans les entreprises de la région d'Elisabethville, 1957-1958. Brussels: Institut de Sociologie, Université Libre de Belgique, and Elisabethville: CEPSI, 1959.

Perrings, Charles. Black Mineworkers in Central Africa. London: Heinemann, 1979.

Phanzu-Nianga di Mazanza. Introduction à l'arbitrage commercial. Kinshasa: Edition Soprodar, 1981.

Poupart, R. Facteurs de productivité de la main d'oeuvre autochtone à Elisabethville. Brussels: Institut de Sociologie, Université Libre de Belgique, 1960.

_____. Première esquisse de l'évolution du syndicalisme au Congo. Brussels: Institut de Sociologie, Université Libre de Belgique, 1960.

Schwantz, Alf. "Croissance urbaine et chômage à Kinshasa," Manpower and Unemployment Research in Africa, vol. 2, no. 1 (1969), pp. 37-44.

_____. "Illusion d'une émancipation et aliénation réele de l'ouvrière zairoise," Canadian Journal of African Studies, vol. 6, no. 2 (1972), pp. 183-212.

United States. Department of Labor. Bureau of Labor Statistics. Foreign Labor Information: Labor in the Belgian Congo. Washington: 1959.

_____. Labor Law and Practice in the Republic of Zaire. Washington: 1972.

Wolter, R.; Devreux, L.; and Régnier, R. Le Chômage au Congo Belge. Rapport d'enquête 1957. Brussels: Institut de Sociologie, Université Libre de Belgique, 1959.

Zaire. Association Nationale des Entreprises Zairoises. Code du travail. Kinshasa: 1972.

Zaire, République du. Code du travail. Kinshasa-Gombe: Editions CADICEC, 1981.

_____. Ministère du Travail et de la Prévoyance Sociale. Code du travail, mesures d'application: Textes officiels diffusés depuis de 9 août 1967 et en vigueur au 1 juillet 1981. Kinshasa: Editions CADICEC, 1981.

8. Transportation, Communications, and Energy

American ORT Federation. Training for Road Construction Repairs and Maintenance, Republic of Zaire, Office des Routes: Final report. Geneva and New York: 1975.

L'Automobile et la sécurité routière en droit zairois. (Colloquium organized by UNAZA.) Kinshasa: Presses Universitaires du Zaire: 1982.

Berenschot-Bosboom N.V. Study of Ports and River Transport: Democratic Republic of the Congo. Washington: International Bank for Reconstruction and Development, 1970.

Bokonga Ekanga Botombele. Communications Policies in Zaire: A Study. Paris: UNESCO, 1980.

_____. Cultural Policy in the Republic of Zaire. Paris: UNESCO, 1980.

Borgniez, G. Donnés pour la mise en valeur du gisement de méthane du Lac Kivu. Brussels: ARSOM, 1960.

Campus, F. L'Aménagement hydroélectrique du fleuve Congo à Inga. Brussels: ARSC, 1958.

Cavallaro, Evaldo. Infrastrutture e decollo economico, il caso dello Zaire. Rome: Istituto Italo-Africano, 1976.

Chelman, W. Le Marché pétrolier au Congo Belge et au Ruanda-Urundi. Léopoldville: IRES, 1959.

Clerfayt, A. Le Développement énergique du Congo Belge et du Ruanda-Urundi. Brussels: ARSOM, 1960.

Comité des Transporteurs au Congo Belge. Transports au Congo Belge. Léopoldville and Brussels: 1959.

Compagnie du Chemin de Fer du Bas-Congo au Katanga. Compagnie du Chemin de Fer du Bas-Congo au Katanga, 1906-1956. Brussels: 1956.

Companhia do Caminho de Ferro de Benguela. Benguela Railway. Benguela, Angola: 1960.

Congo, République Démocratique du. Ministère des Transports et Communications. Transports et communications; brochure de documentation editée à l'occasion de la Foire Internationale de Kinshasa, 1971. Kinshasa: Editions Afrique-Contact, 1971.

Cornet, René Jules. La Bataille du Rail. Brussels: Cuypers, 1958.

Guth, Herbert J. Civil Aviation in the Republic of Zaire. (Prepared for USAID.) Washington: 1972.

Huybrechts, André. Transports et structures de développement
au Congo; étude du progrés économique de 1900 à 1970. Paris:
Mouton, 1970.

Keating, Robert B., and Howell, John T. A Transport Reconnaissance of the Northeast Congo Region. (Prepared for USAID.)
Washington: 1970.

Lederer, André. L'Evolution des transports à l'ONATRA durant les
années 1960 à 1977. Brussels: ARSOM, 1978.

_____. L'Exploitation des affluents du Zaire et des ports de l'in-
térieur de 1960 à 1971. Brussels: ARSOM, 1973.

_____. Histoire de la navigation au Congo. Tervuren: MRAC,
1965.

Malu wa Kalenga. Les Solutions possibles du problème du déficit
energétique de la région du Shaba en République du Zaire. Kinshasa: Office National de la Recherche et du Développement,
République du Zaire, 1972.

Mission franco-belge pour l'étude préliminaire d'un port en eau pro-
fonde. (Joint study in cooperation with the Congolese government's
Ministère des Affairs Etrangères, de la Coopération et du Commerce Extérieur.) Paris: Ovaty, 1971.

"Les Relations SABENA-Air Congo, 1960-1968," Etudes Africaines du
CRISP, nos. 90-91 (March 1969).

Research and Development Consulting Engineers. République du
Zaire, services routiers, 1969-1971. (publisher unknown): 1972.

Rochon, Paul-André. Etude sur la possibilité de réduire la demande
en combustibles ligneux à Kinshasa à partir de mesures d'économie
d'énergie: Bois. Ottawa: Institut de Développement International et de Coopération, Université d'Ottowa, 1983.

Société Nationale des Chemins de Fer Zairois. Rapport au Secrétaire
d'Etat Belge à la Coopération. Lubumbashi: 1983.

United States Information Agency. Research Service. Media habits
of Zairian Priority Audiences. Washington: 1971.

Van Cauwelaert, F. Autoroute Ndjili-Maluku: Chaussée expérimentale,
dimensionnement, exécution, contrôle. Kinshasa: Présidence de
la République, Office National de la Recherche et du Développement, 1971.

9. Foreign Trade and Investment

Bongoy Mpekesa. Investissements mixtes au Zaire: Joint ventures pour la période de transition. Kinshasa: Presses Universitaires du Zaire, 1974.

Communauté Economique Européene. Direction Générale de l'Aide au Développement, Direction de la Politique et des Etudes de Développement. Les Echanges commerciaux entre la CEE et les états africains et malgache associés, 1958-1966/7. 3 vols. Brussels: 1969.

Contracting Parties to the General Agreement on Tariffs and Trade. General Agreement on Tariffs and Trade. Protocol for the Accession of the Democratic Republic of the Congo to the Agreement of October 30, 1947. Done at Geneva August 11, 1971. Washington: U.S. Government Printing Office, 1972.

Fédération des Industries Belges. La Belgique et le développement du Tiers-Monde: Livre Blanc. Brussels: 1967.

Hirsch, Hans G. Credit for Agriculture through Cooperatives in the Democratic Republic of the Congo. Kinshasa (?): U.S. Department of Agriculture, Economic Research Services, 1971.

Kabala Kabunda, M. K. K. "Multinational Corporations and the Installation of Externally-Oriented Economic Structures in Contemporary Africa: The Example of the Unilever-Zaire Group," in Multinational Corporations in Africa, Widstrand, Carl, ed. New York: Africana, 1976.

Lofumbwa Bokila. Les Régimes fiscaux visant à encourager les investissements directs et de portefeuille dans les pays en voie de développement: l'Interaction du système fiscal zairois et des régimes préférentiels des pays de l'O.C.D.E. Brussels: Bruylant, 1981.

Mangungu Ekombe Endambo. Une Communauté autour des grands lacs africains: Zaire-Rwanda-Burundi. Bukavu: République du Zaire, 1977.

Pearson, Scott R., and Cownie, John, eds. Commodity Exports and African Economic Development. Lexington, MA: Lexington Books, 1974.

Phanzu-Nianga di Mazanza. Legal and Fiscal Guide for the Foreign Investor in Zaire. 2nd ed. Kinshasa: Imprimerie Kassale, 1977.

Tshitenge, J. P. "Le Commerce extérieur de la République Démocratique du Congo, 1965-1968," Cahiers Economiques et Sociaux IRES, Vol. 7, nos. 2-3 (1969), pp. 243-263.

United Nations. Economic Commission for Africa. Report by the ECA
Mission on Economic Cooperation in Central Africa. New York:
1966.

United States. Treaties. Agricultural Commodities. Agreement between the United States of America and the Democratic Republic
of the Congo, signed at Kinshasa August 12, 1968. Washington:
U.S. Government Printing Office, 1968.

_____. Treaties. Agricultural Commodities. Agreement between
the United States of America and the Democratic Republic of the
Congo modifying the Agreement of October 21, 1969, signed at
Kinshasa March 24 and July 7, 1970. Washington: U.S. Government Printing Office, 1970.

Van der Steen, Daniel. Echanges économiques extérieurs du Zaire;
dépendance et développement. Brussels: CEDAF, 1977.

Widstrand, Carl, ed. Multinational Firms in Africa. Uppsala: Scan-
dinavian Institute of African Studies, 1975.

Zaire, République du. Département de l'Economie Nationale. Enquête
sur les entreprises, 1969-1970. Kinshasa: 1973.

_____. Le Guide de l'Investisseur. Kinshasa: 1974.

_____. Investir au Zaire: l'Industrie de transformation. Kin-
shasa: 1975.

IV. HISTORY

1. General

Buana Kabue. L'Expérience zairoise: Du Casque colonial à la toque
de léopard. Paris: Afrique Biblio Club, 1975.

Choprix, Guy. La Naissance d'une ville: Etude géographique de
Paulis (1934-1957). Brussels: CEMUBAC, 1961.

Congo, Belgian. Histoire du Congo. 3 vols. Léopoldville: 1959.

Cornevin, Robert. Histoire du Congo (Léopoldville). Paris: Berger-
Levrault, 1963.

_____. Histoire du Congo Léopoldville-Kinshasa: Des Origines
préhistoriques à la République du Congo. Paris: Editions Berger-
Levrault, 1970.

Duffy, James. Portugal in Africa. Cambridge, MA: Harvard University Press, 1962.

Elisabethville, 1911-1961. Brussels: Cuypers, 1961.

Fetter, Bruce. The Creation of Elisabethville, 1910-1940. Stanford: Hoover Institution Press, 1976.

Forbath, Peter. The River Congo: The Discovery, Exploration and Exploitation of the World's Most Dramatic River. New York: Harper & Row, 1977.

Galle, Hubert. Le Congo: De la Découverte à l'indépendance. Brussels: Editions J. M. Collet, 1983.

Hauzeur de Fooz, Charles. Du Congo de Léopold II au Congo-Kinshasa. Brussels: Imprimerie Mondiale, 1966.

Hennessey, Maurice N. The Congo. New York: Praeger, 1961.

_____. Congo: A Brief History and Appraisal. London: Pall Mall Press, 1961.

Lutumba. Histoire du Zaire. Kinshasa: Okapi, 1972.

Mandjumba Mwanyimi-Mbonda. Chronologie générale de l'histoire du Zaire: Des Origines à nos jours. Kinshasa: Centre de Recherches Pédagogiques, 1985.

Mbumba Ngimbi. Kinshasa, 1881-1981: 100 ans après Stanley: Problèmes et avenir d'une ville. Kinshasa: Centre de Recherches Pédagogiques, 1982.

Mendiaux, Edouard. Histoire du Congo. Brussels: Dessart, 1961.

_____. Moscou, Accra et le Congo. Brussels: Dessart, 1960.

Muka. Evolution du Sport au Congo. Kinshasa: Okapi, 1970.

_____. Vers le sommet du sport zairois et africain. Kinshasa: St. Paul Afrique, 1974.

Tshimanga wa Tshibangu. Histoire du Zaire. Bukavu: Editions du CERUKI, 1976.

Vanderlinden, J., ed. Du Congo au Zaire -- 1960-1980. Brussels: CRISP, 1980.

Vellut, J. L. Guide de l'étudiant en histoire du Zaire. Kinshasa: publisher unknown, 1974.

_____. "Le Zaïre à la périphérie du capitalisme: Quelques per-
spectives historiques," Enquêtes et documents d'histoire africaine,
vol. 1 (1975), pp. 114-151.

Verhaegen, Benoît, ed. Kisangani, 1876-1976: Histoire d'une ville.
Kinshasa: Presses Universitaires du Zaïre, 1975.

2. Pre-Colonial

Anstey, Roger. The Atlantic Slave Trade and British Abolition,
1760-1810. Atlantic Highlands, NJ: Humanities Press, 1975.

_____. Britain and the Congo in the Nineteenth Century. (Re-
print of Oxford: Clarendon Press, 1962.) Westport, CT: Greenwood Press, 1981.

_____. Le Royaume du Congo aux XVe et XVIe Siècles. Léo-
poldville: Editions de l'Institut National d'Etudes Politiques,
1963.

Balandier, Georges. Daily Life in the Kingdom of the Kongo: From
the Sixteenth to the Eighteenth Century. (Translated from French
by Weaver, Helen.) London: Allen & Unwin and New York:
Pantheon, 1968.

Batsîkama ba Mampuya ma Ndwâla, R. Voiçi les Jagas; ou, l'histoire
d'un peuple parricide bien malgré lui. Kinshasa: Office National
de la Recherche et du Développement, 1971.

Bertrand, A. "La fin de la puissance Azande," Bulletin des Séances
IRCB, (1943), pp. 264-283.

Boxer, C. R. "The Kingdom of Congo," in The Dawn of African
History, Oliver, Roland, ed., pp. 75-81. London: Oxford University Press, 1961.

Brode, Heinrich. Tippoo Tib: The Story of His Career in Central
Africa. London: Edward Arnold, 1907.

Ceulemans, P. La Question arabe et le Congo (1883-1892). Brussels:
ARSC, 1959.

Curtin, Philip D. The Atlantic Slave Trade: A Census. Madison:
University of Wisconsin Press, 1969.

Denis, P. Histoire des Mangbetu et des Matshaga jusqu'à l'arrivée
des Belges. Tervuren: MRAC, 1961.

Denucé, Jean. L'Afrique au XVIème siècle et le commerce anversois.
Antwerp: De Sikkel, 1937.

Ekholm, Kajsa. Power and Prestige, the Rise and Fall of the Kongo Kingdom. Uppsala: Skriv Service AB, 1972.

Farrant, Leda. Tippu Tip and the East African Slave Trade. New York: St. Martin's Press, 1975.

Filesi, Teobaldo. San Salvador: cronache dei re del Congo. Bologna: E.M.I., 1974.

Gamitto, A. C. P. King Kazembe and the Marave Cheva, Bisa, Bembe, Lunda and other Peoples of Southern Africa. (Translated by Cunnison, Ian.) 2 vols. Lisbon: Junta de Investigaçoes do Ultramar, 1962.

Goma Foutou, Célestin. Histoire des civilisations du Congo. Paris: Anthropos, 1981.

Harms, Robert W. River of Wealth, River of Sorrow: The Central Zaire Basin in the Era of the Slave and Ivory Trade, 1500-1891. New Haven, CT: Yale University Press, 1981.

Hiernaux, Jean. "Cultures préhistoriques de l'âge des métaux au Ruanda Urundi et au Kivu," (Part I), Bulletin des Séances ARSC, no. 2 (1956).

_____. Cultures préhistoriques de l'âge des métaux au Ruanda Urundi et au Kivu (Part II). Brussels: ARSOM, 1960.

_____. Diversité humaine en Afrique subsaharienne: Recherches biologiques. Brussels: Institut de Sociologie, Université Libre de Belgique, 1968.

Hilton, Anne. The Kingdom of Kongo. Oxford: Clarendon Press, 1985.

Hinde, Sidney Langford. The Fall of the Congo Arabs. London: Methuen, and New York: Thomas Whittaker, 1897.

Jadin, Louis. L'Ancien Congo et l'Angola, 1639-1655: d'après les archives romaines, portugaises, néerlandaises et espagnoles. Brussels: Institut Historique Belge de Rome, 1975.

_____. "L'Ancien Congo et les Archives de l'Oude West Indische Compagnie conservée à le Haye (1641-1648)," in Bulletin de Séances, ARSC, vol. 1, no. 3 (1955), pp. 447-451.

_____. "Le Congo et la Secte des Antoniens. Restauration du Royaume sous Pedro IV et la 'Sainte-Antoine' Congolaise (1694-1718)," Bulletin de l'Institut Historique Belge de Rome, vol. 33 (1961), pp. 411-615.

_____. Rivalités luso-néerlandaises au Sohio, Congo, 1600-1675. Tentatives missionaires des récollets flamands et tribulations des capucins italiens, 1670-1675. Brussels: Institut Historique Belge de Rome, 1966.

Johnston, H. H. (Sir Harry). George Grenfell and the Congo. 2 vols. London: Hutchinson, 1908.

_____. The River Congo from its Mouth to Bolobo. London: Sampson Low, 1884.

Kimena Kekwakwa Kinenge. Tippo Tip: Traitant et sultan du Manyema. Kinshasa: Centre de Recherches Pédagogiques, 1979.

Klein, Herbert S. The Middle Passage: Comparative Studies in the Atlantic Slave Trade. Princeton, NJ: Princeton University Press, 1978.

Le Fèbre de Vivy, L. Documents d'histoire précoloniale belge (1861-1865). Brussels: ARSC, 1955.

Lejeune-Choquet, Adolphe. Histoire militaire du Congo. Brussels: Alfred Castaine, 1906.

Lerman, Dragutin. Commissaire Général Dragutin Lerman. 1863-1918. A Contribution to the History of Central Africa, Lopasic, Aleksander, ed. Tervuren: MRAC, 1971.

M'Bokolo, Elikia. Msiri, bâtisseur de l'ancien royaume du Katanga, Shaba. Paris: ABC, 1976.

Meyers, Joseph. Le Prix d'un Empire. Brussels: Presses Académiques Européennes, 1964.

Miers, S. and Kopytoff, I., eds. Slavery in Africa: Historical and Anthropological Perspectives. Madison: University of Wisconsin Press, 1977.

Pigafetta, Filippo. A Report of the Kingdom of Congo and the Surrounding Countries, drawn out of the Discourses of the Portuguese by Duarte Lopez (1591). (reprint of 1881 edition published in London.) New York: Cass, 1969.

Pinto, Francisco Antonio. Angola e Congo. Lisbon: Livraria Ferreira, 1888.

Proyart, l'Abbe. Histoire de Loango, Kakong et autres royaumes d'Afrique. Paris: (publisher unknown), 1776.

Randles, W. G. L. L'Ancien royaume du Congo des origines à la fin du XIXe siècle. Paris, The Hague: Mouton, 1968.

Reefe, Thomas Q. The Rainbow and the Kings: A History of The Luba Empire to 1891. Berkeley: University of California Press, 1981.

Rinchon, Dieudonné. Les Armements négriers au XVIIIème siècle. Brussels: ARSC, 1956.

_____. La Traite et l'esclavage des Congolais par les Européens. Brussels: Imprimerie De Meester, 1929.

Schuler, Monica. Alas, Alas, Kongo: A Social History of Indentured African Immigration into Jamaica. 1841-1865. Baltimore: Johns Hopkins University Press, 1980.

Simpson, W. H. Land and Peoples of the Kasai. London: (publisher unknown), 1911.

Sutton, Smith. Yakusu, the Very Heart of Africa. London: (publisher unknown), 1910.

Swann, A. J. Fighting the Slave-Hunters in Central Africa. (Reprint of 1910 edition.) New York: Cass, 1968.

Thys, A. Au Congo et au Kasai. Brussels: Weissenbruch, 1888.

Tuckey, J. K. Narrative of an Expedition to Explore the River Zaire. London: John Murray, and New York: William B. Gilley, 1818.

Van der Kerken, G. Le Mésolithique et le Néolithique dans le Bassin de l'Uelé. Brussels: IRCB, 1942.

Vansina, Jan. The Tio Kingdom of the Middle Congo, 1880-1892. London: Oxford University Press, 1973.

Verbecken, Auguste. Msiri, roi du Garenganze. Brussels: Cuypers, 1956.

_____. La Première traversée du Katanga en 1806. Voyage des "pombeiros" d'Angola aux Rios de Sena. Brussels: IRCB, 1953.

_____. La Révolte des Batetela en 1895. Brussels: ARSC, 1958.

Weeks, J. H. Among the Primitive Bakongo. London: Seely, Service, 1914.

Womersley, Harold. Wm. F. P. Burton: Congo Pioneer. Eastbourne: Victory Press, 1973.

3. Congo Free State

Alexis, M. G. (Gochet, Jean-Baptiste). La Barbarie africaine et l'action civilisatrice des missions catholiques au Congo et dans l'Afrique équatoriale. Paris: Procure Générale, 1889.

_____. Le Congo Belge illustré ou l'Etat Indépendant du Congo. Liège: Dessain, 1887.

_____. La Traite des nègres et la croisade africaine. Liège: Dessain, 1889.

Ascherson, Neal. The King Incorporated: Léopold II in the Age of Trusts. New York: Doubleday, 1964.

Bateman, Charles S. L. The First Ascent of the Kasai. London: Philip & Son, 1889.

Bauer, Ludwig. Léopold the Unloved. Boston: Little, Brown, 1935.

Belgium. Federation for the Defense of Belgian Interests Abroad. The Truth About the Congo Free State. Brussels: 1905.

Berlin Conference, November 1884 to February 1885. General Act of the Conference of Berlin. (Washington: 49th U.S. Congress, 1st Session of the Senate, Miscellaneous Document no. 68.) Washington: 1886.

Botinck, François. Aux Origines de l'Etat Indépendant du Congo: Documents tirés des archives américains. Paris: Nauwelaerts, 1966.

Castelein, A. The Congo State: Its Origin, Rights, and Duties, the Charges of its Accusers. New York: Negro Universities Press, 1969.

Collins, Robert O. King Leopold, England and the Upper Nile, 1899–1909. New Haven: Yale University Press, 1969.

Comeliau, Jean. Dhanis. Brussels: Libris, 1943.

_____. Stanley et Léopold II. Leverville, Belgian Congo: Bibliothèque de l'Etoile, 195– (c. 1958).

Commission to Investigate the Congo State Territories. The Congo: A Report of the Commission of Inquiry Appointed by the Congo Free State Government; a Complete and Accurate Translation. New York: G. P. Putnam's Sons, 1906.

Conference of Missionary Societies, Representatives of American organizations conducting missionary work in the Independent State of the Kongo. Washington: U.S. Government Printing Office, 1904.

_____. Conditions in the Kongo State. Washington: U.S. Government Printing Office, 1905.

Cookey, S. J. S. Britain and the Congo Question, 1885-1913. (Idaban History Series) London: Longmans, 1968; New York: Humanities Press, 1969.

Crowe, Sybil Eyre. The Berlin West African Conference, 1884-1885. London: Longmans, Green, 1942.

De Lichtervelde, Comte Louis. Léopold II. (official biography) Brussels: (publisher unknown), 1935.

Delcommune, Alexandre. L'Avenir du Congo Belge menacé. Brussels: Office de Publicité, 1921.

_____. Vingt années de vie africaine (1874-1893). 2 vols. Brussels: Larcier, 1922.

Etat Indépendant du Congo. Bulletin Officiel de l'Etat Indépendant du Congo. Brussels: 1885-1908.

_____. The Congo: A Report of the Mission of Inquiry Appointed by the Free State Government. London: G. P. Putnam's Sons, 1906.

_____. Justice Repressive. Brussels: E. Dory, 1905.

Gann, Lewis H. The Rulers of Belgian Africa, 1884-1914. Princeton, NJ: Princeton University Press, 1979.

Gould, Tony. In Limbo: The Story of Stanley's Rear Column. London: Hamish Hamilton, 1979.

Harms, Robert. "The End of Red Rubber," Journal of African History, vol. 16, no. 1 (1975), pp. 73-88.

Institut Royal Colonial Belge. La Force Publique de sa naissance à 1914. Brussels: 1952.

Keith, Arthur Berriedale. The Belgian Congo and the Berlin Act. New York: Negro Universities Press, 1970.

Liben, C. Inventaire, papiers Alphonse Cabra, Lieutenant Général, 1862-1932. Tervuren: MRAC, 1977.

Louis, William Roger. E. D. Morel's History of the Congo Reform Movement. Oxford: Clarendon Press, 1968.

_____. "The Philosophical Diplomatist: Sir Arthur Hardinge and King Leopold's Congo," Bulletin des Sciences. Brussels: ARSOM (1965), pp. 1402-1430.

MacDonnell, John D. King Leopold Second: His Rule in Belgium and the Congo. (Reprint of 1905 edition.) New York: Argosy, 1970.

Massoin, Fritz. Histoire de l'Etat Indépendant du Congo. 2 vols. Namur: Imprimerie Picard-Balon, 1912-13.

Meyers, Joseph. Le Prix d'un Empire. Brussels: Presses Académiques Européennes, 1964.

Morel, Edmund Dane. The Congo Slave State. Liverpool: J. Richardson & Sons, 1903.

_____. Great Britain and the Congo. London: Smith, Elder, 1909.

_____. History of the Congo Reform Movement. Lewis, W. R. and Stengers, Jean, eds. Clarendon: Oxford University Press, 1968.

_____. King Leopold's Rule in Africa. (Reprint of 1904 edition.) Westport, CT: Negro Universities Press, 1970.

_____. Red Rubber: The Story of the Rubber Slave Trade Flourishing on the Congo in the year of Grace 1906. (Reprint of 1906 edition.) New York: Negro Universities Press, 1969.

Reeves, Jesse Siddall. The International Beginnings of the Congo Free State. Baltimore: Johns Hopkins Press, 1894; New York: Johnson Reprint Corp., 1973.

Roeykens, Auguste. Les Débuts de l'oeuvre africain de Léopold II. Brussels: ARSC, 1955.

_____. Le Dessein africain de Léopold II (1875-1876). Brussels: ARSC, 1956.

_____. L'Initiative africaine de Léopold II et l'opinion publique belge. Brussels: ARSOM, 1963.

_____. Léopold II et l'Afrique, 1855-1880. Essai de synthèse et de mise au point. Brussels: ARSC, 1958.

_____. Léopold II et la conférence Géographique de Bruxelles. Brussels: ARSC, 1956.

_____. La Période initiale de l'oeuvre africain de Léopold II (1875-1883). Brussels: ARSC, 1957.

_____. La Politique religieuse de l'Etat Indépendant du Congo. Documents. Brussels: ARSOM, 1965.

Salmon, Pierre. La Révolte des Batetela de l'Expédition du Haut-Ituri, 1897: Temoignages inédits. Brussels: ARSOM, 1977.

Slade, Ruth. King Leopold's Congo: Aspects of the Development of Race Relations in the Congo Independent State. (Reprint of the edition published by Oxford University Press, London, 1962.) Westport, CT: Greenwood Press, 1974.

Stanley, Henry Morton, Sir. The Congo and the Founding of its Free State: A Story of Work and Exploration. New York: Harper, 1885; New York: Negro History Press, 1970.

_____. Exploration Diaries. Stanley, Richard and Neame, Alan, eds. London: Kimber, 1961.

_____. In Darkest Africa. New York: Scribners, 1890.

_____. Through the Dark Continent, 1874-1877. London: Sampson, Low, Marston, Searle, 1878.

Starr, Frederick. Truth About the Congo: The Chicago Tribune Articles. (Reprint of 1907 edition.) New York: Negro Universities Press, n.d.

Sternstein, Jerome L. "King Leopold II, Senator Nelson W. Aldrich and the Strange Beginnings of American Economic Penetration in the Congo," African Historical Studies, vol. 2, no. 2 (1969), pp. 189-203.

Stringlhamber, B. E. M., and Dresse, P. Léopold II au travail. Brussels and Paris: Editions du Sablon, 1945.

Thompson, R. S. Fondation de l'Etat Indépendant du Congo: Un Chapître de l'histoire du partage de l'Afrique. Brussels: Office de Publicité, 1933.

Twain, Mark. King Leopold's Soliloquy. New York: International Publishers, 1961.

United States. Department of State. Congo Conference. Message from President Arthur and Report by the Secretary-of-State on Congo Conference at Berlin. Washington: January 30, 1895.

_____. Congo Conference. (Includes protocols of sessions of the Conference at Berlin and related correspondence.) Washington: 1885.

Vandervelde, Emile La Belgique et le Congo. Paris: Félix Alcan, 1911.

_____. Les Derniers jours de l'Etat Indépendant du Congo.
Mons: Editions de la Société Nouvelle, 1909.

Verdick, E. Les Premiers jours du Katanga (1890–1903). Brussels:
Comité Spécial du Katanga, 1952.

Wack, Henry Wellington. The Story of the Congo Free State: Social,
Political, and Economic Aspects of the Belgian System of Government in Central Africa. New York: Argosy-Antiquarian, 1970.

Wauters, Alphonse-Jules. L'Etat Indépendant du Congo. Brussels:
Librairie Falk & Fils, 1899.

Willequet, Jacques. Le Congo belge et la 'Weltpolitick' (1894–1914).
Brussels: Presses Universitaires, 1962.

4. Belgian Congo

Anstey, Roger T. King Leopold's Legacy: The Congo under Belgian
Rule, 1908–1960. London: Oxford University Press, 1966.

Belgium. Ministère des Colonies. Annuaire Officiel. (35th ed.)
Brussels: 1959.

_____. Rapport sur l'Administration de la Colonie du Congo
Belge...présenté aux Chambres Législatives. Brussels: annual
through 1960.

_____. Receuil à l'usage des fonctionnaires et agents du service
territorial au Congo Belge. Brussels: Several editions with
addenda.

Belgium. Parti Socialiste Belge. Congo 1885–1960. Positions Socialistes. Brussels: Institut Vendervelde, 1960.

_____. Un Program pour le Congo et le Ruanda-Urundi. (Rap-
ports présentés au Congrés Extraordinaire des 30 juin et 1er
juillet 1956). Brussels: Société d'Edition du Peuple, 1956.

Bourgeois, René. Témoignages. Tervuren: MRAC, 1982.

Brausch, Georges. Belgian Administration in the Congo. (Originally published in London: Oxford University Press, 1961.) New
York: Greenwood Press, 1986.

Buel, R. L. The Native Problem in Africa. 2 vols. (Originally
published in New York: Macmillan, 1928.) Hamden, CT: Shoe
String Press, 1965.

Bustin, Edouard. Lunda Under Belgian Rule: The Politics of Ethnicity. Cambridge, MA: Harvard University Press, 1975.

Comité Spécial du Katanga. Compte-rendus du Congrés Scientifique d'Elisabethville, 1950. 8 vols. Brussels: 1951.

Congo, Belgian. Gouvernement Général. Bulletin Administratif. Bestuursblad. (Published semi-monthly in French and Flemish. Merged with the Bulletin Officiel in January 1960 to form Moniteur Congolais.) Léopoldville: 1912-1959.

_____. Bulletin Officiel. Ambjtelijk Blad. (Published monthly and semi-monthly in French and Flemish until merger with Bulletin Administratif in 1960. Together, the two publications provide a record of Belgian administration of the colony.) Brussels: 1908-1959.

_____. Conseil du Gouvernement. Compte Rendu Synthétique des Séances. Léopoldville: annual.

_____. Conseils de Province. Compte-Rendus Analytiques des Séances. Léopoldville: irregular.

_____. Discours du Gouverneur Général à la Séance d'Ouverture du Conseil de Gouvernement. Léopoldville: annual.

_____. Discours. Rede. (Speeches in French and Flemish with statistical section.) Léopoldville: 1911-1959 (annual).

Coppens, Paul. Anticipations Congolaises. Brussels: Editions Scientifiques et Techniques, 1956.

Cornet, René Jules. Maniema, le pays des mangeurs d'hommes. 2nd ed. Brussels: Cuypers, 1955.

Daye, Pierre. Problèmes congolais. Brussels: Les Ecrits, 1943.

De Bauw, A. Le Katanga: Notes sur le pays, ses ressources et l'avenir de la colonization belge. Brussels: Larcier, 1920.

De Hemptinne, J. Le Gouvernement du Congo Belge: Projet de réorganisation administrative. Brussels: Librairie Dewit, 1920.

_____. Le Tournant de notre politique indigène. Elisabethville: Editions de la Revue Juridique du Congo Belge, 1935.

Dehoux, Emile. Le Problème de demain: L'Effort de paix du Congo Belge (colonat blanc et paysannat indigène). Brussels: R. Stoops, 1946.

Delicour, Fernand. Les Propos d'un colonial belge. Brussels: Weissenbruch, 1956.

Demuntur, Paul. "Structure de classe et luttes de classes dans le Congo colonial," Contradictions, vol. 1 (1972), pp. 67-109.

Denuit, Désiré. Le Congo, champion de la Belgique en guerre. Brussels: Editions Frans Van Belle, 1946.

Depage, Henri. Contributions à l'élaboration d'une doctrine visant à la promotion des indigènes au Congo Belge. Brussels: ARSC, 1955.

Dessart, Charles. Le Congo à tombeau ouvert. Brussels: Dessart, 1959.

Domont, Jean Marie. Elite noire. Brussels: Office de Publicité, 1957.

"L'Evolution politique du Congo Belge et les autorités indigènes," special issue of Problèmes d'Afrique Centrale, no. 43 (1959).

Fonds du Bien-Etre Indigène au Congo au Rwanda et au Burundi. Une Oeuvre de coopération au développement: Quinze années d'activités du Fonds du Bien-Etre Indigène...1948-1963. Ghent: Snoeck-Ducaju, 1964.

Ganshof van der Meersch, W. J. Congo: Mai-juin 1960. Rapport du Ministre chargé des affaires générales en Afrique. Brussels: Ministère des Affaires Africaines, 1960.

_____. Fin de la souveraineté belge au Congo. (Sponsored by the Institut Royal des Relations Internationales.) The Hague: Nijhoff, 1963.

_____ and Perin, François. Le Droit électoral au Congo Belge. Brussels: Bruylant, 1958.

Gérard, J. La Monarchie belge abondonnera-t-elle le Congo? Brussels: Editions Europe-Afrique, 1960.

Gilbert, O. P. L'Empire du silence. Brussels: Editions du "Peuple," 1947.

Guebels, L., ed. Relation complète des travaux de la Commission Permanente pour la Protection des Indigènes au Congo Belge, 1911-1951. Elisabethville: CEPSI, 1953.

Haleqijck de Heusch, M. La Charte Coloniale. 3 vols. Brussels: Weissenbruch, 1914.

_____. Les Institutions politiques et administratives des pays africains soumis à l'autorité de la Belgique. (For the Institut Colonial International.) Brussels: Etablissements Généraux d'Imprimerie, 1934.

Henige, David P. Colonial Governors from the Fifteenth Century to the Present. Madison: University of Wisconsin Press, 1970.

Hostelet, Georges. L'Oeuvre civilisatrice de la Belgique au Congo, de 1885 à 1953. Brussels: ARSC, 1954.

_____. Pour éviter l'anarchie puis la dictature, la réalisation de l'indépendance du Congo exige des étapes. Brussels: private publisher, 1959.

_____. Le Problème politique capital au Congo et en Afrique noire. Brussels: Institut de Sociologie, Université Libre de Belgique, 1959.

J. K. (Van der Dussen de Kestergat, J.). André Ryckmans. Paris: Centurion, 1961.

Jadot, J. M. Blanc et noirs au Congo Belge: Problèmes coloniaux et tentatives de solutions. Brussels: Edition de la Revue Sincère, 1929.

Jentgen, P. Les Frontières du Congo Belge. Brussels: IRCB, 1952.

_____. Histoire des Secrétaires Généraux du Ministère des Colonies pendant l'occupation. Brussels: IRCB, 1946.

Jewsiewicki, Bogumil. "African Peasants in the Totalitarian Colonial Society of the Belgian Congo," in Peasants in Africa: Historical and Contemporary Perspectives, Klein, Martin A., ed. Vol. 4, pp. 45-75. Beverly Hills, CA: Sage Publications, 1980.

_____. "Unequal Development: Capitalism and the Katanga Economy, 1919-1940," in The Roots of Cultural Poverty in Central and South Africa, Palmer, Robin and Parsons, Neil, eds., pp. 317-344. London: Heinemann, 1977.

Joyce, Pierre and Rosipe, Lewin. Les Trusts du Congo. Brussels: Société Populaire d'Editions, 1961.

Kanyinda Lusanga. Le Phénomène de la colonisation et l'émancipation des institutions socio-politiques traditionnelles au Zaire. Brussels: CEDAF, 1975.

Lovens, M. L'Effort militaire de guerre du Congo Belge, 1940-1944. Brussels: CEDAF, 1975.

_____. La Révolte de Masisi-Lubutu: Congo Belge, janvier-mai 1944. Brussels: CEDAF, 1974.

Malengreau, Guy. Les Droits Fonciers Coutumiers chez les indigènes du Congo. Brussels: IRCB, 1947.

_____. "Organization of Native Administration in the Belgian Congo," Journal of African Administration, vol. 7, no. 2 (1956), pp. 85-88.

Martelli, George. Leopold to Lumumba: A History of the Belgian Congo, 1877-1960. London: Chapman and Hall, 1962.

Martynov, V. A. Congo under the Yoke of Imperialism. Moscow: Academy of Science, Institute of World Economy and International Relations, 1959.

Merlier, Michel. Le Congo de la colonisation belge à l'indépendance. Paris: Maspero, 1962.

Norton, William B. A Belgian Socialist Critic of Colonialism: Louis Betrand (1856-1943). Brussels: ARSOM, 1965.

Paulus, Jean-Pierre. Congo 1956-1960. Brussels and Paris: "Terre d'Europe," 1961.

Pétillon, Léo A. M. Courts métrages africains: pour servire à l'histoire. Brussels: Renaissance du Livre, 1979.

_____. Témoignages et Réflexions. Brussels: La Renaissance du Livre, 1976.

Pevée, Albert. Place aux noirs. Brussels: Editions Europe-Afrique, 1960.

Phombeah, Dennis. Congo: Prelude to Independence. London: African Research and Publications, 1961.

Pons, Valdo. Stanleyville: An African Urban Community under Belgian Administration. London: Oxford University Press, 1969.

Rhodius, Georges. Congo 1958; ou, Cinquante ans de civilisation. Brussels: Ministère de la Défense nationale, Direction de l'Education des Forces Armées, 1959.

Ryckmans, Pierre. (former Governor-General). Dominer pour servir. Brussels: L'Edition Universelle, 1948.

_____. Etapes et Jalons. Brussels: Larcier, 1946.

_____. La Politique coloniale. Brussels: Editions Rex, 1934.

Salkin, Paul. Etudes Africaines. Brussels: Larcier, 1920.

_____. Le Problème de l'évolution noire, l'Afrique central dans cent ans. Paris: Payot, 1926.

Sauvy, J. Le Katanga: Cinquante ans décisifs. Paris: Société Continentale d'Editions Modernes Illustrées, 1961.

Sépulchre, Jean. Propos sur le Congo politique de demain:

Autonomie et fédéralisme. Elisabethville: Editions de l'Essor du Congo, 1958.

Slade, Ruth M. The Belgian Congo: Some Recent Changes. (Sponsored by the Institute of Race Relations.) London: Oxford University Press, 1960.

Sohier, Jean. La Mémoire d'un policier belgo-congolais. Brussels: ARSOM, 1974.

Sourdillat, Jacques. Les Chefferies au Congo Belge. Paris: Domat-Montchrestien, 1940.

Stengers, J. "Belgian Historiography since 1945," in Reappraisals in Overseas History, Emmer, P. C. and Wesseling, H. L., eds. Leiden: Leiden University Press, 1979.

_____. Belgique et Congo: Elaboration de la Charte Coloniale. Brussels: La Renaissance du Livre, 1963.

_____. Combien le Congo a-t-il coûté à la Belgique? Brussels: ARSC, 1957.

_____. Textes inédites d'Emile Banning. Brussels: publisher unknown, 1955.

Stenmans, Alain. La Reprise du Congo par la Belgique. Brussels: Editions Techniques et Scientifiques, 1949.

Terlinden, Charles; Cornet, René Jules; and Walraet, Michel. Le Comité Spécial du Katanga. Brussels: Cuypers, 1950.

Van Bilsen, A. A. J. Vers l'Indépendance du Congo et du Ruanda-Urundi. Réflexions sur les devoirs et l'avenir de la Belgique en Afrique centrale. Kraainem, Belgium: Privately printed, 1958.

Van der Kerken, G. La Politique coloniale belge. Antwerp: Editions "Zaire," 1943.

_____. Les Sociétés bantoues du Congo Belge et le problème de la politique indigène. Brussels: Bruylant, 1920.

Vanden Bossche, Jean. Sectes et associations indigènes au Congo Belge. Léopoldville: Gouvernement Générale, AIMO, 1954.

Van Grieken, E. and Van Grieken-Taverniers, M. Les Archives inventoriées au Ministère des Colonies. Brussels: ARSC, 1958.

Van Zandijcke, A. Pages de l'histoire du Kasayi. Namur: Grands Lacs, 1953.

Van Zuylen, Baron Pierre. L'Echiquier congolais, ou le secret du roi. Brussels: Dessart, 1959.

Vanhove, Julian. Histoire du Ministère des Colonies. Brussels: ARSOM, 1968.

Verhaegen, Benoît. Le Centre Extra-Coutumier de Stanleyville (1940-1945). Brussels: CEDAF, 1981.

Vermuelen, Victor. Déficiences et dangers de notre politique indigène. Brussels: publisher unknown, 1952.

Vers la promotion de l'économie indigène. Brussels: Institut de Sociologie, Université Libre de Belgique, 1956.

Wauters, Alphonse-Jules. Histoire politique du Congo Belge. Brussels: P. Van Fleteren, 1911.

Wauthion, R. Le Congo Belge à un tournant. Brussels: ARSC, 1959.

Whyms, L. Léopoldville, son histoire 1881-1956. Brussels: Office de Publicité, 1956.

5. Independence (1960-1965)

Abi-Saab, Georges. The United Nations Operation in the Congo, 1960-1964. Oxford and New York: Oxford University Press, 1978.

African Affairs Research Group. Save the Congo, Save Africa: The Bleeding Heart of Africa. Location unknown: 1965.

Ainslie, Rosalynde. The Unholy Alliance--Salazar, Verwoerd, Welensky. London: Anti-Apartheid Movement, 1962.

Amachree, Godfrey, K. J. "U.N. Civilian Operations in the Congo," in Southern Africa in Transition, Davis, J. A. and Baker, J. K., eds., pp. 305-312. New York: Praeger, 1966.

Amalaure, Jean. Les Pourquois de l'aventure katangaise: Etiologie insolite d'une aventure transcontinentale; essai historique et politique sur des événements encore récents. Avignon: J. Amalaure, 1983.

Anciaux, Léon. Le Drame du Congo: La vérité au sujet de la débande de l'Armée Nationale Congolaise. Brussels: CRAOCA and Fraternelle des Troupes Coloniales 1914-1918, 1960.

Belgium. Chambre des Représentants. Rapport de la Commission

Parlementaire chargée de faire une enquête sur les événements qui se sont produits à Léopoldville en janvier 1959. Brussels: Documents Parlementaires. S. 1958-1959, no. 100/3.

_____. Rapport du Groupe de Travail pour l'Etude du Problème politique au Congo Belge. Brussels: Documents Parlementaires. S. 1958-1959, no. 108.

_____. La Table Ronde Economique. Bruxelles, avril-mai 1960. Compte-Rendus et Documents. Brussels, 1960.

Belgium. Ministère de la Justice. Congo, July 1960. Evidence. Brussels: 1960.

Bouvier, Paule. L'Accession du Congo Belge à l'indépendance. Brussels: Institut de Sociologie, Université Libre de Belgique, 1966.

Bowett, D. G., et al. United Nations Forces: A Legal Study of UN Practice. New York: Praeger, 1964.

Burns, A. L., and Heathcote, N. Peacekeeping by the UN Forces: From Suez to the Congo. New York: Praeger, 1963.

Cabanès, Bernard. Du Congo Belge au Katanga. Paris: Editions du Fil d'Arianne, 1963.

Calder, Ritchie. Agony of the Congo. London: Gollancz, 1961.

Le Camp des Baluba: Une Initiative de l'ONU. Brussels: Dessart, 1962.

Centre de Recherche et d'Information Socio-Politiques. "Le Conditionnement politique de l'Opération 'Dragon Rouge' (Stanleyville, novembre 1964)," Travaux Africains du CRISP, no. 38 (1964), pp. 1-20.

_____. Congo: 1964: Political Documents of a Developing Nation. Princeton: Princeton University Press, 1966.

_____. "Les Débats de décembre 1964 au Conseil de Sécurité sur l'intervention belgo-américaine à Stanleyville," Travaux Africains du CRISP, nos. 42-43 (Feb. 8-15, 1965), pp. 19-21.

_____. "Le Kwilu, de la lutte pour l'indépendance à la rébellion muléliste," Travaux Africains du CRISP, nos. 30-32 (Feb.-Mar. 1964).

Chatterjee, Dwarka Nath. Storm over the Congo. Ghaziabad: Vikas, 1980.

Chomé, Jules. La Crise congolaise: De l'Indépendance à l'intervention militaire belge. (30 juin-9 juillet 1960). Brussels: Editions Remarques Congolaises, 1960.

_____. Le Drame du Luluabourg. Brussels: Editions Remarques Congolaises, 1959.

_____. Le Gouvernement congolais et l'ONU: Un Paradox tragique. Brussels: Editions Remarques Congolaises, 1961.

_____. Indépendance congolaise, pacifique conquête. Brussels: Editions Remarques Congolaises, 1960.

_____. M. Lumumba et le communisme. Brussels: Editions Remarques Congolaises, 1961.

_____. Mobutu et la contre-révolution en Afrique. Waterloo: Tiers-Monde et Révolution, 1967.

_____. Moise Tshombe et l'escroquerie katangaise. Brussels: Editions de la Fondation Joseph Jacquemotte, 1966.

Clarke, Stephen John Gordon. The Congo Mercenary; a history and analysis. Johannesburg: South African Institute of International Affairs, 1968.

Congo, République de. Documentation technique du Gouvernement concernant les résolutions de Coquilhatville. Léopoldville: 1961.

_____. Les Entretiens Adoula-Tshombe (Second Livre Blanc du Gouvernement Central sur la séccession katangaise). Léopoldville: 1961.

_____. De Léopoldville à Lagos. Léopoldville: 1962.

_____. Ministère des Affaires Etrangères. La Province du Katanga et l'indépendance congolaise. Léopoldville: 1961.

Davister, Pierre. Katanga, enjeu du monde. Brussels: Editions Europe-Afrique, 1960.

_____, and Toussaint, P. Croisettes et casques bleus. Brussels: Editions Actuelles, 1962.

Dayal, Rajeshwar. Mission for Hammarskjöld: The Congo Crisis. Princeton, NJ: Princeton University Press; Oxford: Oxford University Press, 1976.

De Bosschere, G. Rescapés de Watsa. Brussels: Dessart, 1966.

De Coninck, Albert. Le Drame congolais. Ouvrons le dossier. Brussels: Editions "Communisme," 1960.

De Vos, Pierre. Vie et mort de Lumumba. Paris: Calmann-Lévy, 1961.

Demany, Fernand. S.O.S. Congo: Chronique d'un soulévement. Brussels: Labor, 1959.

Dikoba, Simon J. Matadi sous l'agression des Belges (juillet 1960). Léopoldville: Indépendance-Imprimerie Kongolaise, 1961.

Dinant, Georges. L'ONU face à la crise congolaise. Brussels: Editions Remarques Congolaises, 1962.

Duchemin, Jacques. Notre Guerre au Katanga. Paris: Pensée Moderne, 1963.

Dugauquier, Daphne P. Congo Cauldron. London: Jarrolds, 1961.

Dumont, G. H. La Table Ronde belgo-congolaise. Paris: Editions Universitaires, 1961.

Franck, Thomas M., and Carey, John, eds. The Legal Aspects of the United Nations Action in the Congo. New York: Oceana, 1963.

Gavshon, A. L. The Mysterious Death of Dag Hammarskjöld. New York: Walker, 1962.

Gendebien, Paul Henry. L'Intervention des Nations Unies au Congo 1960-1964. Paris and The Hague: Mouton, 1967.

Gérard-Libais, Jules. "La Liquidation du contentieux belgo-congolais et ses séquelles en 1966," Etudes Congolaises, vol. 9, nos. 5-6 (1966), pp. 1-22.

_____. "Le Rôle de la Belgique dans l'opération des Nations Unies au Congo, 1960-1964," Travaux Africains du CRISP, nos. 68-71.

_____. Séccession au Katanga. Brussels: Editions du CRISP, 1963; Madison: University of Wisconsin Press, 1966.

Gillis, Charles-André. Kasa-Vubu au coeur du drame congolais. Brussels: Editions Europe-Afrique, 1963.

Gordon, King. The United Nations in the Congo: A Quest for Peace. New York: Carnegie Endowment for International Peace, 1962.

Guéry, André. "La Place de Kasa-Vubu dans l'histoire du Congo," Remarques Africaines, no. 335 (1969), pp. 203-206.

Hayes, Margaret. Missing Believed Killed. London: Hodder & Stoughton, 1966.

Heinz, G., and Donnay, H. Lumumba: The Last Fifty Days. (Published originally in French: Brussels: Editions du CRISP, 1966.) New York: Grove Press, 1969.

Hempstone, Smith. Rebels, Mercenaries and Dividends: the Katanga Story. New York: Praeger, 1962.

Henri, P., and Marres, J. L'Etat belge responsable en droit du désastre congolais? Brussels: Editions R. R. Windfohr, 1961.

Hilsman, Roger. "The Congo Crisis," in To Move a Nation. The Politics of Foreign Policy in the Administration of John F. Kennedy. New York: Doubleday, 1967.

Honorin, Michel. La fin des mercenaires, Bukavu, novembre 1967. Paris: Laffont, 1968.

Hoskyns, Catherine. The Congo. A Chronology of Events, January 1960-December 1961. London: Oxford University Press, 1962.

_____. The Congo Since Independence. London: Oxford University Press, for the Royal Institute of International Affairs, 1965.

_____. The Organization of African Unity and the Congo Crisis, 1964-1965; Documents. Dar-es-Salaam, Tanzania: Oxford University Press, for the Institute of Public Administration, 1969.

House, Arthur H. The U.N. in the Congo: The Political and Civilian Efforts. Washington: University Press of America, 1978.

Ilunga-Kabongo, André, and Kalonji, Baudoin. "Les Evénements du Kwilu," Etudes Congolaises, vol. 6, no. 3 (1964), pp. 1-21.

Jacquemyns, G. L'ONU au Congo. Ses Interventions vues et jugées par les Belges. Brussels: INSOC, 1961.

Judd, Charles. The U.N. and the Congo. London: United Nations Association, 1961.

Kalb, Madeleine G. "The C.I.A. and Lumumba," New York Times Magazine, August 2, 1981, pp. 32-56.

_____. The Congo Cables: From Eisenhower to Kennedy. New York: Macmillan, 1982.

Kalonji, Albert. Congo 1960-1964. La Vérité sur la mort de Patrice Lumumba. Documents secrets sur la séccession katangaise et sur Moïse Tshombe. Albert Kalonji révèle et accuse. Brussels: Editions du Ponant, 1964.

_____. Ma Lutte au Kasai pour la vérité au service de la justice.
Barcelona: C.A.G.S.A., 1964.

Kanza, Thomas R. Conflict in the Congo: The Rise and Fall of
Lumumba. London: R. Collings, 1978; Boston: G. K. Hall,
1979.

Kasa-Vubu, Joseph. Receuil des discours, allocutions et messages
prononcés de juin 1960 à juin 1965. Léopoldville: Ministère de
l'Information, Bureau de Documentation et des Relations Publiques,
1965.

Katanga, Etat du. Livre Blanc du Gouvernement katangais sur les
activitiés des hors-la-loi dans certains territoires baluba. Elisabethville: 1962.

_____. Livre Blanc du Gouvernement katangais sur les événe-
ments de septembre et décembre 1961. Elisabethville: 1962.

Katanga, Jean (pseud.). Le Camp des Baluba: Rapport secret.
Brussels: Dessart, 1962.

Kestergat, J. Congo, Congo. Paris: La Table Ronde, 1965.

Kirchmayr, Otto. Mort d'un affreux. Paris: Buchet-Chastel, 1967.

Kitchen, Helen, ed. The Educated African. New York: Praeger,
1962.

_____, ed. Footnotes to the Congo Story: An "Africa Report"
Anthology. New York: Walker, 1967.

Lagos Study Circle. The Tragedy of the Congo. Lagos, Nigeria:
1964.

Lash, Joseph P. Dag Hammarskjöld. London: publisher unknown,
1962.

Lawson, Richard. Strange Soldiering. London: Hodder & Stoughton,
1963.

Le Bailly, J. Une Poignée de mercenaires. Paris: Presses de la
Cité, 1967.

Leclerq, Claude. L'ONU et l'affaire du Congo. Paris: Payot, 1964.

Lefever, Ernest W. Crisis in the Congo: A United Nations Force
in Action. Washington: Brookings, 1965.

_____. Uncertain Mandate: Politics of the U.N. Congo Operation.
Baltimore: Johns Hopkins Press, 1967.

_____, and Wynfred, Joshua. United Nations Peacekeeping in the Congo: 1960-1964, An Analysis of a Political, Executive and Military Contest. Washington: Brookings, 1966.

Mambida-Babinza. Odyssée des événements de Kisangani-Bukavu, 1960-1967. Kinshasa: Forces Armées Congolaises, 1967.

Martelli, George. Experiment in World Government: An Account of the United Nations Operation in the Congo, 1960-1964. London: Johnson Publications, 1966.

Masson, Paul. La Bataille pour Bukavu. Récits et reportages, mai à octobre 1964. Brussels: IMPRESOR, 1965.

Merriam, Alan P. Congo: Background of Conflict. Evanston, IL: Northwestern University Press, 1961.

Meynaud, Jean; Ladrière, J.; and Perin, F. La Décision politique en Belgique. Paris: Colin, 1965.

Monheim, Francis. Mobutu, l'homme seul. Brussels: Editions Actuelles, 1962.

_____. "La Mutinerie de la Force Publique Congolaise," Revue Générale Belge, vol. 98, no. 3 (1962), pp. 37-55.

_____. Réponses à Pierre De Vos au sujet de "Vie et Mort de Lumumba." Antwerp: Imprimerie "De Vlijt," 1961.

Moumié, Félix. Eyewitness Report on the Congo. London: Committee of African Organization, 1960.

Müller, Siegfried Friedrich Heinrich. The Laughing Man: Confessions of a Murderer, Program of a Regime. Dresden: Verlag Zeit im Bild, 1966.

_____. Les Nouveaux mercenaires. Paris: Editions France-Empire, 1965.

Munongo, Godefroid. Comment est né le nationalisme katangais. Elisabethville: Service d'Information du Gouvernement Katangais, June 16, 1962. (mimeo.)

Nguya-Ndila, Célestin. Indépendance de la République Démocratique du Congo et les engagements internationaux antérieurs (succession d'états aux traités). Kinshasa: Université de Kinshasa, 1971.

Niedergang, Marcel. Tempête sur le Congo. Paris: Plon, 1960.

O'Brien, Conor Cruise. To Katanga and Back. New York: Simon and Schuster, 1962.

_____, and Topolski, Felix. The United Nations: Sacred Drama. New York: Ivan Obolensky, 1976.

Pradhan, Ram Chandra. The United Nations and the Congo Crisis. New Delhi: MANAS Publications, 1975.

Reed, D. 111 Days in Stanleyville. New York: Harper & Row, 1965.

Ribead, Paul. Adieu Congo. Paris: La Table Ronde, 1961.

Rivkin, Arnold. Africa and the West. New York: Praeger, 1962.

_____. "The Congo Crisis in World Affairs," Civilizations, vol. 10, no. 4 (1960), pp. 473-479.

Roseveare, Helen. Doctor among Congo Rebels. London: Lutterworth, 1965.

Rouch, Jane. En Cage avec Lumumba. Paris: Les Editions du Temps, 1961.

Rubbens, Antoine. "La Consultation populaire du 22 décembre 1957 à Elisabethville," Bulletin CEPSI, no. 42 (Sept. 1958), pp. 77-81.

Russell of Liverpool (Lord). The Tragedy of the Congo. Wimbledon, U.K.: The Shamrock Press, 1962.

Schöller, André. Congo, 1959-1960: Mission au Katanga, intérim à Léopoldville. Gembloux: Duculot, 1982.

Schramme, Jean. La Bataillon Léopard, souvenirs d'un Africain blanc. Paris: Editions J'ai Lu, 1971.

Scott, Ian. Tumbled House: The Congo at Independence. London: Oxford University Press, 1969.

Simmonds, R. Legal Problems Arising from the United Nations Military Operations in the Congo. The Hague: Martinus Nijhoff, 1968.

Stenmans, Alain. Les Premiers mois de la République du Congo. Brussels: ARSOM, 1961.

Struelens, Michel. The United Nations in the Congo, or O.N.U.C., and International Politics. Brussels: Max Arnold, 1976.

Tournaire, Helène, and Bouteaud, Robert. Livre Noir au Congo. Paris: Librairie Académique, 1963.

Tran-Minh-Tiet. Le Congo ex-Belge entre l'Est et l'Ouest. Paris: Nouvelles Editions Latines, 1962.

Trinquier, R.; Duchemin, J.; and Le Bailly, J. Notre guerre au Katanga. Paris: Editions la Pensée Moderne, 1963.

Tshombe, Moïse. Discours prononcé par le Président du Katanga à l'occasion de la fête du 11 juillet 1962. Elisabethville: Service d'Information du Gouvernement Katangais, 1962.

_____. Moïse Tshombe parle...Les Véritables dessous de l'affair katangaise. L'Avenir du Congo. Brussels: Editions du Ponant, 1963.

_____. Quinze mois de gouvernement du Congo. Paris: La Table Ronde, 1966.

Tully, Andrew. CIA: The Inside Story. New York: Morrow, 1962.

Union de Jeunesses Révolutionnaires Congolaises. Memorandum: L'Agression armée de l'impérialisme américano-belge à Stanleyville et à Paulis. Brussels: Le Livre International, 1966.

United Nations. General Assembly. Report of the Commission of Inquiry into the Events Leading to the Death of Mssrs. Lumumba, Okito and M'polo. New York: 1961.

United States Congress. House of Representatives. Committee on Foreign Affairs. Staff Memorandum on the Republic of the Congo. Washington: August 24, 1960.

United States Government. "Biographic Data on Members of the Tshombe Government," Joint Publications Research Service, no. 27608, pp. 35–40. Washington: 1964.

_____. "Biographic Sketches of Former and Present Congo Ministers," Joint Publications Research Service, no. 33803, pp. 38–47. Washington: 1966.

Valahu, Mugur. The Katanga Circus. New York: Speller & Sons, 1964.

Van Bilsen, A. A. J. L'Indépendance du Congo. Paris and Tournai: Casterman, 1962.

Van der Haag, Ernest. The War in Katanga: Report of a Mission. The UN in the Congo. New York: American Committee for Aid to Katanga Freedom Fighters, 1962.

Van Langenhove, Fernand. Consciences tribales et nationales en Afrique noire. The Hague: Nijhoff, 1960.

_____. Le Rôle proéminent du Secrétaire Général dans l'opération des Nations Unies au Congo. The Hague: Nijhoff, 1964.

300 / The Bibliography

Vandewalle, Frédéric J. L. A. L'Ommegang. Odyssée et recon-
quête de Stanleyville, 1964. Brussels: Le Livre Africain, 1970.

_____. Une Ténébreuse affaire, ou Roger Trinquier au Katanga.
Brussels: Editions de Tam Tam Ommegang, 1979.

Verhaegen, Benoît, ed. Les Cahiers de Gamboma. Instructions
politiques et militaires des partisans congolais (1964-1965). Brussels: CRISP, 1965.

_____. "Consultations électorales et élections au Congo, 1957-
1959," Cahiers Economiques et Sociaux IRES, vol. 3, no. 3 (1965),
pp. 247-289.

_____. "Histoire de Tables Rondes du Congo Indépendant,"
Etudes Congolaises, vol. 1, nos. 2, 4, 5 (1961), pp. 1-14, 1-12,
33-39.

_____. Rébellions au Congo, I. Brussels: CRISP, 1966.

_____. Rébellions au Congo, II. Brussels: CRISP, 1969.

Verhoeven, Jan. Les Otages de Makondo. Journal de l'époque des
Simbas, 1964-1965. Kessel-Lo, Belgium: Europe-Littérature,
1966.

Von Horn, Carl. Soldiering for Peace. New York: McKay, 1967.

Wagoner, Fred E. Dragon Rouge: The Rescue of Hostages in the
Congo. Washington: National Defense University, 1980.

Wauters, Arthur, ed. Le Monde communiste et la crise du Congo.
Brussels: Institut de Sociologie, Université Libre de Belgique,
1961.

Weiss, Herbert P. Political Protest in the Congo: The Parti Solidaire Africain during the Independence Struggle. Princeton, NJ:
Princeton University Press, 1967.

Ziegler, Jean. La Contre-révolution en Afrique. Paris: Payot,
1963.

6. Post-Independence and Mobutism (since 1965)

Adelman, Kenneth L. "The Church-State Conflict in Zaire: 1969-
1974," African Studies Review, vol. 18, no. 1 (1975), pp. 102-
116.

_____. "The Recourse to Authenticity and Negritude in Zaire,"
Journal of Modern African Studies, vol. 13, no. 1, pp. 134-139.

_____. "Zaire's Year of Crisis," African Affairs, no. 77 (1978), pp. 36-44.

Callaghy, Thomas M. The State-Society Struggle: Zaire in Comparative Perspective. New York: Columbia University Press, 1984.

Centre de Recherche et d'Information Socio-Politiques. Dans le cadre de l'Authenticité, nouvelles appelations en République du Zaire. Brussels: March 20, 1972.

Chomé, Jules. L'Ascension de Mobutu: Du Sergent Désiré Joseph au Général Sese Seko. 2nd ed. Paris: F. Maspero, 1979.

_____. Mobutu, guide suprême. Brussels: Complexe, 1975.

Comité Zaire. "Kolwezi '78," InfoZaire, vol. 5, July-August, 1978.

_____. Zaire--le dossier de la recolonisation. Paris: Editions l'Harmattan, 1978.

"L'Enlèvement de M. Tshombe le 30 juin 1967," Travaux Africains du CRISP, no. 76 (March 12, 1968).

Kabongo-Kongo Kola. Zaire, l'ascension d'une nation engagée. Kinshasa: Presses Universitaires du Zaire, 1983.

Kalanda, A. Mabika. La Remise en question; base de la décolonisation mentale. Brussels: Editions Remarques Africaines, 1967.

Kalonga, Ali. Le Mal zaïrois. Brussels: Editions Fati, 1978.

Kambembo. Le Nationalisme congolais, idéologie d'authenticité. Kinshasa: Presses Universitaires du Zaire, 1971.

Hull, Galen S. "Whose Victory in Shaba?" Africa Report, vol. 22, no. 4 (July-August 1977), pp. 4-9.

Mboye Empenge ea Longila. Le Mobutisme et la rupture du concept ancien. Kinshasa: Presses Universitaires du Zaire, 1977.

Mobutu Sese Seko. Discours, allocutions et messages, 1965-1975. Paris: Editions J.A., 1975.

_____. Les Grands textes du Mobutisme. Kinshasa: Institut Makanda Kabobi, 1984.

_____. Mobutu et la guerre de "quatre-vingts jours." Paris: ABC, 1978.

_____. "Speeches and Messages," in Great African Revolutions. Romorantin, France: 1976.

Monguya-Mbenga, Daniel. Histoire secrète du Zaire. Brussels:
Editions de l'Espérance, 1977.

Nguza Karl i Bond. Un Avenir pour le Zaire. Brussels: Vie
Ouvrière, 1985.

_____. "Dix ans de pouvoir idées-forces du Mobutisme," Studie
Diplomatica, vol. 29, no. 1 (1976), pp. 3–39.

_____. Mobutu, ou, l'incarnation du mal zairois. London: R.
Collings, 1982.

Nzongola-Ntalaja, ed. The Crisis in Zaire: Myths and Realities.
Trenton, NJ: Africa World Press, 1986.

Odier, Jeannick. "La Politique étrangère de Mobutu," Revue Française d'Etudes Politiques Africaines, no. 120 (Dec. 1975), pp.
25–41.

Roskam, Karel Lodewijk. Mobutu: de dictatuur in Kongo. Bussum:
Agathon, 1976.

Sergent, Pierre. La Légion saute sur Kolwezi: Opération Léopard:
Le 2e R.E.P. au Zaire. Paris: Presses de la Cité, 1978.

Stockwell, John. In Search of Enemies, a CIA Story. New York:
W. W. Norton, 1978.

Union des Ecrivains Zairois. Authenticité et développement: Actes
du Colloque National. Kinshasa-Gombe: UEZ, and Paris: Présence Africaine, 1982.

Young, Crawford, and Turner, Thomas. The Rise and Decline of
the Zairian State. Madison: University of Wisconsin Press, 1985.

Le Zaire à la croisée des chemins. Lubumbashi: Mwanga, 1975.

Zaire, République du. Département de la Défense Nationale, de la
Sécurité du Territoire, et des Anciens Combattants. Le Bataillon
héros: l'Exploit du 311e bataillon para au cours de la deuxième
guerre du Shaba. Paris: ABC, 1979.

V. POLITICS

1. Constitution and Government

Amnesty International. Memorandum to the Head of State Concerning
Amnesty International's Mission to Zaire in July 1981. New York:
1981.

_____ . Political Imprisonment in Zaire: An Amnesty International Special Briefing. New York: 1983.

Belgium. Ministère du Congo Belge et du Ruanda-Urundi. Constitution 1960. La Loi Fondamentale du 19 mai 1960 relative aux structures du Congo. Brussels: 1960.

Centre de Recherches et d'Information Socio-Politiques. Dans le cadre de l'authenticité, nouvelles appelations en République du Zaire. Brussels: 1972.

Congo, Belgian. La Charte Coloniale Belge. Commentaire de la loi de gouvernement du Congo Belge éclairé par les discussions parlementaires et la comparaison des législations étrangères. (Comments by Halot-Gevaert, Alexandre.) Brussels: P. Van Fleteren, 1910.

_____ . La Charte Coloniale: Commentaire de La Loi du 18 octobre 1908 sur le Gouvernement du Congo Belge. (Commentary by Halewyck, Michel.) Brussels: M. Weissenbruch, 1910-19.

Congo, République Démocratique du. Constitution de la République Démocratique du Congo. 1er août 1964. 2nd ed. Coquilhatville: Bureau Presse-Documentation, 1964.

_____ . Constitution de la République Démocratique du Congo. Kinshasa: Ministère des Affaires Etrangères, 1967.

De Vos, Pierre. L'Enfer katangais. Brussels: private publisher, 1973.

Gatarayiha Majinya. Aspects de la réforme administrative au Zaire: l'Administration publique et la politique de 1965 à 1975. Brussels: CEDAF, 1976.

Gould, David J. Bureaucratic Corruption and Underdevelopment in the Third World: The Case of Zaire. New York: Pergamon Press, 1980.

_____ . From Development Administration to Underdevelopment Administration: A Study of Zairian Administration in the Light of Current Crisis. Brussels: CEDAF, 1978.

_____ . "Local Administration in Zaire and Underdevelopment," Journal of Modern African Studies, vol. 15, no. 3 (1977), pp. 349-378.

_____ . "Patrons, Clients and the Role of the Military in Zaire," in The Performance of Soldiers as Governors: African Politics and the African Military, Mowe, I. J., ed. Washington: University Press of America, n.d.

_____, and Mwana Elas. "Patrons, Clients and the Politics of Zairianization," in Political Patronage, Clientalism and Development, Eisenstadt, S. N. and Lemarchand, René, eds. (Publisher unknown), 1979(?).

Gutteridge, William Frank. Africa's Military Rulers: An Assessment. London: Institute for the Study of Conflict, 1975.

Kmambo, Isaria. "The Rise of the Congolese State Systems," in Aspects of Central African History, Ranger, T. O., ed., pp. 29-48. London: Heinemann, 1968.

La Fontaine, Jean Sybil. City Politics: A Study of Léopoldville, 1962-63. Cambridge, MA: Harvard University Press, 1970.

Lee, J. M. African Armies and Civil Order. New York: Praeger, 1969.

Lefever, Ernest. Crisis in the Congo. A U.N. Force in Action. Washington: Brookings, 1965.

_____. Spear & Scepter: Army, Police and Politics in Tropical Africa. Washington: Brookings, 1970.

Lihau, Marcel. "La Nouvelle Constitution de la République Démocratique du Congo," Etudes Congolaises, vol. 9, no. 3 (1968), pp. 28-70.

M'Buze-Nsomi Lobwanabi. Révolution et humanisme: Essais. Kinshasa: Les Presses Africaines, 1974.

McClennan, Barbara N. Comparative Political Systems. North Scituate, MA: Duxbury Press, 1975.

Mobutu, Joseph Desiré. "Fondement constitutionnel des régimes militaires," Courrier d'Afrique, June 11-13, 1966.

_____. De la Légalité à la légimité. Kinshasa: Editions Graphica International, for the Haut Commissariat à l'Information, 1968.

_____. "Les Problèmes de l'A.N.C.," Eurafrica-Tribune du Tiers Monde, vol. 8, nos. 7-8 (1964), pp. 44-47.

Mpinga-Kasenda. L'Administration publique du Zaire; l'impact du milieu socio-politique sur sa structure et son fonctionnement. Paris: Pedons, 1973.

_____, and Gould, D. J. Les Réformes administratives au Zaire, 1972-1973. Kinshasa: Presses Universitaires du Zaire, 1975.

Promontorio, Victor. Les Institutions dans la Constitution congolaise. Léopoldville: Imprimerie Concordia, 1965.

Ruys, Manu. Vijfentwintig jaar Kongo-Zaïre. Brussels: Grammens, 1985.

Tshimanga Mukala Pawuni. Les structures matérielles et humaines du Conseil judiciaire. Boma: Imprimerie CADEMA, 1981.

Vanderlinden, Jacques. La République du Zaïre. Paris: Berger-Levrault, 1975.

Vengroff, Richard. Development Administration at the Local Level: The Case of Zaïre. Syracuse, NY: Maxwell School of Citizenship and Public Affairs, Syracuse University, 1983.

Verhaegen, Benoît. "ANC Troop Strength and Training," U.S. Joint Publications Research Service, no. 43868, Washington: 1968.

Vieux, Serge A. L'Administration zaïroise. Paris: Berger-Levreut, 1974.

_____. Le Statut de la fonction publique: Le Décret-loi du 20 mars 1965 et ses mesures d'exécution. Kinshasa: Office National de la Recherche et du Développement, 1970.

Wallerstein, Immanuel. Africa: The Politics of Unity. New York: Praeger, 1967.

Warren, J. Division Kamanyola. Paris: Afrique Biblio Club, 1978.

Wembi, Antoine. La Sécurité Sociale au Congo. Origines, possibilités et difficultés de gestion. Louvain and Paris: Nauwelaerts, and Léopoldville: IRES, 1966.

_____. "La Tendance à la centralisation des institutions politiques et administratives du Congo-Kinshasa," Etudes Congolaises, vol. 11, no. 5 (1968), pp. 56-63.

Williams, Jean-Claude. Les Provinces du Congo: Structure et fonctionnement. I: Kwilu-Luluabourg-Nord Katanga-Ubangi. II: Sud-Kasai-Uelé-Kongo Central. III: Nord Kivu-Lac Léopold II. IV: Lomami-Kivu Central. V: Moyen Congo-Sankuru. Léopoldville: IRES, 1964-1965.

_____. "La Seconde Guerre du Shaba," in Enquêtes et Documents d'Histoire Africaine, vol. 3, Leuven, Belgium: 1978.

Young, Merwin Crawford. Politics in the Congo: Decolonization and Independence. Princeton, NJ: Princeton University Press, 1965.

_____, and Turner, Thomas. The Rise and Decline of the Zairian State. Madison: University of Wisconsin Press, 1986.

Zaire, République du. Constitution de la République du Zaire: Mise à jour au 1er janvier 1983. Kinshasa: Journal Officiel, 1983.

2. Law

Balleger, Lois. "La Protection légale du mariage monogamique au Congo Belge," CEPSI Bulletin, no. 11 (1950), p. 87.

Banza, D. S. R. "Du Barreau et de la représentation en justice en République Démocratique du Congo," Revue Congolaise d'Administration, no. 3 (July-Aug. 1968).

Baumer, Guy. Les Centres Indigènes Extra-Coutumiers au Congo Belge. Paris: Domat-Monchrestien, 1939.

Biebuyck, Daniel. Right in Land, its Resources among the Nyanga (Republic of the Congo-Leopoldville). Brussels: ARSOM, 1966.

Bolongo, Likulia, (General). Droit pénal militaire zairois. Paris: Librairie Générale de Droit et de Jurisprudence, 1977.

Braudo, Serge. "Les Etablissements pénitentiaires au Congo (Léopoldville)," Penant, vol. 76 (Jan.-March 1966), pp. 55-72.

Congo, Belgian. Code Economique du Congo Belge. Mise à jour début 1954. Brussels: Agence Economique et Financière, 1954.

_____. Code du Travail. 2 vols. Brussels: Editions du Marais, 1953.

_____. Commentaire du Code pénal congolais. By Mineur, G., 2nd ed. Brussels: F. Larcier, 1953.

_____. Rapport de la Commission pour l'Etude du Problème Foncier. 4 vols. Léopoldville: Gouvernement Générale, 1957.

Congo, République Démocratique du. Ministère du Travail. Code du Travail. Kinshasa: Editions CADICEC, 1967.

Crabb, John H. The Legal System of Congo-Kinshasa. Charlottesville, VA: Michie, 1970.

De Quirini, Pierre. Les Lois que tout citoyen doit connaître. Kinshasa-Gombe: CEPAS, 1983.

Durieux, André. Institutions politiques, administratives et judiciaires du Congo Belge et du Ruanda-Urundi. Brussels: Editions Bieleveld, 1957.

_____. Le Pouvoir réglementaire en droit public colonial belge. Brussels: IRCB, 1952.

_____. Le Problème juridique des dettes du Congo Belge et l'Etat du Congo. Brussels: ARSOM, 1961.

_____. Souveraineté et communauté belgo-congolaise. Brussels: ARSC, 1959.

Falmagne, Etienne. Code du Travail du Katanga: Présentation des textes actuellement en vigueur, accompagnée des notices publiées et d'extraits inédits de jurisprudence, et d'un commentaire par articles. Elisabethville: Société d'Etudes Juridiques du Katanga, 1962.

Grévisse, F. Le Centre Extra-Coutumier d'Elisabethville. Brussels: IRCB, 1951.

_____. La Grande pitié des juridictions indigènes. Brussels: IRCB, 1949.

_____. Notes sur le droit coutumier des Balebi. Elisabethville: Editions de la Revue Juridique du Congo Belge, 1934.

Heyse, Théodore. Congo Belge et Ruanda-Urundi: Notes de droit public et commentaires de la Charte Coloniale. Brussels: G. Van Campenhout, 1952-1954.

_____. Grandes lignes du régime des terres du Congo Belge et du Ruanda-Urundi et leurs applications (1940-1946). Brussels: IRCB, 1947.

_____. Problèmes fonciers et régimes des terres (aspects juridiques, économiques et sociaux). Brussels: CEDESA, 1960.

Kalala Ilunga. Commentaire de la loi relative au nom des personnes physiques. Publisher unknown: 1974.

Kalambay Lumpungu, G. Droit civil. Kinshasa: Presses Universitaires du Zaire, 1985.

Kalongo Mbikayi. Responsabilité civile et socialisation des risques en droit zairois: Etude comparative du droit zairois et des systèmes juridiques belge et français. Kinshasa: Presses Universitaires du Zaire, 1974.

Kengo-wa-Dondo. La Confiscation. (Speech opening Supreme Court on Oct. 20, 1973.) Kinshasa: Cour Suprême de Justice de la République du Zaire, 1973.

_____. Considérations sur le project du nouveau Code de la

Famille. (Speech opening Supreme Court on October 4, 1975.) Kinshasa: Cour Suprême de Justice de la République du Zaire, 1976.

_____. Vers une société sans prison. Kinshasa: Cour Suprême de Justice de la République du Zaire, 1975.

Lamy, Emile. Le droit privé zairois. Kinshasa: Presses Universitaires du Zaire, 1975.

Likulia Bolongo. Droit pénal spécial zairois. Paris: Librairie Générale de Droit et de Jurisprudence, 1976.

_____. Méthodes d'approche de la qualification des faits en droit pénal. Kinshasa: Presses Universitaires du Zaire, 1982.

Louwers, Octave. Lois en vigueur dans l'Etat Indépendant du Congo. Brussels: P. Weissenbruch, 1905.

Lukombe Nghenda. Règles relatives aux organes des sociétés commerciales en droit zairois. Kinshasa: Presses Universitaires du Zaire, 1981.

M'pelekwa Yomputy Yeyele. Index alphabétique du Code pénal et de divers textes de loi: à l'usage des juges de police et des officiers de police judiciaire. Mbanza-Ngungu, Zaire: Parquet de la Sous-Région des Cataractes, 1976.

Mukusa, Jean C. "Le Problème de l'unification et de l'intégration du droit congolais," Problèmes Sociaux Congolais, nos. 75-76 (1966-1967), pp. 55-61.

Nkulu Butombe, J. I. La Question du Zaire et ses répercussions sur les juridictions ecclésiastiques, 1865-1888. Kinshasa: Faculté de Théologie Catholique, 1982.

Paulus, Jean-Pierre. Droit publique du Congo Belge. Brussels: Institut de Sociologie Solvay, Université Libre de Belgique, 1959.

Pauwels, Johan M. La Législation zairoise relative au nom: droit et authenticité africaine. Brussels: ARSOM, 1983.

_____. Répertoire de droit coutumier congolais; jurisprudence et doctrine, 1954-1967. Kinshasa: Office National de la Recherche et du Développement, 1970.

Piron, P.; De Vos, J.; et al. Codes et Lois du Congo Belge. 3 vols. Brussels: Larcier, 1959-1960.

Rubbens, Antoine. Dettes de Guerre. Elisabethville: Editions "L'Essor du Congo," 1945.

_____. Le Droit judiciaire congolais. 3 vols. Kinshasa: Université Lovanium, 1965-68.

_____. L'Indépendance des magistrats dans la République Démocratique du Congo. Brussels: ARSOM, 1966.

_____. L'Instruction criminelle et la procédure pénale. Brussels: Larcier, and Léopoldville: Lovanium, 1965.

Sohier, A. Traité elémentaire de droit coutumier du Congo Belge. 2nd ed. Brussels: Maison Ferdinand Larcier, 1954.

Touchard, G. and Louwers, O. Jurisprudence de l'Etat Indépendant du Congo. Brussels: Weissenbruch, 1905-10.

Verstraete, M. La Nationalité congolaise. Brussels: ARSC, 1959.

Wekerle, Anton. Guide to the Text of the Criminal Law and Criminal Procedure Codes of Burundi, Rwanda, and Zaire. Washington: Library of Congress, Law Library, 1975.

Zaire, République du. Code des contributions de la République du Zaire. Kinshasa: Chambre de Commerce de Kinshasa, 1972.

_____. Le Régime général des biens au Zaire: Loi no. 021 du 20 juillet 1973. Kinshasa: Agence Zaire Presse, 1974.

_____. Statut du personnel de carrière des services publics de l'Etat: Loi no. 81-003 du 17 juillet 1981. Kinshasa: Agence Zaire Presse, 1981.

_____. Département de la Justice. Le Code pénal zairois: Dispositions législatives et réglementaires mises à jour au 31 mai 1982. Kinshasa: 1983.

_____. Tribunal de Centre, Ilebo. Receuil de jurisprudence du Centre d'Ilebo. Kinshasa: Office National de la Recherche et du Développement, 1973.

3. Politics and Political Parties

Artigue, Pierre. Qui Sont les leaders congolais? Brussels: Editions Europe-Afrique, 1960.

Biebuyck, Daniel and Douglas, Mary. Congo Tribes and Parties. London: Royal Anthropological Institute, 1961.

Bossassi-Epole Bolya Kodya. Réflexions critiques pour une authenticité progressiste: l'Expérience zairoise et les macro-contradictions. Brussels: R. Venderlinden, 1976.

Buana Kabue. Citoyen Président: Lettre ouverte au Président Mobutu Sese Seko ... et aux autres. Paris: Editions L'Harmattan, 1978.

Centre de Recherche et d'Information Socio-Politiques. Les Partis politiques congolais. Brussels: CRISP, 1964.

Ceulemans, Jacques. Antoine Gizenga: Hier, aujourd'hui, demain. Brussels: Editions Remarques Congolaises, 1964.

Colvin, Ian. The Rise and Fall of Moise Tshombe. London: Leslie Frewin, 1968.

De Backer, M. C. C. Notes pour servir à l'étude des "groupements politiques" à Léopoldville. Brussels: INFORCONGO, 1959.

De Monstelle, Arnaud. Le Débacle du Congo Belge. Brussels: Leclerc, 1965.

Delière, Line. Katanga rouge. Brussels: Privately published, 1973.

Demunter, Paul. Analyse de la contestation estudiantine au Congo-Kinshasa (juin 1969) et de ses séquelles. Brussels: CRISP, 1971.

_____. Luttes politiques au Zaire: Le Processus de politisation des masses rurales du Bas-Zaire. Paris: Editions Anthropos, 1975.

"M. Gizenga et la fondation du PALU (Parti Lumumbiste Unifié)," Courrier Africain du CRISP, no. 37 (Nov. 19, 1964), p. 22.

Houart, Pierre. Les Evénements du Congo. Brussels: Centre de Documentation Internationale, 1961.

_____. La Pénétration communiste au Congo. Brussels: Centre de Documentation Internationale, 1960.

Kalanda, Auguste, "A Propos du régime communal au Congo: La Consultation de Luluabourg," Mouvement Communal, no. 332 (Sept. 1959), pp. 418-427.

Kamitatu-Massamba, Cléophas. La Grande mystification du Congo-Kinshasa; les crimes de Mobutu. Paris: Maspero, 1971.

_____. Le Pouvoir à la portée du peuple. Paris: L'Harmattan, 1977.

Kanza, Thomas. Congo 196..? Brussels: Editions Remarques Congolaises, 1962.

_____. Le Congo à la veille de son indépendance, ou: Propos d'un Congolais désillusioné. Brussels and Léopoldville: private publisher, 1959.

_____. Eloge de la révolution. Brussels: Editions Remarques Congolaises, 1968.

_____. Propos d'un Congolais naïf. Discours sur la vocation coloniale dans l'Afrique de demain. Paris: Présence Africaine, 1959.

_____. Tôt ou tard...Ata ndele. Brussels: Le Livre Africain, 1959.

Kashamura, Anicet. Culture et aliénation en Afrique. Paris: Edition du Cercle, 1971.

_____. De Lumumba aux Colonels. Paris: Buchet-Chastel, 1966.

Le Katanga devra-t-il prendre sa propre indépendance? Elisabeth-ville: Imprimerie A. Decoster, 1959.

Labrique, Jean. Congo politique. Léopoldville: Editions de l'Avenir, 1957.

Larock, Victor, ed. Le P.S.B. avait raison. Positions socialistes au sujet du Congo, 1959–1960. Brussels: Institut Emile Vander-velde, 1960.

Legum, Colin, ed. Africa Contemporary Record: Annual Survey and Documents. New York: Africana, 1973.

_____. Congo Disaster. Baltimore: Penguin, 1961.

Lemarchand, René. American Policy in Southern Africa: The Stakes and the Stance. Washington: University Press of America, 1978.

_____. "Patrice Lumumba," in African Political Thought: Lumum-ba, Nkrumah and Touré, Skurnik, W. A. E., ed., pp. 13–64. Denver: Social Science Foundation and Graduate School of Inter-national Studies, 1967-68.

_____. Political Awakening in the Belgian Congo. (Originally published by University of California Press, Berkeley, 1964.) Westport, CT: Greenwood Press, 1982.

Lopez-Alvarez, Luis. Lumumba ou l'Afrique frustrée. Paris: Cujas, 1964.

Lumumba, Patrice. Congo, My Country. New York: Praeger, 1962.

_____ . Le Congo, Terre d'Avenir. Est-il menacé? Brussels: Editions de l'Office de Publicité, 1961.

_____ . Lumumba Speaks: The Speeches and Writings of Patrice Lumumba, 1958-1961. (Translated from French by Lane, Helen R.) New York: Boston, Little, Brown, 1972.

Mabaya Ma Mbongo. Le Fascisme au Zaïre. Sartrouville, France: Editions Kolwezi, 1984.

Marrés, Jacques. Le Congo assassiné. Brussels: M. Arnold, 1974.

_____ , with De Vos, Pierre. L'Equinoxe de janvier. Brussels: Editions Eurafrorient, 1959.

M'Buze-Nsomi Lobwanabi. Aux Sources d'une révolution. Kinshasa: Presses Africaines, 1977.

Michel, Serge. Uhuru Lumumba. Paris: Juilliard, 1962.

Monnier, Laurent. "Notes sur l'ABAKO et le nationalisme Kongo," Geneva-Africa, vol. 5, no. 2 (1966), pp. 51-61.

Mouvement Populaire de la Révolution. MPR, 1967-1982: 15 ans au service de la dignité humaine. Kinshasa: Agence Zaire Presse, 1982.

_____ . Rapport d'activité 1967-1972. Kinshasa: n.d.

_____ . Statut du M.P.R. Kinshasa: n.d.

Nkrumah, Kwame. Challenge of the Congo. New York: International Publishers, 1967.

Nzongola-Ntalaja (Georges). "The Bourgeoisie and Revolution in the Congo," Journal of Modern African Studies, vol. 8, no. 4 (1970), pp. 511-530.

_____ . "Urban Administration in Zaire: A Study of Kananga, 1971-1973." Unpublished Ph.D. thesis. Madison: University of Wisconsin, 1975.

Okumu, Washington. Lumumba's Congo: Roots of Conflict. New York: Ivan Obolensky, 1963.

Olsen, Hal C. African Heroes of the Congo Rebellion. Kijabe, Kenya: Africa Inland Mission, 1969.

Le Pari Congolais. Brussels: Dessart, 1960.

Parti Communiste de Belgique. La Lutte pour l'indépendance du Congo: Rapport d'activité du Comité Central du P.C. de Belgique au XIVème Congrés. Brussels: 1963.

Patrice Lumumba, Fighter for Africa's Freedom. Moscow: Progress Publishers, 1966.

Patrice Lumumba: The Truth about a Monstrous Crime of the Co-lonialists. Moscow: Foreign Languages Publishing House, 1961.

Patrice Lumumba. London: Panaf Books, 1973.

Perin, François. Les Institutions politiques du Congo indépendant au 30 juin 1960. Léopoldville: Institut Politique Congolais, 1960.

Reid, Alexander James. The Roots of Lumumba: Mongo Land. Hicksville, NY: Exposition Press, 1979.

Ryckbost, J. Essai sur les origines et le développement des premières associations professionnelles au Congo (1940-1944). Léopoldville: IRES, 1962.

Schatzberg, Michael G. "Fidelité au guide: The J.M.P.R. in Zairian Schools," Journal of Modern African Studies, vol. 16, no. 3 (1978), pp. 417-431.

Schuyler, Philippa Duke. Who Killed the Congo? New York: Devin-Adair, 1962.

Tcha-Malenge, Kibwe. Who Will Win in Congo-Kinshasa? Toronto: Norman Bethune Institute, 1976.

Tribunal Permanent des Peuples. Session sur le Zaire: Rotterdam, 18, 19 et 20 septembre 1982: Sentence. Rotterdam: 1982.

Turner, Thomas. La Politique indigène du Congo Belge. Le Cas du Sankuru. Brussels: CEDAF, 1973.

_____. Le Vandisme (Sankuru-Zaire) et sa signification politique. Brussels: CEDAF, 1974.

Van der Steep, Daniel. Elections et Réformes de la composition des organes politiques. Brussels: CEDAF, 1978.

Van Lierde, Jean. La Pensée politique de Patrice Lumumba. Paris: Editions Présence Africaine, 1963.

Van Reyn, Paul. Le Congo Politique. Brussels: Editions Europe-Afrique, 1960.

Verbeek, Roger. Le Congo en question. Paris: Présence Africaine, 1965.

Verhaegen, Benoît, ed. ABAKO 1950-1960. CRISP, 1963.

Weiss, Herbert and Verhaegen, Benoît, eds. P.S.A.--Parti Solidaire Africaine. Brussels: CRISP, 1963.

Welch, Claude E. Soldier and State in Africa. Evanston, IL: Northwestern University Press, 1970.

Williame, Jean Claude. Patrimonialism and Political Change in the Congo. Stanford: Stanford University Press, 1972.

Young, Crawford. Politics of Cultural Pluralism. Madison: University of Wisconsin Press, 1976.

_____. "Zaire: The Unending Crisis," Foreign Affairs, vol. 57, no. 1 (1978), pp. 169-185.

4. Foreign Affairs and Foreign Assistance

American Council of Voluntary Agencies for Foreign Service. Technical Assistance Information Clearing House. Development Assistance Programs of U.S. Non-Profit Organizations in Zaire. New York: 1974.

Ball, George. The Elements in our Congo Policy. (Based on an address before Town Hall in Los Angeles, CA on Dec. 19, 1961.) Washington: U.S. Department of State, no. 7826, African Series, 25 (1961).

British National Export Council. Africa Committee. Trade Mission to the Democratic Republic of the Congo. London: 1970.

Clos, Max. "The Chinese Role in the Congo: Fact or Fiction?" Africa Report, vol. 19, no. 1 (1965), pp. 18-19.

Gappert, Gary, and Thomas, Garry, eds. The Congo, Africa, and America. Syracuse, NY: Maxwell Graduate School of Citizenship and Public Affairs, Syracuse University, 1965.

Kalb, Madeleine G. The Congo Cables. New York: Macmillan, 1982.

Moshje, Luc. La Pénétration américaine au Congo. Brussels: Editions Remarques Congolaises, 1963.

Rodrigues, J. H. Brazil and Africa. Berkeley: University of California Press, 1965.

Rusk, Dean. "U.S. Policy in the Congo," in The Department of State Bulletin, vol. 46:1180 (Feb. 5, 1962), pp. 216-218. (Text of statement before the Africa Subcommittee, Committee on Foreign Relations, U.S. Senate on January 18, 1962.)

United Nations. Development Programme. Office of the Resident Representative (Democratic Republic of the Congo). Technical Co-operation Programmes of the United Nations and its Specialized Agencies in the Democratic Republic of the Congo During 1966. Kinshasa: 1967.

United States Agency for International Development. Field Budget Submission for Zaire. Washington: annual.

_____. U.S. Overseas Loans and Grants and Assistance from International Organizations. Washington: annual.

United States Congress. House of Representatives. Committee on International Relations. Subcommittee on International Security and Scientific Affairs. Congressional Oversight of War Powers Compliance: Zaire Airlift. (Hearing of August 10, 1978 on Shaba airlift.) Washington: 1978.

_____. Senate. Committee on Foreign Relations. Subcommittee on African Affairs. Security Supporting Assistance for Zaire. Washington: 1975.

_____. Senate. Committee on Housing, and Urban Affairs. Subcommittee on International Finance. U.S. Loans to Zaire. (Hearing on request for guarantees by U.S. Export-Import Bank for additional funds for the Inga-Shaba power transmission line.) Washington: 1979.

_____. Senate. Committee on Foreign Relations. The Political and Economic crisis in Southern Africa. (Staff Report.) Washington: 1976.

United States Library of Congress. (Bibliography of official U.S. publications compiled by Witherell, Julian W.) The United States and Africa. Washington: 1978.

Weissman, Stephen R. American Foreign Policy in the Congo. Ithaca, NY: Cornell University Press, 1974.

Williams, Mennan (Soapy). "The Urgent Need for Congo Reconciliation," in Department of State Bulletin, vol. 47:1222 (Nov. 26, 1962), pp. 803-805. (Text of address before Jefferson Society of the University of Virginia, Charlottesville, VA, Nov. 1962.)

Zaire, 1885-1985: Cent ans de regards belges. (Documents of an exhibition from May 9 to June 30, 1985.) Brussels: European Economic Community Cultural Center, 1985.

Zaire, République du. Report of the Seminar on the Problems of Refugees in Zaire. (Seminar sponsored jointly with the Office of the U.N. High Commissioner for Refugees, held in Kinshasa April 19-25, 1982.) Geneva: UNHCR, 1982.

316 / The Bibliography

VI.   SCIENCE

1. Archeology

Brabant, H. Excavations à Sanga (Contribution odontologique à
l'étude des ossements trouvés dans la nécropole protohistorique
de Sanga). Tervuren: MRAC, 1965.

Cahen, Daniel. La Site archéologique de la Kamoa (Région du Shaba,
République du Zaire) de l'âge du fer. Tervuren: MRAC, 1975.

_____, and Martin, Philippe. Classification formelle automatique
et industries lithiques. Interprétation des hachereaux de la
Kamoa. Tervuren: MRAC, 1972.

_____, and Mortelmans, G. Un Site tshitolien sur le plateau des
Bateke, République du Zaire. Tervuren: 1973.

Inventaria Archaeologica Africana. Nenquin, Jacques, general ed.
Tervuren: MRAC, 1964- (continuing).

Leroy, Pierre. Matériaux pour servir à la préhistoire de l'Uelé: Le
dallage d'Afrique Mégalithe d'Obeledi. Brussels: ARSOM, 1961.

Nenquin, Jacques. "Dimple-based pots from Kasai, Belgian Congo,"
Man, vol. 59, no. 242 (1959), pp. 153-155.

_____. Excavations at Sanga, 1957; the Protohistoric Necropolis.
Tervuren: 1963.

_____. "Notes on Some Early Pottery Cultures in Northern Ka-
tanga," Journal of African History, vol. 4, no. 1 (1963), pp. 19-
32.

2. Geology

Cahen, L. Géologie du Congo Belge. Liège: Vaillant-Carmann,
1954.

_____, and Snelling, N. J. The Geochronology of Equatorial
Africa. Amsterdam: North Holland Publishing, 1966.

Carroll, Paul. Congo: Etudes sols pour la plaine de Kinshasa.
Washington: U.S. Department of Agriculture, 1969.

Congo, République Démocratique du. Service Geologique. Bulletin.
(Replaced the Service Géologique du Congo Belge in 1960.) Léopoldville: 1945-1970.

Danse, A. "Genèse organo-chimique de la latération et de l'argilisation dans les paysages latéritiques," in Bulletin de Service Géologique du Congo Belge, vol. 9, no. 1 (Mar. 1959), pp. 1-8.

Davreux, L. "Quelques considérations sur le bassin hydrographique du Congo," Bulletin du Société Royale Belge de Géographie, vol. 81, no. 1-2 (1957), pp. 67-79.

De Heinzelin de Braucort, J. Le Paléolithique aux abords d'Ishango. Brussels: Institut des Parcs Nationaux, 1961.

Denaeyer, Marcel E. Le Glacis des volcans actifs au nord du Lac Kivu, République du Zaire. Paris: Editions du Muséum, 1975.

Devroey, E. J. Annuaire Hydrologique du Congo Belge et du Ruanda-Urundi (1951-1959). 9 vols. Brussels: ARSOM, 1952-1960.

Egoroff, Boris. L'Eruption du volcan Mihaga en 1954. Brussels: Institut des Parcs Nationaux du Congo, 1965.

Evrard, Carlo. Le Prix de revient des cartes des sols et de la végétation au Congo. Léopoldville, 1961.

_____. Les Recherches géophysiques et géologiques et les travaux de sondage dans la cuvete congolaise. Brussels: ARSC, 1957.

François, Armand. La Couverture katangienne: Entre les socles de Zilo et de La Kabompo, République du Zaire, région de Kolwezi. Tervuren: MRAC, 1981.

Gautier, A. Fossil Fresh Water Mollusca of the Lake Albert-Lake Edward Rift, Uganda. Tervuren: MRAC, 1970.

_____. Geological Investigation in the Sinda-Mohari (Ituri, Ne-Congo); a Monograph on the Geological History of a Region in the Lake Albert Rift. Gent: 1965.

Greenwood, Peter Humphry. Neogene Fossil Fishes from the Lake Albert-Lake Edward Rift (Zaire). London: British Museum (Natural History), 1975.

Herrinck, P. Seismicité du Congo Belge. Compilation des séismes observés aux stations climatologiques entre 1909 et 1954. Brussels: ARSC, 1959.

Lavreau, J. Etude géologique du Haut-Zaire: Genèse et évolution d'un segment lithosphérique archéen. Tervuren: MRAC, 1982.

Lepersonne, Jacques. Structure géologique du bassin intérieur du Zaire. Brussels: ARSOM, 1978.

318 / The Bibliography

Palaeozoic Sporae Dispersae from Congo. 5 vols. Tervuren: MRAC, 1966.

Pecrot, A.; Gastuche, M. C.; Deluigne, J.; and Frippiat, J. J. L'Altération des sols au Kivu. Brussels: INEAC, 1962.

Pire, J.; Berreux, M.; and Quiodbach, J. L'Intensité des pluies au Congo Belge et au Ruanda-Urundi. Brussels: ARSOM, 1960.

Sahama, Thure Georg. The Nyiragongo Main Cone. Tervuren: MRAC, 1978.

Sys, C., et al. La Cartographie des sols au Congo: Ses Principes et ses méthodes. Brussels: INEAC, 1961.

Taverne, Louis. Les Téléostéens fossiles du crétacé moyen de Kipala (Kwango, Zaire). Tervuren: MRAC, 1976.

Tazieff, Haroun. Nyiragongo, The Forbidden Volcano. (Translated from French by Bernard, J. F.) New York: Barron's/Woodbury, 1979.

Tibbitts, G. Chase. Ground-water Resources Investigation Program for the Kinshasa area, Democratic Republic of the Congo. (Prepared by the U.S. Geological Survey in cooperation with Democratic Republic of the Congo under the auspices of USAID.) Kinshasa: 1968.

U.S. Agency for International Development. Bureau for Technical Assistance. Developing Country Coverage of Earth Resource Technology Satellite ERTS-1: July 1972 - June 1973. Zaire. Washington: 1973.

Van Oosterwyck-Gastuche, M. C. Etude des silicates de cuivre du Katanga. Tervuren: MRAC, 1967.

Varlamoff, N. Les Gisements de tungstène au Congo Belge et au Ruanda-Urundi. Brussels: ARSC, 1958.

Wood, Roger Conant. Fossile Marine Turtle Remains from the Paleocene of the Congo, and Gautier, Achilles and Van Damme, Dirk. A Revision of the Miocene Freshwater Molluscs of the Mohari Formation. Sinda Mohari, Ituri, N.E. Zaire. (Published together.) Tervuren: MRAC, 1973.

3. Geography

Annaert, J. Contribution à l'étude géographique de l'habitat et de l'habitation indigènes en milieu rural dans les Provinces Orientale et du Kivu. ARSOM, 1960.

Béguin, H. La Mise en valeur du sud-est du Kasai: Essai de géographie agricole et de géographie agraire et ses possibilités d'application pratique. Brussels: INEAC, 1960.

Choprix, Guy. La Naissance d'une ville: Etude géographique de Paulis (1934-1957). Brussels: CEMUBAC, 1961.

De Blij, Harm J. A Geography of Sub-Saharan Africa. Chicago: Rand McNally, 1964.

Hance, William A. The Geography of Modern Africa. New York: Columbia University Press, 1964.

Kama Funzi Mudindambi. La République du Zaire: Géographie, 3e secondare, programme officiel. Paris: Hatier, 1973.

Mountjoy, A. B. and Embleton, C. Africa: A New Geographical Survey. New York: Praeger, 1967.

Nicolai, Henri. Le Kwilu. Brussels: CEMUBAC, 1963.

_____. Luozi: Géographie régionale d'un pays du Bas-Congo. Brussels: ARSOM. 1961.

_____. Progrés de la connaissance géographique au Congo, au Ruanda et au Burundi en 1964, 1965 et 1966. Brussels: CEMUBAC, 1967.

_____, and Jacques, J. La Transformation des paysages congolais par le chemin de fer: l'Example du B.C.K. Brussels: IRCB, 1954.

Peeters, Leo. La Géographie du pays Logo au sud d'Aba. Brussels: CEMUBAC, 1963.

_____. "Les Limites forêt-savane dans le nord du Congo en relation avec le milieu géographique," Revue Belge de Géographie, vol. 88, no. 3 (April 1965), pp. 239-282.

Raucq, P. Notes de Géographie sur le Maniema. Brussels: IRCB, 1952.

Robert, M. Contribution à la géographie du Katanga. Brussels: IRCB, 1954.

_____. Géologie et géographie du Katanga, y compris l'étude des ressources et de la mise en valeur. Brussels: publisher unknown, 1956.

Robyns, W. "Carte des territoires phytogéographiques," Atlas Général du Congo. Brussels: IRCB, 1948.

Thompson, B. W. The Climate of Africa. Nairobi: Oxford University Press, 1965.

United States. Office of Geography. Belgian Congo: Official Standard Names Approved by the United States Board on Geographic Names. Washington: 1953.

Verbeken, Auguste. Contribution à la géographie historique du Katanga et des régions voisines. Brussels: ARSC, 1954.

Wiese, Bernd. Die Blauen Berge (Mts. Bleus, Zaire): Bevölkerung u. Wirtschaft e. äquatorialafrikan. Berglandes. Wiesbaden: Steiner, 1979.

_____. Zaire: Landesnatur, Bevölkerung, Wirtschaft. Darmstadt: Wissenschaftliche Buchgesellschaft, 1980.

4. Medicine, Health, and Diet

American Public Health Association. Maternal and Child Health Care Service in the Kinshasa Area. (By Mayhen Derryberry et al. for USAID.) Washington: 1971.

Anderson, Barbara, and McCabe, James. "Nutrition and the Fertility of Younger Women in Kinshasa," Journal of Development Economics, vol. 4 (1977), pp. 343-363.

Bakutuvwidi Makani. Planification familiale, fécondité et santé familiale au Zaire, 1982-1984: Rapport sur les résultats d'une enquête régionale sur la prévalence contraceptive. Kinshasa-Gombe: Institut National de la Statistique; Columbia, MD: Westinghouse Public Applied Systems, 1985.

Batangu Mpesa. APHARZA, Association des pharmaciens zairois: 5 ans après. Kinshasa: APHARZA, 1976.

Bervoets, W., and Lassance, M. Modes et coutumes alimentaires des congolais en milieu rural. Brussels: ARSC, 1959.

Centre de Recherches Industrielles en Afrique Centrale. Enquête alimentaire au Shaba: Contribution du CRIAC. Lubumbashi: 1977.

Colbourne, Michael. Malaria in Africa. London: Oxford University Press, 1966.

Cornet, René Jules. Bwana muganga (hommes en blanc en Afrique noire). Brussels: ARSOM, 1971.

De Craemer, Willy, and Fox, Renée C. The Emerging Physician: A

Sociological Approach to the Development of the Congolese Medical Profession. Stanford: Hoover Institution, 1968.

Devisch, Renaat. Se recréer femme: Manipulation sémantique d'une situation d'infécondité chez les Yaka du Zaire. Berlin: D. Reimer, 1984.

D'Heer, A. Une Nourriture saine. Kananga, Zaire: Projet-Soya, 1976(?).

Diocés d'Idiofa. Comment le clan se nourrit, ou, bien manger, est-ce possible?: de la vie ancestrale à une vie nouvelle assumée. Idiofa, Zaire: 1982.

Duren, A. L'Organisation médicale Belge en Afrique. Brussels: ARSC, 1955.

Ermans, A. M., et al. Role of Cassava in the Etiology of Endemic Goitre and Cretinism. Ottawa: International Development Research Centre, 1980.

Fountain, Daniel E. Infirmier, comment bâtir la santé: Manuel de santé communautaire. Kangu-Mayumbe, Zaire: République du Zaire, Bureau d'Etudes et de Recherches pour la Promotion de la Santé, and Kinshasa: Centre Médical de Vange-Bandundu, 1982.

Gelfand, Michael. A Clinical Study of Intestinal Bilharziosis (Schistosoma Mansomi) in Africa. London: Arnold, 1967.

International Colloquium on Ebola Virus Infection and other Haemorrhagic Fevers, Antwerp, 1977. Ebola Virus Haemorrhagic Fever. (Proceedings of colloquium, held in Antwerp, Belgium, Dec. 6-8, 1977.) Amsterdam and New York: Elsevier/North-Holland Biomedical Press, 1978.

Iteke, E. B., and Ermans, A. M., eds. Nutritional Factors Involved in the Goitrogenic Action of Cassava. Ottawa: International Development Research Centre, 1982.

Janzen, John M. The Quest for Therapy in Lower Zaire. Berkeley: University of California Press, 1978.

Jardin, Claude. List of Foods Used in Africa. Rome: Food and Agriculture Organization, and Bethesda, MD: National Institute of Health, 1967.

Jelliffe, D. B. Child Health in the Tropics: A Practical Handbook for Medical and Paramedical Personnel. London: Arnold, 1968.

Lambrechts, A.; Bernier, G.; and Falyse, J.; et al. "Enquête alimentaire parmi les populations rurales du Haut-Katanga," Problèmes Sociaux Congolais, no. 51 (1960), pp. 7-25.

Malanda Dem. Le Développement mental des enfants sourds-muët à Bandundu, Zaire. Kinshasa: Presses Universitaires du Zaire, 1974.

Parent, J. "Le Nourrisson au Katanga," Problèmes Sociaux Congolais, no. 50 (1960), pp. 5-25.

_____. "Le Nouveau-né au Katanga," Problèmes Sociaux Congolais, no. 48 (1960), pp. 45-48.

Rotsart de Hertaing, I. Nutrition: L'Education nutritionnelle dans la pratique journalière. Kangu-Mayombe, Zaire: Bureau d'Etudes et de Recherches pour la Promotion de la Santé, 1975.

Sala-Kiakanda, Mpembele. Social Science Research for Population Policy Design: Case Study of Zaire. Liège: IUSSP, 1982.

Schwetz, Jacques. L'Evolution de la médecine au Congo Belge. Brussels: Office de Publicité, 1946.

United States. Department of Health, Education and Welfare. Division of International Health. Republic of the Congo: A Study of Health Problems and Resources. Washington: 1960.

_____. Syncrisis: The Dynamics of Health - XIV Zaire. Washington: 1975.

_____. Public Health Service. Division of International Health. Republic of the Congo. Washington: 1960.

_____. Walter Reed Army Institute of Research. Republic of the Congo. Washington: 1965.

Van Dooren, F., and Rogowsky, M. Etude cardio-circulatoire de l'indigène du Congo Belge et du Ruanda-Urundi. Brussels: ARSC, 1959.

Vincent, Marc. Les Problèmes de protection maternelle et infantile au Congo Belge et au Ruanda-Urundi. 2 vols. Brussels: FOREAMI, 1959.

Zaire River Expedition, 1974-75. Medical Research Team. Onchocerciasis in Zaire: A New Approach to the Problem of River Blindness. (Rodger, F. C., ed.) Oxford and New York: Pergamon Press, 1977.

5. Natural Science and Zoology

Belgium. Comité Executif de la Flore du Congo Belge et Jardin Botanique de l'Etat. Flore du Congo Belge et du Ruanda Urundi: Spermatophytes. Brussels, 1958.

_____. Division de Phytopathologie et d'Entomologie Agricole. Précis des maladies et des insectes nuisibles rencontrés sur les plantes cultivées au Congo, au Rwanda et au Burundi. Brussels: INEAC, 1962.

_____. Institut National pour l'Etude Agronomique du Congo (Belge). Carte des sols et de la végétation du Congo et du Ruanda-Urundi. Brussels: INEAC, 1955-1958.

_____. Office de l'Information et des Relations Publiques du Congo Belge et du Ruanda-Urundi (INFORCONGO). Monographie des principales essences forestières exploitées au Congo Belge. Brussels: 1958.

Berg, A. Role Ecologique des eaux de la Cuvette congolaise sur la croissance de la jacinthe d'eau. Brussels: ARSOM, 1961.

Bose, M. N. Mesozoic Sporae Dispersae from Zaire. Tervuren: MRAC, 1976.

_____. Some Mesozoic Plants from Western Congo. And Lakhanpal, R. N. Some Middle Tertiary Plant Remains from South Kivu, Congo. (Published together.) Tervuren: MRAC, 1966.

Bultot, F. Estimations...des moyennes vraies journalières, diurnes et nocturnes de la température et de l'humidité de l'air du Congo, au Rwanda et au Burundi. Brussels: INEAC, 1961.

Curry-Lindahl, Kai. Contribution à l'étude des vertébrés terrestres en Afrique tropicale. Brussels: IPN, 1961.

_____. Ecological Studies of Mammals, Birds, Reptiles and Amphibians in the Eastern Belgian Congo. Tervuren: MRAC, 1960.

De Witte, Gaston F. Genera des serpents du Congo et du Ruanda-Urundi. Tervuren: MRAC, 1962.

Dirsh, V. M. Acridoidea of the Congo (Orthoptera). Tervuren: MRAC, 1970.

Dowsett, Robert J., and Prigogine, Alexandre. L'Avifaune des Monts Marungu - The Avifauna of the Marungu Highlands. Brussels: Cercle Hydrobiologique de Bruxelles, 1974.

Du Soleil, G., and Vanderlest, N. Annuaire météorologique du Congo Belge et du Ruanda-Urundi 1957-1961. 5 vols. Brussels: ARSOM, 1957-1960.

Fouarge, Joseph. Essais physiques, mécaniques et de durabilité de bois de la République Démocratique du Congo. Brussels: Institut National pour l'Etude Agronomique du Congo, 1970.

324 / The Bibliography

Germain, R. Les Biotopes alluvionaires herbeux et les savanes in-
tercalaires du Congo equatorial. Brussels: ARSOM, 1965.

Gillardin, J. Les Essences forestières du Congo Belge et du Ruanda-
Urundi: Leurs dénominations indigènes, leur distribution et leur
habitat. Brussels: Ministère du Congo Belge et du Ruanda-
Urundi, Division de l'Agriculture, des Forêts et de l'Elevage, 1959.

Harris, W. Victor. Termites: Their Recognition and Control. London: Longmans, 1961.

Hayman, R. W. The Bats of the Congo and of Rwanda and Burundi.
Tervuren: MRAC, 1966.

Henry, J. M. Analyse d'acclimatation de végétaux en zone équatoriale
zairoise de basse altitude. Brussels: Centre d'Informatique Appliquée au Développement et à l'Agriculture Tropical, 1976.

Inger, Robert, and Marx, Hyman. The Food of Amphibians. Brussels: IPN, 1961.

Institut National pour l'Etude Agronomique du Congo. Carte des
sols et de la végétation du Congo Belge et du Ruanda-Urundi.
Brussels: 1954.

Institut National de Recherche et d'Action Pédagogiques (Congo).
Département de l'Enseignement Secondaire. Section Sciences
Naturelles. Ecologie: Etude de milieux naturels du Congo.
Brazzaville: 1975-1978.

Kabala Matuka. Aspects de la conservation de la nature au Zaire.
Kinshasa: Editions Lokole, 1976.

Lakhanpal, Rajendra Nath. Cenozoic Plants from Congo. Tervuren:
MRAC, 1970.

Lambert, J. Contribution à l'étude des poissons de la forêt de la
Cuvette congolaise. Tervuren: MRAC, 1961.

Laurent, Raymond F. Contribution à l'histoire de l'herpétologie
congolaise et bibliographie générale. Brussels: ARSOM, 1965.

_____. Le Genre Leptopelis Günther (Salientia) au Zaire. Ter-
vuren: MRAC, 1973.

Léonard, A. Les Savannes herbeuses du Kivu. Brussels: INEAC,
1962.

Magis, Noël. Nouvelle contribution à l'étude hydrobiologique des
lacs de Mwadingusha, Koni et N'Zilo. Liège: Editions
P.U.L.R.E.A.C., Université de Liège, 1961.

Malaisse, Françoise. Carte de la végétation du bassin de la Luanza –
Vegetation map of the Luanza drainage area. Brussels: Cercle
Hydrobiologique de Bruxelles, 1975.

_____. Ecologie de la Rivière Luanza – Ecology of the Luanza
River. Brussels: Cercle Hydrobiologique de Bruxelles, 1976.

Maldague, M. E. Relations entre le couvert végétal et la microfaune:
Leur importance dans la conservation biologique des sols tropicaux.
Brussels: INEAC, 1961.

Pierlot, Roger. Structure et composition des forêts denses d'Afrique
equatoriale, specialement celles du Kivu. Brussels: ARSOM,
1966.

Poll, Max. Les Poissons du Stanley-Pool. Tervuren: Musée du
Congo Belge, 1938.

Robyns, Walter, ed. Flore iconographique des champignons du
Congo. Brussels: Ministère de L'Agriculture, Jardin Botanique
de l'Etat, n.d.

Schelpe, E.A.C.L.E. Ptéridophytes – Pteridophyta. Brussels:
Cercle Hydrobiologique de Bruxelles, 1973.

Schmitz, A. La Végétation de la plaine de Lubumbashi (Haut Katanga). Brussels: Institut National pour l'Etude Agronomique
du Congo, 1971.

Schoutheden, H. Contribution à l'ornithologie de la République du
Congo. 8 vols. Tervuren: MRAC, 1961-65.

Shadab, Mohammad Umar. A New Genus of Pseudophloeine Bugs
from the Democratic Republic of the Congo (Heteroptera, Coreo-
idea). New York: American Museum of Natural History, 1972.

Staner, Pierre. Les Eriosema de la flore congolaise. Tervuren:
Musée du Congo Belge, 1934.

Zaire, République du. Reconnaissance des ressources hydro-
électriques dans le Nord-Est. Kinshasa, 1972.

VII. SOCIETY

1. Anthropology, Ethnology, and
Traditional Societies

Actualité et inactualité des "Etudes Bakongo" du P. Van Wing: Actes du colloque de Mayidi du 10 au 12 avril, 1980. Inkisi, Zaire: République du Zaire, Grand Séminaire Mayidi, 1983.

Baxter, P. T. W., and Butt, A. The Azande and Related Peoples of the Anglo-Egyptian Sudan and Belgian Congo. (Ethnographic Survey of Africa, East Central Africa, Part IX.) London: International African Institute, 1953.

Bergmans, Lieven. Les Wanande. Butembo, Zaire: Editions A.B.B., n.d.

Biebuyck, Daniel P. "Fondements de l'organisation politique des Lunda du Mwaan tayaav," Zaire, no. 11 (Oct. 1957), pp. 787-817.

_____. Lega Culture; Art, Initiation, and Moral Philosophy among a Central African People. Berkeley: University of California Press, 1973.

_____. Mitambas: A System of Connected Marriages among the Babembe of Fizi Territory, Kivu Province, Congo Republic. Brussels: ARSOM, 1962.

_____. "On the Concept of Tribe," Civilization, vol. 16, no. 4 (1966), pp. 500-515.

_____. Right in Land and its Resources among the Nyanga (Republic of the Congo-Leopoldville). Brussels: ARSOM, 1966.

_____. Symbolism of the Lega Stool. Philadelphia: Institute for the Study of Human Issues, 1977.

Bittremieux, Leo. Mayombsche Namen. (Mayombe names.) Leuven: Drukkerij Paters de H. H. Harten, 1934.

_____. La Société secrète des Bakhimba au Mayombe. Brussels: IRCB, 1936.

_____. Symbolisme in de Negerkunst. Brussels: Vroman, 1937.

Bleeker, Sonia. The Pygmies: Africans of the Congo Forest. London: Dobson, 1971.

Boelaert, E. L'Etat Indépendant et les terres indigènes. Brussels: ARSC, 1956.

_____. Nsona Lianja: L'épopée nationale des Nkundo-Mongo. Antwerp: Kongo-Overzee, 1949.

_____. "Vers un Etat Mongo?" Bulletin des Séances l'ARSOM, vol. 7, no. 3 (1961), pp. 382-391.

Boone, Olga. Carte ethnique du Congo. Quart sud-est. Tervuren: MRAC, 1961.

_____. Carte ethnique de la République du Zaire. Quart sud-ouest. Tervuren: MRAC, 1973.

Burssens, H. Les Peuplades de l'Entre Congo-Ubangi. Tervuren: MRAC and London: I.A.I., 1958.

Burton, William Frederick Padwick. Luba Religion and Magic in Custom and Belief. Tervuren: MRAC, 1961.

Bwakasa, Tulu Kia Mpansu. L'Impense du discours: "Kindoki" et "Nkisi" en pays kongo du Zaire. Kinshasa: Presses Universitaires du Zaire, 1973.

Bylin, Eric. Basakata: Le Peuple de l'entrefleuves Lukenie-Kasai. Lund: Berlingska Boktryckeriet, 1966.

Colle, P. Les Baluba (Congo Belge). Brussels: A. de Wit, 1913.

Costermans, J. Mosaique Bangba: Notes pour servir à l'étude des peuplades de l'Uelé. Brussels: IRCB, 1953.

Crine, Bruno. L'Avant-tradition zairoise. Kinshasa: Office National de la Recherche et du Développement, 1974.

_____. La Structure sociale des Foma. Brussels: CEDAF, 1972.

Cunnison, Ian G. "Kazembe and the Portuguese, 1798-1832," Journal of African History, vol. 2, no. 1 (1961), pp. 61-76.

_____. The Luapula Peoples of Northern Rhodesia. Custom and History in Tribal Politics. Manchester: Manchester University Press, 1959.

Daye, Pierre. Le Miroir du Congo Belge. Brussels: Editions N.E.A., 1929.

De Beaucorps, R. Les Basongo de la Luniungu et de la Gobari. Brussels: IRCB, 1941.

_____. Les Bayansi du Bas-Kwilu. Louvain: Editions de l'Aucam, 1933.

_____. L'Evolution économique chez les Basongo de la Luniungu et de la Gobari. Brussels: IRCB, 1951.

De Beir, L. Les Bayaka de M'Nene N'toombo Lenge-lenge. St. Augustin: Anthropos-Institut, 1975.

328 / The Bibliography

De Cleene, Natal. Le Clan matrilinéal dans la société indigène. Brussels: IRCB, 1946.

_____. Introduction à l'ethnographie du Congo Belge et du Ruanda-Urundi. Antwerp: De Sikkel, 1957.

De Mahieu, Wauthier. Qui a obstrué la cascade?: Analyse sémantique du rituel de la circoncision chez les Komo du Zaire. Cambridge and New York: Cambridge University Press, 1985.

De Plaen, G. Les Structures d'autorité des Bayanzi. Paris: Editions Universitaires, 1974.

De Sousberghe, L. L'Indissolubilité des unions entre apparentés au Bas-Zaire. Uppsala: Institutionen for Allmän-och Jämförande Ethnografi vid Uppsala Universitet, 1976.

_____. Structures de parenté et d'alliance d'après les formules pende. Brussels: ARSC, 1955.

_____, and Ndembe, J. "La Parenté chez les Lokele," Bulletin des Séances ARSOM, no. 4 (1967), pp. 728-745.

Delhaise, C. Les Warega. Brussels: A. de Wit, 1909.

Denis, Jacques. Les Yaka du Kwango: Contribution à une étude ethno-démographique. Tervuren: MRAC, 1964.

Devisch, René. L'Institution rituelle khita chez les Yaka au Kwango du nord: Une analyse séméiologique. Leuven: Katholieke Universiteit te Leuven, 1976.

Dias de Carvalho, H. Expediçao ao Muatiamvu. Ethnographia e historia dos povos da Lunda. Lisbon: Adolpho Modesto, 1890.

Dictionnaire des rites. Bandundu: CEEBA, 1985.

Douglas, Mary. The Lele of the Kasai. London: Oxford University Press, 1963.

_____. Purity and Danger. New York: Praeger, 1966.

Doutreloux, Albert. L'Ombre des fétiches: Société et culture Yombe. Louvain: Nauwelaerts, 1967.

Droogers, André. The Dangerous Journey: Symbolic Aspects of Boys' Initiation Among the Wagenia of Kisangani, Zaire. The Hague: Mouton, 1980.

Duffy, Kevin. Children of the Forest. New York: Dodd, Mead, 1984.

Elshout, Pierre. The Batwa People of the Ekonda Group in Kiri Territory. Washington: Joint Publications Research Service, 1965.

Evans-Pritchard, E. E. The Azande: History and Political Institutions. Oxford: Clarendon Press, 1971.

_____. Essays in Social Anthropology. New York: Free Press of Glencoe, 1962.

_____. Witchcraft, Oracles, and Magic among the Azande. Oxford: Clarendon Press, 1976.

_____. The Zande Trickster. Oxford: Clarendon Press, 1967.

Franham, Kay. The Pygmies of the Ituri Forest; an Adventure in Anthropology. Agincourt, Ont.: Gage Education Publications, 1972.

Frobenius, Leo. Ethnographische Notizen aus den Jahren 1905 und 1906. Stuttgart: F. Steiner Verlag Wiesbaden, 1985.

Fu-Kiau, André. M'Kongo ye Nza Yakun Zungidila; Nza Kongo. Le Mukongo et le monde qui l'entourait; cosmogonie-Kongo. (Kikongo and French) Kinshasa: Office National de la Recherche de Développement, 1969.

Gelders, V. Le Clan dans la société indigène. Brussels: IRCB, 1943.

Gusimana Wa Mama. Les Origines et guerres pende. Bandundu: Gusimana Wa Mama, 1984.

Halkin, Joseph. Les Ababua. Brussels: A. de Wit, 1911.

Hallet, Jean-Pierre. Pygmy Kitabu. New York: Random House, 1973.

Haveaux, G. La Tradition historique des Bapende orientaux. Brussels: IRCB, 1954.

Hochegger, Hermann. Le Langage des gestes rituels. Bandundu: CEEBA, 1981.

_____. Mort, funérailles, deuil et culte des ancêtres chez les populations du Kwango/Bas-Kwilu. Bandundu: CEEBA, 1969.

_____. Normes et pratiques sociales chez les Buma. Bandundu: CEEBA, 1975.

Hubbard, Maryinez. A la Recherche des Mangbetu, Haut-Zaïre. Brussels: CEDAF, 1975.

Hulstaert, G. Elements pour l'histoire mongo ancienne. Brussels: ARSOM, 1984.

_____. General Survey of the Mongo People in Congo-Leopoldville. Washington: Joint Publications Research Service, 1965.

_____. Le Mariage des Nkondo. Brussels: IRCB, 1938.

_____. Les Mongo: Aperçu général. Tervuren: MRAC, 1961.

Hutereau, A. Histoire des peuplades de l'Uelé de l'Ubangi. Brussels: Bibliothèque Congo, 1922.

Iyeki. Essai sur la Psychologie Bonto. Kinshasa: Office National de Recherche et de Développement, 1970.

Ize-Senze. Symbolique verbale et rituelle chez les Sakata, Lele, Wongo, Kuba, Lulua, Mbole et Vira (République du Zaire). Bandundu: CEEBA, 1984.

Janni, Pietro. Etnografia e mito: La storia dei pigmei. Roma: Edizioni dell'Ateneo & Bizzarri, 1978.

Kalanda, Mabika. Baluba et Lulua: Une Ethnie à recherche d'un nouvel équilibre. Brussels: Editions Remarques Congolaises, 1959.

Kamainda, Thomas. The Cult of the Dead Among the Balambo in the Congo (Leopoldville). Washington: Joint Publications Research Service, 1964.

Kayemba-Buba. Histoire et signification du Djalelo. Kinshasa: Imprimerie de Kinshasa, n.d.

Kezembe XIV, Mwata. My Ancestors and My People. London: Bantu Heritage Series, 1951.

Kimpianga Mahaniah. La Mort dans la pensée kongo. Kinsantu, Zaire: Centre de Vulgarisation Agricole, 1980.

Kopytoff, Igor. "Family and Lineage among the Suku of the Congo," in The Family Estate in Africa, Gray, R. F. and Gulliver, P. H., eds., pp. 83-116. Boston: Boston University Press, 1964.

_____. "The Suku of Southwestern Congo," in Peoples of Africa, Gibbs, James L., ed., pp. 441-478. New York: Holt, Rinehart & Winston, 1965.

Lagae, C. R. Les Azande ou Niam-Niam. Brussels: Vromant, 1926.

Lehuard, Raoul. Les Phemba du Mayome. Arnouville: Arts d'Afrique, 1977.

Lemal, F. Basuku et Bayaka des districts Kwango et Kwilu au
Congo. Tervuren: MRAC, 1965.

Lotar, L. La Grande chronique de l'Ubangi. Brussels: IRCB,
1937.

_____. La Grande chronique de l'Uelé. Brussels: IRCB, 1946.

Louillet, L. Le "Lusalo"; ou mariage monogame par l'échange de
sang. Elisabethville: Editions de la Revue Juridique du Congo
Belge, 1936.

Lucas, Stephen A. L'Organisation politique des Baluba du Katanga.
Elisabethville: Université Officielle du Congo, Faculté de Droit,
1964.

Lumbwe Mudindaambi. Objets et techniques de la vie quotidienne
mbala. Bandundu: CEEBA, 1976.

MacGaffey, Wyatt. Customs and Government in the Lower Congo.
Berkeley: University of California Press, 1970.

Maes, Joseph and Boone, O. Les Peuplades du Congo Belge. Brussels: Imprimerie Veuve Monnom, 1935.

Masson, Paul. Trois Siècles chez les Bashi. Tervuren: MRAC,
1960.

McCulloch, Merran. The Southern Lunda and Related Peoples.
(Ethnographic Survey of Africa: West Central Africa; part I.)
London: I.A.I., 1951.

Merriam, Alan P. An African World: the Basongye Village of Lu-
pupa Ngye. Bloomington: Indiana University Press, 1974.

Mertens, Pierre Joseph. Les Badzing de la Kamtsha. (3 vols.)
Brussels: IRCB, 1935-39.

_____. Les Chefs couronnés chez les Bakongo orientaux. Brus-
sels: IRCB, 1942.

Miller, Joseph C. Cokwe Expansion, 1850-1900. Madison: University of Wisconsin, African Studies Committee, Occasional Papers,
no. 1 (1969). Second revised printing: 1974.

_____. "Kings, Lists and History of Kasanje," in History of
Africa, vol. 6 (1979), pp. 51-96.

Mitchell, J. C., and Barnes, J. F. The Lamba Village. Capetown:
University of Capetown, 1950.

Mudiji-Malamba Gilombe. <u>Formes et fonctions symboliques des masques</u> <u>mbuya des Phende: Essai d'iconologie et d'herméneutique.</u> Louvain-la-Neuve: Université Catholique de Louvain, Institut Supérieur de Philosophie, 1981.

Mulyumba wa Mamba, Itongwa. <u>Aperçu sur la structure politique des</u> <u>Balega-Basile.</u> Brussels: CEDAF, 1978.

Mune, Pierre. <u>Le Groupement du petit-Ekonda.</u> Brussels: ARSC, 1959.

Musée du Pays de Rochefort et de la Famenne. <u>Rochefort et le</u> <u>Congo.</u> (Exhibition organized by the Museum, the French Ministry of Culture and the Musée Royal de l'Afrique Central.) Brussels: Imprimerie Laconti, 1969.

Myanga Gangambi. <u>Les Masques pende de Gatundo.</u> Bandundu: CEEBA, 1974.

Ndambi Munamuhega. <u>Les Masques pende de Ngudi.</u> Bandudu: CEEBA, 1975.

Ngolo Kibango. <u>Minganji, danseurs de masques pende.</u> Bandundu: CEEBA, 1976.

Ngoma, Ferdinand. <u>L'Initiation ba-kongo et sa signification.</u> Lubumbashi: CEPSI, 1965.

Nkiere Bokuna Mpa-Osu. <u>L'Organisation politique traditionelle des</u> <u>Basakata en République du Zaire.</u> Brussels: CEDAF, 1975.

_____. <u>La Parenté comme système idéologique: Essai d'interprétation de l'ordre lignager chez les Basakata.</u> Kinshasa: Faculté de Théologie Catholique, 1984.

Nkudi, Kalala. <u>Le Lilwakoy des Mbole du Lomami: Essai d'analyse</u> <u>de son symbolisme.</u> Brussels: CEDAF, 1979.

Nzamba. <u>Gandanda Initiation et mythes pende.</u> Bandundu: CEEBA, 1974.

Obenga, Théophile. <u>Le Zaire: Civilisations traditionnelles et culture</u> <u>moderne: Archives Culturelles d'Afrique centrale.</u> Paris: Présence Africaine, 1977.

Packard, Randall M. <u>Chiefship and Cosmology: an Historical</u> <u>Study of Political Competition.</u> Bloomington: Indiana University Press, 1981.

Phillippe, René. <u>Inongo: Les Classes d'âge en région de la Lwafa</u> <u>(Tsuapa).</u> Tervuren: MRAC, 1965.

Plancquaert, M. Les Jaga et les Bayaka du Kwango. Brussels: IRCB, 1932.

_____. Les Sociétés secrètes chez les Bayaka. Louvain: Kuyl-Otto, 1930.

Salmon, Pierre. Récits historiques Zande. Brussels: CEMUBAC, 1965.

Schebesta, Paul. Among the Congo Pygmies. (Translated from German by Griffin, Gerald.) New York: AMS Press, 1977.

_____. My Pygmy and Negro Hosts. (Translated from German by Griffin, Gerald.) New York: AMS Press, 1978.

Semaine d'études ethno-pastorales. L'Organisation sociale et politique chez les Yansi, Teke et Boma. (Papers of the 4th seminar organized by the CEEBA.) Bandundu: CEEBA, 1968.

Sendwe, Jason. "Traditions et coutumes ancestrales du Baluba Shankadji," Bulletin CEPSI. no. 24 (1954), pp. 87-120, and no. 31 (1955), pp. 57-84.

Smith, H. Sutton. Yakusu. London: Marshall Bros., 1912.

Soret, Marcel. Les Kongo nord-occidentaux. Paris: Presses Universitaires de France, 1959.

Southall, Aidan. Alur Society: A Study in the Types and Processes of Domination. Cambridge: Heffer, 1956.

Tango Muyay. Leur Bouche crache du feu: Agressions verbales yansi. Bandundu: CEEBA, 1978.

Tayaya Lumbombo. Réparation de l'infidelité conjugale chez les Yansi, République du Zaire. Bandundu: CEEBA, 1981.

Tempels, Placide. Bantu Philosophy. Paris: Présence Africaine, 1959.

Theuws, Jacques A. Th. Word and World: Luba Thought and Literature. S. Augustin, West Germany: Verlag des Anthropos-Instituts, 1983.

Thomas, Jacqueline. Les Ngbaka de la Lobaye. Paris: Mouton, 1963.

Thornton, John Kelly. The Kingdom of Kongo: Civil War and Transition, 1641-1718. Madison: University of Wisconsin Press, 1983.

Thuriaux-Hennebert, Arlette. Les Zande dans l'histoire du Bahr-el-

Ghazal et de l'Equatoria. Brussels: Institut de Sociologie de L'Université Libre de Belgique, 1964.

Torday, Emil. Notes ethnographiques sur les peuples communément appelés Bakuba, ainsi que sur les peuplades apparentées, les Bushongo. Brussels: Ministère des Colonies, 1910.

_____. On the Trail of the Bushongo. London: publisher unknown, 1925.

Tshinkela. Le Miroir Mukongo. Kinshasa: Procure des Frères, 1965.

Turnbull, Colin M. The Forest People. New York: Simon and Schuster, 1961; New York: Holt, Rinehart, and Winston, 1983.

_____. The Mbuti Pygmies: Change and Adaptation. New York: Holt, Rinehart, and Winston, 1983.

_____. Wayward Servants: the Two Worlds of the African Pygmies. Westport, CT: Greenwood Press, 1976.

Turner, V. W. Schism and Continuity in an African Society. A Study of Ndembu Village Life. Manchester: Manchester University Press, 1957.

Valdy, Jacques. Bakongo. Aalter: André de Rache, 1955.

Van der Kerken, G. L'Ethnie Mongo. 2 vols. Brussels: IRCB, 1944.

Van Dorpe, Walter. Origine et migrations des Yeke (de la Tanzanie au Zaire). Bandundu: CEEBA, 1978.

Van Everbroeck, Nestor. Ekmond'e mputela: Histoire, croyance, organisation clanique, politique, sociale et familiale des Bkonda et de leurs batoa. Tervuren: MRAC, 1974.

_____. Mbomb'Ipolu, le seigneur à l'abime. Histoire, croyances, organisation clanique, politique, judiciaire, vie familiale des Bolia, Sengele et Ntomb'e njale. Tervuren: MRAC, 1961.

Van Geluwe, H. Les Bali et les peuplades apparentées (Ndaka, Mbo, Beke, Lika, Budu, Nyari). (Ethnographic Survey of Africa: Central Africa, part V.) London: I.A.I., 1960.

_____. Les Bira et les peuplades limitrophes. Tervuren: MRAC, 1956.

_____. Mamvu-Mangutu et Balese-Mvuba. London: I.A.I., 1957.

Van Noten, Francis. The Uelian. A Culture with a Neolithic Aspect, Uele-Basin (N.E. Congo Republic). An Archaeological Study. Tervuren: MRAC, 1968.

Van Overbergh, Cyrille, and De Jonghe, E. Les Bangala. Brussels: A. de Wit, 1907.

_____. Les Basonge. Brussels: A. de Wit, 1908.

_____. Les Mangbetu. Brussels: A. de Wit, 1909.

_____. Les Mayombe. Brussels: A. de Wit, 1907.

Van Riel, J. L'eau en milieu rural centre africain. Brussels: ARSOM, 1964.

Van Roy, H. Proverbes Kongo. Tervuren: MRAC, 1963.

Van Wing, J. Etudes Bakongo. 2 vols. (2nd ed.) Bruges, Belgium: Desclée de Brouwer, 1959.

Vandeqoude, Emiel J. L. M. Documents pour servir à la connaissance des populations du Congo Belge; aperçu historique de l'étude des populations autochtones, par les fonctionnaires et agents du Service Territorial, suivi de l'inventaire des études historiques, ethnographiques et linguistiques conservées aux Archives du Congo Belge. Léopoldville: Section Documentation, Archives du Congo Belge, 1958.

Vansina, Jan. The Children of Woot: a History of the Kuba Peoples. Madison: University of Wisconsin Press, 1978.

_____. Introduction à l'Ethnographie du Congo. Brussels: CRISP, 1966.

_____. Kingdoms of the Savanna. Madison: University of Wisconsin Press, 1966.

_____. Le Royaume Kuba. Tervuren: MRAC, 1964.

_____. Les Tribus Ba-kuba et les peuplades apparentées. Tervuren: ARSAF, 1954.

Verhaegen, P. Le Problème de l'Habitat rural en Afrique noire. Brussels: CEDESA, 1960.

Verhulpen, E. Baluba et Balubaisés du Katanga. Antwerp: Editions l'Avenir Belge, 1936.

Weghsteen, J. "Origine et histoire des Watabwe," Annali Lateransi, vol. 24 (1960), pp. 364-375.

336 / The Bibliography

Whitely, W., and Slaski, J. The Bemba and Related Peoples of Northern Rhodesia. (Ethnographic Survey of Africa: East Central Africa, Part II.) London: I.A.I., 1951.

Widman, Ragnar. The Niombo Cult among the Babwende. Stockholm: Etnografiska Museet, 1967.

Winter, E. H. Bwamba. Cambridge: W. Heffer (for the East African Institute of Social Research), 1956.

Wolfe, Alvin W. In the Ngombe Tradition. Evanston, IL: Northwestern University Press, 1961.

Yogolelo Tambwe ya Kasimba. Introduction à l'histoire des Lega: Problèmes et méthode. Brussels: CEDAF, 1975.

2. Education

American Council on Education. Survey of Education in the Democratic Republic of the Congo. Washington: 1969.

Babudaa Malibato. Le Citoyen et la conscience nationale, africaine, internationale. Kinshasa: Editions Bobiso, 1981.

_____. Le Citoyen dans le développement national: 4e secondaire, manuel conforme au programme de la République du Zaire. Kinshasa: Mayaka Esongama Nsa, 1975.

_____. Education et instruction civiques: le Citoyen dans la communauté nationale: 3e secondaire. Kinshasa: BEC, 1974.

Barden, John Glenn. A Suggested Program of Teacher Training for Mission Schools among the Batetela. (Originally published, New York: Bureau of Publications, Teachers College, Columbia University, 1941.) New York: AMS Press, 1972.

Belgium. Ministère des Colonies. La Réforme de l'enseignement au Congo Belge: Mission pédagogique Coulon-Deneyn-Benson. Brussels: Editions du Conseil Supérieur de l'Enseignement, 1954.

Bureau de l'Enseignement National Catholique. Les Etudes Supérieures en République Démocratique du Congo. Kinshasa-Kalina: 1971.

Centre Polyvalent pour l'Education Permanente. Education socio-économique: Naissances désirables: Manuel à l'intention des instructeurs d'alphabétisation. Kinshasa: 1978.

Chuma Basukura et al. Profil des professions et des études en République du Zaire: Guide à l'intention des diplômés d'Etat. Kinshasa: Presses Universitaires du Zaire, 1973.

Colloque sur L'interdisciplinarité, Kisangani, 17-20 decembre 1974.
(Documents of colloquium.) Kisangani: Université Nationale du
Zaire, Campus de Kisangani, CRIDE, 1974.

Cornet, C. M.; Vandenbulcke, M. D.; and Kalonji Mutambayi.
Bantu?: Proverbes africains à l'Usage de l'enseignement secondaire. Brussels: A. De Boeck, 1976.

La Culture zairoise à l'école: Actes du Colloque de Kinshasa, 8-11
avril 1980. Kinshasa-Gombe: Presses de l'Institut de Recherche
Scientifique, 1981.

Delvaux, Jean Paul. L'Examen de l'intelligence des écoliers de Kinshasa. Kinshasa: Université Lovanium, 1970.

Dias, Patrick V. Erziehung, Identitätsbildung und Reproduktion im
Zaire. Basel: Beltz, 1979.

Ecole Nationale de Droit et d'Administration. Léopoldville: Imprimerie de l'Avenir, 1962.

Ekwa, Martin. Le Congo et l'éducation: Réalisations et perspectives
dans l'enseignement national catholique. Léopoldville-Kalina:
Bureau de l'Enseignement National Catholique, 1965.

_____. Pour une société nouvelle, l'enseignement national; textes
et discours, 1960-1970. Kinshasa: Editions du B.E.C., 1971.

Enseignement National Catholique. Enseignement National Catholique,
année scolaire 1970-71. (Enrollment statistics, Roman Catholic
schools.) Kinshasa-Limété: Imprimerie St. Paul, 1971.

_____. République du Congo. Annuaire statistique: Enseigne-
ment national catholique. Année 1965-1966. Kinshasa: 1967.

Erny, Pierre. Sur les sentiers de l'université: Autobiographies
d'étudiants zairois. Paris: Pensée Universelle, 1977.

Fullerton, Gary. L'UNESCO au Congo. Paris: UNESCO, 1964.

Gasibirege Rugema Simon. Brève histoire de la formation du personnel enseignant au Zaire. Kinshasa: Maison de l'Education au
Zaire, 1982.

George, Betty G. (Stein). Educational Developments in the Congo
(Léopoldville). Washington: U.S. Department of Health, Education and Welfare, Office of Education, 1966.

Georgis, P. Essai d'acculturation par l'enseignement primaire au
Congo. Brussels: CEMUBAC, 1962.

_____, and Agbiano, Baudouin. L'Enseignement au Congo depuis l'indépendance. Brussels: CEMUBAC, 1966.

Golan, Tamar. Educating the Bureaucracy in a New Polity: A Case Study of l'Ecole Nationale de Droit et d'Administration (ENDA), Kinshasa, Congo. New York: Columbia University Teachers' College Press, 1968.

Hull, Galen. Université et Etat: l'UNAZA-Kisangani. Brussels: CEDAF, 1976.

International Bank for Reconstruction and Development. Zaire: Education Sector Memorandum. (Report by the Consultative Group for Zaire.) Memorandum ZA 77-5. Washington: 1977.

Kapuku Mudipanu. Etude comparative des systèmes d'évaluation des élèves en techniques professionnelles dans les écoles d'infirmiers/-ères de Kinshasa et du Bas-Zaire: 1980-1982. Québec: Université Laval, Faculté des Sciences de l'Education, 1984.

_____. La Valeur prédictive des concours d'admission et des examens de contrôle organisés à l'Institut supérieur des techniques médicales (I.S.T.M.) de 1974 à 1980: Le Cas de l'enseignement et administration des soins infirmiers à Kinshasa. Québec: Université Laval, Faculté des Sciences de l'Education, 1983.

Kasongo Ngoyi Makita Makita. Les Etudiants et les élèves de Kisangani (1974-1975): Aspirations, opinions et conditions de vie. Brussels: CEDAF, 1977.

Kita Kyankenge Masandi. Colonisation et enseignement: Cas du Zaire avant 1960. Bukavu: Editions du CERUKI, 1982.

Knapen, Marie-Thérèse. L'Enfant mukongo. Orientations de base du système éducatif et développement de la personalité. Louvain: Nauwelaerts, 1962.

Koivukari, Mirjami. Rote Learning, Comprehension, and Participation by the Learners in Zairian Classrooms. Jyväskyla: Jyväskylän Yliopisto, 1982.

Massika, Antoine. "L'Education des adultes," Bulletin du Ministère des Affaires Sociales, vol. 5, nos. 5-6 (1965), pp. 5-11.

Mulier, Freddy. La Coopération technique belge dans l'enseignement zairois. Brussels: CEDAF, 1979.

Presses Universitaires du Zaire. Recherche et publications scientifiques à l'UNAZA. Kinshasa: 1972.

Professors World Peace Academy. Ecole, éducation et développement au Zaire. (Documents of the Second Regional Seminar, held in Kinshasa, September 8, 1983.) Kinshasa: 1985.

Rideout, William M. Survey of Education in the Democratic Republic of the Congo. Washington: American Council on Education, Overseas Liaison Committee, 1969.

Rimlinger, Gaston V. Education and Modernization in Zaire: A Case Study. Houston: Program of Development Studies, William Marsh Rice University, 1974.

Sack, Richard, et al. La Langue d'instruction et ses incidences sur les écoliers zairois: Cas du Nord-Kivu. Kisangani: UNAZA, Centre de Recherches Interdisciplinaires pour le développement de l'Education, 1976.

Université Libre du Congo. Université Libre du Congo, République Démocratique du Congo, Kisangani. Kisangani: 1970.

Université Nationale du Zaire. Centre de Recherches Interdisciplinaires pour le développement et l'Education. Rapport général des travaux du Ier Congrés des Professeurs Nationaux de l'Enseignement Supérieur et Universitaire. (Report of congress held at Nsele, 1971.) Kinshasa: Presses Universitaires du Zaire, 1971.

Verhaegen, Benoît. L'Enseignement universitaire au Zaire: De Lovanium à L'UNAZA, 1959-1979. Paris: Editions L'Harmattan, 1978.

Verheust, Thérèse. L'Enseignement en République du Zaire. Brussels: CEDAF, 1974.

3. Religion, Missions, and
Traditional Beliefs

Abel, Armand. Les Musulmans noirs du Maniema. Brussels: Centre pour l'Etude des Problèmes du Monde Musulman Contemporain, 1960.

Anciaux, Léon. Le Problème musulman dans l'Afrique Belge. Brussels: George Van Campenhout, 1949.

Andersson, Efraim. Messianic Popular Movements in the Lower Congo. Uppsala: Almquist & Wiksells, 1958.

Annuaire Catholique du Congo, du Ruanda et de l'Urundi. Brussels: Oeuvres Pontificales Missionaires, 1960-1961.

Annuaire complet des communautés religieuses en Belgique, au Congo et au Grand-Duché de Luxembourg, 1968. Brussels: Bieleveld, 1968.

Arnot, Frederick Stanley. Garenganze; or Seven Years' Pioneer Mission Work in Central Africa. London: Cass, 1969.

_____. Missionary Travels in Central Africa. Bath: Office of "Echoes of Service," 1914.

Arnout, Alexandre. Les Pères blancs aux sources du Nil. Paris: Librairie Missionnaire, 1953.

Asch, Susan. L'Eglise du Prophète Kimbangu: De ses Origines à son rôle actuel au Zaire, 1921-1981. Paris: Editions Karthala, 1983.

Axelson, Sigbert. Culture Confrontation in the Lower Congo. From the Old Congo Kingdom to the Congo Independent State with Special Reference to the Swedish Missionaries in the 1880's and 1890's. Stockholm: Gummesson, 1970.

Balandier, Georges. "Messianisme des Ba-Kongo," Encyclopédie Mensuelle d'Outre-Mer, August 1951.

_____. Sociologie Actuelle de l'Afrique Noire. Paris: Presses Universitaires de France, 1955.

Baptist Missionary Society. 1878-1978: One Hundred Years of Christian Mission in Angola and Zaire. London: 1978.

Bentley, William Holman. Pioneering on the Congo. New York: Johnson Reprint Corp., 1979.

Bernard, Guy. "The Nature of a Sociological Research: Religious Sects in the West of the Congo," Cahiers Economiques et Sociaux IRES, vol. 2, no. 3 (1964), pp. 261-269.

_____, and Caprasse, P. "Religious Movements in the Congo: A Research Hypothesis," Cahiers Economiques et Sociaux IRES, vol. 3, no. 1 (1965), pp. 49-60.

Bontinck, François. Jean-François de Rome. La Fondation de la Mission des Capucins au Royaume du Congo (1648). Louvain: Nauwelaerts, 1964.

Braekman, E. M. Histoire du Protestantisme au Congo. Brussels: Librairie des Eclaireurs Unionistes, 1961.

Brashler, Peter J. Change, my Thirty-Five Years in Africa. Wheaton, IL: Tyndale House, 1979.

Buluku, C. Dieu, idoles et sorcelleries. Bandundu: CEEBA, 1968.

Chinapah, Vinayagum. Swedish Missions and Education in the Re-
    public of Zaire: A Description and Diagnosis. Stockholm: Insti-
    tute of International Education, University of Stockholm, 1981.

Chomé, Jules. La Passion de Simon Kimbangu. Brussels: Les
    Amis de Présence Africaine, 1959.

Combarros, Miguel. Al Ritmo del tam-tam: Negritud y cristianismo.
    Madrid: PS, D.L., 1978.

Commission Diocésaine des Jeunes de Kinshasa. Option fondamentale:
    Thèmes et chants de l'initiation à l'option fondamentale des Bilenge
    ya Mwinda. Kinshasa: Editions St. Paul Afrique, 1978.

Conférence Episcopale du Zaire. Réconciliation et pénitence dans la
    mission de l'Eglise: Contribution de l'Episcopat du Zaire au
    synode romain 1983. Kinshasa-Gombe: 1984.

Crawford, John Richard. Protestant Missions in Congo, 1878-1969.
    Publisher and date unknown. (English translation of Témoignage
    protestant au Zaire, 1878-1970.) Kinshasa: Centre Protestant
    d'Editions et de Diffusion, 1972.

Cuvelier, J. L'Ancien Royaume de Congo. Brussels: Desclée de
    Brouwer, 1946.

_____. Documents sur une mission française au Kakongo, 1766-
    1776. Brussels: IRCB, 1953.

_____. Relations sur le Congo du Père Laurent de Lucques, 1700-
    1717. Brussels: IRCB, 1953.

_____, and Jadin, L. L'Ancien Congo d'après les archives ro-
    maines, 1518-1640. Brussels: ARSC, 1954.

D'Anna, Andrea. Da Cristo a Kimbangu. "Chiese nere" e sincretismi
    pagano-cristiani in Africa. Bologna: Editions "Nigrizia," 1964.

Davies, David Morgan. The Captivity and Triumph of Winnie Davies.
    London: Hodder & Stoughton, 1968.

Dawson, David. Trapped! Ventura, CA: Regal Books, 1982.

De Beir, L. Religion et magie des Bayaka. St. Augustin: Anthropos-
    Institut St. Augustin, 1975.

De Boeck, André. Contribution à l'étude du système moral de la
    jeunesse zairoise. Brussels: Vander, 1975.

De Craemer, Willy. The Jamaa and the Church: A Bantu Catholic Movement in Zaire. Oxford: Clarendon Press, 1977.

De Rome, Jean-François. La Fondation de la mission des Capuciors au Royaume du Congo (1648). (Translated by Botinck, François.) Louvain: Editions Nauwelaerts, 1964.

De Thier, Franz M. Singhitini, la Stanleyville musulmane. Brussels: Centre pour l'Etude des Problèmes du Monde Musulman Contemporain, 1963.

Denis, L. Les Jésuites belges au Kwango. Brussels: L'Edition Universelle, 1943.

Dequeker, Paul. Eglises Tropicales. Kinshasa: Editions C.E.P., 1984.

Devant les Sectes non-chrétiennes: Rapports de compte-rendus de la 31 ème semaine de missiologie. Bruges: Desclée De Brouwer, 1961.

Dieu, Léon. Dans la brousse congolaise: (Les Origines des missions de Scheut au Congo). Liège: Maréchal, 1946.

Fabian, Johannes. Jamaa: A Charismatic Movement in Katanga. Evanston, IL: Northwestern University Press, 1971.

Faculté de Théologie Catholique de Kinshasa. Science et sagesse: Documents du XXe anniversaire de la Faculté de Théologie Catholique de Kinshasa, 23 avril 1957-25 avril 1977. Kinshasa, 1977.

Fourche, T. Une Bible noire. Brussels: M. Arnold, 1973.

Fuller, Millard. Bokotola. New York: Association Press, 1977.

Gérard, Robert. Les Fondements syncrétiques du Kitawala. Brussels: CRISP, 1969.

Gillis, Charles-André, Kimbangu, fondateur d'église. Brussels: Librairie Encyclopédique, 1960.

Heintze-Flad, Wilfred. L'Eglise Kimbanguiste, une église qui chante et prie: Les "Chants captés" kimbanguistes. Lieden: Interuniversitair Institut voor Missiologie en Oecumenica, 1978.

Janzen, John M., and MacGaffey, Wyatt. An Anthology of Kongo Religion: Primary Texts from Lower Zaire. Lawrence: University of Kansas, 1974.

Kaké, Ibrahima Baba. Dona Béatrice: La Jeanne d'Arc congolaise. Paris: ABC, 1976.

Kaufmann, Robert. Millénarisme et Acculturation. Brussels: Institut de Sociologie, Université Libre de Belgique, 1964.

Keidel, Levi O. War to Be Won. Grand Rapids, MI: Zondervan Publishing House, 1977.

Kimplianga Mahaniah. L'Impact du Christianisme sur le Manianga, 1880-1980. Kinshasa: Editions Centre de Vulgarisation Agricole, 1981.

Lagergren, David. Mission and State in the Congo. A Study of the Relations between Protestant Missions and the Congo Independent State Authorities with Special Reference to the Equator District, 1885-1903. Lund: Gleerup, 1970.

Lanternari, V. The Religions of the Oppressed: A Study of Messianic Cults. New York: A. A. Knopf, 1963.

Lory, Marie-Joseph. Face à l'avenir: L'Eglise au Congo Belge et au Ruanda-Urundi. Paris and Tournai: Casterman, 1958.

Lufualabo, François. La Notion Luba-bantoue de l'être. Paris and Tournai: Casterman, and Louvain: Eglise Vivante, 1964.

_____. Orientation pre-chrétienne de la conception bantoue. Kinshasa: Centre d'Etudes Pastorales, 1964.

_____. Vers une théodicée bantoue. Tournai: Casterman, 1962.

MacGaffey, Wyatt. "Comparative Analysis of Central African Religions," Africa, vol. 42, no. 1 (1972), pp. 21-31.

_____. "Cultural Roots of Kongo Prophetism," History of Religions, vol. 17, no. 2 (November 1977), pp. 177-193.

_____. Modern Kongo Prophets: Religion in a Plural Society. Bloomington: Indiana University Press, 1983.

_____. "Oral Tradition in Central Africa," International Journal of African Historical Studies, vol. 7, no. 3 (1975), pp. 417-426.

_____. Religion and Society in Central Africa: The BaKongo of Lower Zaire. Chicago: University of Chicago Press, 1986.

_____. "The West in Congolese Experience," in Africa and the West, Curtin, P., ed., pp. 49-74. Madison: University of Wisconsin Press, 1972.

Makanzu Mavumilusa. L'Histoire de l'Eglise du Christ au Zaire: Nous n'avons pas trahi l'Evangile de Jesus-Christ. Kinshasa: Centre Protestant d'Editions et de Diffusion, 1973.

Malula, Joseph (Cardinal). Directoire de la Pastorale du mariage et de la famille. Kinshasa: Archidiocèse de Kinshasa, 1984.

Markowitz, Marvin D. Cross and Sword; the Political Role of Christian Missions in the Belgian Congo, 1908–1960. Stanford, CA: Hoover Institution Publications, 1973.

Masamba ma Mpolo. Sorcellerie et pastorale. Kinshasa: Centre Protestant d'Editions et de Diffusion, 1977.

McGavran, Donald Anderson. Zaire: Midday in Missions. Valley Forge, PA: Judson Press, 1979.

Middleton, John. Lugbara Religion: Ritual and Authority among an East African People. London: Oxford University Press (for I.A.I.), 1960.

Mosmans, Guy. L'Eglise à l'heure de l'Afrique. Paris and Tournai: Casterman, 1961.

Mulago, G. C. M. La Religion traditionelle des bantous et leur vision du monde. Kinshasa: Presses Universitaires du Zaire, 1973.

Mulago, Vincent, and Theuws, T. Autour du mouvement de la "Jamaa." Léopoldville-Limété: Centre d'Etudes Pastorales, 1960.

Nelson, Robert G. Congo Crisis and Christian Mission. St. Louis, MO: Bethany Press, 1961.

Ngokwey, Ndolamb. Le Désenchantement enchanteur: ou, D'un mouvement religieux à l'autre. Brussels: CEDAF, 1978.

Ntedika Konde. La Faculté de théologie et l'avenir de l'Eglise en Afrique. Kinshasa: Faculté de Théologie Catholique de Kinshasa, 1975.

Nyeme Tese. Munga, éthique en un milieu africain: Gentilisme et christianisme. Ingenbohl, Switzerland: Imprimerie du Père Théodose, 1975.

Pierson, Robert H. Angels over Elisabethville: A True Story of God's Providence in Time of War. Mountain View, CA: Pacific Press Publishers Association, 1975.

Prouty, Robert. Scar across the Heart. Boise, ID: Pacific Press Publishers Association, 1986.

Rodeheaver, Homer Alvan. Singing Black: Twenty Thousand Miles with a Music Missionary. New York: AMS Press, 1975. (Reprint of the 1936 edition published by Rodeheaver Co., Chicago.)

Rencontre des Moralistes Zairois. Morale et société zairoise: Actes de la Première Rencontre des Moralistes zairois, du 1er au 4 novembre 1978. Tshumbe-Wembonyama, Zaire: Centre d'Etudes et de Recherches Anthropologiques du Sankuru, 1982.

Religieux et religieuse en République du Zaire: 1985. Kinshasa: ASUMA, 1985.

Saccardo, Graziano. Congo e Angola: Con la storia dell'antica missione del Cappuccini. Venice: Curia Provinciale dei Cappuccini, 1982.

Semaine d'Etudes Ethno-Pastorales, 2e. Dieu, idoles et sorcellerie dans la région Kwango/Bas-Kwilu: Rapports et compte rendu de la IIème Semaine d'Etudes ethnopastorales, Bandundu, 1966. Bandundu: CEEBA, 1968.

Shaloff, Stanley. Reform in Leopold's Congo. Richmond, VA: John Knox Press, 1970.

Taylor, John V., and Lehmann, Dorothea A. Christians of the Copper-belt. London: SCM Press, 1961.

Toews, John B. The Mennonite Brethren Church in Zaire. Fresno, CA and Hillsboro, KA: Mennonite Brethren Publishing House, 1978.

Truby, David W. Congo Saga: An Authentic Record of Heroes of the Cross during the Simba Rising. London: Unevangelized Fields Mission, 1964.

_____. Regime of Gentlemen: Personal Experiences of Congolese Christians during the 1964 Rebellion. London: Marshall, Morgan & Scott, 1971.

Tshibangu Tshishiku. Le Propos d'une Théologie Africaine. Kinshasa: Presses Universitaires du Zaire, 1974.

Van Caeneghem, R. La Notion de Dieu chez les BaLuba du Kasai. Brussels: ARSC, 1956.

Verner, Samuel P. Pioneering in Central Africa. Richmond, VA: Presbyterian Committee of Publications, 1903.

Vivez donc votre vie!: Les GEN au Zaire disent leurs expériences. Kinshasa: Editions St. Paul Afrique, 1981.

Wharton, E. T. Led in Triumph: Sixty Years of Southern Presbyterian Mission in the Belgian Congo. Nashville, TN: Board of World Missions, Presbyterian Church, 1952.

Womersley, Harold. Congo Miracle: Fifty Years of God's Working in Congo (Zaire). Eastbourne: Victory Press, 1974.

4. Sociology, Urbanization, and Migration

Baeck, L. "An Expenditure Study of the Congolese 'Evolués' of Léopoldville, Belgian Congo," in Social Change in Modern Africa, Southall, Aidan J., ed., pp. 159-181. London: Oxford University Press, 1961.

_____. "Léopoldville, phénomène urbain africain," Zaire, vol. 10, no. 6 (1956), pp. 613-636.

_____. "Une Société rurale en transition: Etude socio-économique de Thysville," Zaire, vol. 11, no. 2 (1957), pp. 115-186.

Benoit, Jacqueline. "Contribution à l'étude de la population active d'Elisabethville," Bulletin CEPSI, no. 54 (Sept. 1961), p. 5-53.

_____. La Population africaine à Elisabethville à la fin de 1957. Son Etat, sa structure, ses movements et ses perspectives d'évolution prochaine. Elisabethville: CEPSI, 1962.

Bernard, Guy. Ville Africaine, famille urbaine: Les Enseignants de Kinshasa. Paris and The Hague: Mouton, 1969.

Capelle, Emmanuel. La Cité Indigène de Léopoldville. Léopoldville: Centre d'Etudes Sociales Africaines, 1947.

Caprasse, P. Leaders africains en milieu urbain. Elisabethville: CEPSI, 1959.

Centner, Th. L'Enfant africain et ses jeux. Elisabethville: CEPSI, 1963.

Comhaire-Sylvain, Suzanne. Femmes de Kinshasa hier et aujourd'hui. Paris: Mouton, 1968.

Conflits familiaux et réconciliation: Rapport du VIe Colloque de Bandundu, République du Zaire. Bandundu: CEEBA, 1975.

De Maximy, René. Kinshasa, ville en suspens: Dynamique de la croissance et problèmes d'urbanisme: Etude socio-politique. Paris: Editions de l'Office de la Recherche Scientifique et Technique Outre-mer, 1984.

De Thier, Franz M. Le Centre Extra-Coutumier de Coquilhatville. Brussels: Institut de Sociologie, Université Libre de Belgique, 1956.

_____. Singhitini, la Stanleyville musulmane. Brussels: Centre pour l'Etude des Problèmes du Monde Musulman Contemporain, 1963.

Denis, Jacques. "Coquilhatville: Eléments pour une étude de géographie sociale," Aequatoria, no. 4 (1956), pp. 137-158 and no. 1 (1957), pp. 1-4.

_____. "Elisabethville: Matériaux pour une étude de la population africaine," Bulletin CEPSI, no. 34 (1956), pp. 137-195.

_____. "Jadotville: Matériaux pour une étude le la population africaine," Bulletin CEPSI, no. 35 (1956), pp. 25-60.

_____. "Léopoldville: Etude de géographie urbaine sociale," Zaïre, vol. 10, no. 6 (1956), pp. 563-611.

_____. "Notes sur le degré de stabilisation des citadins de Léopoldville," Bulletin CEPSI, no. 33 (1956), pp. 151-163.

_____. Le Phénomène urbain en Afrique centrale. Brussels: ARSC, 1958.

Dethier, Robert. Une Famille de citadins du Katanga. Liège: Institut de Sociologie de la Faculté de Droit, 1961.

Jacobson-Widding, Anita. Marriage and Money. Uppsala: Institutionen for Allmän och Jämförande Ethnografi, 1967.

Kazintenkore, E. "La Construction dans les zones de squatting de Kinshasa," Cahiers Economiques et Sociaux, IRES, vol. 5, no. 3 (1967), pp. 327-353.

La Fontaine, Jean S. "The Free Women of Kinshasa: Prostitution in a City in Zaire," in Choice and Change: Essays in Honour of Lucy Mair, Davis, J., ed., pp. 89-113. New York: Humanities Press, 1974.

Leblanc, Michel. Lubumbashi, un écosystème urbain tropical. Lubumbashi: Centre International de Sémiologie, UNAZA, 1978.

_____. Personalité de la Femme Katangaise. Paris: Béatrice-Nauwelaerts, 1960.

Lejeune, Emile. "Les Classes sociales au Congo," Remarques Africaines, (1966), p. 259.

Liniger-Goumaz, Max. Villes et problèmes urbains de la République Démocratique du Congo: Bibliographie. Geneva: Les Editions de Temps, 1968.

Lux, André. "Luluabourg: Migration, accroissement et urbanisation de la population congolaise de Luluabourg. I. Peuplement; II. Facteurs d'urbanisation," Zaire, vol. 12, nos. 7-8 (1958), pp. 819-877.

Masamba ma Mpolo. Older Persons and their Families in a Changing Village Society: A Perspective from Zaire. Washington: International Federation on Ageing; and Geneva: World Council of Churches, Office of Family Education, 1984.

Minon, Paul. Katuba: Etude quantitative d'une communauté urbaine africaine. Liège: Institut de Sociologie de la Faculté de Droit, 1960.

_____. "Quelques aspects de l'évolution récente du Centre Extra-Coutumier d'Elisabethville," Bulletin CEPSI, no. 36 (1957), pp. 5-51.

Moeller de Laddersous, A. Les Grandes lignes de migration des Bantous de la Province Orientale du Congo Belge. Brussels: IRCB, 1936.

Mpase Nselenge Mpeti. L'Evolution de la Solidarité traditionnelle en milieu rural et urbain au Zaire. (Cas des Ntomba et des Basengele du Lac Mai-Ndome.). Kinshasa: Presses Universitaires du Zaire, 1974.

Mpinga, H. "La Coexistence des pouvoirs 'traditionnel' et 'moderne' dans la ville de Kinshasa," Cahiers Economiques et Sociaux, IRES, vol. 7, no. 1 (1969), pp. 67-90.

_____. "Les Méchanismes de la croissance urbaine en République Démocratique du Congo," Etudes Congolaises, vol. 11, no. 3 (1968), pp. 95-103.

L'Organisation de l'espace urbain au Zaire: Séminaire organisé à Kinshasa du 29 avril au 11 mai, 1974: Receuil des Documents. Kinshasa: Institut National d'Etudes Politiques, 1975.

Piérard, J. P. "La Dot congolaise, sa situation actuelle et son avenir," Bulletin des Séances ARSOM, no. 3 (1967), pp. 468-495.

Raymaekers, Paul. "Juvenile Pre-delinquency and Delinquency in Leopoldville," Bulletin of the International African Labour Institute, vol. 10, no. 3 (1963), pp. 329-357.

_____. L'Organisation des zones de squatting, elément de résorption du chômage structurel dans les milieux urbains en voie de développement. Brussels: Editions Univérsitaires, 1964.

Richelle, Marc. Aspects psychologiques de l'acculturation. Recherches sur les motifs de la stabilisation urbaine au Katanga. Elisabeth-ville: CEPSI, 1960.

Roels-Ceulemans, M. J. Problèmes de la jeunesse à Léopoldville. Analyse quantitative de la population juvénile. Léopoldville: IRES, Lovanium, 1961.

Schatzberg, Michael G. Politics and Class in Zaire: Bureaucracy, Business, and Beer in Lisala. New York: Africana, 1980.

Smal, Guy A., and Mbuyi, Joseph W. Femme africaine réveille-toi! Paris: La Pensée Universelle, 1973.

Sohier, J. Essai sur la criminalité dans la province de Léopoldville. Brussels: ARSC, 1959.

_____. Quelques traits de la physionomie de la population euro-péene d'Elisabethville. Brussels: IRCB, 1953.

Turnbull, Colin M. The Lonely African. New York: Simon and Schuster, 1962.

Université Nationale du Zaire and Institut National de la Statistique. La Circulation urbaine à Lubumbashi: Résultats de l'enquête effectuée du 19 mai au 25 février 1973. Lubumbashi: 1973.

Vincent, J. F. Femmes Africaines en milieu urbain. Paris: publisher unknown, 1966.